CW01302449

IN SEARCH OF EDEN

IN SEARCH OF EDEN
ESSAYS ON DOMINICAN HISTORY

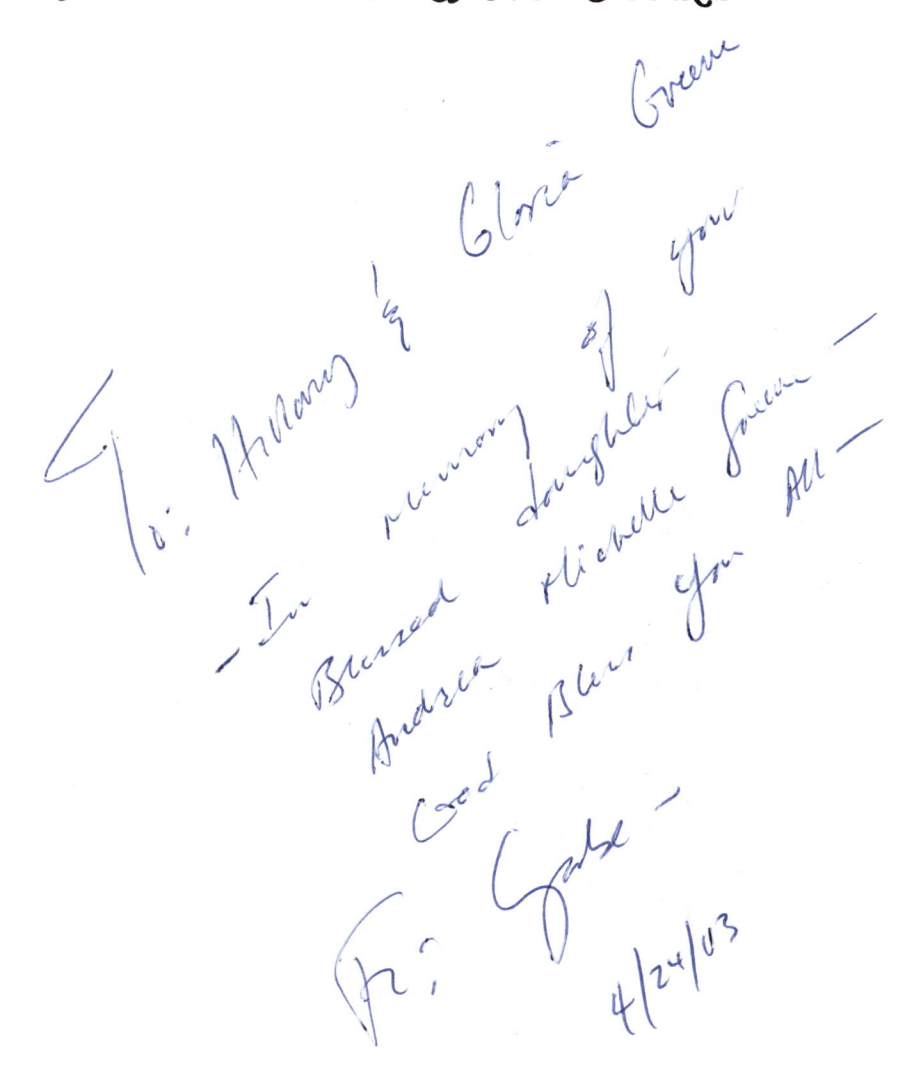

By Irving W. André and Gabriel J. Christian

Copyright © 2002 by Irving W. André and Gabriel J. Christian.

A Pond Casse Press Production

Cover photograph by Irving Andre

All rights reserved, including the right of reproduction in whole or in part in any form.

Eighth Pond Casse publication, 2002.

Pond Casse Press, Brampton, Ontario
Printed in Canada by
The University of Toronto Press Inc.

ISBN NUMBER 0-9699857-5-4

André, Irving W., Christian, Gabriel J.
In Search of Eden
Bibliography p.
Latin America/Caribbean History (Dominica, Society and Politics)

CONTENTS PAGE

1. Acknowledgements vii
2. Photographs... ix
3. Special Foreword. Dr. Thomson Fontaine xix
4. Introduction...1
4. Pond Casse Press..13
5. In Times Crucial..18
   G. Christian
6. Legislation and Repression
   In Dominica in the 1970s................................139
   I. André
7. The Theoritical and Ideological
   Justification For Independence in
   Dominica. 185
   I. André
8. Towards Armageddon. The Attempt to
   Invade Dominica and Its Aftermath........................222
   I. André
9. Domestic and Foreign Policy in the
   1980s..258
   I. André
10. Creative Writing and The Forging of
    a Dominican Identity....................................289
    I. André
11. Rendezvous with History. The Attempts
    at Regional Integration.................................350
    I. André
12. Return of The Prodigal. Dominican
    Migration and its Aftermath.............................374
    I. Andre

| CONTENTS | PAGE |

13. The Rise and Fall of the United
    Workers'Party..418
    I André

14. Roosevelt Bernard Douglas.
    A Dominican Titan......................................459
    G. Christian

15. Diaspora Unbound.....................................520
    G. Christian

16. The Struggle to Preserve Dominica's
    Natural Environment..................................557
    G. Christian

APPENDICES

I. *Why a Rosie Douglas Foundation*..................611
   G. Christian

II. *Notes from The Last Speech by*
    Rosie Douglas on September 22, 2000............619

III. *Ms. Octavia Norde. Profile*
     of a Dominican Migrant to
     Canada..645
     I. André

     Bibliography..656

ACKNOWLEDGEMENTS

This book is intended to be multi-disciplinary in nature, bringing together historical, political and literary analyses. In many instances, the events covered are being published or written about for the first time. As such it necessarily draws from the experiences and ideas of a large number of persons who have all directly, or indirectly contributed to this book. The authors have also benefited from the collective efforts of all those who have contributed at one stage or the other to their education in Dominica and abroad.

Specifically however, there are those whose special contributions to this book must be acknowledged. Gabriel Christian is grateful for the inspiration provided by his parents, Wendel and Alberta. Appreciative of the information provided by Dr. Donald Peters, Hilarian Deschamp, Debbie Douglas, Birdock "Birdie" Shillingford, amongst others. He is also thankful to the staff at the Library of Congress and the Island Resources Foundation, who facilitated his research. He also thanks Lawson, Samuel, Esther, and Theresa Christian, Joan Robinson, along with Simpson Gregoir, Dewanna Maryland, Michele Hotten, Clairmont Walters Dr. and others whose critical comments/encouragement, throughout the time it took to research this book, provided guidance and sustenance.

Similarly, Irving André wishes to thank those who have provided useful insights in the topics covered by this book. Steinberg Henry proved an invaluable source for research material and insights into Dominican culture of the 1970s. Lennox Honeychurch and Alwin Bully offered useful words of advice and encouragement. The respective library staff at York University, the John Hopkins University and the Library of Congress also proved invaluable in obtaining research material for the writing of this book. More recently, Anna Raffoul provided me with important resource material. Finally special thanks to Kathy André who was responsible for doing the final editing and typesetting of this text.

While very grateful for the help received in writing this book, the authors accept responsibility for any errors and omissions in this book. It is our fervent hope that any such errors, omissions or honest divergence of opinion may not detract from the usefulness of this book to the reading public.

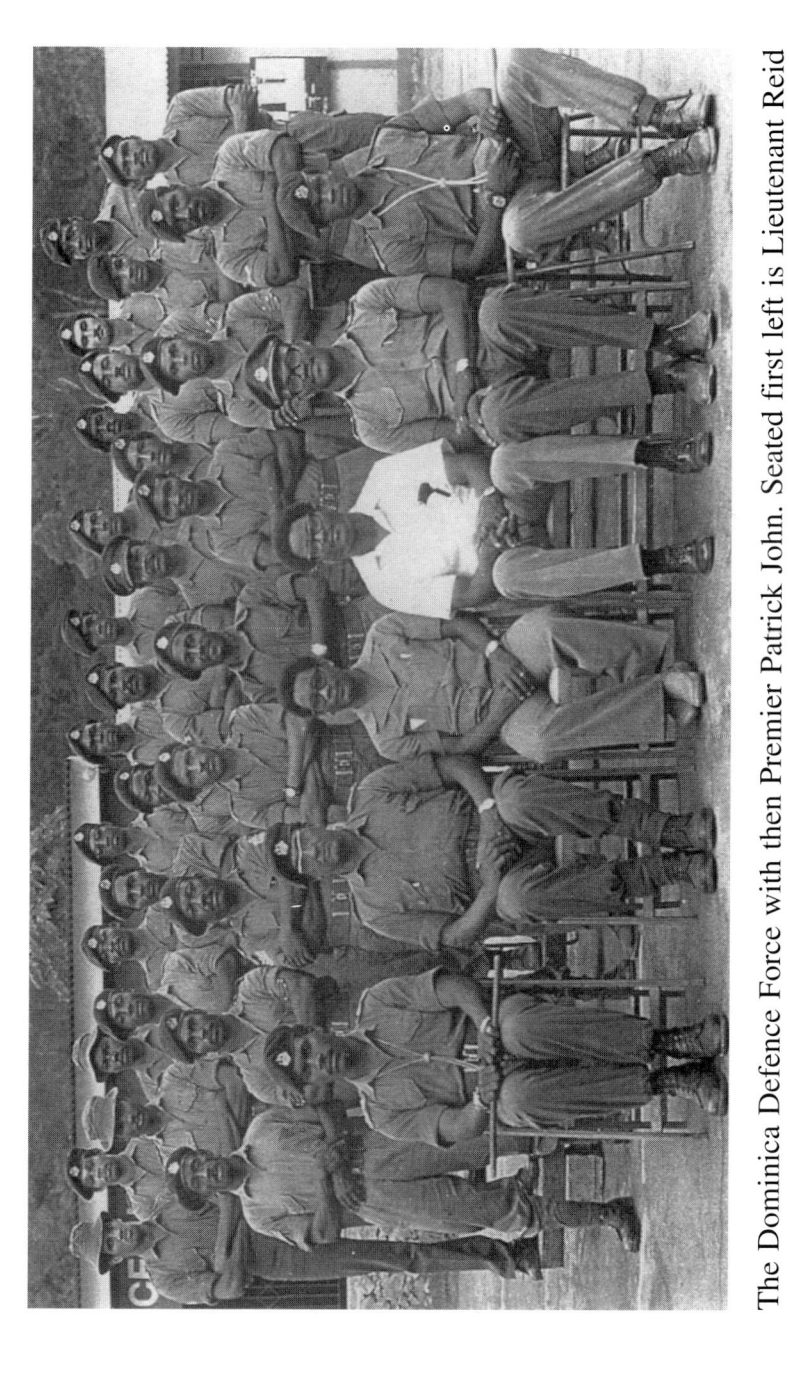

The Dominica Defence Force with then Premier Patrick John. Seated first left is Lieutenant Reid while his counterpart, Frederick Newton, is extreme right. Standing third from left in back row is Sgt. Benjamin, killed by the DPF following the attempted coup in 1981.

THE DOGS OF WAR. Mercenaries Christopher Anderson, Walter Droege, Michael Perdue and Larry Jacklin prior to being sentenced in New Orleans for conspiracy to invade Dominica.

Roosevelt Douglas meets with former Japanese Prime Minister

Douglas in a meeting with University of New Orleans Chanellor, Dr. Gregory O'Brien.

Miss Norde. Early Dominican Migrant poses with Dominican Ferdinand Fortune in Canada.

Gabriel Christian addresses members of Dominica's Cadet Corps in October 2000.

Early Diasporan and lawyer George James Christian

DISTINGUISHED VISITOR. Former Lieutenant Governor of Ontario, Hon. Lincoln Alexander poses with former Carib Chief and his wife and former Dominican President Clarence Signoret.

Nature Island Paradise

The arms and insignia of war. Arsenal of weapons
and Nazi symbol destined for Dominica in 1981

PUBLICATIONS

Other Pond Casse Publications

IN SEARCH OF EDEN. I André and G. Christian 1992.

A PASSAGE TO ANYWHERE. I André 1994.

DISTANT VOICES. The Genesis of An Indegenous Literature in Dominica. I. André 1995.

THE ISLAND WITHIN. I. André 1996.

DISTANT VOICES. I. André 1999.

RAIN ON A TIN ROOF. G. Christian 2000.

THE JUMBIE WEDDING. I. André 2001.

TALES FROM HURONTARIO HIGH. I. André 2002.

DEDICATION

This Book is specially dedicated to the memory of Rosevelt Douglas, Philip Timothy and Eddie Toulon. In their own unique way, they have enhanced our appreciation for and love for our island.

SPECIAL FOREWORD

Dr. Thomson Fontaine

In this fascinating look at the unfolding events in Dominica during the period 1970 – 2002, authors Gabriel Christian and Irving Andre take their readers into the amazing historical events that has helped define a Nation. *In Search of Eden 2* continues from where the first issue, which was published in 1992, left out. Building on the hugely successful *"In Search Of Eden – The Travails of a Caribbean Mini State"*, the authors once again relate in exquisite and pointed detail on the most recent history of Dominica. The collection of essays focus on political upheaval, social unrest, constitutional change, attempted coups, and on the key historical figures like former Prime .Minister Patrick John who defined this period.

Unfolding events in Dominica during the period detailed in this work is at once stunning and insightful. That a former British colony with only a few thousand inhabitants could have survived through such an excruciating historical period is evidence of the uniqueness that defines the Nation and its people. In the essays highlighted in this book, the authors have done a remarkable job of relating those events in a manner that is easily readable and finds resonance for those who may have lived through some of the events detailed within.

The authors intimate involvement with some of the characters and events represented in this work provide an added dimension to the retelling of such events. For instance, in *"Independence Now- The Political and Philosophical Legacy of Rosie Douglas "*, Mr. Christian delves into the minute details of Rosie Douglas role in the Independence movement, his days in the political struggle culminating with his rise to Prime Minister, and his untimely passing in 2000. Mr. Christian's own involvement as a youth leader alongside Rosie Douglas and his close association with him throughout the period detailed in the essay allowed him a unique opportunity to chronicle arguably the most compelling political episode in Dominica's history.

Even where the authors were not intimately involved in the events about which they write, the depth of research and attention to historical detail is admirable. In *Towards Armageddon: The attempt to invade Dominica and its Aftermath,* Mr. Andre portrays a vivid picture of the cast of characters and the sheer audacity of the plot that was contrived to overthrow the Eugenia Charles Government. *"The men involved in the planned invasion were not picadors, or adventurers; not the stuff of legend. Neither patriotism, love of the sea, adventurism or altruism governed their actions. Theirs was no journey of self-discovery, no excursion into the human psyche. Joseph Conrad's 'Heart of Darkness' or Herman Melville's 'Moby Dick' were as far removed from their consciousness as was knowledge of the island they had chosen to invade."*

The plot, in retrospect, seems laughable but could very well have succeeded without the timely intervention of United States federal agents. Mr. Andre argues that *"...their story reveals as much about the island's*

vulnerability, its insignificance in international circles, and its existence on the periphery of the consciousness of the West."

From the radical student uprisings throughout the Caribbean Region in the early seventies, which defined an entire new generation, to the near overthrow of Dominica's government by members of the *Klu Klux Klan* with the tacit support of former Prime Minister Patrick John, to the sudden passing of the late Prime Minister Rosie Douglas in October 2000, *In Search of Eden 2* presents the reader with compelling historical commentary and analysis, which brings to light the events for which Dominica will forever be remembered.

In Search of Eden 2 is therefore a must read for those interested in the more recent history of Dominica, and even for those with just a passing interest in such events. It provides the most complete and exhaustive treatment to date of the characters and events that continue to impact on the evolving Nation State.

INTRODUCTION

Irving André

I. HISTORICAL OVERVIEW

The Commonwealth of Dominica became known to Europeans on November 13, 1493, when Christopher Columbus inadvertently came upon the island. It was then inhabited by Amerindians from South America whose descendents can still be found on the island. The arrival of Columbus irrevocably changed the course of the island's history.

This history can best be analyzed by examining the changing attitudes of the colonial government towards the island since Columbus' voyage. These changes ranged from using the island as a pawn during the 17th and 18th centuries, trying to develop it as a plantation in the nineteenth and finally disregarding it as an impoverished appendage of the British empire in the twentieth century. In the early latter century, the island enjoyed a shortlived prosperity when it became the largest lime producer in the world. However, the advent of crop disease in the early 1920s resulted in the demise of that industry and relegated the island once more to relative obscurity in the eyes of the metropole.

Political events have kept pace with the island's changing social and economic fortunes. In 1832, the British enacted legislation which enabled three local persons to be elected to the House of Assembly. The British abolished slavery in 1834 and by 1838, the local colored elite had taken control over the island's House of Assembly. In 1863, at a time of social unrest in the region, the British government reasserted control over the government by establishing Crown Colony government on the island. In the wake of the collapse of the lime industry, the island received some limited rights of self government in 1924 as a safety valve to dilute indigenous protest over declining economic conditions.

The correlation between economic decline and enfranchising the Dominican public proceeded throughout the twentieth century. In 1951, Britain revised Dominica's constitution to provide for universal adult suffrage, an elected House of Assembly and in 1956, a ministerial system of government. The granting of a limited form of representative government served the British and Dominica well, in the twentieth century. Representation in the House of Assembly provided the local elite an opportunity to protest against the poverty endemic within Dominica by the 1930s. They were allowed to do so with impunity since they did not challenge the sovereign authority of Britain on the island.

The process of co-opting the local elite by increasing opportunities for employment in the civil service and participation in government accelerated following the Second World War. A number of factors explain this. As the economic fortunes of the local white population in Dominica declined, their numbers decreased from about 300 persons in 1900 to approximately 50 persons in 1950.[1] Secondly, the drive towards the dismantlement of the old colonial empires made it unpopular to maintain colonies. The financial burden imposed by the Second World War added a greater impetus to the political reorganization of the old empires. In some instances, such as Rhodesia and Kenya, economic considerations justified retention of the colonial empire. In the West-Indies however, where the economic justification for retention was not as compelling, the British fashioned a Federation in the 1950s to reduce expenses in administering its colonies.[2] The breakdown of the West Indies Federation led to the call for independence from Jamaica and Trinidad in the 1960s. This call coincided with Britain's desire to lessen its financial burden in the West-Indies and independence was granted to these islands accordingly.

---

[1] Patrick L. Fermor, *The Traveller's Tree* (N.Y. Harper and Bros. Publishers, 1950) Page 103.
[2] J.H. Proctor Jr. "Britain's Pro-Federation Policy in the Caribbean: An inquiry into Motivation." The *Canadian Journal of Economics & Political Science* (1956) v.22, No.3, Page 319.

In the case of Dominica, the size of the island and the relative lack of resources militated against the requesting and granting of independence in the 1960s. Further delaying this process was the attempt by the Windward and Leeward Islands to form a Federation among themselves, following the break up of the West-Indies Federation. Instead, the process of granting self government was completed in 1967 when the island became an Associated State. This transitional state was one in which the island received internal self government with the externalities of foreign affairs and defence reposing with the British. In the ensuing period, it was anticipated that the island would learn the rudiments of exercising political power and develop a democratic tradition based on the Westminster form of government. Once this learning process was completed, the island would be granted independence by Britain.

II. THE POPULATION AND SOCIETY

The island's population is approximately 72,000, the vast majority being descendants of African slaves. The population is largely expatriate with the first inhabitants, the Arawaks and Caribs, having originated from South America. Their presence on the island was later augmented by Europeans and with the advent of sugar production, by Africans who had been captured and pressed into slavery. In the early twentieth century, a small number of itinerant traders from the Middle-East settled on the island, whose descendants today wield considerable economic power.

The society is not so much a melting pot of cultures but one with a plurality of cultures existing side by side. The descendants of the Caribs, numbering a few thousand, reside on a 3700 acre reserve where they wage a valiant rearguard battle to preserve their culture and identity. People of African descent are dispersed throughout the island where the majority eke out a living through agriculture. While exposure to the market economy has partly ameliorated their condition, fluctuations in agricultural prices have relegated them to a livelihood which frequently teeters above the marginal.

Social mobility has partly mitigated any latent hostilities among the various ethnic and social groups of the island. Persons of African descent have through education, risen to positions of authority and prestige. For the most part however, the wealthiest persons on the island are persons of Middle East extraction and people of 'complexion'; the latter being largely the result of miscegenation between the races. This social group dominates ownership of the large estates, the island's commerce, agro-industry and also the professions.

While there is fluidity between the social groupings, there are marked social distinctions on the island. These distinctions have persisted since much of the economic wealth on the island reposes in the hands of a few wealthy families. Periodically, the inherent tensions between oligarchic control and the desire for arable land by the rural population has resulted in violence. Such was the case in Castle Bruce and Grand Bay in the early 1970s when the rural peasantry used violence to obtain control of estates controlled by landed interests. Such tensions in the society were to be ameliorated, somewhat, by the Labor Party's ascent to power. Its provisions of opportunity to the vast majority eased social tensions.

Against this social backdrop, three political parties, the Dominica Freedom Party (DFP), the United Workers Party (UWP) and the Dominica Labour Party (DLP) have competed for ascendancy. Dominica's youthful radical intelligentsia of the 1970s which was to be grouped around the Movement for a New Dominica (MND), the popular Independence Committee (PIC) and Peoples Democratic Party (PDP) would later join with Labour, to form its electable core. The United Workers' Party, (UWP) emerged in 1988, and assumed the reins of power in 1995, only to lose them in 2000. This led to the DLP's resumption of power after a twenty one year hiatus.

The DLP and the DFP trace their political lineage to the 1950s with the advent of party politics on the island. They represent opposite ends of the political spectrum. In the 1950s, the Labour Party emerged as a mass worker based party with the primogenitor of the Freedom Party, the Dominica United Peoples' Party (DUPP), representing narrower vested interests on the island. Membership and support of both parties however, now transcend social distinctions and groupings although each party retains its original social identity.

In the 1960s, the Dominica Labour Party wrested control of the island from the DUPP and remained in power until its demise in 1979. Following a transitional period in which the island was governed by a broad based Committee for National Salvation, the DFP assumed power in 1980 and formed the government until 1995, when the UWP triumphed over its two rivals.

III. FOCUS OF THIS BOOK

Dominica's history represents a continuous search for its people to build a genuinely democratic and equitable society on what most consider a nature island paradise. Pre-20th century slavery, along with colonial rule in recent times meant that such an objective remained elusive. The most recent failure of this democratic experiment in the 1970s and its aftermath form the focus of this book. Against a background of declining economic fortunes, marginally ameliorated by financial aid from foreign agencies, the Labour party government enacted legislation which impacted heavily on the lives of all Dominicans. Collectively, this legislation imposed press censorship, curbed rights of free assembly and collective bargaining, among others. These restrictions occurred while the government ostensibly pursued a socialist path of development which seemed to be at odds with the political script written by the British. Instead, the legislation seemed to vindicate the view that there is an inexorable process towards centralized authority within societies in the terminal stages of colonialism.[3]

This spate of legislation triggered opposition from Dominicans throughout the 1970s. Indeed, the period was characterized by social and labour unrest, political upheaval, general discontent and in some cases, disenchantment with the legacy of colonial government. In his essays, Gabriel Christian chronicles the activities of those who advocated a reordering of society to escape the legacy of the island's colonial past. The consolidation of authority by the Labour Party government culminated in the eventual granting of independence from Britain on November 3, 1978.

---

[3] Archie Singham: *The Hero and the Crowd in a Colonial Polity*. (Yale Univ. Press, 1968).

Independence, however, merely exposed the dire financial problems of the island and the need to resolve those problems through foreign investment. Prime Minister Patrick John's attempts to obtain financial aid and his efforts to curb domestic opposition led to the fall of his government in 1979. This paved the way for Prime Minister Mary Eugenia Charles' rise to power following general elections in 1980. In that decade, the Charles government would concern itself with ensuring internal stability while laying the social and infrastructural framework to attract foreign investment to the island.

The superficial banality of those events belies the fact that during this period, successive Dominican governments had to grapple with a number of issues which underpin the quest for a genuinely democratic state. These include:

1. How best to guarantee individual rights and freedoms while ensuring that the exercise of those rights do not undermine the duly constituted government which is the custodian of such rights?

2. To what degree should market forces become the final arbiter of values in an agrarian based economy?

3. How does one inculcate the principle that the art of governing is a privilege conferred by the electorate to some whose very livelihood depends on participation in government?

4. To what extent can the need to maintain a semblance of autonomy and national independence be achieved within the framework of a political union among the islands?

5. To what extent should a political movement whose aims include the overthrow of the existing social and political order be allowed to exist within a democratic country?

6. How can the desire to foster economic growth through exploitation of one's natural resources be reconciled to the desire to preserve the natural environment of the island?

These are some of the issues covered in this book. The fact that these very issues are being faced in numerous countries today gives this assessment a significance transcending the shores of Dominica. Indeed, the brilliant Trinidadian thinker, C.L.R. James, has noted in his book, **Spheres of Existence** that:

> The Caribbean territories have a universal significance far beyond their size and social weight. They seem to be a slice of Western civilization put under a microscope for the scientific investigation of the fundamental predicates and perspectives of that civilization itself.

The essays comprising this book investigate and analyze the most important events in the recent history of

Dominica. They focus primarily on the social, political and economic life of the island. Collectively, they depict an island grappling to come to terms with its own history, as it seeks to forge an identity of its own.

There is a degree of overlap in some of the essays since they were not all written in conjunction with each other. They do not reflect a single ideological viewpoint and in fact may contain different interpretations of the same events. The authors are not only aware of this but are anxious to point it out since implicitly, the book suggests that plurality of thought is desirable in any discussion on the problems which Dominica may have to deal with as it plans for the future.

The book marks the culmination of a period of collaboration between the two authors. This commenced in the mid 1970s when the authors were attending the Dominican Grammar School and the Sixth Form College. They discovered that they shared interests in literature, politics and society. These mutual interests have been sharpened both by higher education and the political and economic developments since the 1970s.

This book is merely the organized expression of the respective views of the authors reinforced by research over a considerable period of time. In a sense, *In Search of Eden* represents our combined efforts to rescue the thoughts, feelings and convictions developed over time from the ethereal, platonic world of ideas which they would otherwise inhabit. By rendering such thoughts in writing, it is our hope that the ongoing examination of Dominica's problems, and the creation of solutions thereto, may receive a new impetus.

THE ORIGINS OF POND CASSE PRESS

In the early 1990s, after a five year sojourn studying law, I came across a box which was filled with the *arcana* of a past life. In that box, which was emblazoned with the word SODABIX on its sides, and which had been shipped from Dominica to Baltimore, Maryland, and finally in 1984, to Brampton, Ontario, was a collection of essays, research notes from the University of the West Indies and Johns Hopkins University, photocopies of works from the US Library of Congress, copies of manuscripts from the University of Toronto, and an assortment of letters, old *Chronicles* and all the literary detritus of an aspiring academic turned lawyer.

It occurred to me that perhaps I could compensate for turning my back on academia by embarking on a literary project, a book on Dominica, focusing on the last twenty- five years (i.e. from 1967) of the island's history. My brief recollection of the limited material on Dominica appeared to justify the plan. Other than Honeychurch's 1984 *The Dominica Story*, Cracknell's 1973 *Dominica*, Trouillot's 1988 *Peasants and Capital*, there was no intellectual probing of the island's fortunes since the 1967 attainment of Associated Statehood. Furthermore, there was nothing by the generation of Dominican students who had been nurtured in the radical chic of the 1970s and who had played a part in the advent of political independence in 1978.

With this in mind, I contacted a few comrades, most notably Gabriel Christian and Steinberg Henry. Gabriel and I had attended the Dominica Grammar School but had had little contact with each other. The school was a microcosm of our community and social distinctions in the broader community were carefully preserved at the DGS. In the mid seventies however, we had met on common ground in a little house overlooking Queen Mary Street in Roseau. We were members of a little radical cell called *Cadre* #1 which had the resources to print a monthly newsletter called *Vanguard*. During our weekly sessions, we would periodically look through the jalousies, with an apprehension akin to that of a youthful Jean Rhys, for the approach of any special constables or other agents of the State, who did not share our enthusiasm for a socialist state. By 1978 I would take my leave, after a giant bearhug and a salutary *a luta continua* instead of a more gentle *au revoir*, bound for the Mona Campus, in Kingston, Jamaica. I would return, first in 1979 and then in 1981, but by then the tide of socialism had ebbed and with it, a desire to remain on the island.

And so in the early 1980s, I blundered out of Dominica, bound for Johns Hopkins University. Gabriel and I maintained contact with each other. In one letter, I suggested that his professional aspirations could only be attained, and his boundless energy assuaged, outside of Dominica and that failure to migrate would result in a daily abortion of all his professional hopes and aspirations. The reason for this advice was simple: The Freedom Party administration in the early 1980s, buffetted by the chilling winds of Reaganomics, would not give a scholarship to an erstwhile radical as he was then. Spurred on by family members, he subsequently left and blazed a trail to Georgetown University Law Center.

I contacted Gabriel with my proposal. A book on Dominica's history from 1967 to the present, with significant aspects of this history being written by notable Dominicans.

He needed no convincing. We set about to persuade other Dominicans to become involved, but for myriad reasons, the response was lukewarm. We ultimately concluded that we should do the book ourselves. *In Search of Eden* was born.

Alongside the decision to forge ahead with *In Search of Eden*, was the decision to establish our own press. The agony of doing a manuscript, foraging for a publisher, sending copies to dozens of disinterested publishing houses, the attendant frustration, the attendant self doubt, were luxuries we could ill afford. We contacted a few printing presses and decided we would bear the cost of this book.

We then looked for a name. Preferentially a local name. Many flitted in and out of our minds. Ballizer, Ainse De Mai, Waitikubuli, Coulibri.

Like a revelation, we settled on Pond Cassé. Why? It was an elevated part of Dominica: almost its centre. It symbolized the very heart of the island, an ideal metaphor for the book.

In Search of Eden, proved a labour of love. We divided the 25 years into focal areas and wrote the chapters accordingly. We agreed on a printer in Virginia, and sent them the necessary floppy discs. My discs proved more sloppy than floppy since the publishing company printed the book with my unedited work.

In 1992, I boarded an airplane to Washington to meet with Gabriel. After breaking bread, we rented a van to Virginia and with great fanfare, received the copies of *In Search of Eden*. Like a precious emerald, we examined the book, staring at it to make sure it was real. The presence of a few errors in the text did not dim our spirits and with great excitement, we announced the newly published work on Dominica.

Since 1992, seven additional works have been published by Pond Cassé Press, most based on Dominica. These include: *Distant Voices, The Genesis of Indigenous Literature in Dominica, A Passage to Anywhere, The Island Within, Rain on a Tin Roof, The Jumbie Wedding* a Revised Edition of *Distant Voices and Tales From Hurontario High*. Other works are in progress. Collectively, they seek to heighten our understanding and appreciation of the island we call home.

The books have been well received even by those with little or no affiliation with Dominica. Our readers encompass all backgrounds and have generally reacted favorably to the books. Indeed, there has been an effervescence of local writing since the advent of Pond Cassé Press in 1992.

This literary renaissance, emerging as it is, from the inertia of the 1980s, augurs well for Dominica's literary future. Hopefully, it will receive a further impetus, as expatriate Dominicans refocus their efforts on the future of their island.

IN TIMES CRUCIAL
RADICAL POLITICS IN DOMINICA 1970-1980

Gabriel J. Christian

INTRODUCTION

The Caribbean, on the eve of the decade of the 1970s was astir with radical thought among certain strata-especially students and the urban young. That arc of English-speaking Caribbean islands, from Jamaica in the north, Dominica at its center, to Trinidad in the south would experience a wave of discontent which would culminate in riots, reformist measures and outright revolutionary attempts at restructuring the social order bequeathed the islands by British colonialism.

On October 16, 1968, thousands of Jamaicans had taken to the streets to voice their grievances at what they considered an inequitable social order inherited from colonialism and maintained by the new ruling elite. The demonstrators, spurred on in some measure by intellectuals such as Guyanese born University of the West Indies (U.W.I) lecturer Walter Rodney were enraged at the sense of powerlessness which was the lot of the mass of black Jamaicans (and Caribbean people in general) in a post-independence era. The response of Jamaica Labour Party (JLP) Prime Minister Hugh Shearer was to ban Rodney from Jamaica and unleash the Jamaica constabulary force and the

Jamaica Defense Force (JDF) against the protestors who he claimed were "semi-literate and illiterate unemployed groups Rodney had zealously recruited for avowedly revolutionary purposes[1]." In the marches which were repressed, three persons were killed and property damage amounted to $2 million. While he was quick to castigate the marchers as unemployed illiterates and communists, not appreciated by Shearer was the resonance that Rodney's message had amongst the new intellectual class not born of the light-skinned Jamaican plantocracy and commercial class. In the debates spurred by *Abeng*, a weekly anti-establishment tabloid in Jamaica, the university educated sons and daughters of ex-slaves had begun to form what appeared as a vanguard for change.[2]

In Trinidad angry voices were being heard through organizations like the National Joint Action Committee (NJAC), which held that independence had only ushered in a new period of misrule. NJAC charged that, under Dr. Eric Williams, white and colored businessmen-Trinidadian and foreign-still owned most of the nation's industries. They sought to overturn such inequitable dominance and, in the words of an NJAC publication ***Slavery to Slavery***, insisted "We need to destroy ...the system from its very

---

[1]. **The Social Origins of Democratic Socialism in Jamaica** (Temple University Press, 1992), Nelson Keith and Novella Keith at 192.

[2]. See Id at 8

foundations..to get out of the economic mess (and build a new society."[3]

By April of 1970, protests calling for "black power" would turn violent and a portion of the army (sent in to crush the protest) would mutiny. The mutiny was scuttled when a Trinidad Coast Guard gunboat, under the command of loyalist officers, shelled the advance party of Trinidadian army insurgents heading from the Chaguaramas peninsula (where the army was based) to Port of Spain. Stunned by the turn of events, Williams (considered a radical in his early days) enhanced legislation which proscribed incitement to racial hatred or violence and bolstered his security forces who soon quelled an incipient guerrilla movement which had erupted in the island's northern mountain range. In addition, Williams ruling Peoples National Movement(PNM),utilized the income derived from the rise in oil prices following the 1973 Arab oil embargo to buy up foreign owned industry, subsidize consumer spending, expand public works projects while fostering programs such as school lunches[4]. His reformist measures at economic nationalism was aimed at co-opting the program of the black power nationalists.

So popular discontent now confronted governments which were led by blacks and which had their roots in the trade union

---

[3] See Jan Rogozinski's *A Brief History of the Caribbean, From the Arawak and Carib to the Present* (Facts on File, 1992) at 276.

[4] See Id at 276.

movement of the 1930s or the post-war quest for universal adult suffrage in the Caribbean. That the misrule vociferated against was in "blackface" was no more tolerable than the previous British variety, of bemedalled geriatric governors decked out in plumed funny hats and peacock feathers. Most important, however, was the feeling that the independence garnered by the countries like Jamaica, Trinidad, Barbados and Guyana in the early sixties, was still held hostage to the *diktat* of foreign capital, be it British, Canadian or American[5]. Rightly or wrongly, the perception of a good many of those who had attained high school or university education was that their local political leaders were nothing more than pliant tools in the hands of old colonial interests. Stung by the challenge and feeling threatened, the local ruling political classes would respond with disdain at the (mostly young) radical "upstarts," speak nervously about "communist instigation," engage in punitive measures, and sometimes make reformist gestures. The criticism being leveled at the status quo in these British colonies had been given resonance by others.

Fellow islander, Martiniquan psychiatrist, revolutionary and scholar, Frantz Fanon had bluntly criticized the new ruling elites of the former colonial territories:

> The national bourgeoisie will be quite content with the role of the Western bourgeoisie's business

---

[5] . See discussion in Herman L. Bennett, ***The February Revolution in Trinidad*** at 132-133 in Franklin W. Knight and Colin A. Palmer ***The Modern Caribbean*** (The University of North Carolina Press, 1984)

agent...it is already senile before it has come to know the petulance, the fearlessness, or the will to succeed of youth.[6]

Via newspapers, travel, and returning U.W.I graduates such sentiments as Fanon's were disseminated. That impatience born of the perceived inadequacies of the status quo would find a vehicle in an increasingly vigorous search by Caribbean people for a more equitable economic order, a non-subservient cultural identity and new forms of political expression. That search would touch Dominica's shores.

Though still a British colony on the eve of that decade, Dominica was, nonetheless, firmly bound by geography, migratory patterns and history to the other English speaking islands. Indeed, it was once part of the ill-fated West Indies Federation[7]. As well, Dominica was well within the cultural and

---

[6]. Frantz Fanon, **The Wretched of the Earth** (Grove Weidenfeld , 1963) 152. Not well known is the fact that Frantz Fanon was one of the nearly 50,000 French soldiers, sailors and civilian refugees who fled the collaborationist regimes in Guadeloupe and Martinique for Dominica between the fall of France to Germany in 1940 and the Normandy Invasion of June 6, 1944. In Dominica the Free French were billeted in homes and hastily built barracks and later shipped to North Africa and England where they joined General Charles de Gaulle Free French Army. After World War II, Fanon studied psychiatric medicine in France and served as a medical doctor with the French occupation army then combating independence fighters in Algeria. There, he was radicalized by his experiences, joined the Algerian National Liberation Front, and became a major exponent of anti-colonial and national liberation ideology. Author's note.

[7]. The West Indies Federation was formed in 1958 and grouped the islands which formed the British West Indies. It collapsed in 1962, when Trinidad decided to withdraw, following Jamaica's earlier decision to withdraw in

political sphere of the United States (and Canada, to a lesser extent) which sought to assume the mantle of an increasingly remote British hegemony in the region. Like all the English-speaking Caribbean territories, Dominica was then, and is (as of this writing), a majority black country, with many of its people having strong Carib ethnic ties. Thus, the ideas spawned by the civil rights struggles of black Americans which convulsed U.S. society in the 1960s were also to filter into the Dominican consciousness.

Sensing the growing ferment, some Caribbean leaders like Forbes Burnham of Guyana sought to associate themselves with that search for Caribbean identity. He dispensed with the suit and tie favored by good colonial servants and made the short-sleeve safari shirt (or shirt jack) formal wear. He championed the Caribbean Festival of Arts, *Carifesta* held in Guyana in 1973, and began to steer his country toward what he termed Cooperative Socialism and support of the African liberation movement.

Other leaders in the English speaking Caribbean took heed and started making even more favorable noises. A renowned historian in his own right, Trinidad's Dr. Eric Williams sought to outflank his critics in the black power movement by speaking thus:

> ..it is absurd to expect black West Indians not to sympathize with and feel part of black American

---

September 1961. See *Dominica,* Basil E. Cracknell, (Stackpole Books Press, 1973) at 176.

movements for the achievement of human rights by black Americans or the emancipation of black Africans from white tyranny in Rhodesia, Portuguese Africa and South Africa, or pride in the historical and cultural past of peoples of the African continent. It is also absurd not to expect young people of the non-white historically dispossessed groups in the Caribbean not to become, as a result of this impact, more conscious of their cultural deprivations and their economic and social disabilities[8]...

In 1968 U.S. civil rights leader, Martin Luther King had been assassinated. The event had shocked islanders and made its way into calypsoes and local debate. His life and death had been followed closely in Dominica and his death was widely mourned[9].

On February 11, 1969, Dominican born Roosevelt "Rosie" Douglas, then a university student at McGill University in Canada, would be part of a major protest by Caribbean students at Sir George Williams [10]University. Douglas had traveled to

---

[8] PNM: Perspectives in the World of the Seventies, Sept. 25, 1970. Quoted in Selwyn D. Ryan's **Race and Nationalism in Trinidad and Tobago**, (University of Toronto Press, 1972).

[9]. At the time of Martin Luther King's death, this author remembers mournful songs on the local radio station and moments of silence being observed in schools, including even kindergarten!

[10]. The Sir George William University protest was to incense many of the exponents of radical thought in the English Caribbean. The protest grew out of a student campus sit-in over racist practices by a biology professor, which had been complained of by Caribbean students. A February 11, 1969 riot ensued in which a $2 million computer center and other campus facilities were destroyed. The arrests of the Caribbean student leaders led to protests in their home-islands. See "Students Riot in Canada," Trinidad Guardian, February 13, 1969; See, generally, Dennis Forsythe's Let the Niggers Burn! The Sir George

Canada to study agricultural engineering at the behest of his estate owning father, Robert B. Douglas. Robert B. Douglas, popularly known as "RBD", had generated savings from his work in the Dutch owned oil fields of Curacao, invested in estates, earned money billeting Free French troops in transit in Dominica during World War II, and ran a major grocery store in Dominica's second town, Portsmouth. Along with his wife Bernadette who was known for charitable works, RBD was active in the local legislative council; representing the northern district of the island for a time during the 1950s. As a shrewd businessman,[11] he was able to escape the confines of a humble beginning and provide advanced educational opportunity for his children. However, though Rosie Douglas came from an upper class black family, his confrontation with racism in Canada showed that his social standing in Dominica had no currency in Canada and he was just another black man; a foreigner at that. That experience changed his life. By the mid-1960s he had been arrested for demonstrating on behalf of black Canadians, Caribbean migrants and indigenous

---

Williams University Affair and its Caribbean Aftermath (Black Rose Books, 1971).

[11]. During the period 1939-1941, I would listen to BBC and American news on Radio at Mr. Douglas' store of the German army's rampage across the low countries, the escape of the British Expeditionary Force from France at Dunkirk and the Royal Air Force's exploits in the Battle of Britain. Guy's like Lowell Thomas, an American, were favorites at the time. If you were outside his store, and he turned up the volume, you could listen for free. However, RBD would charge a penny to those of us who wanted to come inside to listen to his radio. October 11, 2000 statement by this author's father, Wendel M. Christian, British Army World War II veteran, and retired Fire Service Officer.

Canadians. By then he had been swept up in the civil rights and black consciousness movement then ascendant in North America. Arrested in Halifax on a trumped-up charge of loitering, Douglas "boldly declared himself an African living in the Western World by force and not choice. Blacks in Montreal rallied morally and financially to his support.[12]" In October 1968, Rosie was co-chair of the Black Writers Conference in Canada, attended by many considered to be black radicals of the day such as: C.L.R James, Stokely Carmichael, Leroi (Amiri Baraka) Jones and Dr. Walter Rodney. *The main stress of the conference was on the ideology of black power and black nationalism[13]*. It was on his return from Canada, where he was considered to have given incendiary anti-colonial speeches, that Dr. Walter Rodney was barred from returning to Jamaica. His ban incited the October 16, 1968 riots in Kingston, Jamaica, alluded to earlier. Douglas then was part of a burgeoning black pride and anti-colonial movement then sweeping North America, and spreading into the Caribbean islands. Thus, on February 11, 1969, when Canadian police assaulted Caribbean students staging a sit-in strike at the Sir George Williams University Computer Center over racist practices by a biology professor, Rosie was among the leaders arrested.

---

[12] . See Id at 80.

[13] . **Let the Niggers Burn** at 61.

After the Sir George Williams University uprising, he was to author ***Change or Chains***, a stinging rebuke of colonial rule in Dominica. In time, Douglas would be a major player in the upsurge of Dominican radical politics. With such seeds of change being flung far and wide by an increasingly critical Caribbean intelligentsia, whether such seeds took root (and, indeed, to what depth such roots could grow!) would be function of the objective conditions in each country. In that regard, Dominica proved fertile ground.

DOMINICA: 1970

In 1970 Dominica was entering into its third year as an associated state with Great Britain. Dominica had formally become a State in Association with Britain on March 1, 1967[14]. Associated statehood meant that the local Dominican legislature would be responsible for self-government, with Britain retaining responsibility for defense and foreign affairs. Politically, the electorate was divided into two main groups; Labourites (adherents of the Dominica Labour Party); and Freedomites (adherents of the Dominica Freedom Party). The Labour party was born out of the heroic efforts of Phyllis Allfrey (b. 1908) and Emmanuel Christopher Loblack (b. 1898). An unheralded

---

[14]. See ***Dominican Constitution Order*** 1967.

builder of the modern Dominican nation in the 20th Century, Allfrey, female and white, was born to a prominent family of sugar planters on the island. She had studied in England, and written poetry and articles on left-wing politics in pre-World War II Britain. There, she adopted socialist ideas and did volunteer work in support of the Spanish Republic then under assault by fascist troops from Italy and Germany.[15] During the war years she had kept an open house in London for Dominicans who had come to help Britain's war effort, to include then Dominican-born Royal Air Force Officer Edward Scobie[16]. She had been a writer for British Labour Party notable Aneurin Bevan's ***Tribune***, which stood for the proposition that:

> Socialism meant shaking capitalist society to its foundations..the values of capitalist society are profoundly evil and therefore must be profoundly changed..that only socialism could ensure the enlargement of freedom of the individual and his or her beauty and the best things in life..and that a socialism which spurned, or neglected to protect freedom of thought, speech and association was no socialism at all.

Phyllis Allfrey was to abide by the above views and saw the Labour Party as the instrument in building such an easy-going

---

[15] . See Elizabeth Paravisini's ***Phyllis Shand Allfrey, A Caribbean Life*** (Rutgers University Press, 1996)at 61.
[16] . Id at 66. Edward Scobie, a mulatto Dominican, served in the Royal Air Force and was later a founding member of the Dominica Freedom Party. He later became a well known historian and Pan Africanist lecturer in New York City's black community and academic circles in the period 1970-1990.

socialism suitable for the balmy clime into which she had been born and amenable to the values of the romantic visionary and poet that she was at the core. Upon her return to Dominica with such radical ideas of racial justice and workers rights, she had shocked Dominican society by her disregard for the byzantine race and class distinctions of her time. Her invitations of black labourers to her home for tea and her very public association with trade unionist Emmanuel Christopher Loblack had scandalized the upper classes in Roseau. Loblack, a Master Public Works Department mason from Grandbay had experienced the harsh conditions under which Dominican labourers toiled. He had been inspired by the trade union activism which swept the English speaking Caribbean following the Labour riots of the 1930s. His impassioned testimony before the **Moyne Commission** which had been sent to investigate the 1930 Labour uprising in the Caribbean consolidated his place as a leader among the Dominican working class.[17] After vigorous organizing amongst the workers, he co-founded Dominica's first trade union, the Dominica Trade Union on January 11, 1945 along with R.E.A. Nicholls (the uncle of Phyllis Allfrey), Austin Winston and [18]others. In the mold of the British Labour Party the team of Allfrey and Loblack created a Labour Party based on the social reformist ideals of Fabian socialism. The pair, formed the cutting

---

[17] See Id at 104.
[18] See Honeychurch, *The Dominica Story*, 173.

edge of the most exhaustive political organizing Dominica had ever known. Crossing the island by foot, donkey, wading rivers and skidding up and down hills in an old jeep, Allfrey and Loblack made for a fascinating black and white twosome. In that manner, during the 1950s the Labour Party's message of social change was carried from one tiny village to the next. The party appealed to the port workers, ordinary labourers, and rural peasantry; otherwise, that sector of Dominica's population which is made up of what is commonly termed the ***petite bouge*** (or little man) in local French patois.

On May 24, 1955, the Labour party sprang into life from the steps of the Dominica Trade Union Hall in Lagon, Roseau. Labour sought gradual social reform, over revolutionary change, in the Fabian mold. In accordance with its ideals, the party championed the cause of the urban working class and rural peasantry; fought class oppression, colour prejudice and the divide between town and country. Earlier, the Peoples National Movement (PNM) of businessmen Frank Baron and Clifton Dupigny had been formed in the mid 50s to counter the more radical DLP. A relative conservative, Baron later became the island's first Chief Minister. The Freedom Party came into birth later, in October 1968. It grew out of the remnants of the pro-planter Dominica United Peoples Party (made up of followers of the PNM) which had been swept aside by Labour in the general election of 1961. Initially organized by lawyer Eugenia Charles,

Edward Scobie, Anthony Agar, Star Lestrade, Elkin Henry, Martin Sorhaindo and others, the party sought to arrest what was seen by many in the business and professional classes as a drift toward authoritarianism by Labour. To the masses however, the Freedom Party was seen as the tool of a Roseau based elite still mired in prejudice against the leaders of a party which championed the rights of the barefeet peasantry.[19] Labour's ascendancy had its roots in a 1951 revolution in the polling system which had granted every Dominican over the age of 21 the right to vote, without regard to qualifications which previously had sidelined the mass of the population.[20] The Freedom Party, on the other hand, drew its support from (and was perceived by a majority of the population) as representing the interests of the remnants of the old plantocracy, and elements of the Roseau commercial and administrative class. The foregoing sectors grouped the old free-coloured strata who had themselves been radical exponents of a growing Dominican nationalism in the 19th Century struggle against British Crown Colony government.

In the early 19th Century, Dominica had a local legislature, made up of merchants and slave owning landowners. However, Crown Colony rule had, eventually displaced the local legislature with direct rule from London on March 8, 1865. That state of

---

[19] To capitalize on its claim to represent the unshod poor, Labour later took the "Shoe" as its electoral symbol. Thereafter, it would be popularly called the "Shoe Party."
[20] Lennox Honeychurch, *The Dominica Story* (Letchworth Press, Ltd. Barbados, 1984), 176.

affairs continued during the early part of the 20th Century and during World Wars I and II, when many Black Dominicans fought and died making the world safe for democracy while not having the vote in their own country. It was only after the post-World War II balance of forces favored the self determination of colonial peoples did any semblance of democracy become a reality on the island. Labour's rise followed rapidly on the heels of the right to vote which was granted in 1951 and was viewed as a conquest by a black majority, over an urban mulatto elite which had, prior, held the local legislature in its unchallenged sway.

By 1961 a former agriculture extension officer from the remote village of Veille Case, Edward O. Leblanc led the Labour Party to electoral victory. Leblanc, as a banana inspector had become well known around the island, through his work with farmers. He later ascended to leadership of the party, and parted ways with Allfrey. Allfrey by that time had returned from Trinidad where she had been the Minister of Social Welfare in the short-lived Federal Government and the only female in Federal Premier Sir Grantley Adam's cabinet. True to her principles, which sought racial harmony, she had led a walk-out of the West Indian delegation at the 1960 International Labor Organization (ILO) conference in Geneva, in protest at the presence of the South African delegation. In her view the apartheid South

Africans did not represent "...the toiling suffering millions of that country[21]."

Despite such a clear vision of racial harmony which moved Allfrey, it is said that Leblanc resented Allfrey's paternalistic and arrogant attitude toward him. However, supporters of Allfrey came to see him as ungrateful to someone who - by her selflessness, tenacity and vision - had led him from being a mere cog in the colonial wheel to the exalted position of Chief Minister of Dominica. Ultimately, Allfrey's estrangement from Leblanc showed that even the noble efforts she had undertaken to bridge the divide of race and class could come unstuck in an environment fraught with political opportunism and mistrust. Ultimately Leblanc came to lead the country into Associated statehood, thus gaining a greater say for locals in the running of their affairs.

Impelled by Allfrey's vision and under Leblanc stewardship, Labour's social reformist policies had increased funding for health and education. In 1947 there were only 38 primary schools on the island providing education to children 5-12 year's old. Out of a 12,000 school age population only 5,000 actually attended school for any length of [22]time. The remainder laboured in the fields alongside their parents. And even of those who attended, a significant percentage did so spasmodically. A

---

[21]. See Paravisini-Gebert's *Allfrey-A Caribbean Life* at 175.
[22] See Cracknell, *Dominica* at 160.

few hundred of the privileged attended secondary school in Roseau at the Dominica Grammar School (which was the first secondary school, opened in 1893), St. Mary's Academy, Wesley High School or Convent High school. University education overseas catered to, perhaps, one or two students annually. More than a third of the population was illiterate. However, by 1970 there were 80 schools in operation and plans were also afoot to establish a Dominica Extra Mural Center for U.W.I. The Dominica Teachers College project was also on the drawing board and a technical wing (to impart metallurgical, woodwork and electronic skills) had been built to complement the new Dominica Grammar School building. A nursing school had been started in the 1960s to complement the newly built Princess Margaret Hospital. Plans were also in place for a new secondary school, at the second town of Portsmouth as well as a full blown technical college at Bellevue Rawle[23]. Much of the credit for that revolution in education goes to two former teachers, W.S. Stevens and H.L. Christian, both of whom were (at one time or the other) to later head the Ministry of Education under Labour. Their experience in the field, and dedication, earned them respect and support from their former teacher-colleagues within the system. The population had also grown healthier. With, the end of the Second World War diseases such as malaria and yaws were

---

[23] Once built, the institution was later called the Clifton Dupigny Technical College (Dupigny was a local businessman and politician of note during the 1950s). *Author's Note.*

eradicated by government efforts in conjunction with the World Health Organization. In 1956, under the leadership of a dynamic Dominican doctor trained in England, Dr. Dorian Shillingford, the Princess Margaret Hospital opened to provide an additional 240 hospital beds. Smaller hospitals and clinics were set up in the rural [24]areas. As well, several Dominican medical school graduates of U.W.I were beginning to return home to staff the health care system. Even nutrition got a boost from the food aid[25] component to President John F. Kennedy's Alliance for Progress which had been set-up to check any appeal the Cuban revolution might have upon the impoverished Latin American masses. Change had come, but more was desired.

DOMINICA 1970: THE TINDER

By 1970 the children of the rural poor had been granted educational opportunity never, hitherto, realized. With Labour in power, the urban working class perceived that it had powerful friends in the halls of the local legislature. However, such reformist success stirred greater expectations by a significant

---

[24] Id.
[25] The Roman Catholic Church was the primary conduit via which much of the US Alliance for Progress food was dispensed. The doling out of boxes of powdered milk and butter went a long way in giving the Catholic church a charitable image, considering that its support of slavery and tolerance of racial and class prejudice had made it an object of Labour Party criticism. ***Author's note.***

sector of the population that the economic system could not provide. Why so? To properly grasp an answer to that question, a quick review of Dominica's socioeconomic construct during that period is in order.

Though the growth of the banana trade with Britain had proved a boon for the small farmer who had access to land, much of the arable land was held by a few families. ***In a 1961 census it was found that 1.4 percent of the farmers occupied 56.4 percent of the [26]land.*** The big northern estates were held by the Armour, Laville, and Douglas families, the Shillingfords and Rolles dominated the west coast estates, while the Bellots controlled the major part of the estate holdings in the island's southern [27]tier. The landholding pattern had undergone little change since the darkest days of slavery. Thus, the rural peasantry had to squat on mostly inaccessible crown land, generally on sloping rocky soil prone to erosion and landslides.

But even those who were able to eke an existence out of the land, faced the exploitation and gross inequality of a banana and citrus trade totally monopolized in marketing and shipping by the British based transnational corporation, Geest Industries[28].

---

[26] Dominica Environmental Profile (Island Resources Foundation, Washington, D.C. 1991) at 76.
[27] Honeychurch, ***The Dominica Story*** at 164.
[28] See generally Michel-Rolph Trouillot's, ***Peasants and Capital:Dominica in the World Economy***, (The John Hopkins University Press, 1988). Trouillot explains how Caribbean peasants, including those of Dominica subsidized the growth of the Geest conglomerate.

The small light industry sector grouped around handicraft, fruit canning and soap-making was unable to absorb sufficient amounts of the high school graduates, far less the elementary school leavers. To most of those graduates agricultural labour was unappealing, steeped as they were in an education patterned on the British public school system. Though welcomed efforts at economic empowerment, neither the Cooperative Credit Union movement which grew under the guidance of Roman Catholic Nun Sister Alicia and others, or the Cooperative Bank of entrepreneur John-Baptiste "J.B." Charles were wealthy enough assist the improvement of their members precarious economic state.

Emigration was no longer an outlet. Whereas Dominica was part of the massive movement of Caribbean labour to Britain in the mid-fifties and early sixties, severe restrictions had been imposed by the British in 1961[29]. Accordingly, emigration to Britain was no longer an option to the growing mass of literate, unemployed and underemployed youth. Earlier destinations, such as Canada, or the Dutch islands of Curacao and Aruba had dried-up. The U.S. Virgin Islands were an option, but one traversed with great difficulty. Dominica's civil service had expanded to meet the needs of the new health and education initiatives, as well as jobs derivative of political patronage. By 1970, however, the civil service (Dominica's biggest employer) was at saturation

---

[29] See Cracknell, *Dominica* at 154.

point. The financial burden posed by meeting civil service salaries was becoming an increasingly onerous task. There was no state sector in mining, agriculture or fisheries to generate foreign exchange directly into the public coffers to pay for such government expenditures. The biggest government foreign investment deal, a 1966 government contract with a Canadian firm Dom-Can Timbers Ltd. to harvest Dominica's lush forest failed to meet expectations. With $100,000.00 (U.S.) in projected royalties over the first two years of the contract, the government grossed only $15,000.00, as the company saw it fit to cut timber on more easily accessible private land instead of government lands deep in the [30] interior. The old estate families which formed the core of Dominica's national bourgeoisie were content to allow their lands lie fallow, engage, spasmodically, in real estate speculation or, nominally, in the monocrop economy.

With regard to the Roseau based commercial strata, it was the same old pattern of whole-sale retail trade, without any dynamic investment in light industry or hotel development to spur new foreign exchange income. The discord between the government and the commercial sector paralyzed local investment. To many, it appeared that the local business class was content to sit on its money until a government of its liking came to power. Without any control over its foreign affairs the

---

[30] R. Michael Wright, **Morne Trois Pitons National Park in Dominica: A Case Study in Park Establishment in the Developing World**, (Ecology Law Quarterly, 1985).

Labour government could not approach foreign governments for soft loans or grants and was restricted to British assistance, which was minimal. Without new investments in agriculture or industry by the old plantocracy which could absorb the expanding legions of literate school leavers, or assist the economy in any measurable way,[31] tensions were sure to rise.

The Freedom party of 1970 was more a vehicle for criticism of the Labour regime (which the town-based Freedomites saw as an assault by the formerly powerless rural poor upon their citadel of privilege) than a catalyst for systemic change. During that period the Freedom Party did not exhibit any interest in political freedom for Dominica, as in independence from Britain. Neither did the party champion any new program of economic development, agricultural diversification, land reform or indigenous industry. Aside from the modest cannery of the Bellot family at Newtown and the Fort Young Hotel development, the Freedom party allies in the business community seemed caught in the grip of inertia. From her perch as the Editor of *The Star*, an increasingly frail Mrs. Allfrey and her husband Robert castigated the government for becoming increasingly dictatorial and dismissive of civil liberties. **The Dominica Herald**

---

[31] The only significant industrial development was with Dominica Coconut Products. Initiated by a Dominican of Arab extraction, Philip Nasief, it was later sold to US based Colgate Palm-Olive group, amidst much protests from economic nationalists aghast that a vibrant agro-industrial enterprise which had prospered from government protection would now be sold to a foreign firm intent on controlling competition in the Caribbean soap market. **Author's Note.** Also, see Honeychurch, *The Dominica Story* at 160.

newspaper was also critical of government, and took a similar conservative stance. Allfrey allied herself with the Freedom Party on protest marches and the like, calling Leblanc a "Hitler and a Mussolini.[32]" Spurred by what she perceived as the betrayal of her fondest ideals, even the political progressive in Allfrey failed to appreciate Dominica was still a British Colony.

To the restless youth it seemed that "change" for the Freedom Party meant "change-of-party" (i.e. Freedom instead of Labour), not liberation from colonialism or alteration of the bleak social or economic status quo which was a brake on social advancement for the majority. In the meantime, the new political class created by Labour was becoming more entrenched and lacking in new blood or vision. Made comfortable by the perks of political power, the socialist idealism which had motivated Labour in the days of Loblack and Allfrey was gone. Indeed, by the mid-1960s both Allfrey and Loblack had parted ways with Labour.

Returning graduates, some of them children of the rural poor who had found opportunity with the Labour victory, were eyed suspiciously, as if carriers of some fatal virus.[33] To a great

---

[32] Paravisini-Gebert's *Allfrey* at 217.
[33] Indeed, Dominican U.W.I graduates like Dr. William "Para" Riviere, Julian Johnson, Swinburne Lestrade, and others were present, either in Trinidad and/or Jamaica when some of the insurrectionary violence associated with black power protests occurred in 1968 and 1970. On returning home, Roseau youth would gather at the Botanic Gardens or the intersection of Kennedy Avenue and Great George Street (popularly called "Four Corners") to listen and hold discussion with some of the returning U.W.I graduates.

extent, a policy of exclusion, rather than inclusion was the fate of those recent university graduates.

The historical record will show that the failure by the state to absorb the majority of those graduates had a dual underpinning. First, the economic infrastructure to support graduates in the traditional areas like engineering, law or medicine (at the level of remuneration/consumption most desired) was lacking or under great strain. Second, there existed a genuine fear within the new bureaucracy and political class that returning graduates would edge them out of their jobs or disseminate ideas which were not "politically correct." Such a fear was real, considering that the returnees (though small in number) represented the greatest number of university-level graduates yet produced by Dominica in its recorded history, some of whom had taken part in political disturbances on neighboring islands.

Frustrated, some would leave. Others, more defiant, would seek an agency through which to channel their political aspirations. The increasingly literate army of urban youth presented as such an agency. Spawned by the post-war changes and Labour-led reform, that army was in search of direction, in need of jobs, was beginning to question its identity. Were they black-Englishmen? West Indians? Dominicans? What? In 1968, researcher Carleen O'Loughlin of U.W.I had noted:

> [Dominica] has been among those exhibiting little haste in the move towards independence. These attitudes may be ascribed to an emphasis on

caution, but it may also be possible that Dominica is lacking a nationalist feeling because it has not developed a national culture...At the moment it would be hard to find a West Indian people less given to nationalist introspection...

Such a lack of nationalist fervor was changing. Self-government was new to Dominica. Emphasis on celebrating national culture on November 3rd, each year was [34] new. But even with what was new, there were signs of impatience. Coupled with the search for a cultural identity, or national purpose, was a yearning by youth for the creation of new economic and political space. Thus, at the beginning of the 1970s that was Dominica's context. Such was the societal tinder, to which the Dominican intelligentsia was to put a spark.

BLACK POWER: ORIGINS

Black power, as it came to be known in Dominica of the 1970s had a distinct foreign impetus. But it would be to miss the point, entirely, if one failed to recognize Dominica's colonial status, and the unresolved issues of color prejudice, interwoven

---

[34] The Labour government of Leblance had opted to use November 3rd, as National Day, since it was on that date in 1493, that Christopher Columbus became the first European, of record, to encounter the island. Accordingly, formal recognition was given to dress which had evolved out of peasant/plantation wear during the slave era, and the local patois and cultural mores were granted a new respectability. *Author's Note.*

with the economic imperatives of class. As such the issue of whether blacks, i.e. the majority of Dominicans had any power was relevant.

> We were worked like slaves! Labourers worked for less than six pence per day. On the Hillsborough Estate, if you picked up a dry coconut to make sauce for your food and you were caught, is court for you, or they would deduct it from your little pay. Because the best lands were owned by the estates, people were desperate. They had to till rock soil, or move deeper into the mountains. When, we went to town to sell produce and tried to buy things, you would be cheated and the store owners would look down on you...[35]

Simply put, the Dominican "aristocracy", as far as it was perceived, was mulatto and immersed in color and class prejudice which made for the conditions noted above. By 1970 the white population in Dominica was insignificant in its holdings within the island. Also, Dominica fell well within the confines of economic control exercised by foreign, primarily British, capital: Geest Industries and L. Rose & Co. had a monopoly on the export of bananas and citrus, Dominica's main foreign exchange earners; The Royal Bank of Canada and Barclays Bank International, both foreign, dictated the modus operandi of local finance capital, as well as monopolized foreign exchange transactions by local

---

[35] . March 9, 2002, statement by Albertha Christian nee John-Baptiste, born in St. Joseph, Dominica, in 1929, who later became the first local Manager of the National Workshop for the Blind under Labour's rule.

industry or remittances from Dominicans overseas. The foregoing, is not to disregard the fact that Dominicans like J.B. Charles, R.B. Douglas (and others) were significant players in the world of commerce and agriculture. Or that the bulk of the teachers, policemen, firemen, bank clerks, civil servants and others who constituted what passed for Dominica's growing middle class, were of African descent. In fact the political ascendancy of the reformist Labour party had created the space for an enlargement of the middle-class. Nonetheless, all Dominicans resided within a system of economic control that noted Caribbean academic Lloyd Best had described as "plantation economy further modified"; i.e. passively responsive to metropolitan demand and metropolitan investment; with very little of a "residentiary" sector, locally owned, serving domestic markets, using domestically developed technology, and subject to local [36] influence. It may have soothed somewhat that in Dominica, unlike other Caribbean islands like Jamaica or Trinidad (where a significant East Indian or Chinese commercial class existed), most small retail sales, rum shops, and grocery stores were in the hands of a primarily black, commercial strata. Several significant Roseau stores were, however, owned by Dominicans of Arab extraction; i.e. Philip and Elias Nassief, Josephine Gabriel, George Karam, Wadid Astaphan and others.

---

[36] Jay R. Mandle, *British Caribbean Economic History*, at 248 in Knights' and Colin *The Modern Caribbean*.

The old Roseau free colored elite; i.e. the Greens, Shillingfords, Burtons, Edwards, and Philips still maintained stores. However, it was apparent and rather notorious at the time that their businesses were not faring well. It is now commonly felt in Dominica, that several of the Dominicans of Arab extraction threw in their lot with Labour, and so profited from many government contracts.[37] Meanwhile, the old Roseau elite which postured (and was otherwise perceived) as an ally of the Freedom party was denied such access to the public coffers. However, even if Dominicans of African descent had a better foothold in the economic sphere (albeit, on a local level) than their other Caribbean neighbors of African descent, it still rankled that more control was not possible. As well, the recognition that Dominicans had no real control of their trade with Britain, or that colonialism had not benefitted the population after hundreds of years began to gain adherents.

Of equal importance in tracing the origins of black power thought in Dominica, were the psychic scars lashed into the minds of Dominicans by centuries of Western-taught self hate and the ridicule lavished upon Africa and people of African descent. American movies, featuring Tarzan and other white super-heroes lording it over blacks had reinforced that self-hate and ridicule of

---

[37] George Karam, owner of Acme Garage, was the major car dealer in central Roseau. In the mid-1970s he would become Mayor of Roseau under Labour Premier Patrick John, as well as one of John's close confidants. At that time, he appointed a City Council made up of members of his family.

all things black. That maelstrom of prejudice, self-hate and doubting of self among the African descended population, was reinforced by the prejudices of many who made up the mulatto elite. Marrying "White" (i.e., someone of lighter complexion), was sometimes the preferred route of "escape" by many a local black of accomplishment. "Black like butt" (Butt, being the patois term for a small whale with black, oily skin) was a common pejorative before and during that period. There were even gradations of skin color as explained by Deputy Prime Minister and Minister of Education in Dominica's first independence government, Henckell L. Christian:

> There were so many distinctions and gradations based on skin colour as a badge of respectability. Women were described as, Milatwesse, Cabwesse, Sharbine or Negresse.[38]

To undergird Christian's point, Carl Lumumba in *The West Indies and the George Williams Affair: An Assessment*[39] wrote:

---

[38] . See Henckell Lochinvar Christian, MBE, *Gatecrashing Into The Unknown-A Dominica Journal* (ACT Press, Roseau Dominica 1992) at 27. A Milatwesse is the product of a white-black union; Cabwesse, a light skinned black woman with a straight nose and fine hair, as in a Carib/black/mulatto union. A Sharbine would be a red-skinned woman, with black features. A Negresse is a black woman. Comment by Alberta Christian, based on her knowledge of the customs, descriptions and prejudices of the time. March 9, 2002.

[39] See Lumumba at *Let the Niggers Burn!* 151.

Of much more profound importance are those ethno-cultural defects which predispose such pathetic psychological defects as:

The wearing of woolen suits, closed collars
 and ties in 85-90 degree temperatures
A negro attorney general in curled blond wig
The persistent pinching of babies noses
 so they grow straight
The painful process of hair straightening
Purposely cutting the hair short so knots
 wont show
The use of skin bleaching creams
The assessment of beauty on the basis
of "good hair" straight noses, and nearest-to-white skin colour.

Dominican educator, Henckell Christian was to comment:

> Janice Armour (nee Joseph) was to create history when she became the first black girl to be employed at the local branch of the Royal Bank of Canada...the first dark skin beauty who successfully crossed the colour bar...of the Dominica Queen Competition was Evadney Charles of Roseau in 1965...

Such were the distortions in society leading up to the period of black pride politics.

The indigenous Carib people fared little better; castigated by colonizers and brainwashed segments of the population as being cannibalistic, lazy and prone to drink. Commenting on the slanderous tilt to the charge of cannibalism, Carib Chief Irvince Auguiste stated:

> It is a wicked lie...it goes back to the Spanish, the English...Columbus came looking for gold...he met the people inhabiting these islands and tried to enslave them. And the Carib people had enjoyed their freedom for centuries, making their cassava bread and catching fish. Naturally, they would retaliate against anyone trying to enslave them...then when they first brought in enslaved Blacks they told them that Caribs ate Black people, so that the maroons would not seek to join us when they ran away, and would fight us when they did. Like that they kept our two peoples separated for a long time[40].

Auguiste, representative of a new and vibrant Carib leadership, was to take his place among a less subservient Carib generation[41]. Also, as the racial pride spawned by black power thought took root, the frequency of ethnic or color-based insults toward the Carib segment of the population decreased. On September 19, 1930, the Caribs had risen against brutal conduct by the colonial police during an anti-smuggling operation. Suppressed by police reinforcements and a display of force by the **HMS Delhi**, the proud inhabitants who had risen simmered down. However, the incident is cited by many of the new Carib

---

[40]. See *Wild Majesty: Encounters with Caribs from Columbus to the Modern Day-An Anthology* (Oxford University Press, 1999) Edited by Peter Hulme and Neil L. Whitehead at 350.

[41]. That generation was to include one time member of parliament in the 1990's, Dr. Erskine Sandiford, the first Carib medical doctor, trained in modern medicine. He was educated by the Cuban Revolution, as was Kelly Graneau, member of Parliament and Minister of Carib Affairs in the 2000 Labour led Coalition government. *Author's note.*

nationalists as the beginning of their awakening during the 20th century. Soon enough, they would shed the shame heaped on them by the colonial authorities.

Indeed, the radical politics espoused by Allfrey, Loblack, Leblanc and Douglas, lit a fire of dignity amongst the Caribs. Soon, both amongst Caribs and African-descended Dominicans, a new pride would prevail in their racial and cultural heritage.

But self hate ran deep and was perpetuated by the school system and the press. That such prejudice and self hate could find exponents in the press as recently as 1951, is testimony to racism which preceded Labour, and continued (to a lesser extent) afterward. In the Dominica Chronicle of September 22, 1951 what passes for an editorial piece admonished Dominicans thus:

> In England, Englishmen work hard, hard, hard. They can argue and reason in terms of such hardness, but here we would be pure apes to think we can do so...[42]

In that same editorial, the paper told Dominicans:

> There is nothing more laughable or fantastic to convince people here, that for all our ills and requirements past and present, and for all other purposes, there exist in Dominica various political parties any one of which will sooner or later be in power[43].

---

[42] *The Dominica Chronicle*, September 22, 1951 at pg. 6
[43] Id.

The rank servility and thorough inferiority complex engendered by centuries of a white supremacist miseducation is evident in the above lines from **The Dominica Chronicle**. That editorial was commenting on the upcoming 1951 election, the first held under a universal adult suffrage regime. The results in a few years would show how shortsighted that editor was in his predictions.

The foregoing considered, there existed a sufficient local imperative with which to galvanize new cultural awareness and self-respect. Nonetheless Dominicans, their history considered, had shown concern for black struggles overseas. In **La Guerre Negre** (or the Negro War) of June 1844, a William Ellisonde of Stowe Estate testified that one of the insurrectionist of Grandbay, African-born Remy had said the rebellion in Dominica ought take on the pattern of St. Domingue[44] (i.e. the Haitian revolution). It was clear that even before the age of swift communications, Dominicans were observing overseas struggles for freedom, emulating them where possible.

In late 1919 Ralph Casimir, Casimir Morancie and Francis Louis Gardier formed the Dominica Brotherhood Union , "an intended branch of Marcus Garvey's Universal Negro Improvement Association (UNIA). Its history reveals it to be the first black nationalist organization, of record, in Dominica during the 20th Century. Its founders signed a solemn pledge and swore

---

[44] Trouillot, **Peasants and Capital**, 102.

"..to help the Negro...and to give their lives if necessary for the great cause of African Freedom."[45][46] Despite the absence of official recognition from the UNIA's Harlem headquarters in New York City, these energetic supporters of African Liberation in Dominica soon saw their number swell to 800, with their own literary club[47] contingent of Black Cross Nurses and paramilitary African Legion, in black twill, leather leggings, hobnailed boots and Sam Browne belts. Before long they were collecting money and buying shares in the UNIA's Black Star line[48], hopeful that it would assist the uplift of their race. The group solicited funds and membership with such vigor that the British colonial authorities cracked down on the purchase of money orders with new regulations which limited such purchases to a maximum of two pounds.[49] So dynamic was Casimir's own family in that effort that his mother, Maria, was popularly called "Mama Black Star Line!"[50] Unknown to many Dominicans was the fact that

---

[45] . See Dr. Tony Martin, **A Pan-Africanist in Dominica, J.R. Ralph Casimir and the Garvey Movement**, 1919-1923, The New Chronicle, April 12, 1992, page 9.

[46] . Of interesting note, The African Blood Brotherhood was formed in the same year (1919) by early Garvey supporter, West Indian born Cyrill Briggs. Was Briggs in communication with Casimir and the others? The militant and the vigorous Pan African trajectory of both organizations is striking in their similarity, when one notes the focus on military discipline, secrecy, and a "fight to the death against racism" approach of both entities.

[47] . See Dr. Tony Martin, Race First, **The Ideological and Organizational Struggles of the Universal Negro Improvement Association** (The New Marcus Garvey Library, 1976) at page 25.

[48] Id.

[49] Id.

[50] Id.

eminent local entrepreneur and politician, J.B. Charles (father of Prime Minister Dame Eugenia Charles) was a Garvey supporter and corresponded with him with regard to using the Black Star line to ship his lime oil and other agricultural produce to New York. J.B. Charles had also carried on correspondence with renown African American thinker, educator and scholar, Booker T. Washington, adopting some of his views on education and self-reliance as a means to escaping the destitution among blacks left behind by slavery. To that end, Charles sent two of his sons to African American colleges, Morehouse and Tuskegee, in the early part of the 20th Century[51].

Dr. Tony Martin, the leading UNIA historian and chairman of the Black Studies Department at Wellesley College in Massachusetts, notes that Casimir was a steady contributor to the UNIA's *Negro World*, and formed part of the literary flowering which created the Harlem Renaissance. He wrote of

---

[51] 1997 interview, by this author, of Dame Eugenia Charles at Upper Marlboro, Maryland. Her explanation of J.B. Charles history reveals him to have been a Pan-Africanist who, for business reasons, kept many of his opinions private. The Prime Minister disclosed that her father visited Revolutionary Russia in its early days, and was a guest at the Independence celebrations of both Ghana and Nigeria. In her words "...he was very proud of his race...and believed in Africa as his home." Her disclosures, seems to explain why noted Pan-Africanist and Dominican UNIA leader J.R. Casimir was a close associate of J.B. Charles' and later a clerk at her law firm for many years. It also sheds some light on why Casimir was a vociferous early supporter of Eugenia Charles, despite her seemingly pro business conservative politics. Charles relates, that as a child, she would accompany her father to many such Pan African meetings where Casimir spoke.

Casimir, who helped arrange a visit by Garvey to Dominica's shores in 1937, thus:

> One of the most prolific Negro World poets of all was J.R. Ralph Casimir of Dominica, West Indies. He headed the local UNIA and belonged to its literary club. In addition to poems, he also contributed articles on political conditions in Dominica and the activities of his UNIA division. Occasionally, he wrote under the pseudonym "Civis Africanus" (Citizen of Africa)....in 1946 Casimir published in a Garveyite journal,
>
> Persecuted by white folk
> and cheated by his own,
> He fought for Afric's welfare
> To cowardice not prone...
> Bow down ye traitors
> Who tampered with his plan,
> What plan have you to offer
> To help the African?[52]

While the primary goal of the local UNIA member was to seek the improvement of the race on the island, there was also solidarity articles in the *Tribune* and *West Indian Times*, along with efforts such as protest rallies and petitions to the British in support of the Ethiopians under Emperor Haile Selassie then battling the forces of Fascist Italy which had invaded that country in 1935.

---

[52] Dr. Tony Martin, Literary **Garveyism, Garvey Black Arts and The Harlem Renaissance** (The Majority Press, 1983) at 65.

Local members made efforts to reach assembly points in New York from where they hoped to board ships for the journey to the African battlefield[53]. Several prominent members of the Dominica's African Legion were ex-soldiers of the British army who had served in World War I and they were now anxious to strike a blow for African freedom. The record reveals concerns by colonial administrators in Dominica over local UNIA links to New York and the threat posed by such radicalism. However, the process of awakening had just begun.

The exponents of the argument that Black Power thought was a foreign import, were either ignorant of the reality of Dominican society with its origins in European kidnaping of Africans for purposes of enslaving them in the Western hemisphere and the related displacement and decimation of the indigenous Carib inhabitants of the island. Such was the basis of the society. It was also not appreciated by the critics of the new consciousness, that West Indians or their offspring such as W.E.B. Dubois[54] and James Weldon Johnson[55] were major

---

[53] Trinidadian Garveyite, Herbert Fauntleroy Julian, a resident of New York and one of the first blacks to hold a pilot's license actually got to Ethiopia and engaged the Italian airforce in aerial combat, with one of Ethiopia's few planes. Overwhelming Italian air power soon crippled all opposition to the invaders. During World War II, with British and South African assistance, Ethiopia expelled the Italians in 1940. Author's note.

[54]. Dr. W.E.B. Dubois (1868-1963) was born of a Haitian father and African American mother. The first black person to earn a doctoral degree from Harvard University, he was a founder of the Niagara Movement, the National Association for the Advancement of Colored People (NAACP), the Pan African Congress and editor of the NAACP magazine, *The Crisis*. He started

contributors to black liberation thought in the U.S. During the Harlem Renaissance of the 1920's expatriate West Indians, Claude McKay, Marcus Garvey, W.A. Domingo, Arthur A. Schomburg[56], Richard B. Moore[57], among others led the fight for civil rights and overall black liberation in the U.S. and worldwide. Noted U.S. radical Harry Haywood recalls:

> The African Blood Brotherhood was founded in New York City in 1919 by a group of black radicals under the leadership of [Cyril P.] Briggs[58]. A West Indian (as were most of the founders)

---

work on the African encyclopedia project finally completed By Henry Louis Gates and Kwame Anthony Appiah in 1999

[55] . James Weldon Johnson (1871-1938), the first African American NAACP Executive Secretary was of Bahamian parentage. He was a US diplomat, scholar and co-author, with his brother Rosamond, of *"Lift Ev'ry Voice and Sing"* the song that became known as the Negro National Anthem. See Kwame Anthony Appiah and Henry Louis Gates, *AFRICANA, The Encyclopedia of the African and African American Experience* (Basic Civitas Book, 1999)at 1053

[56] . Still considered the pre-eminent bibliophile and collector of books on the Negro, Arthur A. Schomburg was born in San Juan Puerto Rico in 1874 and was a founder of the Negro Society for Historical Research and later became President of the American Negro Academy. His prestigious collection of Black History now forms part of New York Library's Schomburg Center for Research in Black Culture. Its 5 million items makes it the largest repository of Black works in the world. See *World's Great Men of Color* (Collier Books, 1972),by J.A. Rogers and *Africana*, supra, at 1678.

[57] . Barbadian born Richard B. Moore (1893-1978) was one of the leading leftist scholars and organizers in the Harlem community in the 1920s and '30s and one of the leaders of Caribbean independence in the 1940s, '50s and 60s. See *Richard B. Moore, Caribbean Militant in Harlem* (Pluto Press, London, 1992)edited by W. Burghardt Turner and Joyce Moore Turner.

[58] . Cyril Valentine Briggs, born in Nevis in 1888, was the founder of the African Blood Brotherhood, a secret black organization that promoted self defense for black communities following the bloody anti-black riots which gripped the US in 1918-1919. He was founder of the *Crusader* magazine and the American Negro Labor Congress. See *Africana*, supra, at 310.

(sic)....his associate Richard B. Moore, Grace Campbell and others-and The Crusader were among the vanguard forces for the New Negro Movement, an ideological current which reflected the new mood of ilitancy and social awareness of young blacks...[59]

Following on that wave of West Indian contribution to U.S. black consciousness and liberation thought earlier in the 20th Century, came others like Harry Belafonte, CLR James[60], Sidney Poitier, Shirley Chisholm, Malcolm Little aka Malcolm X, Louis Farrakhan, W.E.B Dubois and others who were West Indian born or of West Indian parentage. The oppressive weight of colonialism in their homelands had forced them or their parents, to migrate. In the United States (now mostly forgotten as having its origins in the first successful anti-imperialist revolt of the post Colombus era) they became worthy heirs to, and inheritors of, the revolutionary spirit of 1776, when the American colonists who "held these truths to be self evident, that all men are created equal" set about ejecting the British colonizers from the thirteen colonies. Under the liberal U.S. constitution, despite the burden of racial prejudice, they had rights which recognized them as

---

[59]. See Harry Haywood's **Black Bolshevik: An Autobiography of an Afro-American Communist** (Liberator Press, Chicago, Il, 1978) at page 123. Also, see Howard Zinn's **A People's History of the United States** (Harper Perrenial, 1990) at page 373

[60]. Trinidadian, CLR James (1901-1989)was a distinguished writer, Marxist social critic, Pan Africanist activist and an early ally of Dr. Eric Williams and Ghana's Kwame Nkrumah.

citizens not subjects, and afforded their children better access to education and economic opportunity. If anything a truthful rendition of the facts show a consistent cross fertilization of ideas and experiences between West Indian and U.S. thinkers and activists anxious to better the condition of their people.

BLACK POWER: THE MOVEMENT, THE CHANGES

Organized black thought eventually coalesced around the Black Power Movement (BPM) formed by SMA teacher Hilroy Thomas, and DGS graduates Julian Johnson, Donald Peters and others in 1970. Their pamphlet *Flambeau* came out in several stirring copies, before BPM gave way to new blood.[61]

By 1970-1971 a loose grouping of radical students gathered around Desmond "Destrot" Trotter also issuing several copies of the news-sheet *Black Cry*[62]. It soon disbanded to merge into The Movement for a New Dominica (MND), formed in Roseau on November 16th, 1972. The movement wasted no time in starting its own newspaper *Twavay* (French patois for "Work."). *Twavay* sought the raising of black consciousness, by popularizing the concept of Africa as the ancestral homeland of

---

[61]. Statement by Dominican Academic Dr. Donald Peters on March 17, 1992.
[62]. Statement by Dominican Black Power leader, Birdock Shillingford, June 24, 1992.

Dominica's majority and the need to assist that continent's liberation from colonialism was vocalized constantly. Self respect and black dignity was taught through rap sessions at the botanical gardens, Four Corners, the Goodwill Parish Hall and the St. Gerard's Hall. In the movement, words like "Brother" or "Sister" became common usage when referring to others who were not related to you by blood. If a brother or sister made a solid political point on a platform, they were "Right on!" and those who wore nice-looking dashikis or afro hairstyles were "in the groove." No longer would Dominicans curse their blackness. Black was now beautiful.

An important distinction to be made here, is that black nationalist thinking did not merely fixate its energies on symbols of black pride, but simultaneously waged an anti-colonial battle. Further, black power thought as manifested on the island went beyond a focus on blackness, to also encompass the Carib struggle as one more worthy effort by a captive people yearning to be free. No longer would the young accept the British text book descriptions of Caribs as savages and cannibals simply because they had resisted the colonial invasion with vigor. Such resistance would now be viewed in a noble and heroic light, worthy of acknowledgment and emulation. In that way, black nationalist thought escaped the confines of racial insularity and embraced all those who had been victimized: mulattoes, progressive whites, Caribs, blacks. Nonetheless, the detractors of black power ideology would seek to lay all mindless acts of anti-white prejudice at the door of the movement. For people who had endured 500 hundred years of colonial subjugation, such criticism of black power adherents as anti-white was really a case of blaming the victim for attempting an escape from the cauldron of victimization.

At different times during the 1970s, black power marchers would gather at the Windsor Park, the Botanical Gardens, Peebles (better known as Peoples) Park or Four Corners[63] in central Roseau. They would then wind their way past foreign owned symbols of colonial commerce, such as Barclays Bank, Royal Bank of Canada, Cable & Wireless, the electric power company run by the Colonial Development Corporation (CDC) where marchers would pause and listen to a speech on how much money the particular institution was "ripping-off" from Dominicans. Later, the marchers (sometimes 4,000 to 6,000 strong) would regroup at their point of origin. At that time speakers like Bill Riviere, Desmond Trotter, Nathalie "Sister Nats" Charles, Birdock Shillingford, Donald Peters, or visiting notables like Bernard Wiltshire would speak to the mostly youthful crowd. The highly educated black power orators would

---

[63] . The corner of Great George Street and Kennedy Avenue in Roseau; the popular gathering ground between 1970-1978 of the Roseau radical intelligentsia, student activist and lumpen proletariat or perennially unemployed/underemployed youth. When Cracknell's *Dominica,* at 168 mentions shouts of "honky" and anti-white sentiment as emanating from "street corners" he could be speaking of Four Corners.

delve into history, economics, statistics: hard facts. For Roseau crowds which had hitherto enjoyed the entertainment provided by the saucy political mud-slinging (or *mepuis* in patois) of the traditional politicians, the new oratory was sobering fare; a new form of political education. The mass of Roseau residents, even if they were to later catch-on to the dress code and oratory of radical chic, were still onlookers; listeners, not yet actors in the unfolding drama. Many who considered themselves Freedomites or of the older generation, were openly critical and scornful of these "ungrateful black power boys, for whom white people had done so much[64]".

Another important facet of black power thought in Dominica was the focus on Pan Africanism and the liberation wars being waged in Portuguese controlled areas of Africa such Guinea Bissau. One learnt about Amilcar Cabral's PAIGC in Guinea Bissau, the FRELIMO movement of Mozambique led by Samora Machel and the MPLA of Angola led by Agostinho Neto via films of these guerrila groups in combat or pamphlets from North American support organizations. Resolutions were drawn-up and solidarity calls issued in support of the liberation struggle in Africa. Statements calling for the release of Nelson Mandela and the unbanning of the African national Congress ANC, were

---

[64]. A remark, remembered by this author and made by a scornful (and middle-aged) onlooker at the corner of Virgin Lane and Bath Road, Summer 1973. Such remarks typified Dominica's new generational cleavage between the more radical young and conservative old (be they Labour or Freedom supporters).

issued after clenched-fist resolutions by massed crowds, long before such became popular in many countries of the West. Films were shown at schools, or the Goodwill Parish Hall, educating young Dominicans about the struggles of their African brothers and sisters' portraying them in roles of resistance or governance never before witnessed on film in Dominica. One such depiction which stirred many hearts was the movie **Last Grave at Dimbaza** which gave Dominicans a chilling view of the inside of a South African township. Sometimes, money was collected to be donated to the Organization of African Unity Liberation Committee.[65]

Focusing homeward, the involved urban youth attacked inadequacies of a school curriculum which taught Latin and Shakespeare to the disregard of local, Caribbean or African history. As well, the importance of local control of agricultural production, the heightening of local cultural values and a new search for identity were championed. Real confrontation with the establishment had not come though, except in random cases of police strong-arm tactics. In search of more daring leadership, many followed the trials and imprisonment of Rosie Douglas on charges stemming from the Sir George Williams University protest in Canada and wished his return. At rallies many were

---

[65] . In an effort at establishing his black consciousness credentials Premier Leblanc's government donated US $10,000.00 to the Organization of African Unity, Liberation Committee in 1971. **Author's Note.**

heard to mutter, "They'll see fire in their skin, when brother Rosie comes".

BLACK POWER: THE FLOWERING OF LOCAL CULTURE

In this new social ferment, politics became total; a way of life. No longer would one become a political being simply at election time; or wearing what was considered by the new radicals as the silly party tag of "Labourite", or "Freedomite." Party politics was disdained as a mockery and a cesspool of tribalism which ill served the masses who were fed a steady fare of *mepuis* on political platforms. Instead, emphasis was placed on reading books on black history, culture, art and poetry. To the new thinkers such party loyalty was considered a ruse by devious political rulers to dupe their ill informed adherents. Black power was a movement not a party. Adherence meant to submerge ones whole life into the new nationalist creed. In his thinly veiled autobiography posing as fiction, *A Passage To Anywhere*, Dominican historian and attorney Irving Andre who attended the Dominica Grammar School during that time wrote of his impressions:

> There were also black intellectuals from the university talking about black this and black that. Many wore long multi-colored robes, dashikis..,There were also words, phrases, slogans,

> ...Africa for the Africans...I was so fascinated...I would later refer to myself as Winshoba Wacamba.[66]

Winshoba Wacamba! Even some notable professionals in contemporary Dominican society still carry their African nicknames from that period of activism with pride: Ear Nose and throat surgeon Dr. Irvin "Eipigh" Pascal, renowned attorney Alick "Nkomo" Lawrence and head of the new Bureau of Standards, chemical engineer, Dr. Steve John, also known "Ras Kwame" or "Chu" are part of that proud legacy. Indeed, the passionate spirit of the times went so far as cause many to jettison their Euro-centric birth names forever. Later, an entire generation of Dominican children would bear names with African roots.

In the new dispensation, ones diet, dress and thought pattern was kneaded into the loaf of an upright approach of black consciousness which would be baked in the oven of struggle. Thus, a serious effort was made to undermine the fiction of one being apolitical, since the mere fact of being alive requires one to exist within a particular political construct. Accordingly, it was natural that black power thought was to infuse itself into the very culture.

---

[66] . Irving Andre, *A Passage to Anywhere* (Pond Casse Press, 1997) at 108.

In that new cultural milieu, Black American films of what is now considered the "Blacksploitation" period in Hollywood, would cause massive crowds of Roseau residents to throng the entrances of the two cinemas, Arawak and Carib, in a frantic search for seats. Blacks were now in movies in heroic, not menial roles. Sometimes, they were shown striking out at white oppressors. Featuring black stars such as James Brown, Sidney Poiter, Fred Williamson, or Richard Roundtree, movies such as ***Shaft, Cotton Comes to Harlem, Cleopatra Jones, Buck and the Preacher, Nigger Charlie,*** and ***The Return of Nigger Charlie*** sent their mammoth audiences wild with pride. The prior movie fare dominated by John Wayne was under assault and Dominican crowds no longer reveled in the on-screen slaughter of native Americans by pistol packing cowboys. The audience, once informed of the universality of the struggle against oppression now saw the native American in a sympathetic light. A proud cultural assertion was being furthered by those new heroes of the cinema to whom the vast majority of the audience could relate.

A new introspection created a surge in local artistic endeavors, often times spurred by a Labour administration eager to show its nationalist credentials. Increasingly, Dominican themes gained prominence. The Sisserou parrot, indigenous to the island, now adorned the national coat of arms. By 1970, Dominicans no longer sang ***God Save the Queen***, as their national anthem. Rather, a new national song, ***Isle of Beauty*** written by locals W.O.M. Pond, with music composed by Lemuel M. Christian, took center stage at parades and other official events.

By 1973-1974 a cultural and literary paper *Wahseen* was being published, with contributions by Daniel Cauderion, Alwin Bully, Lennox Honeychurch, and others. The *Waiti Kubuli Dance Group* under Raymond Lawrence introduced modern dance interwoven with elements of Dominican national dress and evoking a rising sense of cultural awakening. The newly formed *People's Action Theater* (PAT), with Alwin Bully, Roger Atherly, and others, was later founded and presented a spectacular play which featured the travails of contemporary Dominican urban life: *Speak Brother, Speak*. The play opened to rave reviews and overflow crowds at the St. Gerard's Hall and Goodwill Parish Hall.

In time, the Carib people joined in this cultural renaissance, forming the dance company *Karifuna* to portray the soul of Carib folk in song and dance. Soon enough, the term "Carib Reserve" went out of common usage when referring to the area of Carib habitation on the island. The respectful word of choice was: Carib Territory.

To crown that flowering of Dominican self-identity, local historian Lennox Honeychurch drew a rapt national audience to their radios every day with his series *The Dominica Story*. A well dramatized affair, the program chronicled Dominica's history from Columbus' time onward. For the first time one could listen to local history which seemed to strive for balance and portrayed local perspectives. The program, and later the book, filled a yawning gap in literature about the island and was less fettered by prejudices prevalent in colonial renditions. Featuring figures like slave rebels Jaco, Balla and Congoree, along with politicians Gordon Falconer and Cecil Rawle in heroic roles, the program remains to this day one of the most popular ever broadcasted by the newly established government-owned **Radio Dominica**. Meanwhile, apart from the themes of resistance in the newly popular Jamaican reggae of Jimmy Cliff, Dominican music was undergoing its own revolution. No longer would local artists be restricted to playing recycled Trinidadian calypsos or those sang at the annual carnival. A new musical genre arose from the womb of the African and French lingual heritage represented by French creole. The insurgent rhythm now heard blasting from every stereo, radio and disco sound system was Cadence-Lypso. Cadence-Lypso, a fusion of French creole language, the Afro-Caribbean tempo and the peculiar speedy beat of *lapeau cabrit* (goat skin) drums would derive its popularity from the efforts of **Exile One** led by Gordon Henderson, **Grammacks**, led by Jeff Joseph, **Midnight Groovers** of Grandbay, **Belles Combo** from Mahaut, and singers Tony Valmond, Ophelia Olivace-Marie, and other Dominican groups based in the French Antilles and Paris.

The fact that these groups produced albums from studios on the French islands, allowed for the constant air play of local songs for the first time in history. Prior, recorded local artists and bands[67] had been restricted to live performances-with the exception of the legendary Swinging Stars Orchestra which had cut its famous calypso album *Splashdown!*

Even the dominant Roman Catholic Church was allowing the use of drums and alternative modalities to a liturgy which increasingly seemed like a lot of uninteresting Latin babble to the restless young. The Charismatic movement took hold, people shook hands in church, clapped, sang lustily and stomped their feet. As a result, the dull traditional masses became more attractive, with the changes and as more local priest such as Fathers' Felix and Alexander came into their own. Even then, the church's membership was depleted during the period by an insurgent evangelistic movement made up of Adventist, Pentecostalist and Baptist faiths. Caught up in the tumult, and egged on by fire and brimstone crusades by Holmes Williams or Jimmy Swaggart on cassette, many simple islanders took fright and saw the changing times as impending doom. Also, the critical

---

[67]. Many credit the Roseau based group, *De Boys and Dem*, with fostering early fusion between local calypso tradition in song and US rock, rhythm and blues. That effort saw the use of electric guitars, accordions, drum sets and electronic mixers. The sound produced was more modern, and a departure from the local tambourin, flute, boom-boom (hollowed bamboo horn) and accordion common to the island's folk song tradition.

thinking spawned by the period caused many to doubt the sanctity of Catholic doctrine or that the Pope was anything but a man, possessed of the worldly vices that entailed. Further, to the converted, their new churches were smaller, with mostly black preachers[68] and offered a warmth and assurance of heaven that the Catholic Church seemed unable to guarantee.

At schools, Caribbean literature and history texts were increasingly common, as were UWI trained teachers who were critical of colonial rule. Woolen blazers, woolen caps, crest emblazoned boat hats and ties soon disappeared from the Dominica Grammar School and St. Mary's Academy. The loose fitting white shirt jacks soon became the replacement garments at both leading high schools, as it was seen as more in keeping with the climate.

Feminism came of age during that period, with women being called "sisters" and a determined effort being made to eradicate the sexist and macho traditions of Dominican society which relegated women to secondary roles in leadership. But even in the black power movement, many of the so-called leaders still insisted on the sisters taking down the minutes at meetings or typing stencils for pamphlets. Aside from efforts at social

---

[68] . In that period the vast majority of the Catholic clergy was Belgian or French, with only two local priests of note Frs. Felx and Alexander. Local clerics like Eustace Thomas, Reggie LeFleure, Monsignor John-Lewis or Fr. Celsus Auguiste came into their own much later, in the late 1970s and 1980s.

equality, women now wore Afro hairdos and avoided "frying" or straightening their hair.

On the cultural side, the government seemed supportive of this search for identity and sponsored national short story, poetry, Quadrille[69], *wob dwiyet* and Bellaire and cultural competitions during the period leading up to every National Day celebration on November 3. On the political front, the Labour party remained suspicious of black power leaders, some of whom like Ronald Green, Peter Alleyne, Joey Peltier, Birdock Shillingford and Desmond Trotter were from families which comprised the old Roseau elite, or were mulatto. Seeking to sow doubt about the true motives of the black power leadership (many of whom were light skinned), The Labour newspaper *The Educator* cried foul:

> bogus...their black power is really mulatto power, a sinister plot ... to return the mulatto to political power.[70]

Nonetheless, that radicalization of the sons of the privileged would, not only bridge the societal gaps created by differences in class and color, but (in an ironic and prophetic-but wholly unintentional-twist) ease the way for the conservative Freedom Party's ascent to power.

---

[69]. Bellaire and Quadrille are national dance styles rooted in a commingled African, French, British heritage. The wob Dwiyet is the national dress which bears the mark of a similar past.

[70]. *The Educator,* May 29, 1974 editorial, quoted in Honeychurch's, *The Dominica Story.*

BLACK POWER: THE TROUBLES

Mass support or not, the societal surge for change fostered by black power thought was building. When the first memorable confrontation would come, high school students would take the lead. Since, 1970-71, students had met at One Hundred Steps at the Botanical Gardens and other places, arguing, discussing; with books on Malcolm X, Angela Davis, Che Guevara, The Black Panthers, Soledad Brothers and other (primarily black American) radical leaders and movements clutched in their increasingly feverish and impetuous grasps.

When the call for action came, it was first answered by students from the most unexpected and, hitherto conservative, of sources. In 1972, the first overtly black power demonstration by high school students took place at Roseau's prestigious St. Mary's Academy. At that time the Academy (as it is more commonly called) was a stronghold of all the "good" Roseau elite names. Run by the (primarily American) Christian Brothers and situated in the heart of conservative Roseau, the Academy stood right behind the massive Roseau Cathedral, adjacent to the Roman Catholic Bishops' Palace. Prior, the government run Dominica Grammar School (D.G.S) which had been created in the last century for sons of the local plantocratic and bureaucratic class held the honor of first place. By the 1970s, the D.G.S was quietly acknowledged by a strongly Roman Catholic Roseau population to be inundated with country folk, especially students from Wesley and Marigot, two Methodist enclaves. Meanwhile, the S.M.A. was (quite ironically) the high school of Reggie Armour, Desmond Trotter, Perceval Marie, Birdock Shillingford and many other known "black powers", as adherents of black racial pride ideology were called. In a 1972 dispute with a student over his afro hairstyle, it was said that a Christian brother administered a kick. Other histories recall, that the student was merely sent home to cut his hair. In any case, the students were outraged. Several statues of white Roman Catholic saints at the nearby cathedral and cemetery were painted black. Placards were prepared with slogans supporting racial pride. Frederick Mongerie (son of 1920s Garveyist radical Mongerie), and other outside sympathizers handed-out red arm bands. At assembly, the day following the incident, a walk-out was staged. The students poured into the streets, "black powers" in the lead. The protest made its way through the Roseau business district. Onlookers from shops, stores, offices were aghast. Roseau had never seen such a spectacle before, except in newsreels about demonstrations in the U.S. and elsewhere. The troubles in Trinidad and Jamaica were still fresh on peoples minds. But there was no violence, apart from a few parents who caught-up with marchers (some during, and others after the march) to administer tongue lashings.

It is remembered by some, that quite a few ultra conservative parents resorted to outright belt lashes on sons who they could grab-out of the crowd. Eventually, the student marchers arrived at the new government headquarters at Bath Road and Kennedy Avenue and appealed to Premier Leblanc. He was attentive, responsive. He was said to have agreed with the students action in principle. For that he was attacked by the conservative Dominica Chronicle and other establishment media. Later, upon resignation from his position as Premier, Leblanc was to remark in an interview:

> ...I accept and welcome change...that is why people said that I was black power and this and that[71].

Whether Leblanc was a black power sympathizer or not, an increasingly radicalized and boisterous youth was proving to be politically oppositional and bold in its challenges to his rule. It seemed that the societal ferment[72] which accompanied black power thought had also added muscle to the voices of the traditional opposition. Henceforth, the Freedom Party and M.N.D. would seek political mileage from any disturbance, black power inspired or not.

---

[71]. Id.

[72]. Earlier, on December 15th, 1971 a riotous crowd of Freedom party supporters had disrupted a House of Assembly sitting which was to have decided a government sponsored Town Council Dissolution Bill. Roseau central, the fulcrum of anti-government feeling in the country, was increasingly part of a restive wave of which black power was part creator, part progeny.

In 1973, the Labour government had declared a state of emergency over a strike by the civil service. Though the issue then revolved over the transfer of popular disc jockey Daniel "Papa Dee" Cauderion, the Freedom Party scored points with its Roseau political base by supporting the strike. Adherents of M.N.D could be seen mingling with and agitating C.S.A crowds at public meetings. In one incident (which served as a harbinger of the future conflict between the security forces and the public) a young Royal Dominica Police Force constable struck academic Rupert Sorhaindo (and relative of Freedom party founder, Martin Sorhaindo) in the head with a baton while he was pacing about with a pro-strike placard at the ministerial building. The constable, nicknamed "Sogo-Fly" was one of a new crop of zealous police officers, like "Groovy-Bat", "Star-Black", "Falcon", "Governor-Cake" and others who would later clash with black power adherents, amidst charges of police brutality. It now appeared that a tumult had been let loose in the land.

Earlier, in mid-1972, the workers on a C.D.C estate at Castle Bruce had revolted under the leadership of a Cornell University educated agronomist Atherton "Athie" Martin. Martin, was from one of the "good" families of Roseau and a graduate of the Academy. Upon his return to Dominica from the U.S., he was made an estate manager at C.D.C. He later disagreed with what he considered to be a draconian managerial directive to fire 53 workers for financial reasons. A move which, in his estimation, would further impoverish the village which depended on the estate for income. As well, Martin was uncomfortable with his role as overseer for a multinational corporation, entities which (like the earlier plantations of the slave era) had exploited Dominica and Dominicans leaving them little to show for their labour. Accordingly, Martin had bridled at the exploitation of village peasant Labourers on C.D.C's Castle Bruce estate and thought they should run it in their interest on a collective basis. Accordingly, he supported a estate workers strike call and threatened unilateral occupation of the land. Initially, the Labour government supported the estate workers. At a gathering, Education Minister and parliamentary representative H.L. Christian claimed that Labour stood for socialism and the petite bouge. Later, the government backed-off stating that the dispute was a private worker-employer matter and broadcasting its fear of "collectives" and preference for cooperatives over radio. The Roseau commercial class shied away and hinted at "communist plotting"[73]. A view its political ally, the Freedom Party, most likely supported.

On November 3, 1973, a contingent of Castle Bruce farmers under the leadership of Martin attempted an entry into the National Day joint military and school parade at the Botanic

---

[73]. See generally, ***Dominica Story*** at 164-165.

Gardens. Forewarned, the police swooped down on the farmers seizing their red and black banners. Black power sympathizers amongst the Academy and D.G.S contingents on parade broke ranks and shouted anti-government slogans. Suddenly, in the background, what sounded like gunshots were heard, escalating the confusion. Later, it dawned that the loud reports came from the backfiring of heavy BSA motorcycles driven by the Easy Riders, Dominica's motorcycle gang of the period who were attempting entrance into the area. School children fled helter-skelter. The Governor, Sir Louis-Cools Lartigue, went into a swoon and had to be escorted away. Premier Leblanc was embarrassed, shocked. Much pandemonium ensued before a semblance of order was restored to the event. However, the pressure tactics worked and the farmers voices were heard. In time, the land at Castle Bruce was purchased and turned into cooperatively farmed property, and Martin would move on to organize the farmers, nationwide, into a strong political force.

By 1973-1974, the radical ferment sweeping the island took root at the Dominica Grammar School (DGS. Founded in 1893, the DGS was the island's academic flagship, with a distinguish stable of "old Boys" such as Dr. Phillip Potter who later went on to head the World Council of Churches and Dr. Clayton Shillingford, a highly regarded scientist with Dupont Labs. An elite institution patterned on the British public schools like Harrow and Eton, its students were fed a daily fare of British literary classics, alongside their core secondary school courses. Up till 1971, Latin was compulsory, and the school's Latin motto **Mens Sana Incorpore Sano** (a healthy mind in a healthy body) was bolstered by a curriculum which included a corp of army cadets who regularly performed musketry drills on the quadrangle and target practice off the school's private shooting range, along with sporting pursuits in cricket, soccer and all-round athletics. But changes were knocking on the door of this all male bastion of conservatism in education.

In 1972, against much opposition from the traditionalist in the old boy network, the school admitted it first batch of female students as it moved toward co-education. Soon, some students who saw that move as a weakening of discipline became intent on wearing "Tams" (knitted headgear common to cooler climes) which sported the red, black and green liberation colors made famous by Garvey's UNIA earlier in the century. Such desire to relax the dress code clashed with a rigid tradition which had just, reluctantly, departed from wool blazers worn with boat hats. Another sore point to the young student radicals, was the presence of a white British principal, Mr. Gough. At the time, both the DGS and SMA had white expatriate principals, as did the Convent which was led by a cadre of stern Belgian nuns. It was felt that there were competent locals who could handle the job and such expatriate dominance fostered a debilitating inferiority complex among Dominicans.

By 1973, the DGS' white principal came under strong pressure to reign. Slogans were painted about the school in black: ***Gough must Go!*** A rather polite chap, Gough was puzzled by this uproar. He yielded with grace and was replaced by the reserved Alfred Leevy, an Indian educated, poet and thinker. Still the radical surge for change in school curriculum persisted. Student advocates of the new nationalism such as Bernard Shaw, Clement "Baba" Richards, Michael Darroux, Nato Maynard, Delmance 'Ras Mo" Moses (Later a poet of note) were in the forefront of efforts to focus on Caribbean history, and dress codes more in keeping with the island's climate. In that regard they were to be roundly dismissed by a majority of the staff which saw the insurgent students as mere "troublemakers" who were in need of stern discipline. Meanwhile, some teachers were sympathetic; among them playwright and artist Alwin Bully who urged compromise and sensitivity to student concerns.

In February 1974, the DGS students threatened to march. Forewarned of the plan that the demonstration would proceed from one of the daily open-air assemblies, the assembly was cancelled on the particular day the protest was planned. When some stubborn students sought to tarry around the assembly area, Deputy Principal Alexander ran out to the milling crowds, whip in hand, and flailed away. The groups of would-be "rebels" took flight and made for their respective classrooms. Later, Minister of Education H.L. Christian and Chief Education Officer Belgrave Robinson visited the school to listen to the students grievances. The government officials offered leniency and a listening air. However, in real terms, security was tightened and a plainclothes police officer was posted on the school compound to root out locks-men and marijuana users. The administration's soothing response was merely cover for a vigorous effort to maintain standards and the status quo; though more Caribbean literature books found their way into the curriculum. It was shortly thereafter that an altercation between a police constable Richards and DGS student Randy Shillingford led to Shillingford's arrest and the near mobbing of the officer by incensed students. Shillingford wore locks and was suspected of involvement with marijuana. The student onlookers considered the officer's handling of Shillingford brutish. Meanwhile, many on the staff thought the unprecedented arrest on the hallowed school grounds a tolerable irritation if they were rid of one more ill-disciplined student with marijuana smoking proclivities.

By 1975, the school returned to some quiet with the departure of some of the student activists: some to the Dominican forests in search of alternative back-to-nature lifestyles. There, several were to perish; some allegedly at the hands of the Special

Service Unit (SSU) of the Royal Dominica Police Force and Dominica Defence Force patrols which combed the forests to dissuade those who they considered subversive of the social order. However, by the end of the decade the students would rise again to add their dissenting voices against an educational system which ill prepared them for the world of work and an economic system which offered little or no hope of employment.

One year earlier, by carnival 1974[74], calypso, that medium of popular Caribbean expression was giving vent to sentiments of outrage and forecasting the death of a society which, in the lingua franca of the time, was called "babylon"; with the police officers being designated as "babylons" or "babylonians". The new terminology had been popularized in Bob Marley's rousing reggae lyrics. Rich in biblical symbolism about oppression, the Dominican young (of whatever party persuasion) had adopted the language of scorn and resistance, with regard to the status quo and its denigration of things black. There was a certain fearlessness which stalked the discourse of the young, of whom the majority could be said to have adopted the basic race pride tenets of black power by 1974-1975. In the tradition of Soul singer James Brown, "Say it Loud. I am black and I'm proud" was a common response by youth to anyone who would make race-prejudicial remarks.

---

[74]. The blatantly incendiary and disrespectful chant of many young carnival goers that year was: "We doh want no babylon; babylon is total fuckries!"

Speaking of the troubles and in defiant reaction to his arrest the previous year under the emergency, the calypsonian and school teacher, the Mighty Caterer, belted-out a number which swept the crowds of revelers in carnival 1974:

> Oh Sogo-Fly why you arrest me?
> State of Emergency, you push me
> in the prison.
> Oh, Sogo-Fly what you do, you do.
> State of Emergency, you use your
> powers on me!
> and:
> I say,
> When the kingdom, fall.
>
> I and I,(refrain)
> Babylon go Kill Babylon![75]

Before any "fall" however, babylon was to be confronted by the masses again and again.

Enter the radical people of "Sout" as the area around the big Southeastern village Grandbay was called. Grandbay, a heavily populated southern village, was a strong hold of opposition: First, as a Freedom stronghold in the early 1970's,

---

[75]. That song was prophetic. On December 19, 1981 officers of the Dominica Defence Force which had been disbanded by the new Freedom Party government of Eugenia Charles, assaulted central police headquarters in Roseau under a barrage of gunfire. When the smoke and confusion, of what was an attempted coup had cleared two former Defence Force personnel and one police officer was dead. Several others were severely wounded. The two punitive arms of the state had clashed and as the calypso foretold years prior: Babylon, killing Babylon.

later as a redoubt of black power thought[76]. The record reveals that Grandbay has always been a cockpit of violent conflict between the masses and the landowners. With its settlement origins rooted in slavery, that conflict has almost invariably made the struggle a black/white issue. However, the root cause reposed in what was an inequitable land distribution in the area of the village. In its heyday Grandbay's main estate, Geneva, was said to employ 300-400 slaves. Apart from that estate, there is very little cultivable land in the area[77]. According to Paul Alexander who recalls the events of 1974:

> Land was tight in Grandbay. The law said one could not even pick up a dry coconut to eat. And at Geneva, nuts were plenty on the ground. So Chubby and Grell picked up two
> nuts in front of the Geneva Estate foreman and dared him to act. Police came and arrested them. Later, we went to the court in Roseau and forced the judge to let Grell go. But Chubby spent some time in jail. When he came out, Chubby's band Midnight Groovers made a hit song about the incident -Pour yon coco[78].

---

[76]. Grandbay would transfer its allegiance to Dominica's left and would be the site of the main library and literary center of Dominica's political left between 1975-1980.

[77]. See P.I. Gomes, **Plantation Dominance and Rural Dependence in Dominica** 1986 (manuscript at U.S.D.A. Library, Beltsville, MD), at 64.

[78]. April 2002, statement by Computer Programmer at the US Department of Labour in St. Thomas, Paul "Larwa" Alexander. President of Waseen Dominique, the main Dominican Diaspora organization in the US Virgin Islands, Alexander was a community leader in Grandbay during the 1970s.

The arrest, referred to above sparked, violence. A March 30, 1974 *New Chronicle* article reported that five buildings on the estate of Elias Nassief, a Dominican of Syrian extraction had been burnt to the ground. Cattle were spirited away, other livestock left behind had their entrails strewn about, coconut trees, the main crop, were chopped down. A police contingent arrived in Grandbay, led by an Inspector Bannis. A cunning and seasoned officer of long service in the police, Bannis promptly seized a young man, whom he felt (on good source) was the leader. Unicef, as the alleged leader was popularly called, escaped as quickly as he was caught. Immediately upon his escape, a good portion of youth in the village moved into a state of general insurrection against the established order. The presbytery was assailed by a hail of stones, telephone links to Roseau were cut, trees were strategically placed along several points of the one road linking Grandbay to Roseau, and an estate shop was seized and its contents distributed Robin-Hood style. School life in the village was disrupted, and students who went to school in the capital were stranded or had to hike all the way over mountain tracks to reach their destination. The ring leaders of the uprising brandishing old muskets and locally made guns, were heard to vociferate against Babylon, the tough praedial larceny laws (enacted to prohibit the theft of crops), and exploitation. The main plantation house itself was consumed in a conflagration. On

Wednesday, April 3rd, a state of emergency was proclaimed. In further attacks, the estate's coconut drier and diesel fuel station were fired. Fire officers sent to extinguish the blaze were fired upon, from nearby bushes. Before calm was restored, the insurrection fever sweeping Grandbay seemingly executed a foray into the capital Roseau. Mysteriously, Nasieff's huge convenience store, near the Dawbiney market on King George the V, street was burnt to the ground. Soon, with Defence Force reinforcements and the re-arrest of Unicef, the uprising was quelled. Later, the estate was to be purchased by the government and sold to the villagers as part of a small-farmers scheme.

Around that same carnival period, February 1974, an American tourist John Jirasek was killed. Police affidavits were later entered into evidence, which purported to show that one Antiguan female visitor (alias Pretty Pig) was in the company of Roy Mason when, black power notable Desmond "Ras Kabinda" Trotter, whispered excitedly, "I just kill a white man". On the basis of that (and other evidence that Trotter was found with the murder weapon) both Mason and Trotter were charged and tried for the crime of murder. The case of the ***Queen v. Desmond Trotter and Roy Mason*** was the most politically charged trial in Dominica at that time, and drew huge crowds which blocked the courthouse entrance and overflowed into the nearby grounds of the Roseau Public library.

To his supporters, Trotter was a valiant black power activist framed by babylon system. To his detractors in both the Labour government and Freedom party (who shared in attacking Trotter and those who shared his political views) he was a troublemaker whose bad influence had "spoilt peoples children" and ruined the tourist industry. Trotter was defended by a handsome and dashing young lawyer from Grenada, who was to endear himself to Dominican youth who adhered to black power thought, Maurice Bishop[79]. Later to-be-foreign minister in the Freedom Party government, Brian Alleyne joined in the defense. Mason was found not guilty. Trotter lost and was sentenced to hang. Though found guilty, a world-wide appeal was launched by black power, humanitarian and liberal organizations. At home pamphlets and wall-slogans alleged a "frame-up" and called for Trotter's release. Trotter's death sentence was later commuted, with his final release occurring during the tumult of 1979.[80]

---

[79]. Maurice Bishop went on to lead the first revolution in the English Caribbean, when his New Jewel Movement (N.J.M) toppled Sir Eric Gairy's regime on March 13th, 1979. He was to perish at the hands of an extremist inner-party faction on October 19, 1983. Shortly thereafter, the U.S., with the encouragement of Freedom Party leader and Prime Minister Eugenia Charles, invaded and occupied Grenada. See generally Reynold A. Burrows, **Revolution and Rescue in Grenada** (Greenwood Press, 1988); Also, Major Mark Adkins, **Operation Urgent Fury**, (Lexington Books, 1989).

[80] . Desmond "Ras Kabinda" Trotter left the island in 1979 and became a guest of Maurice Bishop and the Grenadian Revolution. Later he left for the Rastafarian settlement of Shashamane in Ethiopia and became a community leader there. The settlement had been a gift to Rastas by Emperor Haile Selassie I.

Trotter's trial represented the split in the movement of black power thought. M.N.D. and it organ ***Twavay***[81] were more effective in pointing out problems and agitating, as opposed to identifying long-term goals, solutions, or building a sustainable movement. Though a committed cadre led by Ron Green, Bernard Dinard, Birdock Shillingford, Glen Ducreay, Neville Graham and others remained in country and pursued community development work, many of the academics, like William "Para" Riveire, Joey Peltier, Hilroy Thomas, Bernard Wiltshire and others drifted in and out of the country, between university study breaks and foreign lectures. Accordingly, serious rifts developed between those who stayed behind and those who left; those who were more schooled and those who were less-well schooled. Such stratification between the local base and what was perceived as an itinerant, campus hopping leadership was one problem. Another, was the lack of political foresight by those who could whip a well-intended Roseau crowd into a frenzy over the Angolan peoples struggle for liberation from Portugal, but yet failed to realize Dominica's colonial status under Britain and seek to focus on the mechanics of ending it and replacing it with a new socio-economic order. In addition, the movement had not solidified a base among workers or civil servant unions, as those entities were under the ideological control of the pro colonial

---

[81]. French creole for work.

George Meany Center in Maryland and the West German Frederich Ebert Foundation. The local trade union leadership was well in the grasp of Charles Savarin, Louis Benoit and Frederick Joseph, who were in the mold of the US AFL-CIO; focused, narrowly, on salary negotiation and individual working conditions; not interested in worker control of the means of production or a mass movement for political change with workers at the helm. Conservative, and anti-socialist for the most part, these new union leaders shunned the social-change politics of the old Dominica Trade Union movement and later black consciousness thinkers. Issues of class-colour prejudice and national independence were not high on their list of priorities, if at all. When the Civil Servants Association, Waterfront and Allied Workers Union and Dominica Amalgamated Workers Union did seek national industrial action, it was usually in alliance with the Dominica Employers Federation and against a Labour regime with which they rarely sought compromise[82]. Such meant that the black consciousness movement was restricted to students, younger civil servants, some farmers in areas of Wesley, Castle Bruce and Grandbay, and elements of the unemployed.

---

[82] . While the Dominican workers union did act to inhibit a sometimes authoritarian Labour regime, their political perspectives often seemed anti-national and in the service of foreign interests, in a manner similar to the Chilean and Venezuelan unions which helped overthrow the duly elected nationalist governments of Salvador Allende in 1973 and Hugo Chavez in Venezuela in April 2002. Chavez was restored to power on April 14, 2002, after massive public protests and a military rebellion against the coup makers.

By 1975, the adherents of the new Dominican nationalism would now split into three paths: One would choose cultural resistance to babylon via Rastafarianism or Dreadism. Others, would analyze Dominica's politics, deem political independence from Britain as the next logical step and struggle for the accomplishment of that phase; the other step aimed towards eventual economic independence (as much as such is possible in an interdependent world economy) and full national liberation, inevitably leading to socialism. The third path sought the removal of the Labour party as the immediate objective (before all else) to be followed by some sort of socialization of the means of production. Whatever the avenues followed by the now splintered movement born of the Black Power era, a new and distinct sense of nationalist feeling had taken hold. Further, a disdain for the capitalist mode of production had arisen born of its abject failure to meet the needs of the growing army of unemployed. Thus, a desire for socialism and local control of the means of production became ascendant among wide swathes of the urban and rural young.

By 1974-75 Leblanc was gone; resigned to going back to his distant rural hamlet and family life. A populist who had led a social reformist Labour Party to electoral victories, he seemed at a loss for leadership in the face of the youthful upsurge. An avid supporter of local culture and the petite bouge, he would resign in

1974 before Dominica's radical politics turned violent. His successor was a former trade unionist of humble origins with a populist (yet authoritarian) streak, the diminutive and fiery Patrick Roland John, popularly known as "P.J".

A NEW RADICALISM: THE DREADS

Not many people consider that Dominica fought a small, undeclared and semi-secret internal war between 1975 and 1980, which continued somewhat into the 1980s. That conflict was to continue into the reign of Ms. Charles' government because the root causes which gave it birth were not resolved. The war pitted the machinery of the state against Dominican Dreads who had resorted to guerrilla methods to secure their rights and/or autonomy from traditional society.

Though "Dread" as a term is associated with pejorative establishment designation, it was to become commonly accepted to describe those who accepted some tenets of Rastafarianism as practiced in Jamaica. In 1930, Ras Tafari, the grandson of King Sahela Selassie of Shoa and son of Ras Makonnen, was crowned King Negust Negusta, after serving fourteen years as Prince Regent of Abyssinia-now called Ethiopia. On November 2, 1930 Ras Tafari ascended the throne and became known as Haile

Selassie I, Lion of Judah, Defender of the Faith, Light of the Trinity.[83] The event was captured by a world audience via newspapers, newsreels and books. Blacks the world over took pride in the event and the residual influence of Garveyism propelled segments of the Jamaican population to lock their hair in the style of their Ethiopian brothers; hence dreadlocks. However, the 1970s Dominican locks man or woman was part of a liberation struggle and was not a passive spectator to events on the world stage or in far off Africa. Freedom to smoke marijuana, honor Africa and African identity, partake of a vegetarian diet, squat on government lands and be left alone to enjoy nature's splendor was the desire of the Dominican dread in the 1970's. The Dread convert was also anti colonial and pro socialist, in that the adherents had derived their rebelliousness from the black power movement and favored a collective approach to sustenance. Beyond politics, many Dreads of the time even saw a stylistic similarity between themselves and the long haired Che Guevara, Raul Castro and the other Cuban revolutionary "barbudos"[84] in the early days of their descent from the Sierra

---

[83] . See Horace Campbell's ***Rasta and Resistance-From Marcus Garvey to Walter Rodney*** (Africa World Press, Inc., 1992) at page 70 and generally, for a well written review of the role of Rasta and Dread influence and involvement in the struggle against colonialism and imperialism.

[84] . The bearded ones; early name for the Cuban revolutionaries when they descended from the mountains in 1959.

Maestra. For them, Che's huge Cuban cigar was likened to a solid spliff.[85]

Due to their roots in political rebellion, the government saw the Dreads as subversive and a potential guerilla warfare threat to the regime. Unlike the urban based Jamaican dread, the Dominican Dread would violently resist any attempt by babylon to arrest or curtail his/her activities. Whereas, a classic Rasta in the Jamaican mold, is not known to favor armed resistance but rather await the judgement of Jah[86] upon babylon.

Essentially, the Dominican dread of the 1970s was a youthful (primarily male) adherent of black power thought, who at the time claimed distinct Christian virtues, affection for nature (and unprocessed foods), and an Afrocentric view and faith, separate and apart from the organized religion of babylon system. An obligatory bow was made towards Haile Selassie of Ethiopia, as most Rastas of Jamaica and elsewhere are known to do. Dread notables, in the mold of Tumba, Peter Alleyne[87] or Pokosion[88]

---

[85] . Marijuana cigarette.

[86] . i.e. God

[87] . The son of distinguished Dominican Queens' Counsel Keith Alleyne, and brother of human rights lawyer Brian Alleyne (later Dominica Freedom Party Attorney General. Alleyne (who became famous for allying with Tumba and escaping several police traps) was typical of those who, like Trotter, evolved from black power adherent to dread. Peter Alleyne, like his father and brother later attended law school, graduated and started a law practice after some resistance from the legal establishment which did not recall his rebel-in-the-hills record too fondly.

[88] . Desmond Galloway, aka "Tumba" and Leroy Ettienne, aka "Pokosion" (i.e Precaution) were two Dreads who became legendary during the 1970s and

were more like modern day variants of the escaped slaves who had earlier founded guerilla camps in Dominica's mountain fastness in the 1700s and early 1800s. In contrast to Jamaica, where the Rastas are primarily an urban phenomena, not known to occupy the mountain fastness of cockpit country[89], Dominica locksmen sought to turn the thickly forested mountains into an impregnable redoubt and an Eden found.

Unemployed, mostly literate, youth for whom the social reforms of Labour had fostered greater expectations, those who became Dread had opted out of established society when those expectations for jobs, higher education, a respected and meaningful role in contemporary Dominican society, went unmet. Many had attended M.N.D meetings and had felt a need to go beyond mere mouthings of black nationalist jargon. A need was felt to go back to the land, to nature, to create an entirely new and pure social alternative to babylon. Yet, Dreads, as a group, were never organized in any manner adequate to push their agenda. Rather, groups would coalesce among certain leaders, in certain geographic spots, at certain times. Only rarely did they petition

---

1980s for their numerous escapes from attempts at capture and resistance to the established order. Tumba was accused of a mid-1970's double kidnapping, while Pokosion was linked to the murder of a local planter and Farmer's Union notable, Ted Honeychurch in 1981. Both were eventually killed by the security forces, though some (as with most legends) believe that they were able to escape the island.

[89]. Cockpit country being the location, deep in the Blue Mountains, from which Jamaican maroons like Cudjoe and Nanny fought off British military expeditions sent to re-enslave and/or defeat them in the 1700s.

government, but then with no clearly definable aim than to "reason out". Witness one such missive:

> ..so come let us reason-out in Zion...at which time time we will provide you with plenty itals, brother man..[90].

Overall, Dreads felt that contemporary Dominican society had failed them. Yet, they did not seek to engage in organizing the masses, issuing a program or printing pamphlets as the M.N.D had done.

In rejecting babylon's dress codes (to the degree of using loin clothes, or grass skirts on occasion), its iron implements (sometimes fashioning knives out of coconut shell) and Western values, Dreads placed themselves outside the societal mainstream, and as such prone to attacks from the establishment, without any base of support which would mitigate such attacks[91]. Dreads, for their sustenance, relied on "itals" or natural foods; those who touched pork were deemed "swine" or "swine-ish". They, would also engaged in craft making, or small-time subsistence

---

[90]. A mid-1975 note from Tumba, who had allegedly kidnapped two young women from Portsmouth to staff his mountain camp. The note was addressed to then Minister of Home Affairs Isaiah Thomas and was to prove a futile attempt at negotiation.

[91]. Articles in the *New Chronicle, Twavay,* and from the pulpits of outspoken catholic priests like Father Alexander or diverse Calypsonians, would chastise police brutality. However, no mass movement in support of Dreads, or their human rights, ever took root. The Dominica Human Rights Commission, of Brother Egbert Germaine, Brian Alleyne, Stanley Boyd and rotating student representatives from the United Students Council, was vigilant, mostly ineffective.

agriculture where possible. Mostly though, for cash income necessary to maintain contact with the money economy, they traded in marijuana. Though mostly noble in their objectives, the Dreads were to be penalized by opportunistic criminal elements within their ranks. Such elements may have been responsible for the theft of crops, attacks on farmers, and other misdeeds, as a result of which the entire movement was tarnished. Even where thefts were committed by ordinary crop thieves, Dreads were blamed. In so doing they came into conflict with small farmers with whom they competed (for increasingly scarce land) upon the difficult-to-farm foothills of Dominica's mountainous crown (i.e. government) lands. Most fatally, the Dreads came up against anti-drug legislation and a local security conscious regime swift to enforce it.

Unorganized, without a political leadership or program, Dreads represented political alienation at its worst and most self-destructive. For such, the price would be paid with blood. In November 1974, ***The Prohibited and Unlawful Societies Act***, better known as the ***Dread Act*** was passed by the Labour government under Premier Patrick John. Its aim was to weed out the Dreads and at the same time garner support among small farmers (a traditional Labour Party base) who felt threatened. The Act drew the outrage of some in the political opposition,

Twavay, and newspapers further afield[92] when it made the killing of Dreads a lawful act. However, Dreads were to be killed, or have their locks forcibly cut, in many cases for no better reason than being classified as a member of an "unlawful society". In what was commonly perceived as retaliation, a few farmers were threatened or killed[93]. Such only brought stronger measures from the Dominica Defence Force and the Special Service Unit (SSU) of the Royal Dominica Police Force. In several gun battles between 1975-1981 at Fond Figues, Fond Cole, Belles, and Giraudel several Dreads were killed. About two or more members of the security forces were killed in a conflict which could have been avoided. It is commonly thought that many more Dreads were slain in the woods, their deaths left unannounced. The remainder, with the woods now being thoroughly combed by roving patrols of joint defence force/police expeditions, fled the hills and took to the city. Meanwhile, Patrick John's anti-dread campaign had helped Labour's March 24, 1975 election victory over the Freedom Party.

The old radicalism, centered around the M.N.D, had splintered. Alienation, as epitomized by the Dreads retreat into the mountains, away from political struggle, did not suffice as an alternative. When the crack-down came, none in the Labour Party were strong or wise enough to compel a national debate on

---

[92]. See **Dominica Story** at 190.
[93]. Id.

the issue of state sanctioned and/or societal violence (or the reformist alternatives thereto), so that government and dread oppositionist could meet face to face. It did not matter that those who were killed were, for the most part, the sons and daughters of the "roots" people that Labour had sworn to protect. In the anti-dread hysteria, the Freedom Party allied itself with Labour, even though individual members and sympathizers (as members of the Dominica Human Rights Society[94]) sometimes condemned a government too quick to resort to the mailed fist. The old M.N.D.'s voice, though shrill in opposition to the unslaught on human rights, was ineffective; its members searched, harassed, harried. With new tactics, Dominica's radical thinkers and adherents would soon regroup and build new strength.

THE NEW RADICALISM OF "LEFTIST POLITICS"

Such regrouping took hold in 1977, with the return to Dominica of Rosie Douglas. Influenced by Communist party of Canada cadres, Rosie brought an orthodox Marxist-Leninist view to Dominican radical politics. In his view, simple black nationalism, or opposition to the governing political class would

---

[94]. Generally S.M.A Principal Egbert Germaine, writer Stanley Boyd, Lawyer Brian Alleyne, and rotating student representatives from the United Students Council.

not suffice. Now it would be clearly enunciated that the analysis of choice would be class based, not merely color based (though the legacy of slavery, racism and color prejudice would be acknowledged). Alliances, loathsome as they sometimes might be, would be forged with whomsoever assisted Dominica's accomplishment of what was termed the National Liberation Revolution. Such a path would entail an alliance, grouping progressive elements of the national bourgeoisie, petty bourgeoisie, farmers, labourers, students, and lumpen proletariat. Collectively, such an alliance would forge an anti-imperialist policy to eliminate as much of the foreign control over Dominica's economy as possible. The idea was never to build socialism at that stage, but rather to push policies, such as education, industry, land reform, equal rights for women, narrow the gulf between town and country, promote health, popular participation in political decision-making, and thus create a rise in the standard of living and national consciousness. Once that consciousness level were reached, the new radical thesis held that National Revolutionary Democracy had been arrived at. ***Only*** at that phase would the strugglers then begin to push for socialism, having already prepared its basis, by concrete achievements.[95]

---

[95]. See Jorge Heine, Introduction, ***A Revolution Aborted at 6. K.N. Brutents National Liberation Revolutions Today*** (Moscow, Progress Publishers, 1977) was the standard text used by Cadre No. 1 and other Marxist groups in Dominica 1977-1980 which supported the position of the P.I.C. Sessions would commence with a reading, followed by references to the local

The first objective, in that national liberation struggle, would be the attainment of political independence from Britain.

Apart from the return of university trained Dominicans like Rosie Douglas, U.W.I Extra Mural Department tutor Bernard Wiltshire, or Harvard trained Ph.d Hilroy Thomas, another impetus to the growth of the new Dominican left, was the rising influence of the Cuban Revolution on local political thought. The early U.S. response to the Cuban revolution had been an economic and information blockade which essentially insulated the English speaking territories from Cuba since 1960. However, by 1975 Barbados, Jamaica, Guyana and Trinidad and Tobago had independently resumed commercial and diplomatic ties with Cuba[96]. Most dramatically for the region, the November, 1975 Cuban intervention on behalf of the M.P.L.A in Angola was the first time in history that a Caribbean island had provided concrete military assistance for an African liberation struggle. Prior, Caribbean support for African liberation had been restricted to diplomatic initiatives at the U.N. and within the British Commonwealth group, or local solidarity marches. Cuba's action was granted more emphasis when it's special forces successfully repulsed an armored column of the hated South African apartheid regime's army sent in to assist a competing Angolan faction,

---

manifestations of foreign imperialist control; i.e. Barclays, Cable & Wireless, Geest, C.D.C., Royal Bank, L. Rose & Co. etc.
[96]. Franklin W. Knight, *The Caribbean: The Genesis of A Fragmented Nationalism* (Oxford University Press, 1990) at 252.

U.N.I.T.A. The Garveyites who longed to assist Ethiopia resist Italian aggression in the 1930s, but were unable to effectively do so, would have been impressed. Many Dominican youth who followed world news, and may not even have considered themselves radical, were moved and supported Cuba's action as assisting a fellow black people. In addition, a Dominica-Cuba Friendship Society was launched in the last quarter of 1976, under the leadership of Rosie Douglas. That followed the first trip to Cuba by a semi-official delegation from Dominica, which included Desire John (the wife of then Premier Patrick John) and Alwin Bully, noted playwright, artist and English teacher at the Dominica Grammar School and others. On their return, positive reviews were to be heard of the Cuban situation, especially in education and health. Mrs. John, who had previously experienced difficulty in child-bearing, was to bear her first child soon after. An event commonly attributed to a much-touted Cuban medical prowess. Such developments, with regard to Cuba, eased the appeal of the new leftist politics of freedom from colonial rule and socialism.

In that ferment new organizational structures were to be set up to replaced the, by now dormant, M.N.D[97]. On Thursday,

---

[97]. By late 1977, for all practical purposes, the M.N.D had been replaced by the Peoples Democratic Party led by former U.W.I lecturer Bill "Para" Riviere. Former M.N.D stalwarts like Ron Green, Bernard Dinard, Neville Graham, Birdock Shillingford etc. were considered P.D.P sympathizers, where they were not outright members. The P.D.P was then involved in community work

July 28th, 1977 Cadre No. 1 was established in the Roseau suburb of Pottersville as a model of what was to become known as the Popular Independence Committees (P.I.C's); the main objective of the P.I.C. cadres being to organize and agitate the masses towards support for Dominica's independence from Britain. Other cadres were established in Portsmouth, Mahaut, Wesley and Grandbay and elsewhere. These committees, centered around a political core[98] of Hilarian Deschamps, Gabriel Christian, Lorden Warrington, Sonny Felix, Erickson Romaine, Lennox Waldron, Johnson Christian, Irving Andre, Augustus Lebruine, Smiley Burnette, Joseph Guiste, Weston Seraphin and Curtis Victor (Roseau) Rosie Douglas, Romus Lamothe, and Steve John (Portsmouth), Lloyd Pascal (Boetica), Francisco Esprit (Mahaut), Pierre Charles, Paul Alexander (Grandbay), Angus Aulard (Wesley) would provide "critical support" to any Labour move towards political independence. Further, as cadre they were to operate as the spearhead of political organizing at the schools, within youth groups, the entire government structure, workers and farmers so as to fire the spirit of a weak Dominican nationalism.

---

in the Portsmouth area and environs, as well as some continued solidarity work on behalf of the imprisoned Desmond Trotter.

[98]. The P.I.C executive was also called the "**Core**", and grouped senior cadres like Rosie Douglas, Pierre Charles, Francisco Esprit, Bernard Wiltshire etc.

These sectors were to be organized to support independence first and foremost[99].

In a deeply Catholic country, with a population brought-up on the milk of anti-communism, the cadre felt that it was important to make an impact in peoples lives in a direct manner. In that regard, rhetoric as set aside and the library at Grandbay set-up to serve as the spear-point of a village literacy campaign. In no time Grandbay alone produced six monthly magazines, all with a left wing inclination. Modeled on the Jamaica literacy project, JAMAL, DOMAL (Dominica Literacy) organized literacy classes and issued completion certificates. Bonty Liverpool, Pierre Charles, Paul Alexander and other were keen leaders in that quest to shed light in a place of darkness. All the while all public talk of socialism or communism would be left for a later stage when popular consciousness would be ripe.

In the city, radical student activists energized their student councils to hold debates and elocution contests on the issue of independence and socialism. To champion their positions the students would seek to influence the United Student Council or form new entities. In the north of the island, Agricultural

---

[99]. In discussion cadres viewed British imperialism as the main enemy, with local adherents being the secondary enemy. Once Britain was out of the picture, then Dominicans could deal with locals who supported the neo colonial status quo. As example, cadres would reference Mao Zedong's alliance with Chiang Kai Chek to defeat Japanese imperial conquest over China, and the later expulsion of Chiang from the mainland once China made its revolution in 1948.

cooperatives would be formed at Castle Bruce, Portsmouth, Wesley, and Marigot with Rosie Douglas, Richard Charles and Athie Martin being heavily involved in setting up such structures.

The system of culture, education, economics, all came in for criticism with socialism being touted as the alternative. The divide between the education system and the agricultural economy was lamented. The need to pursue value-adding to local products and not merely be the supplier of raw cocoa with which transnational food processor Nestle would make Milo and re-sell to Dominicans, was trumpeted. The role of Dominica Coconut Products as an example of such value adding (turning coconut oil into soaps) was emphasized. Advances in Soviet and Cuban science were studied and the importance of the Soviet Five (5) Year Plans in building a modern state on the ruins of feudal Czarist Russia was highly praised. If the USSR, in less than fifty (50) years could move from industrial backwardness and serfdom, to being the first country in the space race, with superior production in many areas of industry, then the new leftist thinkers saw hope for the undeveloped former colonials in the Caribbean, Latin America, Africa and Asia. That the Soviets favored and armed the blacks engaged in a life and death struggle against Ian Smith's racist regime in Rhodesia and John Vorster's Apartheid regime in South Africa endeared them to local leftists, oftentimes causing them to overlook the distortions in democratic access to decision making and economic inefficiency which were, even then, hobbling the socialist bloc.

Carried along by the ferment, many student members gained election to student council executives and, several of them such as Romus Lamothe (Portsmouth Secondary School) and Gabriel Christian (DGS) becoming Head Boy and Deputy Headboy of their respective schools. From such positions, the students played a key role in the 1977 National Youth Council election of Pierre Charles to the position of President of that body. A position which was to launch his political career and carry him, ultimately, to the seat of Prime Minister after the sudden death of Rosie Douglas on October 1, 2000.

However, from early, a confrontation developed between the P.I.C and the old M.N.D. leadership. In retrospect, that schism seems akin to the conflict which later led to a bloody denouement and collapse of the Grenadian revolution six years later, on October 19th, 1983. Then, as with Grenada, it pitted those who had kept the embers of struggle burning within Dominica against those who had been abroad; those who had a more populist feel, from those who were too doctrinaire[100]. Grouped around the P.D.P), the old M.N.D. leadership may have well viewed Rosie Douglas as a "Johnny-Come-Lately", who had not endured the

---

[100]. For a reasonably balanced and well researched analysis of Grenada's intra-left ideological battles, see Jorge Heine's *A Revolution Aborted: The Lessons of Grenada* (University of Pittsburgh Press, 1991)

"roughing-ups", arrests and other tribulations of the early 1970s radicals. In response, Rosie pointed to his struggle against racism in Canada and his analysis that one should (in his paraphrase of Ghana's Kwame Nkrumah) "seek ye, first, the political Kingdom [i.e. independence], and all will follow". Further, he openly criticized the old left (by that time, all radicals were popularly lumped together as "leftist") for not supporting the Labour government's move to independence and for aligning with the Freedom Party's call for a referendum on the issue.[101]. An attempt by Riviere to meet with Roseau's Cadre No. 1 to smooth out such disagreements over tactics foundered[102]. In the notes of that November 3, 1977 meeting, Riviere was said to have argued "uselessly...an obscure theory of ill-defined two stages (of national liberation struggle). He was "made to see the light" (i.e. on the necessity of political independence) before being wished adieu in the spirit of "left-wing unity". The records of Cadre No.

---

[101]. It should be noted that suspicion (by the old radicals from M.N.D., historically opposed to Labour) may have focused on Rosie because he, at the time, resided (and may have been thought to be colluding) with his older brother Michael Douglas, Minister of Finance in the Labour government and a member of parliament from Portsmouth.

[102]. Earlier, the P.I.C had disagreed with the M.N.D/P.D.P's position on Desmond Trotter solidarity work. The P.I.C. position was that to ally with the Freedom Party to demonstrate on behalf of Trotter was in error, since Freedom had never supported what Trotter stood for. Accordingly, P.I.C. members shied away from a demonstration in early 1977 at the Roseau New Bridge in which the police riot squad tear gassed the demonstrators, causing them to flee into the river. S.M.A. principal, Brother Egbert Germain was detained and roughed-up, almost spurring a demonstration by incensed D.G.S and S.M.A student radicals.

1 reveal that Riviere's theories were characterized as "revisionist" and "faulty". It was clear that the old Black Power thinkers such as Riviere and Ron Green were suspicious of Rosie's method of work and were displeased with his popularity among significant segments of young Dominicans.

At the same time, with the Labour Party increasingly disorganized and restricted to an unmotivated membership, Patrick John was only too happy to have the youth support provided by the P.I.Cs. In March 1977 P.I.C supporters flooded the Dominican parliament during the independence debate[103], which Labour won. In what can only be analyzed as a tactical sop to the left, John started voicing support for "New Socialism"[104]. Following May 1977 constitutional talks at London's Marlborough House between the government, Freedom Party parliamentarians headed by Eugenia Charles and the British Office of Colonial Affairs, the government negotiating team returned home jubilant. Disagreements with the opposition (which favored a nationwide referendum on the issue) notwithstanding, it seemed that independence was at hand. The

---

[103]. See generally *The Dominica Story* at 195.
[104]. In a major address at the Dominica Labour Party's 22nd Annual Convention on August 28th, 1977 (called the "Newtown Statement"), John told the gathering that his aim was a socialist society, one based on "New Socialism". John condemned "any system which advocates or promulgates that profit must be the key motive for economic progress...private ownership as the sole means of production". He admitted that "New Socialism" would recognize the existence of God and the freedom of religious worship.

Dominica Student Federation, formed that year by Gabriel Christian, Romus Lamothe, Alick Lawrence Angus Aulard, Steve John, Debbie Douglas and others from Roseau, Portsmouth and Wesley, as a counterweight to the old United Student Council[105] planned to capture attention for a socialist path of development at speeches planned at the welcoming ceremonies for the government team. However, following a rousing speech in which Portsmouth Secondary School Federation leader Romus Lamothe lambasted the failures of colonial society and called for socialism, the government team, enroute to Roseau by motorcade, had a change of mind once it arrived at the Windsor Park rally. At Roseau, the Dominica Student Federation President, Gabriel Christian, was discreetly called aside by Mayor of Roseau, George "Jojo" Karam and told that his portion of the program was cancelled. His speech, which called for an unrelenting battle against the colonial legacy and for socialism, was never delivered. That incident is notable for it signaled John's change of gears. He had used the P.I.C. to mobilize popular support for independence in the face of significant Freedom party opposition to the manner in which it was being sought. Now, he would reneged on his talk of socialism and approach right-wing

---

[105]. The United Student Council had its genesis in the 1972 S.M.A demonstration, and attempts by Reggie Armor, Samuel Christian, Peter Azille and others to build a strong political movement to foster student representation on a national level, and push for education reform.

characters from Texas, South Africa and elsewhere to support his development strategy, even though a thin veneer of socialist rhetoric was maintained.

By the end of January 1978, John cleared his cabinet of those he considered "communist", claiming that there existed a communist plot to overthrow his government once independence was obtained. In so doing, he dismissed Minister of Agriculture Michael Douglas and Ministry of Agriculture Parliamentary Secretary Ferdinand Parillon. Douglas, amplifying his Catholic school upbringing, affirmed that he was a democratic socialist, *not* a communist. The Cuban Friendship society, in its first ever criticism of government, challenged John to arrest the communist plotters and send a top level mission to Cuba to investigate, arguing that anything short of that would reveal a government engaged in a diversionary tactic[106]. Certainly, the Labour-left honeymoon was over; the politics of "critical support" was in shambles. During parliamentary debates, Vic Riviere and Eustace Francis, both Labour government parliamentarians, could be heard boasting about their service with the Royal Air Force during the Malaysian Emergency[107] and their impeccable anti-communist credentials. In parliament, Francis himself was heard to say, *"every time is comrade this, and comrade that; I myself*

---

[106]. Dominica's *New Chronicle*, February 4th, 1978 at pg. 2.
[107]. Aimed at thwarting the post-World War two influence of the Malyasian communist movement.

fed-up with this comrade business". Nonetheless, the P.I.C. maintained its principled support for independence (even though with more reserve towards John's regime which seemed to be drifting rightward). That position was well stated by Michael Douglas who maintained a reasoned and moderately left-wing voice in parliament:

> I wouldn't like the British government or anyone else to believe that they can toy around with independence because two ministers have been dismissed... independence of my country remains paramount to my mind and I shall continue to work harder than anybody else in the [Labour] party to bring independence to Dominica[108].

The period between January 1978 and Independence day, November 3, 1978 saw the left adrift as its top leaderships quarreled amongst themselves. It was estranged from a government into which it had sought to inject new blood and have conform to its social-democratic roots. Attempts at enshrining a more socialist ethos to Dominica's constitution failed.

Yet, organized efforts by the P.D.P leader, historian and former U.W.I lecturer Bill "Para" Riviere, was beginning to bear fruit in the second town of Portsmouth. A traditional Labour base, and constituency of Douglas, Portsmouth saw the first official electoral victory of the new socialist left. In June-July 1978 town

---

[108]. Dominica's **New Chronicle**, February 4th, 1978 at pg. 2

council elections, Para won a seat (only narrowly missing the spot of top vote getter by 75 votes) along with two of his other party members Neville Wade and Helen Nanthan on the five seat city council. Mike Douglas was the top vote getter and secured a seat alongside one of his candidates, Joseph Hunter. Para's strength emanated from his community work, which included construction of a bridge. Indeed, the new radicalism' immersion in organization and the meeting of relevant community needs was solidifying its hold among certain sectors of the populace, especially in the rural areas and in urban sectors in the north of the country. The Freedom Party candidates had all lost; Labour, itself, had failed to contest that election.

Nonetheless, the anti-communist posturing of the government made political work by the left more difficult. In March of 1978, the Roman Catholic Bishop of Roseau, Arnold Boghart, Education Minister Henckell Christian and the Governor Louis Cools-Lartigue hurriedly convened a gathering of all secondary school and Sixth Form College Students at the Goodwill Parish Hall. The students were warned to beware of those who spread foreign ideologies (i.e. anti-imperialist or socialist concepts). The Bishop gravely intoned that ***Granma's***[109] had been found at the library of the Convent High School and that

---

[109]. Official organ of the Cuban Communist Party (English edition); circulated by left-wing organizations in Dominica since 1975.

some teachers were teaching communistic atheism[110]. If anything, the over reaction by the authorities drew smirks and guffaws from the crowd, which was otherwise happy at getting-off from classes early.

Later, in Summer 1978, student organizers, youth leaders and community activists returning from Havana, Cuba where they represented Dominica at the 11th World Festival of Youth and Students, were detained by the police department's special branch led by inspector Desmond Blanchard. Among that group was Pierre Charles, President of the National Youth Council, Steve John, Agnes Esprit, Debbie Douglas and Gabriel Christian representing the Federation of Students along with representatives of farmer, cooperative society and village council groups. The customs area was efficiently cleared of all taxi men and other visitors and shut. Extra customs personnel, Norman Letaing and Val Obed were called in from Roseau. Arriving tourists were rushed through. Meanwhile, the books and other possessions of the native Dominicans were searched for several hours, much of it seized for a review which lasted months before release. It was later found-out that, in the delegations absence, a totally false

---

[110]. A remark aimed at Extra Mural tutor Bernard Wiltshire who, while teaching a Sixth Form College Cambridge G.C.E. 'A' Level course in General Paper mentioned dialectical materialism and atheism. Some students were startled. His remarks had been passed on to the higher authorities in the church and state. As a result pressure was brought to bear on the Sixth Form, then a hotbed of left-wing radicalism.

charge had been made in parliament that the delegates had actually gone to Cuba for a bomb-making jamboree under the tutelage of none other than the P.L.O's Yasir Arafat. Such was the anti-left hysteria which gripped the government.

A September 1978, by-election to replace the recently deceased Labour Parliamentarian Isaiah Thomas, was won by a little known Labour Party candidate, ex-police corporal Wordsworth Lanquedoc. John reveled in his political strength by baiting his opponents:

> We shall confound their politics, we shall frustrate their dirty tricks and we shall give them endless licks![111]

The left did not partake of that St. Joseph campaign. However, Freedom Party stalwart Alvin Armantrading was soundly thrashed, leaving the party crestfallen. The Freedom Party's media ally the *New Chronicle* was to lament:

> ...the Freedom Party is still not able to effectively relate to the masses, it is still not able to capitalize on the enormous and countless mistakes of
> the Labour Party and to blow the myth of Labour for Labourers.[112]

By November 3rd, 1978 the student leadership at the Sixth Form College had decided to take the lead and protest the

---

[111]. Dominica's *New Chronicle* September 23rd, 1978 at pg. 4.
[112]. Id.

exorbitant sums lavished on fireworks and bunting which had been imported for the independence celebrations. Cooler heads cautioned against rash moves and spoke in favor of national unity at a time of independence celebrations. Earlier in the year, Principal of the Sixth Form College, Kay Polydore had spoken forcefully against the radical surge at the school, concerned that it would draw government scrutiny, while jeopardizing the future careers of the radical students. Taking heed, the protest planners could only watch sullenly, as monies which could have been spent on sorely needed textbooks and lab equipment went up in puffs of colorful fireworks from the heights of Morne Bruce overlooking Roseau on the morning of November 3, 1978. Hot on the heels of independence, a new season of radical political activism was to awake, of which students at Sixth Form College, along with their other allies in the organized political left were to be part creators, part progeny.

By Sunday January 22nd, 1979[113] the National Youth Council hosted a massive national youth conference at the St.

---

[113]. The N.Y.C., the official national umbrella organization for youth, had elected a new executive in 1977. That executive was composed of P.I.C. members and other youth sympathetic to a left-wing program which spoke to wide-ranging reforms in Dominican politics, education, and the need for a less-dependent economic approach to development. The election, in time, was to be criticized as a rigged affair by the political right. However, an objective examination of the period reveals that the Freedom Party and Labour Party lacked mass influence among youth and student organizations and so were without the votes within the N.Y.C. to ensure election of their candidates, if

Joseph government school. The conference chaired by Pierre Charles, saw several panels, on the economy, health, education, equal rights for women, youth problems, unemployment, drugs, culture etc. deliberate throughout the day. Fraternal messages from left wing regional organizations were read. Guyana's Peoples Progressive Party representative (doubling as representative of the Prague-based World Federation of Democratic Youth) spoke in support of the N.Y.C program. The event ended with a call for land reform and new initiatives in education, trade and industry to insure that Dominica's recently won independence would be more than mere "flag independence". The pressure upon the Labour government to deliver, was on.

Nonetheless, a split had developed within the P.I.C. Bernard Wiltshire had become increasingly critical of Rosie's lack of detail and seeming disregard for strong a "vanguard" organization which would lead the working class and its allies in the struggle for complete national liberation. Wiltshire himself came under criticism from P.I.C members, as being "rude", "uncomradely", and an "ultra-leftist" who articulated Marxist concepts like atheism which "frightened the religious masses," thus making political work more difficult for all. Wiltshire's retort, was that P.I.C. leadership cuddled "herb (i.e. marijuana)

---

any. It was at that time the Freedom Party started the Young Freedom Movement (YFM), with modest success.

users" and had otherwise failed to organize and prepare for the de-linking between P.I.C. and the Labour government. Francisco Esprit, Hilroy "Castor" Thomas, Sobers Esprit, Pierre Charles, and Greg Rabess, and most Core members agreed somewhat with the criticism of Rosie. Only Cadre No. 1, and portions of the Portsmouth and Grandbay cadres supported Rosie in the factional fight. His brother Michael, who had by then formed a group of his constituents into a grouping called Dominica Democratic Alliance, remained outside the fray. In a final rejoinder, a meeting of P.I.C.'s Roseau affiliate Cadre No. 1, dismissed Wiltshire as an *"autocrat...a Trotskyist caught within a web of ultra-leftism, which is an infantile disorder in the words of Lenin."*[114]

The language of that factionalism reflected more the hoary and irrelevant concepts of purge-politics under Joseph Stalin, than it did Dominica's reality. Nonetheless, serious questions over the nature of "critical support", personal discipline in organization, over-intellectualizing and sloganeering, and whether or not cadres should smoke marijuana were raised.[115]

---

[114]. Minutes of April 9th, 1979 Cadre No. 1 meeting

[115]. Documents now in the U.S. Archives in Washington D.C. collected from the files of the Grenadian politburo point to similar problems with marijuana and Dread influence in that revolution. In fact plans were actually discussed to imprison Grenada's Dreads and expel dread notable Desmond Trotter, who had sought refuge in Grenada since the Revolution. Also, the lack of organizational discipline was to prove fatal to Bishop in his conflict with the

These factional problems would continue to dog Dominica's new left, leaving it unable to adequately capitalize on the results of its activism, thus allowing the Freedom Party to capitalize on the fruits of its agitation.

In late 1978, early 1979, a serious crisis affected Dominica's banana industry, the life-blood of Dominica's economy. A disease, called leaf-spot (for the manner in which debilitating brown spots appeared on the banana tree leaves) threatened to cripple fruit production. The Dominica Farmers Union (D.F.U.) led by Athie Martin was quick to organize around the seemingly slow-response of the Ministry of Agriculture. Mike Douglas, leading the P.I.C. aligned D.D.A, added his voice to concerns at the parliamentary level[116]. After a consultation with farmers and students, the D.F.U led a January 29th, 1979 march through the streets of Roseau. Since the S.M.A walk-out it was the first time students had poured into the streets for a political cause. The tone of the protests, though ostensibly showing concern over the leaf-spot crisis, was definitely anti-government. The alliance between students and farmers was new; and the involvement of left-wing personalities, like Martin and others in and outside the student and farmers movement was

---

more bureaucratic and systematic Coard whose supporters were to, arrest, imprison and murder Bishop.

[116]. Having retained his position as MP from Portsmouth Douglas was the sole voice espousing left-wing causes in parliament, after Patrick John began his right-ward shift in 1978.

significant. D.F.U leaders, like Ted Honeychurch and Alvin Armantrading (known or perceived as Freedomites), spoke at the massed meeting following the march. The leaf-spot march prefaced an alliance of the left, Freedom Party, students and farmers which was to slowly take shape over the coming months.

In the midst of that upsurge in activism came a thunderclap of an event, heard as far away as London and Washington, and which was to shake the political establishments of the English speaking Caribbean to the core. That event was the March 13th, 1979 revolution by the New Jewel Movement (N.J.M) under the leadership of Maurice Bishop, which overthrew Sir Eric Gairy's regime on Grenada. It was the first overthrow of government of its type, ever, in the history of the English speaking Caribbean territories. More so, the N.J.M represented the type of radicalism which had derived from the upsurge in black power thought in the earlier part of the decade. As an organization, it had counterparts in almost every English Caribbean territory. With Jamaica and Guyana under leaderships (Michael Manley and Forbes Burnham, respectively) which espoused socialism, the Grenadian revolutionaries even had access to friends in high places. But the greatest impact was to be felt on the ground, specifically in the Windward islands of St.

Lucia[117] and Dominica. Relations between the N.J.M leadership and Dominica's left was strong. Bishop had represented black power activist Desmond Trotter; Kenrick Radix had caucused with the P.I.C and P.D.P over differences in tactics during the lead-up to Dominica's independence. Just a year prior, in the Summer of 1978, N.J.M activists led by Liam James[118], had argued, consulted on tactics, strategy and otherwise shared living space with Gregory Rabess, Pierre Charles, and other P.I.C members at the Villa Lenin, the sprawling residential site for Latin American delegates to the 11th World Festival of Youth and Students, located on the outskirts of Havana. Now, the N.J.M was in power. Apart from sending congratulatory telegrams, and promises of support, the left was now imbued with a new zest and determination to assume the levers of state control. However, without members in parliament, aside from a sympathetic Michael Douglas, the P.I.C. needed to build alliances with the trade unions and others sectors of the burgeoning opposition to Patrick John. Immediately, the P.I.C. fashioned a slogan which was to become legendary, as it was spray-painted and popularized

---

[117]. In St. Lucia a tumultuous general election was to take place in mid-1979, which replaced the conservative leadership of John Compton with a Left leaning St. Lucia Labour Party under the leadership of George Odlum and retired Judge Allan Louisy.

[118]. later to rise to the rank of Lt. Colonel and head of Grenada' State Security apparatus, 1979-1983.

around the country: **"GAIRY GONE, PJ NEXT! ALLIANCE IS THE ANSWER"**.

Before the leaf-spot crisis and the echoes of the March 13th, 1979 revolt were able to fade away, another issue exploded on the political scene. It concerned the plan by the John government to lease 45 square miles of prime agricultural land in Dominica's north, to a group of Texan investors led by one Don Pierson. Dominica's treasury would receive a measly $99.00 per year for a 99 year lease, in exchange for granting the investors what would be virtual autonomy in the free-port area. Once the news hit the streets, the left sought to coordinate the outrage felt by many that this a was down-right colonial land grab which made a mockery of Dominica's struggle for independence from Britain. To the left, it seemed that we were replacing one colonial master with another. Quickly the P.I.C. framed a nationalist slogan which resounded around the island: **"TEXAS FOR TEXANS, DOMINICA, FOR DOMINICANS"**. Without land reform, or good job prospects, Dominica's youth were receptive to the anti-free-port opposition which considered the deal a "sell-out" to foreign interests. With nationalist feelings stirring, the P.I.C and D.D.A. worked with the Freedom Party, D.F.U and student leadership to stop the deal from going through. At a March 2nd, 1979 meeting organized by Sixth Form College students, held at the Dominica Grammar School, Don Pierson's response to a barrage of questions from the students was found woefully inadequate. His face red with exasperation, and unprepared for the student's verbal onslaught, Pierson limped out of the room. A momentum was building against the deal. For the first time the left and Freedom Party activists spoke on the same platform, at numerous anti-free-port meetings held nation-wide (that unity was a far cry from the left/Freedom Party schism over independence barely two years earlier!). In response to public disapproval, and wary of a demonstration planned for May 8th, 1979 John cancelled the free-port deal.

By that time, the John government was floundering. The party, as organized along structured units of branches all over the island, was a shell of its former self. The rural core of Labour could only passively watch as a government, acting ostensibly on their behalf, failed to consult with them. Though a former trade union leader, John now increasingly surrounded himself with a Roseau-based coterie of businessmen, considered by many to comprise opportunists, and others hoping to secure a government position, or some largesse from an increasing bare government till. Foreign trips, of dubious worth, were regularly criticized in the *New Chronicle* [119]. Though Labour had won a majority of the vote at the 1975 election, the government found its supporters unwilling to come to its defense over issues, such as the free-port

---

[119]. See *New Chronicle*, **"The Prime Minister of On Secret Mission"** December 9, 1978 at pg. 9.

or leaf-spot crises. The Labour government's achievements in spurring beneficial social change in the 1960s, was fast becoming a distant memory. Labour's efforts in founding a National Commercial and Development Bank, building a new airstrip at Canefield a few miles outside the capital (to avoid business travelers the sometimes dizzying two hour trip through mountainous terrain from the Melville Hall Airport to Roseau),a spanking new Social Security System, and new housing schemes at Bath Estate, River Estate and Canefield were not enough to blunt the criticism that Dominica seemed adrift under John's leadership. Within the Labour Party democracy seemed at its nadir as John seemed to have cowed any opposition to his increasingly autocratic rule. No dissenting voices were to be heard from within the government to assure the still-silent Dominican majority that all was well. With the muting of any critical internal discourse over divisive development issues, the opposition felt emboldened.

To make matters worse, Prime Minister John, now addressed the citizens over national radio wearing the title of "Doctor" or "Colonel."[120] Such titular embroidery seemed immodest at best, and bordered on buffoonery at worst. As a result, his leadership was increasingly losing respect among the

---

[120]. By 1977 John had assumed the rank of colonel, as commander-in-chief of the local defence force. Later, he was to claim having earned a doctorate in metaphysics from a U.S. university.

population, especially the young. To add to the atmosphere of drift and the bizarre, news began leaking that the government had approached the South African government with a proposal to access petroleum in exchange for a fee.[121] The instigator of that proposal was thought to be Guyanese-born Attorney General, Leo I. Austin whose letter to the South African embassy in London was to wind up in the hands of the P.I.C.. A B.B.C. documentary, on the program "Panorama", seemed to shed further light on the subject. The government was increasingly hard-pressed to dispel the rumors of a South African plot to use Dominica as a base for the purchase and storage of petroleum; with the earlier proposed free-port being a cover. As well, the link between the government and Barbadian right-winger and confessed gun-runner Sydney Burnette Alleyne seemed to confirm the worst fears of the left that John had linked-up with the most fascist and racist elements in the world[122]. The

---

[121]. By that time, the South African government (without oil resources of its own, and staggering under the costs of an oil-from-coal program-SASOL) was desperately searching the world for allies who could assist its efforts to surmount the OPEC embargo. Earlier, South African attempts at obtaining oil by military means (i.e. its 1975 invasion of oil rich Angola) had been crushed by the joint Cuban-M.P.L.A armies.

[122]. Alleyne claimed a relationship with the "Wild Geese" mercenaries who, under the leadership of South African based mercenary Colonel Mike "Mad Mike" Hoare, savaged the Congo during its 1960s civil war. Hoare was later convicted of an attempted invasion of the Pacific island nation of Seychelles, then ruled by a left-wing government. Later, in 1981, Patrick John would be arrested for plotting, with Klu Klux Klan and American Nazi party operatives, to overthrow the newly elected Freedom party government. One of the persons

Dominican left now feared for its very physical survival. For, though none of its top leadership had been imprisoned or killed, it was the common wisdom that John would have to resort to strong-arm tactics if his plans with such foreign interests (as those he were courting) were to have any chance of success. To this day, it remains uncertain as to whether or not John and/or his advisors had any idea as to the eventual outcome of that alliance being forged with shady elements of the international right-wing and pariah nations like South Africa. Or who, in reality, was the mastermind behind these efforts (if indeed a mastermind was required for deals which can only be described as outlandish).

Events were moving swiftly to confrontation, however. By May 29th, 1979 the government proposed two amendments: One, to the Industrial Relations Act, the other to the Libel and Slander Act. The twin amendments would have the effect of cramping union activism, and muzzling a press[123] which (led by the *New Chronicle*) was increasingly strident in its opposition to recent government policies. The major unions decided to confront the government effort, the official Freedom Party opposition and left joined in the effort.

---

investigated for complicity in the plot was none other 1992 U.S. Presidential candidate David Duke, a notorious Nazi and Klu Klux Klan sympathizer.

[123]. It is notable, that radio opposition was via the critical, but generally objective, reports of Radio Antilles reporter Elsworth Carter, a Dominican. The government had little or no control over Antilles, since it was located on another island, Monsterrat. However, government control over Radio Dominica reigned supreme.

May 29th, 1979, as an event (and its aftermath) will be examined in more detail elsewhere. Suffice it to say, it led to the final conflict between the radical politics which had developed in Dominica during the 1970s, and a government which had become increasingly viewed by the majority as authoritarian and unresponsive to the voice of the people. As a result of protests on that day, May 29th 1979, the government of Patrick John was to be overthrown. In its place, an interim government grouping, rump elements of the former Labour administration, Freedom Party activists and leftists grouped under the newly formed Dominica Liberation Movement was to be installed.

The crisis, had forced the Leftist dispersed amongst, the P.I.C., P.D.P, and D.D.A to come together, under one banner: The Dominica Liberation Movement. It was Rosie Douglas who pressed for such functional unity and suggested the name- Dominica liberation Movement (DLM) at a May 30, 1979 meeting held at the Roseau offices of the Dominica Christian Council. For the Dominican left, May 29th, 1979 represented an ascension to power of the Dominican radicalism which had steadily grown in strength during the decade. Its stay in power, albeit brief and limited, was notable for what was revealed. Soon after ascension to power, the left wing encouraged Dominica's participation at the July 14th-15th, 1979 **Grenada Summit**.

At the summit, Prime Ministers Oliver Seraphine of Dominica, Allan Louisy of St. Lucia, and Maurice Bishop of Grenada embraced a decision to strengthen inter-island cooperation and work towards the "liquidation of all traces of colonialism in and out of the Caribbean." That summit also attended by interim government ministers, Attorney General Brian Alleyne and Agriculture Minister Athie Martin, was remarkable for its anti-imperialist oratory and resolute calls for Eastern Caribbean unity. Even the conservative, and usually reserved former St. Lucian judge Prime Minister Allan Louisy, in a fit of zeal, leapt to the lectern shouting "long live the Revolution!" Back home, however, he was to be bedeviled by the same factionalism faced by Dominica's left when Deputy Prime Minister George Odlum accused him of reneging on a deal to vacate the top job, once the elections had been won. The plan, according to Odlum, was that he was to occupy the top job. Feeling that Louisy had been used as a Trojan horse for left wingers, many St. Lucians soured on the St. Lucia Labour Party. Such acrimony, while for different reasons, would plague the Dominican left.

Adept management of internal conflict or dispute resolution was not the strong point of the Eastern Caribbean left wing. Such internal dissension was to later spell the death of the Grenada Revolution, cause the early removal of the St. Lucia

Labour Party from political office and frustrate the electoral chances of Dominica's newly revamped Labour party for about twenty years. Ascension to the halls of political power exposed the left's weaknesses among organized urban Labour and the depth of its inter-personal feuds and ideological dissension. However, the left also faced other substantive issues with regard to tactics and strategic objectives.

How could a movement pursue real social change where the media and means of production were in antagonistic private hands? How could one overcome the inherent conservatism of an overwhelmingly Roman Catholic country of small landholders, hucksters and shopkeepers anxious to stake out their own very private economic niche, in contradiction to any leftist inspired collectivist vision? How could one inspire Dominicans to sacrifice for social change in the fight against foreign economic domination, in the face of a weak nationalist tradition? Such were the questions which derived from the left's difficulty in broadening its base, beyond students, some conscious farm cooperatives and a narrow intellectual strata. In addition, in a society which had known stability, the squabbling amongst the political left amounted to self destruction of its political line.

Despite the missteps and misgivings noted above, political power allowed the left an opportunity to operate some of the levers of state and show-off its talent. Athie Martin, in the

Ministry of Agriculture and Michael Douglas, in Finance, were to gain plaudits for efficiency and hard work. There was hope aplenty, especially among students, that better things were yet to come. Nature, however, had different plans. Shortly after entering office the interim government was faced with Dominica's biggest natural disaster in the 20th Century: The August 29, 1979, Hurricane David.

THE POLITICS OF HURRICANE AID

Hurricane David devastated Dominica's agricultural economy and took about 56 lives on August 29, 1979. Its destruction was to result in the presence of British, French and Venezuelan troops who, in some areas, constituted the only organized authority for some time. The British arrived early, the Royal Navy frigate ***HMS Fife***[124] cutting through the still choppy seas on the very next day and its contingent of sailors performing valiantly under trying conditions.

The Venezuelans manned the airport at Melville Hall and their French made Alouette helicopters scoured the island for survivors, while dropping off tons of supplies to villages which had been isolated by landslides. The French established a major

---

[124] See Honeychurch's, ***Dominica Story***, 2nd ed. At 209.

base on the Goodwill savannah and fanned out from there to clear roads and distribute relief supplies. The U.S. presence came later, was massive, and much appreciated. Huge twin engine chinook heavy-lift helicopters, using the Windsor Park soccer field as a staging area disgorged tons of c-rations for the population. Later, the U.S. Aid program was to be crudely politicized when some elements sought to make further assistance to Dominica conditional on the interim government engaging itself in its anti-Cuba campaign. None of the other donors of that period attempted to assert such a quid pro quo for assistance.

When Agriculture Minister Martin urged volunteerism by suggesting that Dominicans form work brigades to assist the foreign rescue workers, his efforts were assailed and he was condemned as an acolyte of Godless communism. A pious church going man, Martin's drive for self reliance was deemed an attempt at "regimentation." He was spurned for wanting, in the words of a very vocal Freedom partisan of the time, one Destouche of Pottersville, "make Dominicans work hard, like we in Cuba." Shortly afterwards, US flags sprouted on houses around Roseau. Many saw the flags as attesting to their well founded appreciation of the US assistance, others as a device to ward-off some alleged Cuban attempt to seize their land and homes to share with the poor and "lazy."

That devious anti-Cuba campaign persisted, and grew to a crescendo, shortly after Cuban Economic Development Minister Hector Rodriguez Llompart and Grenadian Prime Minister Maurice Bishop visited Dominica in early September, 1979 on an aid assessment mission for the Non-Aligned Ministers Conference then being held in Havana. Earlier, Rosie Douglas had gained credit for his diplomatic mission to Fidel Castro, who (along with Grenada's Maurice Bishop, Guyana's Forbes Burnham and Jamaica's Michael Manley) urged the Non-Aligned Movement heads of state then meeting in Havana to contribute money to Dominica's relief effort following the devastating hurricane of August 29th, 1979. Douglas was later joined by Bernard Wiltshire in mobilizing support for Dominica from the gathering. That effort was later able to realize contributions in the region, of U.S. $13 million, from distant sources like Saddam Hussein's Iraq and Ayatollah Khomeini's Iran.

Llompart and Bishop came bearing substantive assistance which would empower Dominicans in the long term. Out of a proposed Cuban assistance package which included offers to build a new hospital, along with one hundred university scholarships, only eleven university scholarships were accepted. The government also accepted a Cuban donation of $100,000 U.S. dollars. The left-wing members of the interim government were disgusted, as they had lobbied hard for acceptance of the whole deal. Later, the left was to continue the scholarship program, first via the DLM and then later via the reformed Labour Party. Eventually, even the conservative post-1980 election Freedom Party regime was to embrace the virtue of the Cuban scholarship program. Today, the majority of university educated Dominicans in the fields of medicine are Cuban trained and, as of May 2002, four hundred Dominican students attended Cuban various universities free of charge.

THE 1980 ELECTIONS

Despite the compromise on Cuban assistance by the interim government, a withering propaganda regime was to flourish during the reign of US Ambassador's Sally Shelton whose influence on Prime Minister Seraphine was suspect. Many believing that he had succumbed to her charms. In fact after the revolutionary rhetoric of the **Grenada Summit**, Seraphine had offered the U.S. military base facilities on Dominica. It was claimed, on the inside, that such efforts were aimed at wooing the U.S. away from its preference for the Freedom Party. However, the U.S. would not be wooed. Thereafter, the opposition profited from U.S. monetary assistance in painting the local left as some voracious communist menace bent on doing Russia's bidding.

Never mind that such was blatant intervention in the affairs of a sovereign country, the U.S. kept up its involvement in ways covert and overt. As a result the populace was to chase the communist bogey through a thick mist of propaganda, instead of seeking solutions to the very real problems of under-development left by colonialism. Issues of university education, land reform, the lack of local technical competence in many areas, health care, local control over financial institutions and the energy company (owned by the British Colonial Development Corporation) export markets, agro processing, fisheries were not on the agenda during the election. Rather, the populace was misdirected into resurrecting the ghost of self destructive *mepuis* politics which the left had struggled against in the early part of the decade.

However, struggle in the name of the masses and an approaching election was not long able to dampen the personal animosities rife among the old leadership of Dominica's left wing. An unseemly squabble had erupted over leadership with Athie Martin, William "Para" Riviere and Pierre Charles arrayed against the P.I.C leadership of Rosie Douglas, student movement activists and Mike Douglas' D.D.A. Under the constitution, elections were due by July of 1980. The interim government which took power in Summer 1979, was mandated to serve-out the term of the Labour party which had been elected in 1975. In the lead up to the 1980 election, the left had again split.

Elements of the left, cognizant of the shift in public sympathies, favored an alliance with the anti-John Labour Party elements now coalescing around interim Prime Minister O.J. Seraphine's Democratic Labour Party (Dem. Lab.), which considered itself a social democratic party. Specifically, the P.I.C and D.D.A broke away in supporting the Dem. Lab. while, the P.D.P. of Bill Riviere (now joined by Bernard Wiltshire) decided to run a "purist" campaign under the Dominica Liberation Movement-Alliance cover.

Bolstered by U.S. financial assistance, Freedom Party supporters wearing t-shirts emblazoned with the message: NO RUSSIA! NO CUBA! NO TRAITOR! swung around the island on a "Freedom Train" motorcade. In propaganda salvoes which verged on the comical people were told: "Alliance[125] will take your house and split it in half and share it with the lazy; Alliance will turn churches into dance halls; Alliance will cut your cows in pieces and share it amongst the lazy; Alliance will take your shoes and share it, if you have more than one pair..." Under such an onslaught of misinformation and outright lies, the left's popularity was weakened.

Though the Freedom Party had a role in the interim government, it purposely separated itself from the administration in order to better its chances at the polls by not being associated

---

[125] . Now the popular name of the Dominica Liberation Movement, having adopted the slogan "Alliance" popularized all over the island by the PIC.

with any of its missteps. By January 1980, both Charles Maynard and Brian Alleyne had resigned their positions in the interim government, so that by Election time, Dem. Lab, felt free to revive the standard criticism that the Freedom Party was the tool of Dominica's bourgeoisie. It was clear that the Freedom party had escaped its elitist tag and narrow class base when it offered election candidates like Henry "Bab's" Dyer (Roseau North, constituency), or Alleyne Carbon (Cottage constituency) who came from humble origins. Frustration showed in the speeches of the Dem. Lab. campaigners when the reality that the Freedom party had democratized its base hit home. In the words of London University educated barrister, then Attorney General Eustace Hazelwood Francis, better known to his working class supporters as "Woy!":

> Ladies and gentlemen, who is the Freedom Party? The Freedom Party is the party of the Burtons, the Shillingford's, the Agars, the Green's, the this, the that....the aristocracy. But they get smart. They have learnt the tricks of the Labour Party. They put some of our little people in front to fool you, making you believe that is the real Freedom Party and that you really in something....Some of you poor people running behind their motorcade saying you "hooked-on Freedom." Really, you not hooked on anything, but second class citizenship. Like slaves, some of you still want slave masters to adore.[126]...

---

[126] . Address by Eustace Francis to a mammoth crowd of Dem. Lab. supporters on the Goodwill Savannah at its biggest pre-election rally in July 1980.

He further sought to revive Labour's socialist credentials in face of criticism that the administration was dealing with the Bahama-based Shah of Iran who was then seeking refuge after being overthrown by Ayatollah Khomeini the year prior.

> ...They say we have Shah money. We do not have Shah money. The Shah is their kind of people; their thing. They belong to the capitalist world and they invest their money on the rivieras... We are socialist people; Non-Aligned people. This business of Shah money is nothing more than political humbug....

On that same day, Prime Minister Seraphine, followed up with a volley, in a similar vein:

> When they asked me to head the interim government, they said I was the best man. The cleanest one. The one who was not corrupt. Who wanted me to save the country, ladies and gentlemen? It was the Freedom Party. It was the Alliance. It was the Civil Service Association. It was the Employers Federation. It was the churches. They all wanted me. Now, they think they can use me...as if I am some little boy they send to do message in a shop for them. Ladies and gentlemen...massa[127] day done!

---

[127] Massa, a term used to address planters or white persons during the slave and colonial period, denoting submission by blacks to their power.

However, to a national audience where conservative middle class values now reigned, such verbal jabs did not resonate with the Dominican public as they would have thirty years earlier, when poverty and class and color prejudice was more widespread on the island.

Dem. Lab's last minute campaign was an all-out affair and included use of a white Goodyear blimp (towed around the island by a trawler leased to the P.I.C by Guyana's government), emblazoned with the red painted words, "Vote DemLab!" Herculean efforts by a helicopter borne O.J. Seraphine, who criss-crossed the island on election eve wearing a cowboy hat with Dem. Lab. insignia - while dramatic - could not turn the tide. The government's attempts at strategic distribution of galvanize roofing for constituencies where homes still suffered from the damage inflicted by Hurricane David, came undone as it was viewed with poor taste by many as an outright attempt at vote-buying. Efforts at quickly releasing donated clothing, popularly called "brogodow!"[128] did not play in the government's favor either. Though, the campaign of July 20th, 1980 was fiercely fought and was described by chroniclers of the period as "one of

---

[128] Brogodow! The sound said to be made by boxes of food and clothes dropped by helicopters immediately after Hurricane David. It came to be the term used to describe all donated food or clothing. As in "He wearing brogodow"...or "I had some brogodow for breakfast."

mutual animosity, character assassination, and blatant lies[129]," it went ahead in relative peace.

The Dominican populace sought stability in the 1980 election and saw the Freedom Party as the entity best able to assure that. It was the prevailing view that Freedom's US alliance would ensure development assistance. It did not hurt such a result any that the U.S. had a heavy pro-Freedom Party thumb on the scales of decision when electoral options were being weighed[130].

At the end the Left lost, garnering roughly 15% of the vote. The Freedom Party won, garnering a slight majority of approximately 52% of the popular vote. Dem. Lab. secured another 20% of the vote, with old Labour led by Patrick John and a few die hards gathering somewhere between 10% and 12%, the remainder going to independent candidates. In defeat, the left garnered more votes than any other Marxist-Leninist led organization has ever done in any of the other British Commonwealth Caribbean territories, even where hobbled by unfavorable external and internal factors.

---

[129]. Honeychurch's, *The Dominica Story*, at page 213, quoting the Caribbean Insight.

[130]. In Bob Woodward's *Veil: The Secret Wars of the CIA* (Simon & Schuster, 1987) it is related that CIA records reveal a $100,000 sum had been passed to the Freedom Party's government at some point, a sum a key senator on the Intelligence Committee considered a "payoff". Prime Minister Charles firmly denied any knowledge of a secret payment to her, her party or government. Id at 290.

In some constituencies, like Castle Bruce, Grandbay, Paixe Bouche, Carib Reserve and others, the left would have secured electoral victories, had its vote not been split.[131] If the left wing voter support, dispersed among the DLM and Dem. Lab vote were counted in one bloc, it would surely have approximated a third of the electorate. When the dust had settled only Michael Douglas (Portsmouth) and Elford Henry (Wesley) emerged triumphant on the side of the political left.

CONCLUSION

By the end of the decade the left had become an accepted part of Dominica's political life. Issues, such as greater emphasis on free education, land reform, opposition to police brutality where it occurred, scholarships for higher learning, women's rights, a foreign policy in support of African Liberation movements, greater economic self reliance and control over local resources, relations with a U.S. blockaded Cuba, greater emphasis on local culture, and a pride in the African and indigenous roots of the Dominican population are now commonly accepted as valid; no longer radical.

---

[131]. In later elections in the 1980s, the left (or candidates who espoused similar policies and earned its support) would win Grandbay, Carib Reserve, Wesley, Marigot and Paixe Bouche.

The radicalism which rocked Dominica in the 1970s lessened the bite of class and color prejudice, lent renewed focus to democracy, and the need for accountability by government to the governed. Indeed, many of the policies espoused by the left found resonance even within the conservative confines of a Freedom Party government eager to keep within the good graces of a populace which had exhibited revolutionary democracy, by taking to the streets. Dominica, had changed in a way that strengthened the dignity of blacks, Caribs and women. The Freedom Party had, itself, been forced to democratize and reach out to the working class and peasantry, in a way courting the voting power of the petit boug as Labour had earlier done. Accordingly, though still the flag bearer of Dominican conservatism, the Freedom party leadership was pragmatic enough to manage an escape from the class and color politics that long frustrated its political ambitions. In time, the left and Labour would fuse. Intent on serving the masses, and coming (historically) from the same socialist perspective, the left would come to constitute the core of electable Labour. As well, the left's radicalism would find a niche in Dominican enterprise, as many who took part in that flowering of radical thought sought to contribute, in a concrete way, to economic self reliance. Such a contribution, by enterprises like Frontline Bookstore, Star Brite Candle Factory, The Small Projects Assistance Team (S.P.A.T),

Farm-to-Market (which exported local fruit) and others, met real needs and ensured continuity of a radical vision of social security, access to higher education, the development of local technology, economic self reliance, social justice and dignity.

By the end of the Twentieth Century, the years of effort led the Labour Party from the two decades in opposition to the halls of power. Ironically, their former bitter opponent, the Freedom Party (weakened by the departure of Eugenia Charles from the political scene) shared power with Labour, as its junior partner in a coalition government which came to power on February 1, 2000. At the end of the Cold War, the new United Workers Party claimed the same social democratic principles as did Labour; thus a consensus on the primacy of social justice seemed engraved in the national consciousness. Simply put, but for the years of radical activism, Dominica may have long become another corrupt failed-state, so many of which now litter a world subjugated by a pernicious globalization which serves the interest of a wealthy few at the expense of the many. Fortunately, despite its disabilities, Dominica has favorable indices in health care which makes for the island to have the highest per capita concentration of centenarians and the oldest human being, as of this writing: Elizabeth "Ma Pampo" Israel, born in 1875. The life expectancy for males on the island is at a respectable 79.5 and 83.2 for females. Unlike many developing countries, Dominica is not riven by calcified racial, ethnic and class divisions so rampant in the Western hemisphere and beyond. A vibrant nationalistic press, led by local electronics engineer Ronald Abraham's *Marpin Televison* and its eminent commentator Lennox Linton, maintain a close scrutiny of public and private sector conduct. With press coverage by newspapers such as *The Sun*, *The Chronicle*, *Independent*, *The Tropical Star* and the island's first internet news magazine, Dr. Thomson Fontaine's *The Dominican*, along with the privately owned *Kairi FM* radio, Dominicans are generally well informed. That reality is not perfect and there is much to improve, as the island now battles economic fallout from the World Trade Organization's (WTO) ruling which destroyed the protected market for English Caribbean bananas in the United Kingdom. Keen vigilance has to be maintained to prevent any diminishing of the gains made over the years of radical activism, in light of the backsliding toward racial and class animus now plaguing Europe and North America; in particular after the tragic attacks on the Twin Towers in New York on September 11, 2001. With such a noble legacy of service toward the least among us and in accord with a universal vision of human brotherhood and peace among nations based on equity and mutual respect, the forces of Dominican radicalism are assured a continued existence for the foreseeable future.

LEGISLATION AND REPRESSION IN DOMINICA IN THE 1970s

Irving André

INTRODUCTION

The year 1979 is perhaps the single most important year in the recent history of Dominica. Between May and August, the island experienced a popular revolt against the national government, and a disastrous hurricane which paralleled the devastation caused by political upheaval.

The fall of the Patrick John government led to the ascendancy of the rival Dominica Freedom Party in the island's 1980 General Elections. Subsequently, the Dominica Labour Party was relegated to the fringes of the island's politics with internal conflict becoming a permanent characteristic of its existence. More importantly, and what may be the apotheosis of national betrayal, the events of 1979 led to the former Prime Minister contracting with a band of Klu Klux Klan members to invade the island which government he headed less than 15 months earlier!

What accounts for such a momentous chain of events in the island's history, less than one year after attaining political independence from Britain on November 3, 1978? In one sense, the events of 1979 marked the culmination of the conflict between the government and the island's trade Unions evident throughout the *1970s*. In 1977, government workers brought the island's business to a virtual standstill after a protracted 47 day strike. The John government yielded and was forced to pay millions of back pay to its workers.

In the ensuing years, the government was forced to deal with industrial unrest from teachers, garbage collectors and nurses. This unrest emanated from sectors of the labour force regarded as essential. Prior to March 29, 1979, the prevalent view in government was the need for legislation to rid itself of the burden of legitimate union militancy.

Proponents of this interpretation of the events of 1979 will no doubt point to the actions taken by the John government, which precipitated the mass action on May 29, 1979. The events which led to the Dominica Defence Force opening fire on Dominicans demonstrating against the government started with the declared passage of legislation aimed at curbing the unions' ability to initiate industrial action.

On May 22, 1979, the Minister of Health Industrial Relations, and Women's Affairs, sent a copy of a proposed Bill to amend the *Industrial Relations Act, 1975,* to the island's four trade unions, inviting them to discuss the proposed Bill later that day.[1] In their collective response to the invitation, the unions implicitly advised the Minister that such discussion was pointless, since the House of Assembly was scheduled to meet on May 29, 1979, to discuss the contents of the Bill. In any event, the unions noted, discussion would be useless since the proposed amendments militated against their continued existence and their enactment would lead to and *open invitation to industrial unrest in the country.*[2]

The trade unions had cause for alarm at the proposed amendment to the *Industrial Relations Act*. The progeny of the Attorney General, the amendment banned all strikes by civil servants and workers in *essential services*, the latter term to be defined by the government as suited its fancy. It also sought to prohibit financial aid to strikers; a provision which would emasculate the unions in any industrial dispute they would have with the government. Striking workers could be arrested and if found guilty, fined $250.00 or jailed for 3 years. Union leaders on the other hand, could be fined $2,000.00, jailed for 18 months and be banned from holding office in any union for five years. A proposed amendment to the *Libel and Slander Act* would force

---

[1] Report of the inquiry into the Dominica Defence Force and **Report of the Commission of Inquiry** into the events of May 29th, 1979, March 27, 1981, Prime Minister's Office, Government Headquarters, Roseau, Commonwealth, page 1 hereinafter referred to as **The Report**.
[2] As in above footnote, page 2.

editors of any local paper to disclose sources of any anonymous articles which they published.

After the unions rejected the initial invitation of the government, the Prime Minister, accompanied by Attorney General Leo Austin, met with the union leaders. Again the union leaders expressed disapproval of the proposed amendment and the dire consequences which would result if it became law. Austin reiterated the government's intention to amend the *Act*, dismissing the caution of Charles Savarin, General Secretary of the Civil Service Association (CSA) that industrial unrest would likely result.[3]

The following day, the CSA adopted a unanimous resolution that its members would absent themselves from work on May 29, 1979, and assemble outside the Government Headquarters building to demonstrate the unions' opposition to the new legislation.[4] To thwart this development, the Prime Minister proclaimed that public meetings in Roseau would be prohibited between May 29 and June 4, 1979.[5] He also cautioned the Acting Commissioner of Police and Commander of the Defence Force that the security forces should take all measures to prevent the breakdown of law and order and to avoid the reoccurrence of the December 16, 1971, storming of the House of

---

[3] **The Report**, page 2.
[4] As above.
[5] As above.

Assembly. Later that day, the Acting Commissioner of Police and Commanding Officer of the Defence Force held a meeting to discuss security measures at the House of Assembly.[6] Later that evening, the unions held a public meeting during which the plan for the proposed demonstration on May 29, 1979, was affirmed.

The inevitable confrontation occurred the following day when the Defence Force opened fire on the 10,000 – 15,000 demonstrators assembled outside government headquarters. The confrontation was short and bloody, with one person killed and nine others wounded. In a scathing indictment of the actions of the Defence Force, an inquiry into the events of May 29, 1979, concluded that:[7]

> In our opinion, the use of firearms to ensure the entry of the Prime Minister... was wholly unjustified and may properly be made the subject of criminal investigation by the proper authorities.

It further concluded that the Defence Force officer who authorized the use of gunfire to disperse the crowd:

> [I]gnored the principles that govern the actions of the military when assisting the civil power in maintaining law and order. In our opinion, serious consideration should be given to the question whether Captain Reid

---

[6] As above, page 3.
[7] as above, page 23.

is a fit and proper person to hold any rank whatsoever in the Dominica Defence Force.[8]

The pace of events prior to May 29, 1979 was matched by those following that date. The actions of the Defence Force triggered regional and international condemnation. The Prime Minister of Trinidad and Tobago withdrew a $12 million dollar soft loan to the island. The Caribbean Trade Union Movement imposed an embargo on food to and from Dominica. Dominicans resident in New York staged a protest outside the United Nations Headquarters while their Canadian counterparts established a Committee of Concerned Dominicans to coordinate condemnation of the May 29th incident.

Soon after, the Ministers of Government resigned from the John government. A broad based Committee for National Salvation was set up on June 12, 1979, as an interim government and quickly appointed a new President of the island. One of the first acts of Jenner Armour, the new President, was to revoke the appointment of John as Prime Minister of the island.[9] It was an ignominious exit for one who had become his own nemesis.

The fall of Patrick John has all the elements of Greek Tragedy. The population of Dominica acted as the Chorus clamoring for John's resignation. Sympathy over the fall was

---

[8] As above, page 26.
[9] As above.

generated by the spectacle of Ministers of Government resigning while their leader resolutely refused to resign as Prime Minister of the island. Finally, the tragic flaw of John himself, undone by his own obsession to become the messiah who brought economic salvation to his land and people.

In any event, the events of May 29, 1979, appear to have been caused by the attempts of the John government to curtail the power of the local trade unions through legislation. However, historical events of this magnitude hardly lend themselves to interpretation based on a single causative or precipitatory factor. Rather, those events must be seen in the context of the period when economic problems and the need to secure external economic help, forced the government to adopt repressive measures to remain in power.

These measures were both economic and legislative in nature. On one hand, the government pursued a number of ill-fated economic ventures which did nothing to alleviate economic hardship on the island. These hardships engendered resentment and unrest on the island, thereby precipitating the enactment of a number of laws which set the stage for the clash between the two parties in 1979.

Throughout the 1970s, the government enacted legislation to perpetuate itself in power. It enacted the *Dread Act*[10] to protect

---

[10] As above.

the State from subversives who ostensibly sought to overthrow the government. Furthermore, it amended the *Praedial Larceny Act*[11] to protect estates from *vagrants* while in 1975, it passed the *Industrial Relations Act* to curtail the powers of the trade unions. Concomitantly, the government enacted or amended existing legislation to guarantee the loyalty of the Police and Defence Forces. Each of these enactments will be examined since collectively, they form a prologue to the events of 1979. However, their significance in these events cannot be properly assessed without an examination of the economic background against which they unravelled.

THE ECONOMICS OF DESPERATION IN THE 1970s.

A. THE ECONOMIC PROBLEM

The international oil crisis of the early 1970s had far-reaching consequences in Dominica. The cost of the island's imports increased dramatically, imposing a great strain on foreign exchange reserves. On the other hand, this increase in the cost of imports was not offsetted by a 10% rise in the price for the

---

[11] As above.

island's main agricultural export, bananas; from 5.2 cents per pound to 11 cents.[12]

In November 1974, the price of bananas, which accounted for 75% of the island's import revenues, fell from 9 cents a pound to 5 cents[13] at a time when the price of fertilizer rose from $7.50 to $23.00 a bag.[14] Farmers who sought relief from the fluctuating banana prices got little help since they faced an equally volatile market with other products. For example, the production of bay oil enjoyed a short-lived success until prices crashed in 1974.[15]

Whatever revenues which accrued to the government from its exports were largely spent to finance importation of consumer goods. In 1975, the country had to use $14 million of its revenues to finance food imports.[16] In 1976, the value of the island's imports amounted to $45 million or almost double the value of total domestic imports.[17]

The island's precarious economic system was further exacerbated by the paucity of aid from traditional donor countries. In his 1976 Budgetary Address, Minister of Finance, Victor Riviere, noted that:

---

[12] W. Riviere, "A Report on Dominica", **Trinidad and Tobago Review**, March 1979, 11 at 12.
[13] Hansard of the Proceedings of the Eighth meeting of the Fourth Session of the Second Parliament under the **Dominican Constitution Order 1967**, November 1974, page 77.
[14] As in footnote #13, page 79.
[15] W, Riviere, "A Report", **Supra**, footnote #11, page 11.
[16] As in footnote # 16, page 16.
[17] Budget Address by V. A. J. Riviere, July 20, 1976, page 11.

> Dominica will now have to rely on Emergency Aid Fund through which the Caribbean MDC's and the British Government will channel their aid contribution in support of the budget of the Associated States.

The espousal of socialism by the government likely proved to be an additional factor in perpetuating the island's dismal economic condition. This ideological shift in 1975 militated against foreign investment in the island at the very moment when it was most needed. Even when the Minister of Finance was proposing a *rearrangement and redirection of our economic and social systems*[18], he conceded that the island had to look to the British government for budgetary grants to finance the $5 million budgetary deficit in the fiscal year 1975 – 1976.[19] At the time, the Premier advised the island's civil servants that his government could not pay their salaries and had *appealed to the British government in vain for a loan to assist in (their) payment.*

The critical problem facing the government therefore, was how to generate revenues at a time when traditional sources of revenue had all but dried up on the island. The problems of unemployment, declining consumer purchasing power,

---

[18] Budget address, page 18.
[19] Hansard of the Proceedings of the Third Meeting of the Second Session of the Third Parliament under the **Dominica Constitution Order 1967**, on Monday, July 20, 1976, page 39.

production and the paucity of new capital formation[20] all combined to create a very bleak economic future.

What was needed were new sources of revenue to stimulate the local economy and generate revenues to finance the island's annual budget.[21] As the Finance Minister noted:[22]

> There are certain limits beyond which the government cannot prudently go, in this period of price inflation, to extract appreciably more revenues from virtually the same heavily-taxed pockets, whether by direct or indirect tax measures.

The desire to increase revenues through any means received a new impetus with the August 29, 1976, declaration that the government wished the island to become a sovereign nation on the 2nd of November, 1977.[23] It became incumbent on the government to achieve some breakthrough in the economic impasse which it found itself. It became necessary to justify the drive towards political independence by the announcement of some massive investment program, on a magnitude which would make independence palatable to the Dominican population. But where would such investment be found when the traditional sources of investment had apparently shrivelled like a pod?

---

[20] As above, page 10.
[21] As above.
[22] As above.
[23] Hansard of the Proceedings of the Sixth Meeting of the Second Session of the Third Parliament under the **Dominica Constitution Order 1967**, held on December 1976, page 3.

B. THE ECONOMIC SOLUTION

In July 1975, the government established the Dominica Development Corporation as the vehicle which would put into effect an agreement with the Alleyne Mercantile Corporation in Barbados. The agreement called for the building of an oil refinery, construction of a thousand room hotel and a jet airport. The government lost little time in purchasing the 375 acre Compton Hall Estate at Woodfordhill for the proposed jet airport. The ink had not completely dried in this agreement when the Alleyne Mercantile Bank folded in Barbados.[24]

Undaunted, Patrick John, Victor Riviere and Leo Austin met the principal of the failed bank, Sidney Burnett Alleyne, in England in September 1978. A new development scheme proposed by Alleyne was even more grandiose than that originally conceived in 1975. Estimated to involve some $11 billion, the scheme would incorporate a petro chemical plant, an oil refinery and 250, 000 houses for the island's 80,000 inhabitants! To facilitate this mammoth project, the parties contracted with a firm called Promoters Conglomerate to send 150 engineers to the island with sufficient money to cover a year's salary for all the individuals involved.

---

[24] **The Nation**, Bridgetown, Barbados, Friday June 1, 1979.

Far from being a *bona fide* development agreement however, the whole scheme proved to be cynical ploy by the South African government to circumvent economic sanctions. On January 18, 1979, a letter from Alleyne to the South African Coal Oil and Gas Corporation Ltd. (SASOL) revealed that the Dominican Government had given its approval to Alleyne for the purchase and sale of crude oil from SASOL.[25] Another letter dated February 6, 1979, from Leo Austin, to the South African government indicated that:[26]

> [W]e have agreed that mutual interests will be served in the promotion, stockpiling, re-sale and re-fining of crude oil and petro-chemical products to meet the needs and exigencies of our respective countries.

One month later, Austin met with a representative from a South Africa-affiliated construction firm in London to finalize the agreement for work to commence on the proposed airport.

Similarly in February 1979, Don Pierson, a Texas businessman disclosed an agreement with the John government granting him 45 square miles of the northern part of Dominica for the establishment of a Free Port Zone. A 99 year lease, which provided for the payment of $100 annually to the Dominican government, granted Pierson *extreme and exclusive rights* and

---

[25] As above, page 4.
[26] As above.

powers to authorize any type of business activity within the Free Port Zone. The Dominica Caribbean Free Port Authority would exercise unfettered control over the area with veto powers over the sovereign powers of Dominica.[27] Alarmed at the prospect of mass demonstrations protesting the sale of 40% of the cultivated land of the island, the government cancelled the agreement on May 2, 1979.

That within one month of this action and two months after the London meeting, Leo Austin would risk confrontation with the island's trade unions by enacting the *Industrial Relations (Amendment) Act* reflects the government's reliance on repressive legislation to ensure social and economic stability on the island. It actively pursued this policy throughout the 1970s commencing with the passage of the *Prohibited and Unlawful Societies and Association Act, (The Dread Act)* and culminating in the events of 1979.

THE PROHIBITED AND UNLAWFUL SOCIETIES AND ASSOCIATION ACT 1974 (THE DREAD ACT)

The racial violence evident in the United States in the 1960s manifested itself in Dominica, albeit by a number of uncoordinated attacks against a few white persons and locals.

---

[27] As above.

These random acts of violence, infused with the rhetoric of the Black Power Movement, were transformed by the government into a sinister plot by a terrorist organization *working on a communist takeover*.[28]

As proof of its contention that the threat of such a takeover was imminent, Premier John referred to a 1973 document by the radical Movement for a New Dominica (MND) which stated that the government and police are unable to assess the kind of revolutionary violence the people are capable of, force will be met by force.[29]

He construed the document *as a programme leading up to the ultimate revolution*. It outlined a programme for community development and proposed the redistribution of arable land on the island. It suggested that the MND should establish a dialogue with all sectors of the economy including the trade union movement, students, nurses and teachers. The document outlined a strategy where members of the MND would *focus attention* on a number of areas in the island:

> I suggest before beginning the grounding session, that MND members <u>must</u> attempt to educate themselves of the peculiar objectives, conditions of the particular

---

[28] Hansard of the Proceedings of the Eighth Meeting of the Fourth Session of the Second Parliament under the **Dominican Constitution Order 1967**, on Tuesday, November 19, 1974, page 24.
[29] As above, page 25.

area, for e.g. peasant holdings vis-à-vis estate holdings, extend of estate production, unproductivity, etc....

To clinch the case proving the existence of a Leninist plot, John referred to the call to arms at the conclusion of the document:

> [C]e pour tout malheureux travail en semme pour changer Dominique. Ce pour nous tout travail pour faire revolution la. (All poor people must work together to change Dominica. We must all work to make the revolution.

John preyed on the fears of the public to set the stage for the legislation which followed. He hinted that Dominican youth were stealing guns for Dreads.[30] He heightened the tension by stating that schoolboys had been kidnapped by *boys from the Society* and had not been seen since.[31] He transformed this fear into anger and support for the proposed legislation by solemnly declaring how *this group go around and deface any property irrespective of ownership, irrespective of law.*[32] Finally, he channelled the public's determination to *restore law and order in this country*[33] by proposing the *Dread Act*, which received smooth passage in the House of Assembly.

---

[30] As above, page 27.
[31] As above.
[32] As above.
[33] As above.

John's address to the House of Assembly in November 1974, introducing the Prohibited and Unlawful Societies and Associations Act, crystallized the public's pent up fury and concern over perceived subversion by radicals during the period:

> Mr. Speaker, there was a shooting of a visitor during the Carnival season. Surely unemployment could not have motivated this. There was the slashing by cutlass of another person...during the National Day Celebrations this year, unemployment could not have motivated this. There is a system of walking in on to peasants' lands and reaping the crops and threatening the peasants.... There has been constant abuse of young girls who walk the streets if they do not respond when they are called "sister" they may be called *leggobeast* and slapped or abused....

He derided the alleged public outcry over the arrest of Desmond Trotter for the murder of a white person during Carnival in 1974:

> Mr. Speaker, only two weeks ago we had a certain situation. After a certain sentence was passed in the Courts, children from the ages of ten and twelve were amassed in groups and they were marching up and down in front of the Police Station chanting, "Free Trotter, Babylon is fockeries."

He gave his parliamentarians a lesson on the language of the Dreads:

> Mr. Speaker, if we watch the type of English they now teach the younger people, while when they write their other branches and associates from overseas, Mr. Speaker, they write in perfect English. We have heard some of them in the court when they defend certain brothers speak fluent English. But Mr. Speaker, if I may go in slight

detail in the dictionary of the *Dread language* to hear how the people speak now, Mr. Speaker, if one of the members of this association wants to walk away he says, *let us make a small motion*, if he is in possession of an illegal firearm, he tells you *I got a piece*, if there is any person in society who is against their ideologies, you are called *Babylon*. Immense buildings like this, the Police Station, and other buildings are called *endless concrete*. Mr. Speaker, in an Assembly like this when you watch the gallery filled with people and you see a tremendous crowd, you call that *endless man*. On a question of the food, the food they eat, particularly vegetables and provisions, this is called *itals* and in order to create confusion in the minds of the law enforcement authorities, when they are in possession of marijuana, they are in possession of *itae*, the meats and fish, Mr. Speaker, are called *jot* or *swine*, and if there is any food that has rice or salt in it, it is called *swine jot*, that differentiates between vegetables and food which is *swine* and food mixed with salt *swine jot*, because they don't eat salt. Now Mr. Speaker, if there is a lady for instance, who may not accept their ideologies she is called a *leggobeast*, and persons who own a lot of wealth they are called *the controller* and the security officers and the policemen, Mr. Speaker, they are called *swine-man*. Now, this is the type of language that persons who have gone to Universities and have come back are inculcating in the younger people. People whom the people of Dominica were hoping would have contributed not only to the education of the younger people but to the economic development of the country.

He detailed how members of the unlawful society posed a threat not only to property but to young people:

> Mr. Speaker, we had a situation in July this year with a lady who lives in Bath Road opposite Central Water

> Authority, her name is Mrs. Piper. She has a young boy; he goes to the Academy, I think he was in Form III, when these boys from the Society got the boy out of school, and he was away from his family. After the first week, the mother went to the Police and the boy was apprehended and brought back. He returned to school, but after two days at school he was again taken away from the school and that time he went for 17 days. The mother again went to the Police, the boy was found again, this time in the jungle. He came back home and during the night while the mother was asleep, he disappeared and his mother has not seen her son since July – a young boy under 18, wild, living like Tarzan boy.

John finally declared his government's intention to rid the island of the menace which threatened to engulf it:

> We will use Moses law and the Communist terrorists are bound to yield – it's tooth for tooth, an eye for an eye, gun for gun, and bomb for bomb, hand grenade for hand grenade, raid for raid, blade for blade, knife for knife, and Mr. Speaker, life for life.

The *Dread Act* declared a number of organizations to be *unlawful societies*. Activities which would bring an organization within the ambit of the new legislation included:

a) acts of terrorism;
b) threatening a public official, magistrate or juror;
c) assaulting or interfering with anyone because of their race, colour, class or creed;
d) destroying crops or livestock.

Organizations deemed to be unlawful included those:

a) which members were required to take an oath of office; or
b) which members or governing body was unknown to the public

The few organizations which were not covered by the new legislation included Free Masons, Foresters and the Odd Fellows.

Any member of an unlawful society who *appeared in public or elsewhere wearing any uniform, badge or mode of dress, or other distinguishing feature or hairstyle was guilty of an offence and subject to arrest without warrant.* Such persons would not be eligible to receive bail and anyone committed an offence, who aided and abetted any unlawful association or harboured a member wanted by the police.

Furthermore, anyone convicted of being a member of an unlawful association faced imprisonment for a first offence and two years for a subsequent conviction. Someone convicted of harbouring a member or counselling an unlawful association faced a mandatory jail term of two years. Any individual convicted under the *Dread Act* had no right of appeal. The *Act* protected any civilian who killed or injured a member of an unlawful association found illegally inside a dwelling house, from civil or criminal liability and extended a similar immunity to the island's security forces.

HUMAN RIGHTS AND *THE DREAD ACT*

The *Dread Act* ran roughshod over many of the rights and privileges enjoyed by the citizens of Dominica. It extinguished a plethora of rights established under the British Common Law tradition which had become part of the fabric of the island's legal system. In sanctioning the arrest of someone with long matted hair, it deprived the individual of his right no to be arbitrarily arrested. In denying bail to such a person, it discarded the presumption that no one should be denied his liberty unless charged with the most serious offences.

Furthermore, the *Dread Act* criminalized the act of having a hairstyle although the individual may not necessarily have had the intention of becoming part of an unlawful association. In doing so, it created offences of absolute liability where the wearing of distinctive clothing or hairstyle created an almost irrefutable presumption of an intent to be a member of an unlawful society.

As a result, the *Dread Act* shifted the burden of proof in a trial on an accused instead of the Crown. In any criminal proceeding, the Crown must prove every element of the offence including the wrongful act and the intent to perform the act. For example, in a typical criminal prosecution, the Crown would have to prove that the accused was wearing a *dread* type of clothing or a *dread hairstyle*. In addition, the Crown would also need to prove that the accused intended to be part of an unlawful association. However, all that was required of the Crown to convict under the *Dread Act* was to prove the wrongful act. The onus then shifted to the accused to disprove that he was a member of an unlawful society.

The new legislation also denied the person's right to belong to an association of his or her choice. It also denied that person's freedom of movement since he or she was liable to be summarily arrested if found in a public place. Additionally, it extinguished the right of a person not to be deprived of life, liberty, integrity except in accordance with the principles of fundamental justice, since an accused was only to be tried summarily without the procedural and substantive safeguards of an ordinary trial.

More importantly however, the *Dread Act* denied the persons suspected of being *Dreads*, the right to pursue civil claims or resolve disputes they may have with other individuals. For example, a person belonging to an unlawful society attends at the dwelling of an individual where the ownership of that dwelling is in dispute. Exercising his "rights" under the *Act*, the individual could kill the *suspected dread* with impunity in resolving what really amounted to a civil dispute between two individuals.

Members of an unlawful society were further denied the right against unreasonable search and seizure. The slightest suspicion of a law officer could result in his being arrested and subsequently imprisoned. He could then be held for up to 48 hours under the *Act* before being taken before a magistrate to be summarily tried and imprisoned. Anyone so unfortunate to be convicted and sentenced to the mandatory jail term would then be deprived of the right of appeal guaranteed to all persons convicted of a criminal offence.

DEBATE ON THE *DREAD ACT*

In proposing this legislation in the House of Assembly, Premier John relied on patriotism as his last refuge to garner support for the proposed legislation. In his address to the island's House of Assembly, he declared that:[34]

> I look forward for every member of this Honourable House, members of the public, members of groups who are peace-loving citizens

---
[34] As in footnote # 28, at 30.

of Dominica to come out now and to assist the Police in bringing back the peace and harmony in Dominica...

His appeal for support did not fall on deaf ears. Virtually every member of the House of Assembly present supported the passage of the *Prohibited and Unlawful Societies and Associations Act*. The Third Nominated Member of the Opposition, Mary Eugenia Charles, found it *regrettable that the day should have arrived when we ourselves must take away one of our human rights enshrined in the constitution.* She nevertheless proceeded to support the legislation in amended form. Such support was unfortunate but necessary since, *a greater majority of people's freedom is being eroded and that is freedom from fear.*

However, Charles cautioned that *we must not allow it to stand on our statute books, one day more than necessary.* She further noted that she desired *the law to come up for review every six months.* Finally, Charles pleaded unsuccessfully to ameliorate the dreads from the finality of a conviction under the *Dread Act*, by providing them with a right to appeal.[35]

Other members of the House of Assembly expressed reservations about the *Dread Act*. One former member of the

---

[35] As above, # 28, page 67.s

government, R.O.P. Armour, described how the *Act* would criminalize the innocent by noting that:[36]

> I am saying this, a young man of 17 decides that he is going dread, he has not yet beaten up anybody, he has not yet stolen, he has not yet cursed anybody, he is still hesitant, but in fact one day he is anxious to grow his hair long and comes in public and you hold him.... He goes before a magistrate, the magistrate has no alternative but to send him in for 18 months in the first instance and first offence.

Government members gave their unqualified support for the new legislation. The government's First Nominated Member, A.C. Active, declared solemnly that:

> This is not the first group of violent people we have seen in Dominica. We have had the *Kay passas...* the *howlings*, and peoples lives were in danger, but never has Dominican lives been more in danger or Dominicans more scared than they are today with regard to the dreads.

Minister of Education and Health, H.L. Christian described the dreads as *a monstrous organization [with] roots outside of the Caribbean.* Other government members attributed the dread problem to the activities of well connected intellectuals.

John identified two pieces of evidence which convinced him that the MND was planning to initiate guerilla activity on the island. He referred to an organization purportedly led by Ernest

---

[36] As above, at 39.

Merrill, of the Organization for the Development of Dominica (ODD) which identified the trails within Dominica's hinterland. John viewed the ODD as an organization engaged in training persons to effect the overthrow of his government. Secondly, he attributed the dreads' habit of *eating only vegetables and ground provisions to a desire to get the body accustomed to the jungle way of life.*

One after another, the labour party electives trooped to the lectern and with macabre humor, exposed how this group of intellectuals was misleading the youth. Premier John fired the opening salvo by noting that:

> Only two weeks ago, Mr. Speaker, one young man by the name of Aurelius Jolly, who works in the Ministry of Education and Health, brought down some dreads from Fond Cole to his home to make a "jot", that is food… and he prepared the meals for the guys – meals without salt, that is "swine jot". However he prepared a separate dish for himself in the presence of the boys.

Minister of Communication and Works Earl Leslie, lamented that:

> It is sad to see young people who call themselves literate people who have had all the opportunities in life starting off from Elementary school right up to Secondary school and they can also boast that they have been to a University and they carry little titles behind their names "A, B, C, D."

Not to be outdone, Minister of Agriculture, Thomas Etienne waxed philosophically that:

> I have to say that man is but an ape. He likes to copy, he likes to do things which he sees other people do. He likes to do things because he has the belief that other people are better than he is, or other people are better educated than he is, and if they can do that he can also do it and this is one of the reasons I believe why we have come to this state we are in.

If the John government attributed the Dread problem to the activities of privileged subversives, the opposition Freedom Party regarded it as the logical outcome of the social policies of the Labour government. They regarded the dread problem as the culmination of the social activism of the Labour government in seeking to break down class distinctions on the island. Specifically, Charles complained that if *we continue... talking about "gros bourg" and "petit bourg, "bourgeoisie" and "massa day done" then it is obvious that we have not yet decided to come to grips with the problem.* Charles further related the Dread problem to the breakdown of respect for law and order and to the Labour government's attack on the bastions of privilege including the Church, the banks, the courts and landed interests. She argued that the lack of respect for property and destabilization from abroad could be mitigated by instituting a National Service programme, film censorship and reinforcing law enforcement on the island.

The arguments of the government and opposition in explaining the genesis of the Dread problem were in reality flip sides of the same coin. The catalyst for the activism of the Dreads was the return of educated Dominicans either from North America or from the University of the West-Indies. However, the soil in which they sowed the ideological seeds garnered from abroad had already been tilled by the social activism of the Leblanc government. That these seeds were able to germinate in the minds of Dominican youth was also a reflection of the social policies of the Labour government. Increasing access to secondary education, the rejection of a Eurocentric mode of dress, the subtle attacks on established institutions such as the Church, had all imbued in the minds of youth the notion that challenging the social order was not sacrilege after all. This became even more apparent when the purveyors of the new radicalism, the so-called Black Power Boys, were themselves with few exception, from the middle class. Once that psychological bridge had been crossed, it was inevitable that random acts of violence against persons and property would result.

AMENDMENTS TO THE *DREAD ACT*

The onslaught against human rights in the *Dread Act* continued with the passage of the *Prohibited and Unlawful Societies and Associations (Amendment) Act 1974* in December, 1974. The new legislation made provisions for public officers who contravened the *Dread Act* and provided for the burden of proof in charges under the *Act*.[37]

The amendments to the *Dread Act* provided that no member of an unlawful society or association should hold an appointment in the public service, and that any public officer *acquitted* of an offence under the *Act*, should be investigated by the Public Service Commission to assess whether the officer was a fit and proper person to resume his appointment in the public service.

Additionally, the legislation formally shifted the burden of proof on an accused, making him or her obliged to prove in court that he or she was not a member of an unlawful association. All that was required of the Prosecution in a trial was to adduce some evidence that the accused wore certain clothes or had a particular hairstyle ubiquitous to members of an unlawful society. The burden of proof then shifted to the accused to prove that he was

---

[37] Hansard of the Proceedings of the Ninth Meeting of the Fourth Session of the Second Parliament under the **Dominica Constitution Order**, 1987.

not a member. If unsuccessful in doing so, he was summarily convicted.

JUSTIFICATION FOR THE *DREAD ACT* AND RELATED LEGISLATION

Despite the political rhetoric, economic considerations, more than any other, accounted for the new legislation. The *Praedial Larceny Act* for example, sought to ensure that agricultural production on the island was not adversely affected by the *dread crisis*. Criminalization of the theft of a coconut for example, would discourage individuals from stealing the produce of local farmers.

The government enacted the *Dread Act* for two purposes. The *Act* sought to prevent a reduction in the number of visitors to the island who no doubt would be turned away by the reports of random acts of violence against white persons. More than the preservation of the tourist industry however, the *Act* sought to preserve the social order from individuals who espoused an ideology which called for land redistribution and peasant ownership. While those who advocated such goals did not become powerful enough to challenge the government at the polls, they forced the government and opposition to join together in passing the legislation since both political parties had a vested interest to preserve the social order and more importantly, to be seen by the electorate to be preserving that order. Passage of the *Dread Act* was therefore a cynical ploy by the government to pander to public opinion with the opposition paying lip service to the legislation for fear of paying a heavy political price for its failure to do so.

A number of indicators suggest that at the time of the passage of the *Dread Act*, the island's economic well-being was not being threatened by dreads or subversives. For example, the number of visitors to the island increased steadily from 15,212 in 1972 to 22,018 in 1976. (See Chart No. I)

CHART NO. 1

	1972	1973	1974	1975	1976
Business Visitors	4153	4413	5401	5775	2042
Day Tour	415	540	821	1129	4970
Intransit	312	346	528	784	39
Immigration Perm.	142	83	33	28	8
Immigration Temp.	63	47	60	65	20
Holiday Visitors	10114	10027	9996	11143	14939

Unclassified	13	19	10	10	-
TOTAL	15212	15475	16819	18934	22018

SOURCE: **Statistical Digest No. 5** (Statistical Division, Ministry of Finance, Government of Dominica, Table No. 12a.)

The number of business visitors dropped significantly in 1976 or two years after passage of the *Act*. However, this drop was compensated by a fourfold increase in visitors to the island on day tours in 1976. The number of holiday visitors increase steadily over the whole period with only a small drop (61) in 1974 over the preceding year.

The only significant drop in the number of visitors to the island which may be attributable to the threat of violence on the island in 1974 appeared to be in the number of cruise ship arrivals within the period. In 1974, 9 cruise ships docked in the island's harbour carrying a total of 1, 889 passengers. By 1975, only 1 ship carrying 248 visitors had docked on the island. The figures rose dramatically in 1976 and 1977 with 13 ships in each year carrying 1,908 and 7,500 passengers respectively. It is uncertain however, whether the drop in the number of cruise ships visiting the island in 1075 was precipitated by activities of the Dreads themselves or by the notoriety which the island gained following passage of the *Dread Act*.

Furthermore, it cannot by concluded that a decrease in agricultural production justified passage of the *Dread Act*. No figures exist for banana production in 1974. However, banana production increased from 27,917 long tons in 1975 to 43,319 long tons in 1978. The production and value of livestock products showed a similar increase with beef production increasing from 297,000 lbs. in 1975 to 350,077 lbs. in 1978. Apologists for the passage of the *Act* would no doubt parry by submitting that this increase in production only became possible because the government enacted the *Dread Act*.

Lacking any economic justification, it is also clear the *Dread Act* and related legislation did not serve any purpose of national security. The legislation did not proscribe any activities aimed at undermining national security or overthrowing the duly elected government. It did not seek to restrict the possession of weapons or to prescribe penalties for possession of such weapons. The *Act* criminalized membership in an *unlawful association* although the reason for such membership may not have been for a purpose dangerous to the public peace. The real reason for so doing was to increase the powers of the island's security forces and in effect, those of the government. Instead of enacting specific legislation which would infringe democratic rights as little as possible to deal with a perceived security problem, the government passed legislation with the broadest possible application.

Based on the foregoing, it can reasonably be concluded that passage of the *Dread Act* was essentially a political act to further the interest of the party in power. The MND had embarked on a political programme, the ideological orientation of which bore strong affinities to that of the government. The MND's emphasis on land redistribution reflected the policy of the Labour Party government. Support for the MND would only be achieved at the expense of the Labour government. What better way to prevent that possibility than discrediting the MND through passage of the *Dread Act*? What better way to pre-empt a Freedom Party victory in 1975 by enacting legislation which would cast the government in the role of savior of the island?

The fact that within one year of its electoral victory, the government would officially espouse *socialism*, lends support to the above conclusion. In July 1976, then Minister of Agriculture, O.J. Seraphine, advised the House of Assembly that *there exists in this Society a group numbering less than twenty who possess about 80% of the land masses of this country and they are withholding the production and development of our State.* In words strongly reminiscent of the MND programme discredited by his own government prior to the 1975 election, Seraphine proceeded to note that:

It's a shocking thing and I am sure that when in the coming months the Government of Dominica and more specifically the Ministry of Agriculture shall be making every effort possible towards the realization of the redistribution of lands, we will be called Communists, Socialists or whatever you like.

OTHER LEGISLATION

The John administration enacted other *satellite* legislation to create a dragnet to ensnare anyone so unfortunate to be considered a dread. One such piece of legislation was the *Abolition of Corporal Punishment (Amendment) Act 1974 (Abolition Act)*. In the surreal atmosphere in which the *Dread Act* became law, this new legislation was appropriately named since ironically, it reintroduced rather than abolished corporal punishment. Its objective was *getting at the type of act which the society is now frowning on and which have been the basic tactics of the Dreads.*[38]

The *Abolition Act* sought to identify offences which would result in corporal punishment. Those included: rape, malicious destruction of crops or livestock, and the wounding of, maiming, or shooting of visitors or members of the island's security forces. The penalty for any of these offences included flogging with the

---

[38] Hansard of the Proceedings of the Dominica House of Assembly, December 6, 1974., page 2.

cat-o-nine tails which, according to a government member, was good *for the people who cut coconut trees merely to drink the nut and move on [and for] those who cut down the young cocoa trees for making dread locks.*[39]

A few members of the House of Assembly realized that the penalties prescribed in the *Abolition Act* constituted cruel and unusual punishment. R.O.P. Armour cautioned that *Dominica may well find itself in trouble internationally for bringing in this sort of law.*[40] Eugenia Charles solemnly declared that *I only agree to the whipping but not to cat-o-nine tails.*[41] In an effort to put as much distance between himself and the *Abolition Act*, Armour actually sought to abstain from voting on the legislation *after* the Bill had been passed by the House of Assembly.[42]

THE PRAEDIAL LARENCY (*Amendment*) ACT[43]

This legislation constituted the final act in the government's drive to impose a penal sanction for the most trivial offences involving loss of property. The legislation sought to

---

[39] As in footnote # 38, at page 72.
[40] As above, page 72.
[41] As above, page 75.
[42] As above, page 76.
[43] Hansard of the Proceedings of the Sixth Meeting of the Second of the Third Parliament under the **Dominican Constitution Order 1967**, on Monday, December 20. 1976, page 43.

remove the monetary penalty and to increase the term of imprisonment for an offence prescribed in the *Act*. Despite the corporal punishment set out in the *Abolition of Corporal Punishment (Amendment) Act*, the declared intention of the *Praedial Larceny (Amendment) Act* was *to make sure that the agricultural farmers are in fact protected by law.*[44]

CONSOLIDATION OF POWER IN THE 1970S; THE ROAD TO THE EVENTS OF MAY 1979

The suppression of the Dreads in 1974 and the goodwill engendered by the *Dread* Act, paved the way for the John government's electoral triumph of 1975. The Dominica Labour Party won 16 of 21 seats of the House of Assembly compared to 3 seats for the opposing Dominica Freedom Party, with the remaining 2 seats being won by independent candidates. With the reins of power firmly in its grasp, the John government proceeded to consolidate and perpetuate its tenure in office.

---

[44] As in footnote # 43.

A. CURBING THE PUBLIC

From 1975 to 1979, the John government passed a number of statutes entitled the *Public Order Act* to restrict any popular protest in the island. On December 20, 1976, it introduced the *Public Order(Amendment) Act*.[45] The *Act* sought to define a public procession, to provide for the control of slogans or banners or clothing and to revise the penalties provided in case of infringement of the Public Ordinance.[46] The *Act* restricted the circumstances in which a public meeting could be legally held. However, while its avowed purpose was the maintenance of law and order, the real reason for its passage was to discourage any opposition to the drive towards independence planned for 1977. As noted by government minister Michael Douglas:[47]

> [If] they (*sic*) are any indications to go by I expect that indiscipline will hot up during 1977 in this country. This is why I consider this bill timely because within it are the instruments to deal very efficiently with that sort of situation.

---

[45] Hansard of the Proceedings of the Sixth Meeting of the Second Session of the Third Parliament under the **Dominica Constitution Order 1967**, on Monday, December 20, 1976, page 27.
[46] As above, page 28.
[47] As above, page 28.

B. LOYALTY OF THE SECURITY FORCES

The Dominica Defence Force (DDF) was embodied in August 1974, just three months prior to the passage of the *Dread Act*. Originally conceived as a volunteer force to assist the Royal Dominica Police Force in maintaining law and order during a civil disturbance, it gained prominence as the major factor in the neutralization of the dreads in 1974 – 1975.

The attractiveness of such force to the government was that it could operate without the constraints under which a traditional police force operated. It also lacked the elaborate hierarchy of leadership which the established police force possessed, making it easier to control. Furthermore, whereas the police force was dispersed throughout the island thereby making full control difficult, the Defence Force remained in the island's capital making it more malleable to the wishes of the Premier.

The government enacted legislation in November 1975, to establish a permanent Defence Force with the loyalty and inclination to suppress domestic strife. The Force had a score to settle with the Roseau based Freedom Party going back to the 1971 storming of the House of Assembly. Many of its junior officers felt that there would be no repeat of its failure to curb political activism on that occasion.

John moved quickly to exercise control over the Defence Force. He arrogated to himself the title of Colonel-in-Chief with personal control of the Force. This process of co-optation was complete when he shifted control of the Force from the Commissioner of Police to the office of the Prime Minister after November 3, 1978.[48]

By 1976, a few junior officers and soldiers of the DDF viewed themselves as an important arm of government in transforming the State along the socialist lines propagated by the John government. Then Lieutenant F.C. Newton, who would attempt a violent overthrow of the Charles government in 1981, wrote ominously in the DDF's magazine, *Forward,* that:

> It is unrealistic to imagine that the Defence Force would be unaffected by the social, political and economic revolution going on around it, in fact in some cases it may be called upon to be the principal instrument of them.

Newton rejected what he perceived to be the antiquated role of the DDF in upholding the privileged position and power of the ruling class and at the same time ensuring that the masses and peasants remain in a state of subjugation.

Not all members of the DDF agreed with Newton's dream of a peoples army. Its Commanding Officer from November 3,

---

[48] **Report**, as in footnote # 1, page 15.

1970, to June 1976, Major Twistleton St. R. Bertrand, was a W.W. II veteran and quintessential military man. He was schooled in the belief that the army was separate from government and should not become embroiled in political controversy. While the role of the army was to serve the State efficiently, it was not subject to the whims and fancies of the leader in office. Major Bertrand's departure from the DDF in 1976 avoided the inevitable confrontation between himself and the junior officers of the DDF. His successor, Major Hamlet, maintained a semblance of respectability until his departure in 1978.

The ascendancy of Major Frederick Newton however, marks the point when the DDF degenerated from being a fairly well disciplined body to one lacking an esprit de corps and plagued by doubts about its own professionalism. By 1979, the DDF would become a mere incubus of its former self, wracked by discipline and drug problems.

From August 1975 to August 1977, the DDF's main duties involved providing security at the Government House, the prison and at the Court House. With the subsiding of the Dread problem, the Force existed as an appendage of government which had become obsolete despite its brief existence. One indication that the Force had outlived its purpose was that in 1978, members were still receiving the *bush* allowance of $60.00 they'd received during the Dread era, even if they had not visited the bush since 1975.

Bloated by a regular income and burdened by the absence of any clearly defined purpose, by May 1979, the DDF had degenerated into a motley crew of 77 men, plagued by discipline problems and waiting for some new mission from its Colonel-in-Chief. The passage of new legislation in May 1979, and the need to keep the population in check provided just such a mission for its members.

THE ROYAL DOMINICA POLICE FORCE (RDPF)

The Force, numbering 225 officers and constables in the mid-1970s[49], proved capable of coping with the daily maintenance of law and order but singularly incapable of handling the crises which the government periodically faced. For instance, on December 15, 1971, when the government sought to dissolve the Roseau Town Council after it came under the control of the opposing Dominica Freedom Party, the Force proved unable to

---

[49] Hansard of the Proceedings of the Fifth Meeting of the Second Session of the Third Parliament under the **Dominica Constitution Order 1967**, held at the House of Assembly, Government Headquarters, on Friday, November 19, 1976, at page 4.

prevent 3,000 demonstrators from smashing through the police cordons and taking over the House of Assembly.

The government perceived the RDPF to be ineffective in serious industrial disputes as in 1973, when the government declared a state of emergency. During the Dread crisis of the mid-70s, the ranks of the police force were augmented by a unit of special constables who relished the opportunity for exacting calculated acts of brutality on the public.

The John government sought to deal with the perceived inadequacy of the police force in two ways. First, it bolstered the ranks of the Force by providing the special constables with a financial incentive to perform their duties more vigorously than they otherwise would have done.

The *Police Act* of 1974 provided the special constables with all the powers, privileges and immunities of regular policemen. In November 1974, along with the passage of the *Dread Act*, the government amended the *Police Act to enable special constables to be entitled to a pension or gratuitous payment like the policemen.*[50]

Secondly, the government amended the *Police Pensions Ordinance Cap 237*, in November 1974, to establish better

---

[50] Hansard, as in footnote # 13, page 11 / 53A,, IBID, page 15.

provision for the dependents of all policemen killed in the line of duty.[51] Special constables who died in the line of duty would be deemed to have been receiving the same rate as a constable regularly employed in the Police Force. Where the dependent of the deceased officer would benefit, the new legislation also provided for lump sum payments in lieu of monthly pension benefits the deceased would have received following his retirement. Finally, in November 1976, the government increased the pension allowance paid to the children of non commissioned officers or police constables.[52]

By 1976, the government opposition viewed the island's security forces with great trepidation.[53] Certain police officers and special constables, openly supported the government,[54] indiscriminately shot at civilians and wantonly disregarded their commanding officers.[55] A few officers spoke on political platforms and Cabinet Ministers interfered with transfers of policemen[56] to various parts of the island.

---

[51] As above.
[52] Hansard of the Proceedings of the Fifth Meeting of the Second Session of the Third Parliament under the **Dominica Constitution Order 1967**, on Friday, November 19, 1976, page 12.
[53] Hansard of the Proceedings of the Second Meeting of the Second Session of the Third Parliament under the **Dominica Constitution Order 1967**, on Monday, June 14, 1976, page 42.
[54] As above, page 53.
[55] As above, page 53.
[56] As above.

These negative influences on the members of the police force took their toll on morale and discipline. Disinterested service actuated by nothing more than a desire to do one's job professionally, became in the 1970s , a quality to be derided rather than emulated. The leadership of the Force held the view that they were distrusted by the political leadership of the island because they felt that the maintenance of law and order was not a political question.

Nothing illustrates the process of relative decline in the police force more than the events of May 1979. By then the RDPF was *ill –equipped and under strength* to the extent that it could not provide a riot squad from its own ranks.[57] Relative neglect by the authorities had engendered a sense of inferiority among members *vis-à-vis* the Defence Force.[58] There was little cooperation between the two forces. Indeed, when members of the Defence Force on May 29, 1979, used tear gas to disperse the crowd as a prelude to gunfire, many policemen on the scene had to beat a hasty retreat since none had respirators to protect themselves nor did they know that tear gas would have been used.[59]

---

[57] **Report**, as in footnote # 1, page 16.
[58] As above, page 17.
[59] As above.

CONCLUSION

The direct control exercised by Patrick John over the island's security forces best explains his willingness to forge ahead with his proposed legislation in May 1979, even with the knowledge that such legislation would be universally opposed. Throughout the 1970s, John pampered and protected these forces in a conscious effort to make them loyal to his administration. Successful in his efforts to eradicate the Dread problem, the Prime Minister formed the opinion that he would be successful in preserving his government from any challenge by the island's trade unions and opposition party. As the events of 1979 indicate, it was a grave though unfortunately not the last miscalculation of Patrick John.

THE THEORETICAL AND IDEOLOGICAL JUSTIFICATION FOR INDEPENDENCE IN DOMINICA.

Irving André

INTRODUCTION

The island achieved political and constitutional independence from Britain on November 3, 1978, on the 485th confirmation of its location by Christopher Columbus in 1493. Unlike former colonies of Britain, such as Kenya, Ghana and Zimbabwe, independence for Dominica was not the culmination of a bitterly fought war of nation liberation against forces aligned to the imperial power. Neither was it the result of a thorough analysis into the problems which bedeviled the island's development since independence could not give the island any greater control over its resources than it already had. Independence was not a question of wrestling control from an intransigent colonial power. Rather, it was a question of when such control should be accepted from a colonizer which appeared only too willing to relinquish its constitutional ties to the island.

Indeed, the major issue facing Britain in granting political independence to the island was whether or not the holding of a national referendum on independence should be a condition precedent to the granting of independence to Dominica. On

March 1, 1967, the island had received the Dominican Constitution Order which provided, under section 34, that fundamental changes could only be achieved through the holding of a national referendum. Furthermore, the British Parliament enacted the *West-Indies Act* in 1967 which provided that the holding of a referendum must precede the granting of political independence to the Associated States of the then British West-Indies. The Act also made provision for the British government to voluntarily release the constitutional ties which bound it to the island. Indeed a number of Caribbean countries, including Trinidad and Tobago in 1964 and Grenada in 1973, achieved independence without holding a referendum.

The fact that by May 1977, the British government was prepared to jettison this minimum requirement before granting independence reflects the significance (or the lack thereof) of the issue of Dominica's independence to Britain. All what was required, according to the British Minister of Government who chaired the Dominica Constitutional Conference in London, was *for some further process of consultation to take place if there remain areas of serious disagreement*, between the Dominican government and the Opposition. The British government agreed with the Dominica government delegation that having 16 of 21 seats in the island's House of Assembly invested the government with the mandate to seek independence on behalf of the Dominican people.

With the British government willing to grant independence on a platter, the attainment of this goal in November 1978 proceeded as a political *fait accompli*. Being the main source of financial aid to Dominica, Britain had no economic justification for opposing the request for independence. The island would still be obliged to sell its main agricultural export to Britain. The necessity of carrying such produce in Britain ships would still exist. British companies in Dominica, such as the Barclays Banks and the fruit processing company of L. Rose and Co. Ltd., would continue to operate in the island with impunity.

The insistence of the Freedom Party Opposition that a referendum should preceed the granting of independence reflected not so much an aversion to independence but a distrust of the Labour Party government. The government formally announced its intention to seek independence from Britain in August 1976. However prior to that date, and commencing with the Speech from the Throne in 1975, the government had evinced a desire to assume control over significant sectors of the island's economy under the guise of socialism. It sought to make inroads in the financial sector by announcing plans to establish a national bank. It further sought a foothold in the agricultural sector by proposing to acquire arable land for redistribution purposes. Finally, it moved to consolidate itself in power by the passage of legislation which aligned the interests of the security forces to those of the government. Far from being a genuine effort to wrest control from an imperial power, independence, despite the government's rhetoric, was merely the culmination of its efforts to cast itself in the role of socialist saviour of the island.

EMBRACING THE TENETS OF SOCIALISM

The espousal of socialism did not result from the staking out of any well articulated theoretical or ideological claim by the island's leadership. Rather, it resulted inevitably from the shared experiences and indeed the social background of the founders of the Dominica Labour Party (DLP). Ironically, the party was founded by Phyllis Shand Allfrey in 1955, a white Dominican who, as a member of the British Labour Party, was an avowed Fabian Socialist.

In the social milieu in Dominica in the 1950s, a white person, of whatever political hue, was a person of privilege, commanding a degree of respect akin to reverence not bestowed on her *native* party members. This undoubtedly attracted public attention to the new party. One of Allfrey's local counterparts,

Emmanuel Loblack, made the DLP a mass party[1] between 1955-1962 to the point that in the early 1960s, the DLP would wrest political control of the island from the DUPP, Dominica United People's Party, a party supported by business interests in Roseau. By then, both Allfrey and Loblack had been expelled from the party by E.O. Leblanc, a local agriculturist turned labour unionist in September 1961.

The genesis of *socialism* was in large measure, a reflection of the antipathies of E.O. Leblanc towards his political foes and erstwhile colleagues. He resented the social ostracism to which he was subjected by the *gros bourg* of Roseau.[2] This resentment found expression in the embracing of land redistribution schemes in which estates owned by wealthy interests would be acquired for distribution among small farmers. It was also reflected in Leblanc's scrupulous efforts to promote indigenous cultural activities in rural areas at the expense of the pretentious cosmopolitan life in Roseau.

Leblanc's aversion to Western values and disdain for the privileged position occupied by white persons on the island led to the enactment of a ***National Dress Act*** in 1971. The ***Act*** replaced the traditional suit with the long sleeve shirt jack worn over long

---

[1] Cuthbert J. Thomas, "From Crown Colony to Associated Statehood", Unpublished Ph. D. Thesis. University of Massachusetts 1973, page 173-74.
[2] See Honeychurch, **The Dominica Story**, 1984, page 181.

trousers, closed shoes or sandals with socks, as the national dress of Dominica. To mitigate the influence of vested interests, Leblanc fostered rural development to a point where he significantly undermined the old class assumptions which had subordinated the interests of the *petit bourg* to those of urban social and business interests on the island.

In addition to these initiatives which accentuated the social distinctions in the island, Leblanc forged links with Guyana's Forbes Burnham who was establishing the tenets of a Co-operative Socialist state in his country. Burnham advocated nationalization of the country's primary industries, state control over its financial institutions and the fostering of community self-help programmes though the establishment of a national service scheme and a system of co-operatives. More than this, Burnham relied on the doctrine of the paramountcy of his party to guarantee himself unlimited tenure in office, unencumbered by the periodic inconvenience of holding elections.

The Guyanese Prime Minister visited Dominica in November 1969 and Leblanc received a first hand account of the tenets of a co-operative socialist state. This initial visit was followed by a 1971 leadership conference in Grenada when Guyana, along with leaders from the islands, signed the Grenada Declaration, which promoted the formation of a political union between the islands and Guyana. With an area encompassing 83,

000 square miles compared to the 305 sq. miles of the largest of the *small islands*, it was inevitable that the proposed union would not be as palatable to the island leaders as it appeared to Forbes Burnham.

The presence in Dominica of Guyanese-born Leo Austin, former school teacher and later Attorney-General of Dominica, lubricated the Dominica – Guyana **entente** and added another impetus towards the Dominica government's adoption of Burnham's socialist rhetoric. As Attorney General, Austin would become the architect of a spate of legislation which would ultimately make the Labour government the repository of unprecedented power in the 1970s. Such legislation encroached on the private sectors such as banking and land acquisition. They also served as the harbingers for the 1976 formal declaration of the government to embark on socialism and to seek national independence in 1977.

LAYING THE FOUNDATION FOR SOCIALISM

Following its electoral triumph in March 1975, the Labour government presented it's economic plan for the upcoming fiscal year in its Speech from the Throne on April 29, 1975. This speech set out the ritualistic promises to expand banana production, foster product diversification, lessen the tax burden and to reduce the budget deficit. In addition, the government promised to institute the following measures in the upcoming fiscal year:[3]

1) to institute an effective system of price and supply control.
2) to institute a system of import substitution.
3) to continue to enact Incentives Legislation to attract industry to Dominica especially those of the enclave and assembly types.
4) Establishment of a comprehensive Social Security Scheme to foster social justice.
5) Negotiate a loan from the Caribbean Development Bank for the development of a 200 low income housing scheme in the Bath Estate Emshall area.
6) Co-operative development in the various fields of human endeavour.

To the opposition listening attentively to the government's Speech from the Throne, there was a sense of *déjà vu* about the policies outlined in the Budget. Indeed Mary Eugenia Charles, the leader of the Opposition, observed flippantly that she had to *admire His Excellency the Governor coming here year after year reading vague generalities and bits and pieces of former speeches from the throne strung together without any philosophy of development.* Charles proceeded to lament that while the

---

[3] Hansard of the First Meeting of the First Session of the Third Parliament of the Dominican Constitution Order 1967 held at Government Headquarters, Roseau, on April 29, 1979, page 5.

government *calls itself a Socialist Government*, there was not *one indication of socialism* in the Speech from the Throne.

Members of the John government disagreed with Charles' assessment of the government's policies. One government member, Eden Bowers, retorted that the introduction of a Social Security Scheme, price control and low income housing was consistent with the *Socialist and co-operative approach* of the government. Another government member, Ferdinand Parillon, advised the House that *presently on the desks of Heads of Departments...there is a draft policy statement on Co-operative development in Dominica*. The scheme sought to expose the youth to co-operativism and secondly, to integrate *co-operative education* into the island's education system. To that end, Parillon reported a government initiative wherein the efficacy of co-operative practices in boosting citrus production would be studied under the auspices of the International Labour Organization.

Lacking any coherent policy towards the introduction of socialism, the government flirted with the tenets of socialism for the political mileage which would accrue from embracing such policies. This was done on a piecemeal basis with the government reserving a role for the private sector in its *socialist economy* through its enactment of *incentives legislation* to stimulate foreign investment. However, the role of the private sector in the economy was limited because of government encroachments in the form of price control and import substitution.

In the months following April 1975, the government continued to make inroads in the role of the private sector in its proposed socialist economy. In October 1975, it enacted the **Bonds and Securities Act**,[4] which purported to enable the issue of bonds by the Dominica Government in payment of any debts incurred by the State. However, Part IV of the *Act* provided for the acquisition of lands for public purposes through the issuance of Treasury or Saving Bonds to facilitate such purpose. In explaining the genesis of this legislation, Ferdinand Parillon advised the House of Assembly that:

> *Mr. Speaker, this government has pledged itself to leading our people along a socialist path. What we have is human and land resources, it follows therefore that our development must be based upon those two resources.... Our Constitution provides, Mr. Speaker, for the acquisition of land. It also provides for the payment of adequate compensation in reasonable time. We have no money. We cannot therefore continue to offer cash payment for lands which have to be acquired. This bill seeks to fulfill a need in difficult circumstances without breaching constitutional rights.*

---

[4] Hansard of the Fourth Meeting of the First Session of the Third Parliament under the Dominica Constitution Order 1967 held at Government Headquarters, Roseau on 31st October, 1975, page 17.

The other legislative initiative taken by the government in furtherance of its agenda of imposing state control in the economy was the establishment of a National Commercial and Development Bank in 1975.[5] In establishing the bank, the government sought *to create a financial institution which shall have responsibility for acting as banker, fiscal agent and trustee of the Government.* The bank was not intended to operate as a central bank and would ostensibly be free from political influence. The Finance Minister however, would be involved in appointing a Chairman of the bank. The *Act* called for the government owning 51% of the shares of the Bank with the public owning the other 49% shares. In further justifying the creation of the bank, Eden Bowers noted that it *represents a very important step towards...the fight against colonialism (and furthered the) approach to independence.*

The third initiative by the government in gaining hands on control over the economy was in the passing of a resolution in 1976 to purchase the Melville Hall and Castle Bruce Estates for development purposes. On September 27, 1973, the government had undertaken to purchase the two estates. Further to this undertaking, the Land Management Authority had taken control

---

[5] Hansard of the Proceedings of the Fifth Meeting of the 2nd Session of the Third Parliament under the Dominica Constitution Order 1967, held at the House of Assembly, Government Headquarters, on November 19, 1976, page22.

of the estates on October 1, 1973. The agreement provided for the government to pay the full purchase price and accrued interest at any time after execution of the agreement in September 1973 in *full settlement* of the Government's liability. A resolution in November 1976 authorized the Ministry of Finance to borrow $1M from the Commonwealth Development Corporation to consummate the 1973 purchase agreement by paying the vendors the full purchase price of the estates.

The government continued to tantalize the opposition in 1976 with the prospect of fully embracing socialism. The 1976 Speech from the Throne surpassed that of 1975 in adumbrating policies which appeared to reflect a commitment to socialism. The government reiterated its policies of distributing Crown lands for production, promoting the Cooperative approach to destroy *the social evil of exploitation of man by man*, and building low income housing. New initiatives included the intention to publish a five-year Agricultural Development Plan, legislation *designed to stabilize and systemise house rents* and a five year Economic Development Plan. The Speech also hinted at the government's ties with the Guyanese government in noting that Dominica had been *granted a line of credit by the government of Guyana for supply of rice...and negotiations are currently underway for the grant of similar facilities for sugar and fish from the government of Guyana.*

Despite these areas of projected government involvement, the 1976 Throne Speech provided a role for private sector activity in the future economy of the island. It anticipated the establishment of an Industrial Free Export Zone *to accommodate joining ventures between foreign and local investors*. Priority was to be given *to highly technical and labour intensive projects*. The Speech made no mention of any restrictions on the ability of foreign investors to repatriate any profits or any limits on their ability to operate in Dominica.

The July 1976 Budget address by Finance Minister Victor A. Riviere, further emphasised the need to reorder the island's revenues and expenditures to reflect the *socialist path* of the government. Riviere proposed to broaden the island's tax base on the grounds of equity and to foster the goals of economic development. To enhance import substitution, he sought to increase stamp duties on imports and to remove a number of exemptions to those duties. He also proposed to raise the consumption tax on products such as apples, peaches, and confectionery for which local substitutes existed.

The Budget address also proposed a withholding tax on the repatriation of income from Dominica. The tax would apply to money sent out of Dominica to non-residents, or that taken out of Dominica by non-residents. Riviere also sought to implement a nation-wide valuation of all real property in Dominica to determine the income earning potential of all property for taxation purposes.

The tax initiatives in the 1976 Budget promised to promote import substitution, discourage the export of capital from Dominica, and increase the tax burden on all landowners on the island. Such policies, Riviere noted, were *necessary and urgent in order that the worker, the little man. may be able to gain substantial control of the economic structure, concomitant with his political influence and participation.* If implemented, the taxes would place a larger tax burden on property holders in the island, in addition to restricting their ability to consume foreign products.

In John's contribution to the Budget debate in July 1976, he formally declared that his government *embraces the philosophy of socialism not of communism; nor of confiscation of property or land.*[6] His brand of socialism contemplated government's *participation in enterprises with the public sector (since) that is the only true means of encouraging the development of the nation....* Under his new regime, John anticipated that through measures such as import substitution, the expansion of co-operative practices and also a national service,

---

[6] Hansard of the Proceedings of the Third Meeting of the Second Session of the Third Parliament under the Dominica Constitution Order 1967, held at the House of Assembly, Government Headquarters, Roseau, on 20th July 1976, page 40.

Dominica would achieve economic self-sufficiency in much the same way that Puerto Rico was *said to have pulled itself up to economic viability by its own boot straps.*

This grandiose vision of economic self-sufficiency however, belied the precarious economic situation which plagued the country in the mid – 1970s. The regional Caribbean Development Bank in its 1975 annual report, expressed grave doubts about the viability of the small islands, including Dominica. In his 1976 budget address, John lamented that government *could not service out loans and only the kindness and benevolence of the well disposed managers of commercial banks enabled us to get overdrafts to tide us over from day to day.* He further noted that as of June 1976, aid from the British was not as forthcoming as in previous years given the British's newfound *doctrinal aversion to bilateral budgetary aid* to the Associated States. Henceforth, the British government would contribute half of a projected 2m pounds emergency fund held by the Caribbean Development Bank, which would be disbursed by the bank to the islands when the need arose.

These economic problems show clearly how essentially lacking in economic justification was the drive towards socialism and ultimately political independence. Even while outlining his vision of the new self-reliant state, John admitted to having *appealed to the British Government in vain for a loan to assist in the payment of our civil servants.*

In one sense however, the Labour government had no viable option to seeking independence since Britain had already taken a number of steps which unequivocally reflected its desire to jettison its colonial empire. To that extent, the attainment of independence from Britain would not so much be a fight but a *fait accompli*, with the only impediment being the resolution of any differences between the Dominica government and Opposition.

THE DRIVE TOWARDS POLITICAL INDEPENDENCE

Between December 8th-10th, 1975, the Heads of Governments of the Caribbean convened in St. Kitts for discussion of matters of mutual concern. During their deliberations, the island leaders passed a unanimous resolution mandating the Associated States of the region to approach Britain *at the earliest possible date to seek an end to associated statehood*. Furthermore, the resolution called for the abrogation of Associated Statehood and the concomitant granting of independence without the necessity of a national referendum. In a national broadcast celebrating the 21st anniversary of the Dominica Labour Party on 29 August 1976, John issued the

Salisbury Declaration in which he promised to keep *the ball of independence rolling into the appointed day of self-determination in 1997*.

In December 1976, hastily appointed Deputy Governor and Attorney General, Leo Austin, addressed the House of Assembly on the independence proposals for the island. He indicated that the government had talks earlier that year in which the British Under-Secretary of State for Commonwealth Affairs was advised that the Dominica government intended Dominica to become a sovereign state on November 2nd, 1977. The Under Secretary had invited the government delegation to submit a Green Paper on independence to the nation and to the Foreign and Commonwealth Office. The contents of Austin's speech comprised the government's Green Paper on independence.

In his speech, Austin outlined the reasons for seeking political independence. Foremost among these was the alleged disadvantage of associated statehood which, according to Austin, manifested itself *whenever a step forwards is being made by the Commonwealth Caribbean on a regional basis, and an agreement is called for*. Before such agreement could be executed, it had *to be submitted to Her Majesty's government with a request to allow the Associated States to adhere to it*. Such a requirement noted Austin, constituted *a fetter* on the Associated States' ability to realize their *true identity*.

The second proffered justification for independence was liberation. The Green Paper declared the government's belief that all persons possessed a right to freedom and political and constitutional freedom. Anything less would be an anachronism, or so the government intoned.

The third reason adduced for independence was historic. The island had been under British tutelage for 400 years. That was ample time in which the island could learn to fully govern itself. In any event Austin noted, *the British...themselves faced...grave economic problems* that threatened its survival and therefore could not help Dominica anymore. Other nations who otherwise would have filled in for Britain in granting aid to Dominica refrained from doing so while the island remained a colony of Great Britain.

To those who opposed independence because of the inadequacies of the government, Austin indicated that the government had acquired experience in governing the country on democratic principles. Such experience was essential to the realization of full independence and fortunately such experience reposed in the ranks of the government.

In any event, the government intended to establish a nation founded on democratic principles with an independent judiciary, a constitution which enshrined the rights and freedoms of all citizens. To allay any fears, the new constitution would incorporate the rights and freedoms in the exact form as they stood in the Constitution of 1967 and with which, Austin noted, the country had *lived happily for the past ten years*.

The foregoing assurance of respect for democratic rights and freedoms did nothing to assuage the concerns of the Opposition which had absented itself from the House of Assembly during Austin's presentation. In the 1970s, the government enacted legislation such as the ***Dread Act*** and related legislation which had significantly curtailed the rights enshrined in the Dominica Constitution Order of 1967. A State of Emergency had been declared in 1973 in the midst of a national strike. The island was still recovering from a 47-day civil servants' strike when the John government announced its independence proposals to the nation.

If the promise to adhere to the 1967 Constitution was not persuasive, so too was the government's foremost reason for seeking independence. The necessity of obtaining the British government's approval as a prerequisite to being bound by an agreement was at worst an irritant rather than a hindrance to economic development. Such a requirement did not preclude the Associated States from concluding agreements on their own and therefore did not impede the individual states from exploring any possibilities of economic aid.

The libertarian reason was really an appeal to the emotions. The post-World War II period had witnessed the growth of nationalism and the proliferation of independent states. The United Nations had passed resolutions on the right of colonized persons to self determination. In the region, the collapse of the short-lived West-Indies Federation in 1962 precipitated a march towards independence by Jamaica, Trinidad, Barbados and most recently Grenada. Other islands were in the process of following suit and it would have been incongruous for the island to have reversed that trend.

The most persuasive argument for independence however, was that the island had no viable option to do otherwise. As indicated, the drive to independence occurred at an historical juncture when grave economic problems militated against Britain's continued ability to provide financial aid to the islands at past levels. In June 1976, Britain signaled its intention to reduce its financial commitment to the island. Any doubts that Britain wanted to end Associated Statehood evaporated when in May 1977, its Undersecretary of State advised a Dominica delegation that Britain would in effect renege on its original undertaking in 1967 to require the holding of a referendum before granting independence to Dominica.

Despite the Labour government's dismal record for respect of human rights' in the 1970s, it was pointless to oppose independence because of fears concerning the John administration. With internal government being the exclusive preserve of the Dominican government, the British had maintained a stolid silence in the 1970s when the government systematically encroached on democratic rights on the island. The colonial government had not been able to ameliorate the conditions of citizens burdened by the ***Dread Act***, and ***Praedial Larceny Act***, amongst others. Conversely, John had not tempered his onerous attack on human rights in the 1970s in deference to Britain. He would certainly not have done so following independence. In effect, the John administration would have been no worse after independence than it had been prior to independence. There was therefore no substantive reasons for opposing the quest for independence in 1977.

In retrospect, it may well be suggested that had independence not been granted, the events of 1979 and then 1981 would not have occurred. This suggestion however, is implausible since the onerous legislation which led to the events in May 29, 1979 was not dissimilar to that enacted by the John administration in the 1970s. In fact, the willingness of the Labour government to enact such legislation reveals that there was no change in the conduct of the government after independence was attained in 1978.

LOCAL REACTION TO THE CALL FOR INDEPENDENCE

A. SUPPORT FOR INDEPENDENCE

A number of individuals and organizations supported the message of independence though not necessarily its messenger. Foremost among these supporters was Rosie Douglas, who had developed a penchant for radicalism as a student activist in Canada. Following his arrival in the island in 1976, he formed a number of Peoples Independence Committees to garner support for independence among the populace. In addition, Douglas established a series of study groups which members studied the precepts of Marxism and in the process, the importance of political independence to former colonized people.

The study group established in Roseau, known as Cadre #1, soon established its own newsletter, **The Vanguard**, which it disseminated throughout the capital. In addition, the group held discussions with youth groups, church organizations and the youth wing of the Dominica Freedom Party to propagate the message of independence. The activities of Douglas through his personal efforts and his organization *made independence a little more palatable to many Dominicans....*[7]

---

[7] **The New Chronicle**, Roseau, Dominica, November 3rd 1978, page 6.

Another supporter of independence and associate of Rosie Douglas was Bernard Wiltshire, a British-trained historian and Resident-Tutor of the University of the West-Indies in Dominica. A brilliant public speaker, Wiltshire used his position to organize discussions about the advantages of the socialist/communist system vis-à-vis the colonialist/capitalist system. He also showed films on a number of issues such as apartheid and the anticolonialist struggled in Africa.

Two factors enhanced Wiltshire's influence particularly among the students at the Sixth Form College. The Extra-Mural Department and the Sixth Form college occupied the same building and this enhanced contact between Wiltshire and the students. Secondly, Wiltshire assembled a well-stocked library of books on Marxism/Leninism, Third World politics, and other related topics. Combined with the occasional lecture at the Sixth College, the Extra-Mural Department became a powerful magnet to many students, drawn by Wiltshire's powerful oratory and the Extra-Mural library.

Primarily because of the personalities of Douglas and Wiltshire, the strongest areas of support for independence in the island were Portsmouth and Grandbay. Rosie Douglas drew on the political support for his brother Mike in finding a very receptive audience to the message of independence. Support for independence in Grandbay however, was more problematic since the parliamentary representative for Grandbay was a member of the Dominica Freedom Party, the main voice opposing independence under the John administration.

Furthermore, the John administration had not endeared itself in the past to the residents of Grandbay. In April 1974, the government declared a State of Emergency in Grandbay following a riot involving the destruction of property on the 1,300 acre Geneva Estate. Secondly, a major offensive against the Dreads had been carried out in the village. Thirdly, one of the notorious cases decided under the **Praedial Larceny Act** involved the lead singer, of the popular Grandbay band *Midnight Groovers*. He was convicted of stealing a coconut and had been sentenced to eighteen months in jail.

The activities of Wiltshire and then youth leader Pierre Charles dissipated the latent animosity towards John in Grandbay. Charles had become the President to the National Youth Council in 1977 and commanded great respect among the youth of his village community. Both men garnered support for independence by emphasizing that its importance superseded any concerns about the leadership of Patrick John. Grandbay, which historically, had been the cradle of radicalism in the island,[8] formed a natural base of support for the message of independence on the island.

---

[8] See Lennox Honeychurch, **The Dominica Story**, 1984, page 166-67.

The prevalent view expressed by the left in support of independence was that Associate Statehood represented the legal relationship in which Dominica languished in a perpetual state of under-development. This under-development resulted from the island's dependence through foreign control of the economy; dependence on trade and foreign aid finally on patterns of consumption reflecting a preference for foreign products over local products.[9] The severing of the legal relationship through independence would be the first stage in the process whereby the society's value system would be reoriented away from its dependency on traditional sources of aid, trade and indeed consumption. The country would necessarily have to look beyond Britain and the traditional Western sources of aid to achieve true development and independence.

In Rosie Douglas's Black Power Manifesto, **Chains or Change**, the thinking of a significant number of Dominica's intelligentsia was summarised. Independence he intoned, *is not something that is given in the form of a new flag and a piece of sheep skin with some writing that one calls a constitution; [it] involves the right of a people to self determination.* It involved forging new relationships. According to Douglas, *our import and export channels must extend to embrace several countries in*

---

[9] Athie Martin, "The Role of the Farmer in the Development of an Independent Dominica", **The New Chronicle**, Independence Magazine, November 1978, page 40.

various parts of the world. Such a move is absolutely necessary so that no one country can hold Dominicans to ransom.

However, the John administration perceived independence as anything but a definitive break from the traditional way of enticing Western investors or aid from Western sources. If anything, independence signaled the removal of any impediments, real or imagined, on the government's ability to vigorously pursue investors from the United States, Germany and France among others. Indeed, within five months of independence, the Attorney General concluded an agreement with the South African government providing for the building an oil refinery in Dominica. At the same time, the government concluded an agreement with a U.S. investor relinquishing its sovereign control over 40% of the arable land of Dominica.

These developments do not necessarily indicate that members of the left misjudged Patrick John and his fidelity to socialism. Indeed, some members, most notably Dr. William Riviere, were united with the Freedom Party in their common antipathy towards John's administration. Unlike the Freedom Party however, the left largely believed that independence should be the first priority with the possible disposal of John following soon after. Deposing John prior to independence might have prompted the British, who were still the sovereign power, to restore John if he was deposed.[10] The British would not have countenanced the substitution of John by a communist government in Dominica any more than it tolerated the communist Cheddi Jagan government in Guyana in 1964. On the other hand, it would not have intervened if John was deposed after independence, as was the case in Grenada when Maurice Bishop deposed Prime Minister Eric Gairey.

Media support for independence originated from the government-owned Dominica Broadcasting Corporation (DBS). According to one contemporary observer, *the pro- independence voice of the Radio Service of (DBS) is like the lone, forlorn hollow voice of one crying desperately and unheard in the wilderness.*[11] This support stood in strong contrast to the views espoused in the **Dominica Chronicle** which views were less than conciliatory to the prospect of independence under the John administration. Support for independence reflected the philosophy of Dennis Joseph, General Manager of the Dominica Broadcasting Corporation and a supporter of the ruling Labour Party. As he noted in the Independence issue of the **Dominica Link:**

---

[10] Hansard of the Proceedings of the Fourth Meeting of the Fifth Session of the Second Parliament under the Commonwealth of Dominica Constitution Order 1978, on 22nd October, and Tuesday 26th November, 1984, page 138.

[11] Wolsey P. Louis, **The Dominica Link, Independence Issue**, November 1978, page 74.

> It must be remembered that the Broadcaster is first and foremost a National and may not be able to afford the professional luxury of sitting on the fence in order to achieve partiality when matters relating to the goals and objectives of the nation are at issue.

B. OPPOSITION TO INDEPENDENCE

i. THE DOMINICA FREEDOM PARTY

The main opposition to Independence emanated from the Dominica Freedom Party. However the party opposed not so much independence itself which it regarded as inevitable, but independence under the current leadership of the island. As explained by the Party's 1977 publication, **Think it Over;**

> We will have no change if the style of leadership remains the same. Independence may come, but as long as we are burdened with the same leaders, conditions will remain stagnant and Dominica will make no progress.

The publication also stressed the need not to *rush blindly* into ***independence and the necessity for the population to voice their opinion on its desirability.***

The party's major attempt to involve the population in the decision to proceed to independence failed when on May 2, 1977, the British rejected the submission that a referendum should be a prerequisite to independence. At the Constitutional Conference held on that date, the government delegation argued that it represented the majority of people and a referendum would therefore be unnecessary. Secondly, a referendum on independence would dredge up latent racial animosities towards Britain, given the island's colonial history.

These submissions found favour with the British, but only because a referendum would inevitably delay the granting of independence. Furthermore, a referendum may have revealed a low level of public support for independence on the island.

On the other hand, independence had to be granted to Dominica with at least the semblance of agreement between the government and the opposition. This explains why the British gave the Freedom Party a pyrrhic victory by calling for the resolution of any serious areas of disagreement between the government and opposition at the Constitutional Conference in London in May 1977.

The apprehension about the John administration placed the Freedom Party in a quandary. On one hand, it asserted that independence was inevitable. On the other hand, it was forced to oppose what it declared to be desirable because of its concern over the John administration.

This concern manifested itself in two ways. The DFP attempted to mitigate John's power after independence by proposing a constitution which had a series of checks and balances on the powers of the Prime Minister. These included a proposal that the island become a republic immediately after independence with a President elected by popular ballot. The President would be in charge of security, defence and external affairs. This executive president would be an effective check on the Prime Minister and would prevent him from assuming the dictatorial powers which the Freedom Party feared. A precedent for such a system existed in France where the government functioned smoothly despite the bifurcation of authority between an executive president and Prime Minister.

Furthermore, the Party proposed a House of Legislature comprised of 13 elected members, instead of the 21 then existing and 8 members nominated by proportional representation. These 8 senators would be allocated on the basis of the percentage of the popular votes received by either Party in the general elections.

As a third bulwark against government control, the Freedom Party proposed that the Attorney General should not be in charge of state prosecutions. It also proposed that the Director of Public Prosecutions (DPP) should be separate and independent from the Attorney-General. The party did not address the question of who would appoint the DPP or what role the Attorney

General would play, other than enacting legislation, alongside an independent office of Director of Public Prosecutions.

The Freedom Party did not find a sympathetic air at the May 1977 Constitutional Conference in London. Based on the objections of the government delegation, the Conference Chairman, Mr. Luard, held that there would be no republic. The government later retracted its opposition to a republic but indicated that while a republic would be acceptable, the President would be nominated. Furthermore, he or she would be assigned such functions as the Parliament periodically decided instead of the executive functions envisaged by the Freedom Party.

In explaining this unanticipated but limited concession, Miss Charles noted that:

> It was something that was thought of in the last minute because the British government felt that if we agreed to that, I would withdraw everything else...[12]

The British also decided to keep the 21 elected member House of Assembly intact but with 9 nominated members or senators. Finally, the Conference held that there would be no formal bifurcation of the offices of the Attorney General and the Director of Public Prosecutions.

---

[12] Hansard of the Proceedings of the Fourth Meeting of the Fifth Session of the Second Parliament under the Commonwealth of Dominica Constitution Order 1978, on Monday 22nd October, 1984, p. 146.

The call to the people in the booklet, **Think It Over** did not result in a groundswell of support for the Freedom Party proposals, forcing the British government to modify its support for Dominica's independence. In July 1978, an adviser to the British government visited the island to assess public opinion and reported that he met *no more than one or two people who were opposed to independence.*[13] This was surprising to contemporary observers since the Freedom Party had organized a massive rally in Roseau following the May 1977 Constitutional Conference, to gain public support for its proposals. Such support was one factor explaining why independence was not granted in November 1977 as originally anticipated. However, the British adviser could hardly have concluded otherwise since his government had already rejected a call for a referendum in May 1977. Neither could he have found otherwise since in October 1977 and again in April 1978, the Dominica House of Assembly voted overwhelmingly in favour of independence.

ii. THE NEW CHRONICLE

If the Dominica Broadcasting Service was unwavering in its support for independence, so too was the **New Chronicle** in its

---

[13] See Honeychurch, **The Dominica Story**, for a chronology of events leading to Independence on November 3rd, 1978.

opposition of independence. The concerns of the paper reflected those of the Opposition party. The paper voiced concerns about the protection of human rights in the newly emergent state and the repercussions of *socialism* in the lives of the people. The paper organized essay competitions in 1977 with topics including *The Differences between a Socialist and a Capitalist Economy* and *Discuss the Steps that people can take to Safeguard Human Rights Provisions of a Constitution*. Indeed an October 27, 1978 editorial in the news magazine **The Dominica Link** berated the New Chronicle for its *consistently anti-Government* stand and considered the justification of press censorship *on the grounds of protecting our country's image overseas.*

For the most part however, political allegiances determined the public's attitude towards the desirability of independence. The strongest areas of support were in the Portsmouth and Grandbay areas while opposition was concentrated in Roseau. Pockets of support for or opposition to independence, existed throughout the island. However, a significant part of the electorate remained stolidly obliviousness to the issue of independence and its apparent advantages to the island. This obliviousness has been attributed by one observer to a more fundamental lack of a sense of history by Dominicans.[14]

---

[14] Jonathan Wylie "The Sense of Time, the Social Construction of Reality, and the Foundations of Nationhood in Dominica and the Faroe

However, it merely reflected the public's fears that despite the rhetoric, independence would not materially alter their lot in life.

TAKING THE FINAL STEPS TOWARDS INDEPENDENCE

Apprehension over the John Administration cast the Dominica Freedom Party in the role of the devil's advocate in the debate over independence. In October 1977, the Opposition brought a Motion of No Confidence against the government. Not unexpectedly, the government easily defeated the Motion given its overwhelming majority in the House of Assembly. After the House of Assembly affirmed the plan for independence in April 1978, the Opposition objected to the composition of the electoral Commission set out in section 56(3) of the draft constitution. The section provided for a supervisor of elections appointed by the government, who would be nominally subservient to the wishes of the government. To preserve the integrity of that position, the Opposition proposed the Electoral Commission to be comprised of three members, with Government, Opposition and the President choosing one member. The final composition provided for the Chairman of the Commission to be appointed by the President in his own discretion with four other appointments being made under advisement from both sides of the House of Assembly.

One significant development in January 1978, clearly reveals that the issue of independence was severed from its ideological roots prior to November 1978. Up to that point, the John government had justified independence on the need to attain self sufficiency, to develop a new spirit of co-operativism and to organize production to ensure that the rewards would be distributed among the population. His ministers of government had propagated the virtues of socialism and the need for the reordering of the society along socialist lines. However, on January 1978, John unexpectedly dismissed Ferdinand Parillon and Michael Douglas, two ministers who had been among the most vocal in propagating socialism.

The reason adduced for Parillon's dismissal was that of a conflict between himself and the powerful Attorney General.[15] According to some, John dismissed Douglas following pressure from foreign investors who disapproved of Douglas's socialist proclivities. Both explanations appear plausible but the reasons for the dismissals run much deeper.

Although distrusted by a section of the electorate, Douglas had earned the respect of many as a capable minister and possible challenger for the Leadership of the Party. He also had the

---

[15] **The New Chronicle, Independence Magazine,** November 1978, page 6.

potential of carving out a political enclave in the North with a little help from Parillon, the representative of contiguous Colihaut. With a firm support base, Douglas could easily have risen to challenge John as leader of the Labour Party.

Secondly, John may have dismissed Douglas because of anticipated hostility to the type of foreign investments he sought for Dominica. In his 1976 address, John indicated a desire to establish a Free Port Zone in Portsmouth, given the town's natural harbour. With the relinquishment of sovereign control over such an area, Douglas's political strength would have been gravely undermined. Indeed, Douglas precipitated the *revolt of the Northerners* against a proposed Free Port Zone in 1979, when the John government granted a Texas investor a 45 square mile area encompassing Portsmouth, for such a scheme.

More significant however, the dismissal of Michael Douglas may have reflected John's fear and distrust of Mike's association with his brother Rosie Douglas. The Douglas brothers had been in the vanguard of the efforts to gain support for independence. At a rally in Portsmouth, Michael Douglas had called for a unilateral declaration of independence much to the delight of the crowd in attendance. The brothers had carried the momentum after May 1977, while John, Vic Riviere and Leo

Austin visited Europe in search of investors.[16] Momentarily alienated from the one issue which preoccupied the population, John dismissed Douglas to pre-empt his possible rival from upstaging him on the issue of independence.

In any event, the firing of these two men severed the connection between socialism and independence. As events subsequently revealed, the massive foreign investment which John contemplated for the island was antithetical to the mixed economy he had envisaged as part of his brand of socialism. Indeed, the dismissals revealed that John had essentially jettisoned his socialist rhetoric in favour of unbridled foreign investment on the island. Such a change of policy, if successful, would necessarily require a compliant work force and uncritical local press. Ironically, John's efforts to establish the legislative groundwork to revert to an unfettered market economy led to his eventual downfall.

---

[16] **The New Chronicle, Independence Magazine,** November 1978, page 6.

TOWARDS ARMAGEDDON: THE ATTEMPT TO INVADE DOMINICA AND ITS AFTERMATH

Irving André

The dismissal of Patrick John by the newly appointed President of Dominica in June 1979 threw the Dominica Labour Party into a political tailspin from which it barely recovered. In the 1980 general election, the Dominican Freedom Party routed its nemesis by winning 17 of 21 seats in the National House of Assembly. However, within one year of this victory, the government would have to deal with one of the gravest crises which an elected government had to deal with - that of an invasionary force trying to supplant the legitimate government with one recently rejected by the island's electorate.

What accounts for this desperate attempt by the island's first Prime Minister to regain leadership and power? That John felt that he had been illegally deprived of the island's leadership in 1979 emerges in his refusal to resign as Prime Minister after the events of May 29, 1979. John had defiantly clung to the reins of power even after widespread looting and destruction of property owned by members of his political party. The justification for this defiance seemed to have sprung from the belief that in as much as John had been democratically elected in

1975, only the electorate could have legitimately removed him from office.

However, the reasons for John's attempt to regain power by non-democratic means run much deeper. In an essay on West-Indian politicians, writer C. L. R. James noted that:

> All personal distinction and even in some cases the actual means of life and the means of improving the material circumstances of life, sprung from participation, direct or indirect, in the government, or circles sympathetic to or willing to play ball with the government.[1]

James argues that within the context of a small island, politics is not so much the art of governing the country as being a means of earning a living. This may be less true today than in the 1970s. At the time however, the typical politician derived his sense of self importance almost exclusively from participation in government. Consequently, loss of office caused a degree of economic disruption to the local politician which was unparalleled in the region. As calypsonian Cleve Jean-Jacques sang in the 1980s, *I've seen ministers (i.e. government) become bus drivers.*

The island's first Prime Minister seemed the epitome of the political type described by James. Prior to becoming involved in politics, he had been General Secretary of the *Waterfront and*

---

[1] James, C. L. R., **Spheres of Existence**, 1980, page 132.

Allied Workers Union (WAWU) and had progressed to become Mayor of the island's capital. Significantly however, these bastions of support for John were systematically eroded after his entry into national politics. In 1971, the Roseau Town Council came under the control of the Dominica Freedom Party and by 1974, the rank and file of WAWU regarded its erstwhile leader as a *traitor*.

Severed completely from his original bases of influence and even livelihood, the Premier had no option but to contrive to remain in power at all costs. He tried assiduously and succeeded in co-opting the island's security forces to buttress his tenure in office. He inevitably developed a proprietary interest in the task of *governing* the island. He enjoyed the trappings of success; the prestige attendant on the position of Premier. John soon developed a heightened sense of self-importance with the result that he assumed a number of roles which would elevate his stature as a leader.

For example, the Prime Minister made himself Colonel of the island's Defence Force in 1974. In the 1970s, he indicated to the House of Assembly that he had been the recipient of a Doctorate Degree in Philosophy. In his numerous overseas trips, John invariably surrounded himself with a number of *advisors*. He also developed a penchant for chartering airplanes even for the most mundane assignments abroad.

Such idiosyncrasies may not normally warrant attention except where, as here, they demonstrate the extent to which the Premier became enamoured with his job. They also show in retrospect, that if this individual lost this job through means he considered unjust, not only would he fight to maintain that job, but if unsuccessful, would do anything to regain it.

The economic compulsion to become Prime Minister however, does not fully explain John's involvement in the planned invasion. Archie Singham in his book, *The Hero and the Crowd in a Colonial Polity*, has explored the emotional relationship between the West-Indian folk leader and his audience, the electorate. The folk leader becomes a hero to his people; as in the case of Eric Gairey in Grenada, Robert Bradshaw in St.Kitts, or Vere Bird in Antigua. Inevitably, the role of hero assumes a life of its own with the result that loss of the exalted position necessarily involves, loss of face. As V.S. Naipaul has noted in his book, **The Overcrowded Barracoon**; *to lose is to be without a role, to be altogether ridiculous.*

Within Dominica, Edward Leblanc had avoided this fate in the 1970s through voluntary resignation from office and self-imposed exile in Thibaud. His successor was less fortunate. Political defeat meant a loss of prestige in the eyes of John's political supporters; he could no longer bask in their adulation. Depressed over the enormity of paradise lost, he inexorably turned his attention to plotting how paradise could be regained. This was almost a reflex action, engendered by the need to act out the role of leader foisted upon the ex-Prime Minister by his fickle supporters. Indeed, it would be inconceivable that John would have contracted with Mike Perdue without the assurance that a significant part of the electorate would overlook the reprehensible manner of his assumption of power.

THE AGREEMENT

Following his fall from office in June 1980, John reactivated his links to the dubious investors which he had adroitly managed to court while in office. He soon established links with a New Orleans businessman, Mike Perdue, who listed membership in the *Klu Klux Klan* as one of his credentials for doing business with the island. John's contract with Perdue was merely the extension of the policies he had pursued in office and more specifically, a likely successor to his Government's partnership with SASOL, the South African Oil and Gas Company Ltd..

Both parties soon crystallized their partnership into a formal agreement on September 20, 1980. In consideration for Perdue's arranging his reinstatement as Prime Minister of

Dominica, John undertook to pay Perdue $150,000.00 to meet the expenses of the operation. The task of planning the operation reposed in the hands of Mike Perdue. Pursuant to the agreement, Perdue would receive Dominican citizenship and a top government position.[2]

Perdue then used his *Klu Klux Klan* affiliations to hire a number of individuals to join the enterprise. He recruited Wolfgang Droege and Alexander McQuirter, National Director and Grand Wizard of the Canadian chapter of the *Klu Klux Klan*. He later hired a female member of the Klan, Marian McGuire, who preceded the men to Dominica in 1981, on an intelligence gathering mission. To complete his army, Perdue would place an ad in an Illinois newsletter, **Le Mercenaire**, seeking men of *disciplined character* who were interested in *security duty for a private employer on [a] Caribbean island*. His recruits would include an Alabama Klan leader, a disgraced racist Sheriff, two security guards and a Klansman convicted of assault against black children.

The plan to reinstate John called for the neutralizing of the island's Police headquarters and the arrest of the government. It involved an expeditionary force embarking from New Orleans and sailing to the island where the mercenaries would team up with former members of the then defunct Defence Force. To that

---

[2] **Toronto Star**, Friday, May 8, 1981, page A16

end, Perdue chartered the 52 foot research vessel, the *Manana*, at a cost of $15,400.00 to take the men to their destination.[3]

The mercenaries anticipated that they would attack the Roseau Police station and seize its radio communications centre, armoury and barracks. The attacking force would comprise 45 men or three attacking units, code named Red Dog 1, 2, and 3. The latter two, comprising 18 and 17 men respectively, would largely be responsible for securing the radio communications centre, armoury and barracks . The Dominican complement, Red Dog 1, would be made up primarily of members of the disbanded Defence Force including two of the top men of the force.

THE ECONOMIC PLAN

The 32 year-old Perdue from Houston, Texas, anticipated a tremendous economic windfall from his involvement in the planned invasion. In May 1979, a business enterprise in which a fellow Texan contracted with the John government to establish a 45 square mile Free Trade Zone was terminated because of popular disapproval in the island. Distrustful of the local population, Perdue intended to rely on military might to stifle any

---

[3] **The Globe and Mail**, Toronto, Canada, Wednesday, May 13, 1981, page 4.

opposition to his bid for unrestricted access to the island's natural resources.

The hope of economic aggrandizement provided a powerful impetus to the foreigners implicated in the attempted invasion. For example, those involved hoped to establish a business consortium known as *Nortic Enterprises,* the principal of which would be Mike Perdue.[4] The company would invest in agricultural development, the construction of an international airport, tourism and gambling and the cutting and exploration of timber found on government land.[5] To ensure the smooth operation of these enterprises and to stifle any opposition to the overthrow of the elected government, the conspirators planned to increase the Dominica Defence Force by 200 men.[6] Perdue's men would then be hired *as specialists used in training and maintaining the National Defence Force.*[7] That would create the necessary atmosphere conducive to foreign investment. As noted by McQuirter:

> The only reason people don't invest in the (black) countries is because you can't trust the government. As soon as everything was secure, there'd have been an awful lot of people down there, people like us, with the same ideas.

---

[4] **Toronto Star**, Friday, May 8, 1991, A16.
[5] As footnote in # 3.
[6] As in footnote # 3.
[7] As in footnote # 3.

This thinly disguised intention to create what amounted to a foreign controlled police state had a broader economic justification than Perdue's *Nortic Enterprises*. Preliminary reports indicated that a group of wealthy U.S. businessmen bankrolled the operation in the amount of $75,000.00.[8] Further reports suggest that an influential Toronto mob figure contributed $10,000.00 to members of the Canadian Knights of the *Klu Klux Klan* towards the success of the project.[9] James McQuirter, Grand Wizard of the *Canadian KKK*, noted that his secret partners intended to set up a modern airport, casino, hotels and off-shore banking operations on the island.[10] In a letter to McQuirter, Perdue also suggested that his *business people* could arrange an $8,000,000.00 loan *within a few months*.[11]

It becomes clear that what was perceived by John to have been foreign investment to facilitate economic development really would have amounted to economic devastation by the conspirators. McQuirter contemplated using the island's vast rain forest to establish a lucrative lumber industry. He indicated that in the past, the Dominican government had refused to promote lumber cutting for environmental reasons. His men on the other

---

[8] **Toronto Star**, Thursday, April 30, 1981, A2.
[9] **The Globe and Mail**, Wednesday, May 13, 1981, page 4.
[10] As in footnote # 8.
[11] **Toronto Star**, Wednesday, May 13, 1981, page 1.

hand had no such scruples and would cut down lumber as fast as they could be sold.[12]

While McQuirter planned to pillage the island's natural resources, his associates sought to exploit its newly independent status as a refuge for shady individuals and capital. One investor sought to issue diplomatic passports to criminals seeking asylum.[13] Reports further indicated that investors in the expedition included a number of drug dealers who contemplated making the island a lucrative entrepot for the illicit drug trade.[14]

THE CONSPIRATORS

The early history of the Caribbean is replete with tales of swashbuckling buccaneers, pirates and adventurers who roamed the region in search of easy prey. While the exploits of these are steeped in ignominy, they have nevertheless survived the censure of historians who have painted a largely romanticized picture of their exploits.

No amount of historical *objectivity* however, can mask this aspect of the island's history. The men involved in the planned invasion were not picadors, or adventurers; not the stuff

---

[12] As in footnote # 10.
[13] As in footnote # 9.
[14] As in footnote # 8, page A2.

of legend. Neither patriotism, love of the sea, adventurism or altruism governed their actions. Theirs was no journey of self-discovery, no excursion into the human psyche. Joseph Conrad's **Heart of Darkness** or Herman Melville's **Moby Dick** were as far removed from their consciousness as was knowledge of the island they had chosen to invade.

And yet their story reveals as much about the island's vulnerability, its insignificance in international circles, and its existence on the periphery of the consciousness of the West. In an October 17, 1981, feature story for the **Toronto Star**, senior editor Judy Stoffman has given a profile of the men involved in the planned invasion of the island. That two reporters from the Toronto radio station CFTR delayed reporting the scheme to preserve the impact of the story says as much about journalistic sensationalism as it says about the island's significance in the eyes of the West.

In her article, Stoffman describes the invasionary force as *a ragtag band of Klu Klux Klanners, neo-Nazis, weekend mercenaries and an alcoholic girl.* More than that however, the conspirators were the human detritus washed ashore by the neo-conservative storm which struck Canada and the United States in the early 1980s. As odd an assortment of men as the crew of Melville's P*equod*, they were nevertheless united by a deep seated hatred of black, Jews and minorities of all shades.

In 1979, Michael Perdue initiated the scheme after reading about the overthrow of Grenadian Prime Minister Sir Eric Gairey by Maurice Bishop. His familiarity with magazines such as **Soldier of Fortune** and **Le Mercenaire** had acquainted him with the exploits of mercenaries in the tiny Comoro Islands and Fernando Po off the coast of Africa and the idea of replicating their activities in the neighbouring Caribbean began to take shape.

Perdue reportedly met Sir Eric Gairey in San Diego. Gairey initially endorsed the idea since it included his resumption of power. Perdue then methodically proceeded to assemble his band of invaders. He contacted David Duke, then head of the National Association for the Advancement of White People and later U.S. presidential candidate.

Duke introduced Perdue to Don Andrews, ex-convict and former head of the Canadian-based Neo-Nazi Western Guard. Andrews suggested using Dominica as a beachhead for the invasion of Grenada, to avoid the inevitable detection if launched from the United States or Canada. An associate and itinerant businessman, Arnie Poli, later suggested to Andrews that he should have a front in Dominica. In a move fraught with symbolism, Andrews chose to start a company which would grind, roast and package the black beans of Colombian coffee in Dominica.

When Perdue finally met Andrews in the fall of 1979, the plans for an invasion of Grenada had already been made. Perdue met an additional person in Toronto whose pedigree as a Nazi sympathizer appeared to legitimize their enterprise. Andrews introduced him to German-born Wolfgang Droege whose grandfather had related Nazi stories to him as a child.[15] Other Canadians introduced to Perdue, would include unemployed Klan organizer Larry Jacklin who blamed his employment difficulties on Asians, blacks and Jews[16] and Marion McGuire, a recovering alcoholic with ties to the Irish Republican Army.[17]

The plan to invade Grenada was a simple one. Gairey's supporters within the island would foment dissension and opposition to the Marxist regime of Bishop. In this atmosphere of uncertainty, the mercenaries and Gairey would sail from Dominica to Grenada where, with help from Gairey's supporters, Bishop would be overthrown and Gairey reinstated as the legitimate authority on the island. International opposition would be muted since the Reagan administration was vehemently opposed to the Bishop government. The conspirators perceived no threat from regional governments since without U.S. backing, they lacked the resources to intervene. In any event, certain

---

[15] Droege stirred up controversy in 1992 by clandestinely joining a local Ontario chapter of the Reform Party, Canada's third most influential political party, **Toronto Star**, Saturday, February 29 1992, A5.
[16] As in footnote # 8.
[17] **Toronto Star**, Sunday, May 17 1981, A4.

regional governments such as the Adams and Charles regimes in Barbados and Dominica respectively were as much opposed to the left-leaning regime in Grenada as the Reagan administration in America.

Despite these assurances of success, Sir Gairey reportedly rejected the idea of landing in Grenada before the army and police headquarters had been neutralized. An astute politician, Sir Gairey was aware of the militarization of Grenada in the wake of Bishop's ascendancy. The arrogance of his new allies provided no comfort when he remembered the Cuban military personnel on the island and the Peoples Militia which supported the immensely popular Bishop. He was also sanguine about the prospect of failure since he could expect the worst from the Bishop government if the invasion failed. He understandably had no trust in the ability of the regional island governments to protect him. He therefore refused to be part of an invasionary force which did not hold all the cards for the successful takeover of the island.

This new development placed Perdue in a quandary. Attempting the coup without the support of Gairey's sympathizers would have been foolhardy. However, he could not abandon his plan since he had incurred a great deal of expense in assembling his men. Another deposed leader in another small island would equally fit the bill for invasion as Grenada. Indeed, Dominica afforded better chances for success given its smaller population, antiquated police force, sympathetic ex-soldiers with a score to settle with the Charles government, and fairly significant grassroot support for the ex-Prime Minister. Furthermore, the Charles government had only been in power for a very short time and had not consolidated its authority on the island. Finally, the problem which forced Gairey to back out of the scheme was obviated since John would be there on the island marshalling required support for the invasion.

Prior to the September 20, 1980 agreement executed by John and Perdue, Droege travelled to Dominica in December 1979 and unsuccessfully tried to contact John. Perdue was similarly unsuccessful despite sending John several telegrams. The breakthrough came after the general elections in 1980 which shattered John's hopes of resuming power through the ballot. In August 1980, he agreed in principle to Perdue's scheme. Preliminary discussions were held in Antigua with two members of the disbanded Dominica Defence Force. These discussions were crystallized in the formal agreement on September 20, 1980.

By October 1980, Perdue had virtually everything in place for the attempted invasion of Dominica. He had a duly executed contract with the island's ex-Prime Minister, investors committed to the project and like-minded individuals ready to join his enterprise. While visiting Canada in October, he was introduced to another individual interested in the scheme.

Alexander McQuirter had served as National Direction or Grand Wizard of the Canadian Knights of the *Klu Klux Klan*. His United States counterpart was David Duke, candidate for the Governship of the state of Louisiana and Grand Wizard of the U.S. Knights of the *Klu Klux Klan* until 1979. At their trial on conspiracy charges, Perdue would testify that Duke introduced him to McQuirter and helped arrange transportation of the mercenaries to Dominica. Duke established the *National Association for the Advancement of White People* (N.A.A.W.P.) to offset the N.A.A.C.P. in America. McQuirter did not establish a sister organization in Canada since he felt that such an organization would have less appeal to Canadians than to Americans.[18]

From his office on Dundas Street East in Toronto, McQuirter ran the Canadian Branch of the *KKK* and was the point man for Mike Perdue, his U.S. counterpart. He received a three year contract from Perdue pursuant to which he would become Dominica's minister of propaganda following the overthrow.[19] In that capacity, he would be responsible for propagating the views espoused by the *KKK* and other North American Neo-Nazis.[20]

---

[18] Barnet, Stanley, "White Supremacists and Neo-Fascists" in **Racism in Canada**, Ormond Mckague ed. (1991) (Saskatoon, Saskatchewan) pages 85-10 at page 92.
[19] **The Globe and Mail**, Wednesday, May 13, 1981, page 4.
[20] **The Globe and Mail**, Wednesday, May 13, 1981, page 4.

That would enable the plotters to achieve their goals which, according to McQuirter, was *to put the world right so to speak.*[21]

In their involvement in the projected overthrow of the Charles government, McQuirter and his cohorts wedded economic self-interest to their racist ideology. According to him, Dominica needed *white order and white government.*[22] The island had not been successful in attracting investment since according to McQuirter, potential investors could not trust the black government.[23]

If the country needed white government, why then would McQuirter and Perdue consent to supplanting the Prime Minister, with Patrick John, a black man? Such a move would forestall international criticism of the coup and would certainly mask its nature and that of the men who engineered it. Loss of life occasioned by the event would have been kept to a minimum but in any event would not constitute a problem, since according to McQuirter, *it would have been Negroes doing it to Negroes, which is one of the characteristics of their race.*[24]

Based on the foregoing, it becomes apparent that the conspirators regarded this enterprise as anything but an attempt to reinstall John in the seat of power. They regarded him merely as the black face who would give the imprimatur of legitimacy to a

---

[21] As in footnote # 18.
[22] As in footnote # 8.
[23] As in footnote # 8.
[24] As in footnote # 8.

regime set up by themselves. They were the very antithesis of the *investors* needed by the island to develop its natural resources. John merely provided them with the ideal opportunity to establish a beachhead for the propagation of their supremacist ideology and to get rich in the process.

Assuming without deciding that John knew the full agenda of the men he had hired to regain power, his alliance with Perdue represented the logical outcome of the economics of desperation which he had pursued throughout his tenure in office. It bore continuities with the agreement made with the agents of the South African government in 1979. It marked the culmination of the policy pursuant to which the government was courted by offers of free air travel and hotel accommodation throughout the 1970s. Furthermore, it revealed how the drive towards political independence by the John administration was partly a move to remove any impediments on some members of government, real or imagined, to reap economic benefit for themselves.

One example of an *investment* project illustrated this desire for self-aggrandizement. During a sitting of the House of Assembly in October 1975, the Opposition inquired about government involvement in a project entitled the **Planet Earth Development and Finance Corporation.** The Premier explained that the Corporation was locally registered and that the government had secured three Directors on its Board of Directors with veto control over all its financial activities.[25] However by 1979, an investigation revealed that the Corporation had been somehow re-christened the Federal Bank of Dominica with an address in Cheshire, England.[26] The Dominican government owned 71% of the bank and listed one of its Directors as Leo Austin, the island's former Attorney General. The bank had no staff and was located in a room above a small shop in Trodsham, Cheshire. This metamorphosis from the Planet Earth Corporation to the Federal Bank of Dominica had occurred without the knowledge of the opposition or the public.

While the Agreement between John and the conspirators represented the logical extension of his economic policies in the 1970s, it marked an ironic reversal of the social policy followed by John during his tenure in office. For instance, the enactment of the *Dread Act* in 1974, partly resulted from an attempt to prevent acts of violence against white persons on the island. In the throne speech of April 1975, the government declared its policy to *further continue to oppose racial discrimination, violence and terrorist actions.* The island's 1978 *Constitution Order* prohibited discrimination on the basis of race, amongst others. However, the agreement contemplated a number of white

---

[25] Hansard of the Fourth Meeting of the First Session of the Third Parliament under the Dominica Constitution Order1967 held at Government Headquarters, Roseau, on Friday, October 31st, 1975, at
10:00 a.m..
[26] **The Nation**, Bridgetown, Barbados, June 1, 1979, page 4.

mercenaries wreaking acts of violence against the largely black population of the island. The government had also agitated for and achieved political independence in 1978 on a platform which stressed the need for the island to sever colonial ties to Britain and to establish a proud independent state with full citizenship for its nationals. On the other hand, the former leader contemplated trivializing the value of citizenship by conferring it on foreigners who had no relationship with the island.

FAILURE OF THE INVASION PLAN

The attempted invasion of the island failed when on April 27, 1981, 40 U.S. Federal agents reinforced by 60 policemen from New Orleans, arrested 10 mercenaries including Perdue, Droege and Jacklin as they prepared to board the *Manana* in New Orleans, Louisiana. The mercenaries had stacked 33 automatic weapons, ammunition, sticks of dynamite and various blasting caps for the journey. McQuirter had luckily been deported from the United States prior to April 1991, and was not with the boarding party at the time of the arrest.

The men were immediately indicted on 7 counts of conspiracy, alleging violations of various weapons and explosive law and the *U.S. Neutrality Act* which made it a crime to launch a coup against a friendly nation.[27] The charges carried penalties of up to 50 years jail and $33, 000.00 in fines. All ten were subsequently held in custody on bonds totalling some US $4.6 million.[28]

The indictment against the ten men revealed that the planned invasion had been infiltrated when Perdue gave an undercover U.S. Treasury agent, the captain of the *Manana*, $5,000.00 as partial down-payment for the trip to Dominica. Authorities then installed a listening device aboard the boat as part of its surveillance, code named Bayou of Pigs, of the operation.

The arrest was precipitated by information provided by the Charles government which had been advised abut the planned invasion by Rastafarian Albert Maffei who, along with two members of the DDF, had met Perdue in Antigua in January 1981. Following the U.S. arrest in April 1991, the Charles government wasted little time in arresting John and his Defence Force conspirators for their intended role in the alleged conspiracy.

Prior to the arrest in Louisiana however, events in Dominica had reached a climax. In February 1981, amidst rumors of collusion among Defence Force personnel disgruntled at John's loss of power in 1980 and *dread* individuals, the father

---

[27] As in footnote # 15.
[28] As in footnote # 4.

of the Government's Press Secretary, Lennox Honeychurch, was kidnapped.[29] The kidnapping precipitated the declaration of a state of emergency during which John and seven others were arrested following reports of the attempted coup. Those arrested included Captain Reid and three other men, the former being the architect of the attack by the Defence Force on demonstrators on May 29, 1979. Just one month earlier, Reid had met with Perdue in Antigua to discuss the overthrow of the Charles government.[30]

While languishing in jail, Reid sent a letter to the former head of the Dominica Defence Force, Fredrick Newton, advising the latter to contact Perdue and outline how the government was to be overthrown. Newton, along with two others, were immediately arrested and imprisoned.

The imprisonment of John placed the mercenaries in a quandary. If they abandoned the agreement they stood to lose the $100,000.00 already invested in the project. If they continued, they would lose the ground support necessary to ensure the neutralization of the island's security forces. The immediate effect of John's arrest however, was to make McQuirter cancel a reservation to Dominica where he would have acted as spy or

---

[29] See Lennox Honeychurch, **The Dominica Story**, 1975, 1984, pages 214-217 for a full chronology of these events.

[30] **The Globe and Mail**, Toronto, Thursday, April 30, 1981.

liaison officer for the attacking group.[31] Perdue had already advised him that:

> Your position will be Red Dog 3. You will lead the reinforcements into the police station and your men will secure the fire station. Know who will be working with and have knowledge of the fire station....Check out any potential landing by the sea and air. Check out the airport at night, any personel, etc.. See if its possible to get around 10 to 11 men in and then land the equipment. These are items I need to know.

Following John's arrest, Mary Ann McGuire replaced McQuirter as liason person in Dominica. On April 17, 1981, she sent a message to Wolfgang Droege, advising him that the mercenaries should leave New Orleans on April 27, 1981. After the arrest of the mercenaries on that date, McGuire was herself arrested in Dominica on April 28, 1981.

AFTERMATH OF THE ABORTED INVASION

1. INTERNATIONAL LAW AND MERCENARIES

The attempted invasion underscored the vulnerability of the islands to external influence and the precarious economic

---

[31] As in footnote # 9, page 4.

situation which exacerbate this vulnerability. Furthermore, it exposed the lack of a democratic tradition on the island where the deposed leader could not accept his political demise as merely part of the ebb tide and flow of the political process. Thirdly, it illustrated the comity among nations when the United States authorities alerted the Dominican government about the impending attack and took active steps to abort it.

More than this however, the incident reinforced international attention on the mercenarism phenomenon in international affairs. International attention on this phenomenon had become quite intense in the post World War II period when European countries unwilling to voluntarily relinquish their colonies, employed mercenaries to maintain their colonial empires.

In 1949 for example, the Geneva Convention condemned the use of mercenaries by Portugal against indigenous movements for independence in its colonies. In the 1950s and 60s, when wars of national liberation had become endemic in Africa, the United Nations General Assembly outlawed mercenaries and their use as a criminal act.[32] Furthermore, the assembly declared in its Resolution on *Basic Principle of the Legal Status of the Combatants Struggles against Colonial and Alien Domination and Racist Regimes*, that:

---

[32] A/Res. 2548 (XXIV).

> The use of mercenaries by colonial and racist regimes against national liberation movements struggling for their freedom and independence from the yoke of colonialism and alien domination is considered to be a criminal act and the mercenaries should accordingly be dealt with.

The conspirators involved in the aborted invasion of Dominica, if considered mercenaries, do not fit under these resolutions since they contracted with the very individuals who had ironically achieved independence for the island. However, they share affinities with their counterparts in the 1950s and 1960s in that they ultimately sought to perpetuate white rule in part of a former colonial empire. While not acting under the auspices of a former colonial power, they were driven by the same economic self-interest which motivated their counterparts in the 1950s and 1960s.

The vulnerability of island nation states and the need to prevent the recruitment of mercenaries in foreign countries resulted in a report of a United Nations Ad Hoc Committee on the drafting of and International Convention Against the Recruitment, Use, Financing and Training of Mercenaries. The Committee, including Canada, France, Germany, the United Kingdom, Italy, and the U.S., comprised 35 member states. It presented its findings to the General Assembly in 1984 in the form of a

Consolidated Negotiating Basis of a Convention against the recruitment and employment of mercenaries in 1984.[33]

The Convention prohibited the recruitment of a mercenary as a criminal offence. Activities of mercenaries including destruction of property and the attempted overthrow of a foreign government were now deemed to be criminal offences. These offences were now noted to be extraditable offences to deprive any mercenaries of safe havens for planning the overthrow of a foreign government.

This initiative by the UN represented a move to declare mercenarism an international crime. However, it is unclear what will happen where no extradition treaty exists between two countries and one country fails to adopt the Convention as the legal basis for extradition. The efficacy of the Convention depends on the willingness of the States to abide by its provisions and also the ability of the U.N. to ensure that the nations abide by the Convention. Where however, the U.N. lacks the capacity to enforce the provisions of its Convention, then the effectiveness of the proposed Convention will be severely mitigated.

Despite the laudatory efforts of the United Nations, the efficacy of international law dealing with mercenaries rests largely upon the consensus of the international community. A Convention is only binding on the individual nations if they

---

[33] United Nations General Assembly, **Official Records; Thirty-Ninth Session, Supplement no. 43** (A/39/43).

evince a willingness to be so bound by the convention. That willingness will only be forthcoming if the nations which constitute the United Nations voluntarily accept a derogation of their powers as sovereign states for the common good of preserving the integrity of the borders of the island nation states.

2. EVENTS IN DOMINICA

Revelation of the attempted coup had a sobering effect on the public, underscoring once again the vulnerability of the island to external influences. However, public knowledge of the aborted invasion raised the political ire of the population when confronted with the knowledge that one of their own had invited and in the process legitimized the attempted overthrow of the current government. Such knowledge on the other hand, was tinged with the realization that the island would have proven singularly incapable, either through legislation, or military capability, to neutralize this threat.

In 1980, the government enacted legislation which anticipated a period in the future when it would have to deal with issues related to the threat of international criminals or mercenaries. For example , the government enacted the

Extradition Act in 1980 to facilitate the extradition of fugitives from the island.

The legislation also dealt with *Extradition from Foreign States* and gave the island the flexibility of seeking the extradition of someone charged with a crime enumerated in the *Act*. Extraditable crimes included culpable homicide, manslaughter, assault causing bodily harm and kidnapping, abduction or false imprisonment. The legislation also empowered the Attorney General of Dominica to make requisition to a foreign country for the surrender of a fugitive who may be in that country.

Secondly, the government enacted the *Foreign Incursions and Mercenaries Act* in 1980, the purposes of which included a prohibition against the recruiting of mercenaries within or from Dominica. The legislation proscribed the recruitment of Dominicans or persons ordinarily resident in Dominica to engage in hostile activity outside Dominica. However, the new legislation was limited to those who have actually been in Dominica. Offences were held to be punishable by a fine of $25,000.00 or imprisonment for five years or both.

The third legislative initiative taken by the Charles government after coming into power resulted in the passage of the *Anti-Terrorist Act*. This statute gave the island's Police Forces wide authority to apprehend anyone suspected of being a terrorist. The threat of terrorism was exacerbated by the events of April

1981, and the foiled bid to overthrow the Charles government by former soldiers of the Dominica Defence Force. By 1982, Amnesty International reported that between 1980 and 1982, the island's security forces had killed 13 persons, an unprecedented number for a two year period.

Neutralizing the perceived threat by the security forces proved easier than bringing John and his fellow conspirators to justice. Their foreign counterparts had been dealt with very quickly when on May 7, 1981, they were indicted on charges of multiple conspiracy to use firearms to commit a felony, organizing an expedition against a friendly state and various weapons charges. On May 20, 1981, Perdue pleaded guilty to the charge of plotting to overthrow a government friendly to the United States. Through his testimony, the remaining nine men were found guilty of the same charges and subsequently sentenced to imprisonment for various terms.

THE CASE AGAINST JOHN

Without the benefit of Perdue's testimony, the Dominican government had more difficulty in successfully prosecuting John for his complicity in the aborted invasion. The indictment sworn against John alleged that *between September 19, 1980 and April*

29, 1981, in the Commonwealth of Dominica and elsewhere, he conspired with Michael Perdue and Wolfgang Droege and with other persons to forcefully overthrow the lawfully constituted government.

A second count charged John with allegedly *conspiring with Perdue and Droege to assault police officers at the police headquarters at Roseau, Dominica.* In October 1981, following a preliminary inquiry to determine the sufficiency of the evidence against John and his eight companions, John and three others were committed to stand trial on the offences alleged in the indictment.

The burden on the prosecution in the case of D. P. P. *v. JOHN* was twofold. It had to prove that John was a signatory to the agreement. Proving the agreement was easy, given the document found in Perdue's possession. However, absent any testimony from Perdue indicating that John signed the agreement in his presence, the Crown had to rely on expert testimony identifying the signature on the agreement as being that of the island's former Prime Minister.

In proving a) the existence of the agreement and b) the fact that John was a signatory to it, the Prosecution relied on both oral and documentary evidence. The principal oral evidence was given by Albert Maffie. Sensational cases are invariably made by controversial characters and Maffie was no exception. He had a lengthy criminal record of violence and at the time of trial was an escaped convict with an outstanding murder charge.

The Prosecution proved the existence of the agreement with the testimony of John Osburg, a United States Agent. Osburg testified that in April 1981, he had taken a briefcase from Perdue containing documents including one purportedly signed by ex-Prime Minister Patrick John.

Without the benefit of the testimony from Perdue that he had seen John sign the agreement, the Prosecution had to rely on other evidence to prove that John was a part of the plan to overthrow the government. It sought to do this by putting into evidence a passport application form allegedly signed by John to enable a handwriting expert to compare the signature on the application form and on the agreement. The expert would then determine whether the signatures were in effect one and the same. Making that determination would require the expert to be familiar with John's signature.

The Prosecution relied on Commissioner of Police for Dominica, Oliver Phillip, to give evidence that the signature on the application form was genuine. Phillip testified that as Chief Immigration Officer, he had received passport applications which would ultimately be filed in the immigration office under his control. He was then shown a passport application form dated June 29th 1979. The defence objected to the passport being put in evidence since it was not relevant and since Phillip had not personally processed the application. The trial Judge finally ruled the form to be inadmissible since Phillip had not processed it and in effect, could not testify that the form had been signed or written by John.

Further efforts by the Prosecution to rely on Phillip's testimony with respect to the application form proved futile. Philip further testified that he had witnessed John write and sign his name. Furthermore, he had received handwritten papers from John's office. The Prosecution unsuccessfully tried to prove John's handwriting by relying on further documents received by Phillip from then Assistant Superintendent of Police Blanchard. As with his prior rulings, the trial Judge rejected the Crown's attempts to rely on the documents. In doing so, he substantially weakened the State's case. In the result, he instructed the jury that the State had not made out a case against Patrick John which warranted a defence. The jury had no option but to enter a finding of not guilty.

John's acquittal was successfully appealed to the Court of Appeal of the Eastern Caribbean States. A further appeal by John to the Privy Council was dismissed. In the subsequent re-trial of the ex-Prime Minister and three of his cohorts, John was convicted and sentenced to twelve years in jail.

Aside from the successful prosecution of John, the attempted invasion had other repercussions on the island. The planned invasion crystallized the relationship between John and members of the defence force. Recognition of this relationship and the threat it posed to the island's fledgling democracy had prompted the Charles government to disband the force soon after it assumed power in 1980. Similarly shorn of the power which it once held in the 1970s, the interests of John and some members of the force, insofar that they still coveted the privileges of power, coalesced.

On December 19, 1981, members of the force led by their former commander Major Frederick Newton, simultaneously attacked the police headquarters and the state prison. The plan to neutralize the police forces and to eradicate the government appeared to have been patterned on that drawn up by Perdue with the added objective of freeing John. But for the men's inability to open the armoury and the death of one of the ex-soldiers at the prison, the plan may have been successful. Their failure to free John and to gain access to the weapons in the armoury spelt the doom of the plan. They dispersed into the night but not before killing one policeman, Constable Alexander and injuring several others including the Commissioner of Police. In a ironic twist of fate, Mary Ann McGuire had sent a cable to McQuirter the previous April with the prophetic words: *Alexander is Dead.*

In the ensuing investigation, seven former soldiers were arrested and subsequently tried for murder. The case of the seven men proceeded in June 1983 when the acquittal of John was still under appeal. The trial Judge convicted six of the seven, and sentenced all six to hang. Execution of sentence was stayed pending appeal of the conviction by the six men.

The West-Indies Court of Appeal heard the appeal on the week of September 23, 1984. The appellants argued that the confessions of the appellants, relied on by the prosecution at the trial, had not been voluntarily given and to that extent should have been held to have been inadmissible. The appellants submitted that the failure of the trial Judge to exclude such evidence constituted an error in law and the conviction should be overturned.

The Court of Appeal deferred its decision but ultimately dismissed the appeal against the convictions. There was a sense of inevitability about the final outcome of the case given the overwhelming evidence against the six men. The condemned men may have realized the futility of the appeal since one of the six went on a hunger strike in September for fear of being poisoned. In the end however, the prerogative of mercy saved the lives of five of the ex-soldiers with only their leader, Frederick Newton, being led to the gallows.

CONCLUSION

The events of 1981 robbed the island and its citizenry of its political innocence and introduced a new degree of sobriety in the political process. Formerly a matter of idle conjecture in the relaxed atmosphere of the island, politics became regarded with a new seriousness where political differences became more sharply defined. Nuances in political opinion, formerly the subject of leisurely debate, became a matter to be discussed in hushed and muted terms. Mutual suspicion and distrust permeated the society with criticism of government muted for fear of reprisals. In a community where the government employs as much as 45% of the registered work-force, the imperatives of political conformity became a powerful force defining social relations in the 1980s.

More than this however, the attempted invasion exposed the vulnerability of the island and its reliance on the comity between states for the preservation of its democratic institutions. The reliance on U.S. intelligence for information about the attempted coup initiated the process whereby the island's foreign policy would be closely allied to the United States. Reciprocally, the island would become the beneficiary of significant economic aid from Western sources. This process would become cemented in October 1983 with the U.S. invasion of Grenada, following an invitation to do so by the *Organization of Eastern Caribbean States* (O.E.C.S.) over which Charles presided as Chairperson. This alliance would transform the island into an American bulwark to keep communism at bay. In the process, Charles became a principal advocate of a U.S. trained regional security force to ensure the territorial integrity of the island states of the Caribbean.

DOMESTIC AND FOREIGN POLICY IN THE 1980s

Irving W. André

THE EAGLE HAS LANDED

On the 22nd February 1984, 20,000 persons, gathered in Roseau to celebrate the annual carnival, peered anxiously upwards at the clear blue sky. They seemed unmindful of the faint breeze which murmured through their midst or the green hills which stood impassively to the east. First a speck appeared and then another. The silence of the crowd teetered precariously, about to be broken. As the specks assumed the shapes of human beings, the crowd gasped and then cheered in unison. The roar of approval arose to a deafening crescendo as two unarmed United States soldiers, their brightly colored parachutes matching the riot of colors below, slowly landed among the carnival revellers. The display was a fitting symbol of the course charted by the Charles government following the prior events on the island and the U.S. invasion of Grenada in October 1983.

The Charles government assumed power in the 1980, after fending off challenges from the Dominica Labour Party, the Democratic Labour Party and the radical Democratic Alliance, to gain an overwhelming mandate from the electorate. The

Dominica Freedom Party won 17 of 21 seats or 51.4% of the 30,555 votes cast, compared to 16.7% for the Dominica Labour Party, 19.7% for the Democratic Labour Party and 8.4% for the Democratic Alliance.

In achieving this victory, the Freedom Party campaigned on a platform advocating the rejection of communism on the island. Prior to its political demise in May-June 1979, the Dominica Labour Party sought to establish 'democratic socialism' on the island. After the fall of the John government, a broad-based Committee for National Salvation appointed Oliver Seraphin, a former member of the John government as interim leader prior to the elections constitutionally due in 1980.

Nominally accountable to the Committee for National Salvation, Seraphin sought to consolidate himself in power through political patronage and disbursements of government funds for political purposes. He publicly disavowed being answerable to the Committee. Widespread disenchantment with all splinters of the Dominica Labour Party resulted in his eventual rejection at the polls in 1980.

With her background as an attorney, Dame Eugenia Charles, along with Edward Seaga of Jamaica, soon rose to be one main voices of continuity within the region. She became Chairman of the Organization of Eastern Caribbean States in 1981, an organization comprising the heads of government of

Dominica, St. Lucia, St. Vincent and Grenada. Originally conceived by the former prime minister of Grenada, Maurice Bishop, as an organization to foster regional solidarity against U.S. 'imperialist' influence in the region, the O.E.C.S. under Charles leadership, gave the U.S. the stamp of legitimacy to launch its invasion of Grenada. This marriage, according to Bob Woodward, in his 1987 **Veil: The Secret Wars of the CIA. 1981-1987**, came with a wonderful dowry from the United States - $100,000.00 U.S. which ultimately went to the Dominica Freedom Party.

INTERNATIONAL REACTION TO THE U.S. INVASION OF GRENADA

Reactions to the United States invasion of Grenada oscillated from condonation in the region to denunciation internationally. The October 27, 1984 issue of the Jamaica's **Daily Gleaner** observed that *we trust that this drastic step...will be swift and successful in restoring freedom and democracy to the ill-fated island.* The October 26, 1984 issue of **The Trinidad and Tobago Express** put it more bluntly by noting that *we are not overly concerned with the pious protests about territorial integrity.*

Public opinion in Latin America, where U.S. interference had been endemic since the 19th century, was not supportive of the U.S. actions. The October 26, 1984 issue of the Mexico City **El Universal** asked rhetorically, *with what sort of moral authority can the U.S. government condemn the Soviet invasion of Afghanistan if it acts the same way in its own hemisphere?* The Colombia newspaper, **El Espectador,** in its October 26, 1984 issue, warned that the *first victim in...the invasion is the principal of self-determination of nations...Grenada had become an abscess, but invasion was the indicated remedy.*

The Western Press reacted with no less indignation at the events in Grenada. The conservative Toronto **Globe and Mail** on October 26, demurred that *America has yielded to an atavistic impulse to wield its power for the purpose of reordering the world in its own image and its own liking.* In London, **The Times,** noted on the same day that the *US and its Caribbean allies are in breach of international law and the Charter of the UN.* The next day the London **Financial Times** cautioned that the *more the U.S. indulges in ill-considered unilateral actions, the more essential it is that the European allies should concert their own policies.*

The European press reacted similarly to the Grenada invasion. The liberal French Paper, **Le Monde** noted categorically on October 27, 1984 that *the reasons invoked (for* *the invasion) are unacceptable...President Reagan has seriously slipped.* Public opinion in Germany, ever sensitive to the threat of invasion from what was then the Communist bloc, found expression in an October 26, 1984 article in the **Dusseldorf Handleblatt:**

> One question is the creditability of the
> claim that the landing is the result of
> a call for assistance, Eastern actions
> of a similar nature are invariably
> cloaked in that justification.

REACTION WITHIN DOMINICA

Local reaction to the Prime Minister's trip to the United States to deliver an 'invitation' for the invasion of Grenada was quite overwhelming. On her return to the island, 15,000 people assembled in a massive show of approval. A motorcade transported her to Roseau where she addressed a huge throng of supporters. The assembled multitude hailed Charles as the island's messiah and gloried in the prominent role she had played in the invasion.

However, not everyone approved of the Prime Minister's actions. Amidst increasing accusations of encouraging U.S. interventionist policies in the region, Charles was forced to explain her government's foreign policy *vis-a vis* that of the United States. Indeed by February 1984, the initial euphoria over the intervention had significantly dissipated. As one local calypsonian sang in the 1984 calypso competition:

> rules an regulation you make in the house
> must drive us crazy;
> If I had a choice to stay with you
> 'mama" here in Dominica,
> I'll go and cut cane in Cuba.

Reference by the calypsonian to the harsh economic realities on the island best explains the Charles government's policy of courting U.S. approval in exchange for economic help. The government had come into power in 1980 with the economy facing near ruin and the island's foreign policy totally discredited. For example, in 1979, amidst accusations that Mr. Patrick John had been involved in a plan to overthrow the Barbados government, Prime Minister Adams of Barbados had taken the unprecedented step in declaring John a *persona non-grata.*

The island's economy occupied a similar abyss. In 1978, bananas accounted for 60% of the island's export earnings or $42,401,000. By 1979 however, Hurricane David devastated the banana industry, causing a 42% ($17,700,000) drop in exports. One year later, Hurricane Allen caused significant damage to the industry.

A slow process of recovery characterized the period following 1980. However, the problems facing the banana industry remained intractable to the extent that by May 1984, the industry was in an advance state of bankruptcy with a $21 million debt. Financial resources needed to reinvigorate the agriculture were diverted into non-productive activities such as the prosecution of ex-prime minister John and the ex-defence force of soldiers who had attempted to overthrow the government in December 1981.

Despite its economic problems, the Charles government took credit for a gradual improvement in the country's economic well-being. By 1984, Charles indicated that in the four years of her Party rule, unemployment in the island had decreased from 23% to 13% annually.[1] Furthermore, inflation on the island had dropped from 30% in 1980 to 4.3% in the financial year ending June 1984.

Similar successes could be pointed out in the infrastructural development on the island. By September 1984, at least four major road rehabilitations projects were in progress all financed by international lending agencies. For instance, the European Development Fund (EDF) financed the 15 km long Pond Casse- Castle Bruce Road project. Another project, the Roseau-Point Mitchell-Grandbay road received funding from the

---

[1] **The New Chronicle**, October 5, 1984, page 1.

International Development Association while the Portsmouth-Hatton Garden project was funded by the Canadian Development Agency. Finally, the United States Agency for International Development (USAID) financed the 49 km long Roseau Pond Casse- Hatton Garden Project at a cost of U.S. $7,651,424.[2]

The fact that at least two of these projects, the Roseau-Grandbay and the Roseau-Hatton Garden projects commenced in November 1983, within one month of the Grenada invasion, indicated that support for the invasion translated into financial aid from international agencies. If anything, the invasion propelled the island into the limelight and undoubtedly increased its visibility, internationally.

That visibility became evident when the island's Prime Minister appeared as a guest of the popular U.S. television programme **Sixty Minutes** on October 14, 1984, which reportedly translated into at least eight inquiries from prospective investors about investment opportunities on the island.[3]

INTERNAL STABILITY AND FOREIGN INVESTMENT

The events in Grenada forced the Charles government to direct its attention to internal stability for two reasons. Firstly,

---

[2] **The New Chronicle**, September 21, 1984, page 5.
[3] **The New Chronicle**, October 19, 1984, page 1.

there was evidence of possible linkages between the local left and communist or even terrorist countries. To expose those linkages, the government targeted the United Democratic Labour Party (UDLP) and specifically, the party's General Secretary, Rosie Douglas. In September 1984, Charles accused Cuba of seeking to engineer an opposition victory in the 1985 general election.[4]

She further accused a member of the UDLP of going to Libya to get support for elections.[5] Furthermore, in a November 1984 interview with Newsweek's Ron Moreau, Charles indicated that there were persons who were prepared to assist local dissidents with the purpose of bringing a totalitarian ideology into this part of the world.[6] When pressed about the nationality of these saboteurs, Charles indicated that they originated from Libya and North Korea.

A corollary to the Charles' government's distrust of the Cuban/Libyan influence in the island was its support for the United States policies in the region. Not surprisingly, the reelection of President Reagan in November 1984, was good for the Caribbean according to Charles, since Reagan was a leader *who knew that the Caribbean exists and who had placed some importance in the Caribbean.*[7] Charles lamented that in the democratic primaries to select a nominee for President, none of

---

[4] **The New Chronicle**, September 21, 1984, page 1.
[5] **The New Chronicle**, September 21, 1984, page 1.
[6] **The New Chronicle**, November 2, 1984, page 23.
[7] **The New Chronicle**, November 9, 1984, page 1.

the six nominees had even referred to the Caribbean in their respective campaign speeches.[8] Better known for his obsession to contain communism in the region than for his intellectual acumen, Reagan provided a receptive ear for Charles' exposure of the alleged 'communist threat' to the island. What better way of parlaying the fear of foreign intervention into the unrestricted flow of foreign investment into the island?

The desire for foreign investments formed the second justification for the government's assessment of domestic stability in the wake of the incidents in Grenada culminating in the U.S. intervention. Foreign investors require some assurance of domestic peace prior to investing in any country. In 1981, the island had to deal with a proposed invasion by foreign mercenaries and an attempted coup by ex-soldiers. The events in Grenada underscored the vulnerability of the islands to external influences; a condition exacerbated by dependence on external aid. Efforts in attracting foreign investments were futile without the potential investor having some guarantee that his investment would not be nationalized or production disrupted by attempts to overthrow the existing government.

The Charles government enacted legislation to create the ideal environment conducive to attracting foreign investment on the island. The need to safeguard against future destabilization

---

[8] **The New Chronicle**, November 9, 1984, page 1.

found expression in the passage of the *State Security Act* in 1984. One section of the *State Security Act* provided that:

> A person may arrest without warrant another person if there is immediate danger that person will commit or attempt an offence against this act… and the arrested person may be detained in proper custody to be dealt with according to law.[9]

Under the *Act,* harboring persons suspected to be spies and passing information hostile to the island were declared to be criminal offences. The statute provided a maximum penalty of fourteen years for persons convicted of espionage.

The Charles government also exacted the *Treason Act*. The *Act* imposed the death penalty on Dominicans convicted of forming an intention, manifested by an overt act, to violently overthrow the government. Any other person similarly convicted or who overtly induced an alien to invade Dominica, faced life imprisonment following conviction. Failure to report a treasonous act was declared an offence punishable by a fine or imprisonment. Finally, anyone charged under the *Treason Act* was automatically imprisoned, pending the outcome of the trial.

The Dominica Labour Party condemned the new legislation *as a threat to the existence of genuine democratic opposition in the state and a breach of the constitutional rights of*

---

[9] **The New Chronicle**, February 17, 1984.

citizens.[10] One parliamentary representative described the legislation as draconian in nature and proof that the party in power was rapidly preparing for 'some kind of war'. While the government viewed the legislation as necessary safeguards for preserving parliamentary democracy in the island, the opposition criticized the legislation as evidence of the *'total militarization of this beautiful island of ours.*[11]

Public reaction to the legislation was mixed at best. The widespread support enjoyed by the Freedom Party mitigated sustained opposition to the controversial legislation. Indeed a large section of the population seem to have taken a vicarious pleasure in the spectacle of their lady Prime Minister, the first in the Caribbean, assume a leadership role in the October intervention. In March 1984, Charles announced to a jubilant public that she'd been invited to participate in the annual convention of the United States Democratic Party, an invitation she subsequently declined.[12] Far from being perturbed at the government's affinities with the US, a significant section of the public prided itself in this flirtation with its powerful northern neighbour.

This support however, did not manifest itself among all members of the public. To the more discerning eye, there was

---

[10] As in footnote #6.
[11] As in footnote #6.
[12] **The New Chronicle**, March 30, 1984, page 1.

something of the overkill about the new legislation. One regular columnist in the weekly newspaper, **The New Chronicle**, noted that:

> The Freedom Party could...immortalize itself by looking beyond the timely but unrefined bits of State Security legislation enacted this week towards identifying elsewhere a lasting solution to the problem of social unrest that leads to the tendency for antistate activities.[13]

Others wondered whether the legislation would not simply provide the island's police force with a licence for making arbitrary arrests and detention. Indeed, passage of the new legislation coincided with allegations of police torture and brutality in a north-eastern village on the island. Not only did these developments bring into focus the nature of the US presence on the island but also the extent of the government's ties with the Reagan administration.

DOMINICA AND THE UNITED STATES

In the immediate aftermath of the Grenada intervention, the US established military teams in Antigua, Barbados, St. Vincent, St. Lucia and Dominica to train the local military or para-military forces on the island.

---

[13] **The New Chronicle**, February 24, 1984, page 4.

In February 1984, Barbados proposed the establishment of a 1500 member force stationed on that island, comprised of personnel from each island to be funded at an annual cost of $20 million. In principle, the U.S. supported the establishment of a military presence in the region but balked at the cost suggested by the Barbados plan. The islands for the most part could not make any significant financial contributions to force and responsibility would inevitably fall on the U.S. for upkeep of the force.

Instead, the U.S. favoured a plan to provide mobile training teams to train special Service Units in each member island, comprised of 40-80 members from local police or security forces. The training would focus on acquainting the Service Units with SWAT like tactics to facilitate quick and effective response to any indigenous uprising on the respective island.

The assumption underlying this approach, as opposed to a standing army in one island, was that the threat to the island democracies originated within each island and not from any foreign expeditionary force. Furthermore, these training units would not attract adverse international reaction about the U.S. establishing a military presence in the region. They would also be less costly than financing a standing army in any one Caribbean island. Finally, the Service Units enabled the United States to establish hands on contact with the security forces of each island

and to assess their ability to neutralize any indigenous threat to the security of the island.

In addition to this initiative, each island received a thirty-two ton armed patrol boat from the US to help patrol the seas which surround them. Unlike the other islands, Dominica possessed no military force and hence relied on the local police force for the preservation of stability within the island. This role was greatly facilitated by the $7.4 m allocated by the US to provide military assistance to the Eastern Caribbean in 1984; a sum subsequently increased by $15m in the aftermath of the Grenada invasion.[77] Dependent on the local police to guarantee its tenure in office, the government, according to some, seemed inclined to overlook any excesses committed by the police in maintaining law and order.[14]

The threat of an encroaching police state however, did not unduly alarm the public when the government enacted the new legislation. Of much greater concern was the fear that this increased militarization would result at the expense of increased financial assistance to the island's beleaguered economy. The concern appeared to have been that the U.S. had no interest in the welfare of the people but only in promoting its regional interests.

---

[77] **Latin America Regional Reports**, December 9, 1983.
[14] The police slaying of a youth after an abortive coup attempt in 1981 remains unsolved.

This concern underlined a 1984 article entitled *After Grenada...our Own Realities* in **The New Chronicle.** The article pointed out the glaring anomaly between the region's economic needs and the sum of $10m allocated to the Caribbean under President Reagan's Caribbean Basin Initiative (CBI). Indeed a 1981 Caricom Study indicated that Caribbean countries which came under the CBI required $4.7 billion in external financing in the five year period 1982-1986. The article proceeded to caution that the US should not make it a habit *to come in with guns and play Saviour, waving the flag and spreading the magic of baked beans and Campbell soup, in clear instances where US negligence positively contributed to the crisis.* The writer expressed the view that the approval granted by the O.E.C.S. to the US implicitly contained an element of reciprocity. He noted that:

> After innocently providing Mr. Regan with
> a reason for going to Grenada to find out
> why a US intervention in the Spice Isle
> (Grenada) was in fact necessary, one would
> hate to believe that we don't deserve the
> suggested current level of US aid to that
> 'rescued' OECS member, or maybe we need a war before
> the funds start flowing.[15]

The perceived paucity of US monetary aid to Dominica vis-a-vas that to Grenada mellowed the US connection

---

[15] **The New Chronicle**, February 12, 1984, page 4.

significantly. In April 1984, the Reagan administration sought an additional $40m in aid to Grenada, bringing the total US aid to the island since the October invasion to $72.2m.[16] The magnitude of this aid can be appreciated when compared to the fact that Grenada's G.N.P. in 1981 was $100m. Furthermore, total US assistance to Grenada between October 1983 and April 1984 amounted to more than seven times that allocated to the entire Eastern Caribbean Basin Initiative

FOREIGN AID AND ECONOMIC 'PROGRESS' IN DOMINICA

The Charles government adopted a model of economic development originally devised by economist, Sir W. Arthur Lewis, in his 1951 booklet 'Industrialization of the West Indies. Later referred to as the *Lewis strategy of 'industrialization by invitation'*, the strategy called for the wooing of foreign investors as the main catalyst for industrial development in the region.

The Lewis model of development had two other components. Lewis reasoned that the region's main asset was a large supply of cheap indigenous labour. If the region could attract labour intensive industries, then given the low cost of labour, such industries could easily complete with their

---

[16] **The Washington Post**, Washington, D.C., Friday April 13, 1984, page A18.

metropolitan markets. The industries established in the region would necessarily be export oriented since, according to Lewis, the domestic market was too small to support more than a fraction of the total projected output of the region.

Secondly, Lewis proposed that fiscal exemptions and other financial incentives would be required to entice foreign companies to the region. In the post World War II period, several Caribbean Countries enacted legislation specially designed to attract foreign investment as contemplated by the Lewis model.[17] The attractiveness of the model resulted in part from the continuation in power of elites *weaned in the post colonial era on the radical –as it was- prescriptions of the model and to whom there might seem to be no alternative...*[18] In the 1970s, the government of Patrick John announced its intentions to enact 'incentives legislation' to attract labour intensive industries to the island. The Charles government continued this policy in the

---

[17] See Terrance Farrell, "Arthur Lewis and the Case for Caribbean Industrialization", **Social and Economic Studies**, V.29, #4 December 1980, page 52 and page 59.
Frank Long, "Industrialization and the Role of Industrial Development Corporations in a Caribbean Economy: A Study of Barbados 1960-1980. **Inter-American Economic Affairs**, v.37 (1983) No.3, page 33.
Norman Girvan and Owen Jefferson eds. **Readings in the Political Economy of the Caribbean**. (1971) pages 109-152.
Stacey H. Widdicombe, Jr., **The Performance of Industrial Development Corporations** (New York: Praeger Publishers, 1972).

[18] E.B.A. St. Cyr, "On Lewis' Theory of Growth and Development", **Social and Economic Studies**, 1980, v.29, no.4, page 16.

1980s at a time when the government enjoyed a warm relationship with the U.S. and its traditional Western allies.

Since taking office in 1980, the government therefore sought to entice foreign investors to set up shop on the island. It pursued a policy of attracting labour intensive industries to the island.[19] To facilitate foreign investment, the government established an Industrial Development Corporation. Tax holidays, cheap labour factory shells, duty free importation of equipment and a favourable political climate represented the prime inducements offered to foreign capital. The *pull* factors combined with the *push* factors in the C.B.I. Programme served as the stimuli to initiate economic development in the island.

To facilitate the speedy establishment of factories, the government established the Industrial Estates Programme pursuant to an agreement with the Organization of Petroleum Exporting Countries (OPEC). The programme involved the construction of a number of industrial sheds at Canefield comprising over 110,000 square feet of space for foreign companies. By October 1984, eight sheds had already been built with another under construction. The government further created the Dominica Industrial Development Corporation (IDC) which duties included courting potential foreign investors to the island.

---

[19] For a critical assessment see Gordon K. Lewis **Puerto Rico**, (New York: Harper and Row Publishers, 1963), p.p. 113-159.

The Charles government did not confine its search for foreign investors to traditional Western sources. In May 1983, Charles established diplomatic relations with the Republic of China on Taiwan. In October of the same year, a six man investment delegation from Taiwan visited the island to study the investment environment and to identify potential projects for investment. At the same time, the government signed a bi-lateral agreement with West Germany in September 1984, enabling Dominica to benefit from the West German Government's initiatives to induce its nationals to invest in Dominica.

By September 1983, the strategy had experienced some success. Twelve foreign firms and 26 local ones received approval for their operations on the island. In 1982/83, Dominica experienced a 3.3% rate of economic growth while manufacturing output grew by 9.6%. Between 1980 and 1984, unemployment had been reduced from 23% to 15% while inflation had reportedly dropped form 30% to 4.3%.

The government achieved similar success in obtaining funding for infrastructural development. In January 1984, the European Development Fund approved a $2.2m grant for improvement of a road in the eastern part of the island.[20] Another road project, linking the island's capital, Roseau, to Hatton Garden, became the main repository of funding from the United

---

[20] **The New Chronicle**, October 2, 1983, p.2.

States Agency for International Development, USAID. The financial aid from the United States partly fulfilled those elements of reciprocity implicit in the Dominica government's support of the Grenada invasion of 1983.

Significantly, the Roseau-Hatton Garden road project was officially launched by Prime Minister Charles and US Ambassador to the Eastern Caribbean, Milan Bish. On completion it would cost an estimated $43.5m, $9.3m of which would be contributed by the USAID. The grant reflected the mutually beneficial collusion between the US and Dominica. At the ground breaking ceremony, U.S. Ambassador Bish noted that the project was:

> The first major bilateral USAID capital project authorized for the Eastern Caribbean... and that the agreement was conceived in the spirit of President Reagan's Caribbean Basin initiative...[21]

If financial aid to Dominica, made the U.S. military actions in Grenada more palatable to Dominicans, it also provided consulting and construction jobs for U.S. companies on the island. For example, the firm of Louis Berger International provided the initial consulting services while the 30.5 mile road rehabilitation programme was assigned to US construction firm, Nello L. Teer.

---

[21] **The New Chronicle**, February 3, 1984, page 9.

FREE ENTERPRISE AND NATIONAL DEVELOPMENT

However, infrastructual development could not materialize solely as the result of external aid. From the standpoint of the Prime Minister, providing investment opportunities for foreign companies did not preclude promoting indigenous development based on the island's own natural resources. While the government fostered free enterprise, it tended to support those firms which sought to utilize local resources in their operations. Where a conflict arose between the policies of certain foreign companies and the perceived interests of the island, the Charles government infrequently responded in a manner contrary to its widely known free enterprise predilections.

This explains the government's move in 1984 to gain control of the local banana industry; a move facilitated by a $4.7m E.C. grant from the USAID. Coupled with this, the government enacted the Banana Marketing Corporation and the Banana Growers Association Acts both of which guaranteed the authorities unprecedented control over the banana industry.

Another case in point relates to the nationalization of the Dominica electricity services. Hitherto, these services had been provided by the Commonwealth Development Corporation, a multinational company operating out of the United Kingdom. Much of its plant and operations had been severely damaged in

1979 by Hurricane David. In the post –1980 period, the company embarked on an extensive expansion programme to improve its services to the public. The problem with government arose over the Corporation's intention to install comparatively low capital diesel plants which ultimately would have increased dependence on fluctuating oil prices. Instead, the local authorities proposed establishing hydro-electric plants which not only would reduce dependence on external fuel supplies but also energy costs to the local consumer. The divergence of views led to the government's decision to acquire a fifty-one percent interest in the company.

That this action illustrates the administration's desire to at least maintain some semblance of autonomy in managing and overseeing the island's development is pretty obvious. While a general desire to attract foreign investors prevailed in official circles, the authorities manifested a singular reluctance to completely accede to the dictates of foreign investors. It is a precarious position; that of steering an enlightened course between eternal dependence in virtually all matters relating to development and the promotion of local welfare and interests. The essence of statecraft in this context is how best to prevent the mask of acquiescence to foreign interests from becoming functionally autonomous to the detriment of the national interest.

SATTELITE OF THE U.S.?

Ostensibly, the island panders to US policy dictates in the region. That seemed to have been the case but only insofar as it served the island's interests. Dismissing the island's leadership as being merely a rubber-stamp for U.S. interventionist excursions in the region is too simplistic an explanation of the policies of the Charles government. Such a view is predicated on the erroneous assumptions that the desire for the U.S. aid is synonymous with a desire to support the U.S. foreign policies in the region and elsewhere.

The voting record for Dominica at the United Nations General Assembly however, does not bear out that assumption. Two elements are identifiable in the island's contribution to the deliberations of the UN General Assembly in this period (see following chart). In the first place, the voting record of both nationals manifests a general dissimilarity. Secondly, Dominica maintained a high level of absenteeism, almost 50% of the sample. It may well be that non-participation in the U.N.'s voting process reflected the island's lack of a UN representative resident in the US. On the other hand, it might be illustrative of the government's reluctance to assume a rigid position on issues which might unduly alienate it from those best in a position to proffer financial aid in the future.

TABLE

Comparison of the Voting Record of Dominica and the US During the Thirty –Eight session of the United Nations General Assembly.[22]
September....20 December, 1983.

Resolutions	**Dominica**	**US**
Commending Foreign Intervention in Grenada	no	no
Condemning interventions in Afghanistan	yes	yes
Affirming Rights of Palestinian People	absent	no
Poor Record of Human Rights and Freedom in Chile	abstention	no
Poor Record of Human Rights and Freedom in El Salvador	abstention	no
Poor Record of Human Rights and Freedoms in Guatemala	abstention	no

---

[22] **The New Chronicle**, January 27, 1984, Page 3.

Resolutions	Dominica	US
Banning Chemical and Bacteriological Warfare	yes	no
Implementation of the Declaration on the Granting of Independence *To Colonial Countries and People*	*yes*	*no*
Support for Swapo in Namibia	absent	no
Condemning South Africa's new constitution	absent	abstention
Invoking Governmental Action against Apartheid	absent	no
Proposing Support for South Africa's Liberation Movements	absent	no
Condemning South Africa's Raids on Angola, Mozambique And Lesotho	absent	no

Notes
1. 'no' implies a vote against the resolution.
2. 'yes' implies a vote in favor of the resolution.
3. 'absent' represents the failure to be present when the vote was taken.

4. 'abstention' represents the failure to vote on a particular resolution.

Source   *United Nations:* **Resolutions and Decisions Adopted By the General Assembly During the First Part of Its Thirty- Eight Session**. Press Released GA/6939 (N.Y., N.Y.: United Nations Department of Public Information Press Sections, 1984).

Only in the resolutions on intervention in Afghanistan and Grenada did the votes of the two countries coincide. While Dominica abstained on the issue of Human Rights in El Salvador, Guatemala and Chile, the US opposed the resolutions. In all the resolutions repudiating Israel's right to occupation of the Left Bank; its military excursion into Lebanon and hegemony over Jerusalem, Dominica absented itself while the US either abstained or voted against the resolutions.[23] The voting record on chemical warfare manifests a similar divergence. Hardly the case of a proxy nation.

However, it is very likely that absenteeism and abstention have become the tools of the small island state, in this case Dominica, to minimize conflict with the US. Certainly in this instance, the maxim 'Don't bite the hand that feeds you' holds true. Occasionally, the island asserted its identification with 'Third World' solidarity, as in the case of the vote on the

---

[23] **United Nations**, pp. 86-88.

dissemination of information on colonization. On more controversial issues such as South Africa, the island maintained a discreet aloofness. The economic realities facing the island probably mitigated uninhibited participation in the UN General Assembly. Hence non-participation represents another aspect of the precarious balance between independence and dependence on the US..

To be sure, the balance appeared to be under siege by the dictates of US security considerations in the region. But it would be wrong to conclude that, the Dominica government's final capitulation to those imperatives is inevitable. The government undoubtedly realizes that in order to rationalize the use of scant resources and provisions of services, a need exits to institute action at variance with its avowed free-enterprise policies. In the future, the government would be forced to face the hiatus between the realization of profit and its eventual distribution. Likewise, the increased militarization would be forced to give way to economic aid to the island's ailing economy.

The price of this aid has not been slavish support of US positions on issues in the United Nations General Assembly. However absenteeism and abstention, both tantamount to a form of diplomatic paralysis, seem to be cost of economic aid from the US. It would be interesting to assess the particular configurations of the island's UN participation in the future. One thing remains certain though. Caught in the thicket of international diplomacy, the island's leadership will find it increasingly difficult to achieve a pristine policy of independence in light of its economic dependence on traditional Western Countries.

CONTINUITIES INTO THE NEW MILLENNIUM

Successive Dominican governments have tried to foster economic growth by attracting foreign investment and assistance from friendly governments. In the early 1990s, the Charles government announced the Guinness Project, a massive development project dated for Point Round in the north. This was followed by the economic citizenship programme and its offshoot, the five star Layou River Hotel Project.

Both of these projects have foundered. Declining banana production and revenues, the ending the Cold War and the reduction of U.S. aid as the fear of communism subsided, forced Dame Eugenia Charles to forge relationships outside its traditional sources for revenue. Her anti-Cuba rhetoric of the 1980s dissipated under the continued advent of scholarships from Cuba. The government solicited aid from the Republic of China on Taiwan, instituted an Economic Citizenship Programme and actively pursued the goals of regional integration.

Following its 1995 electoral victory, the UWP pursued some of these goals even more vigorously to an extent which would ultimately prove detrimental to the island's economic well being. The island's citizenship would become reduced to a chattel, its financial institutions an avenue for money laundering and its investment policy nothing more than an undignified declaration, **Open Sesame**. The inevitable fallout of these polices, widespread allegations of corruption, led to the demise of the UWP government by January 2000.

The ascension of the now deceased Roosevelt Douglas in 2000, resulted in a discernible shift in efforts to garner assistance to the island. Douglas wooed the Dominican communities in England, United States and Canada, African Americans, the European community, Libya and Cuba for assistance. In foreign policy, he eschewed his ideological proclivities and sought an accommodation with traditional Western sources and a closer political identification with the European Union. He also supported Japan's right to whaling, much to the chagrin of some within his own party

Douglas's untimely demise significantly reduced the likelihood that these initiatives will come to fruition. The events of September 11, 2001, significantly reduced air travel, and the advent of a new anti- terrorism campaign waged by the United

States, made closer relations with Libya and Cuba politically unwise.

In a world dictated by the imperatives of anti-terrorism, globalization and the proliferation of trading enclaves, the island will have to rely increasingly on its own resources to provide a modest standard of living for Dominicans. The steps required will include a rationalization of laws and tariffs restricting free movement of goods and persons in the Caribbean and a greater effort to persuade Dominicans in the Diaspora to become stakeholders on the island. Grandiose schemes generated by foreign investors, such as the recently resuscitated Layou River Hotel Project, will not bring economic salvation to the island, and it is only the concerted efforts of Dominicans, at home and abroad, which will bring meaningful change in the fortunes of the island.

CREATIVE WRITING AND THE FORGING OF A DOMINICAN IDENTITY

Irving André

The European contact with the island on November 03, 1493, set the stage for the eventual settlement of Europeans and the eventual displacement of the island's first settlers, the Caribs. With the advent of Columbus, the island was irretrievably drawn into the vortex of European expansion and until 1763, when it irrevocably became a British Colony, its destiny would be moulded first by the Spanish and then by French colonists.

Columbus's arrival did not lead to the establishment of any permanent Spanish presence on the island. In the sixteenth century, Spanish ships would drop anchor at Dominica for supplies and occasional trade with the Caribs but showed no inclination to blunder into the island's interior.

It was the advent of the French in the sixteenth and seventeenth centuries which led to the description of the island in the literature of the period. French priests and friars were the vanguard of French expansionism and they were able to clothe the French's desire for new territories in the habit of their proselytizing activities. Early priests such as Fathers du Tertre and Breton wrote a Carib dictionary and translated part of the Bible into the Carib language.

The focus of these Dominican priests established the mythology of Dominica as an alien forboding place which harboured warlike cannibals. One such priest, de Rochfort, wrote in 1658, that the Caribs were not only cannibals but with great delicacy, differentiated between the Europeans. Not surprisingly, they regarded the French as the tastiest, the English a little less tasty, the Dutch did not please their palates while the hated Spanish was totally unedible. "Thank God, they know not seasoning", one Spaniard is noted to have said.

Another priest, Pierre Labat demurred. The Caribs did not have any inherent cannibalistic traits, he opined. Their unpleasant tendency to feast on other humans was only done in the ecstasy of military triumph; an appeasement of the Gods of War. They did not dine on their female captives and indeed allowed them to retain their own cultures.

One aspect of the Carib people however, was not capable of exaggeration by these early colonists. A few hardy French settlers, particularly from Nantes, La Rochelle, Bordeaux and the Loire Valley, moved to Dominica from Martinique and Guadeloupe and by 1763, some 349 had settled on the island. There they engaged in growing crops such as tobacco, coffee, cotton and spices and established a brief trade with their counterparts in Martinique and Guadeloupe.

The Caribs however, were not enamored by the sedentary lives established by these French colonists. Between 1640 and 1681, they twice laid siege to the English colony in Antigua, slaughtered all the French colonists on Marie Galante, and destroyed the English settlement on Barbuda. In 1659, the English and French agreed to leave the island alone while in 1731, they agreed to treat the island as neutral. When both repudiated the agreement, they signed the Treaty of Aix to Chapelle in October 1748, ostensibly to establish the neutrality of the island and preserve the sovereignty of the Caribs.

Neutrality however, was antithetical to the imperatives of colonial aggrandizement. The French increased their numbers in areas such as Vielle Case and Roseau, particularly after the British capture of Guadeloupe in 1759. The Caribs were pushed further into the near impenetrable interior and as the Europeans established themselves on the island, the Caribs miraculously lost their cannibalistic proclivities.

ADVENT OF THE BRITISH

By 1763, the Treaty of Paris placed Dominica into the hands of the British. About 1700 white persons, some 5800 slaves and about 1000 Caribs resided on the island. To encourage settlement, land previously occupied by French settlers were auctioned off and henceforth, as a number of English settlers migrated to the island where, they established sugar plantations. Continuous warfare between the English and French, first in 1778 and then between 1793 and 1815, led to the departure of large numbers of English settlers and following the French Revolution, the arrival of 5,000-6,000 Frenchmen on the island.

The advent of slave labour on Dominica became the focus of the imagination of colonial observers. Thomas Atwood's 1791, **The History of the Island of Dominica**, purports "to give an account of the civil government...and manners of the different inhabitants of Dominica". Not surprisingly, the slaves are described as little more than savages who of necessity, must be enslaved to ensure their upliftment. He therefore notes that:

> Negroes are in general much addicted to drunknennefs, thievery, incontinency, and idlenefs. The first vice very few of them will retain from when they can get liquor, and in their fits of this kind, many of them are very mifchievous.

Furthermore, that the negroes "diflike of labour is fo great, ... it is fometimes abfolute by neceffory to have recoufe to ensfures that appear cruel, in order to oblige them to labour."

These two themes-that of the forboding landscape and later the subhuman slaves whose traits mandated violence for them to be kept in abeyance, permeate much of the early colonial writing on Dominica. In the early nineteenth century however, a transformation occurred. The abolition of the slave trade in 1807 and the advent of the movement for the Emancipation of Slavery caused a discernible shift in the perception of the island. The growth of the Abolition Movement was the handmaid of the movement for free trade and this marriage happily transformed the indolent African slave into a most industrious worker.

Nowhere is that more evident, than in the published letters of American bishop Joseph John Gurney in his 1840 book, **A Winter in the West-Indies**. Gurney's letters were written to a Southern slaveholder, Henry Clay of Kentucky. Gurney described his strange courtship of Clay in the following manner:

> Notwithstanding the conspicuous part which that statesman has of late years taken in defence of the slavery of the United States, we had abundant proof, that his mind is not steeled against a lively feeling of interest in the cause of emancipation, and we have a strong hope, that the practical views developed in the present volume will ere long be embraced by him...

What "practical views" did Gurney propose to be embraced by Clay of Kentucky? It is this. Free labour was cheaper than coerced labour and more productive. Such labour would lead to an increase in the two predominant West Indies crops - sugar and coffee. "These and other articles will be produced by free labor, both in the West and East Indies-not to mention Africa itself in such abundance and at so reasonable a price, that similar slave grown produce will be driven from every market, even without the end of prohibitory prices...."

What Gurney was therefore proposing was a marriage between Mammon and Manumission. The anticipated profits from this union fuelled his imagination as nothing else and it is this motivation which explains his account of the island.

Gurney's therefore marvels at "the desire of the negroes of Dominica for education." The former slaves, he intones, despite speaking " a barbarous French patois" are nevertheless "orderly, quite and peaceable." Furthermore, that "the negro loves his home, humble though it be, and has no wish to exchange it for a wild life upon the mountains."

He was no less enthralled by the island's beauty. He waxed poetic on beholding the prodigality of nature at Watten Waven:

> Before us was an amphitheatre of mountains, of romantic shapes and covered with foliage, and at their feet, an uncultivated often of extreme luxuriance. The scene was lovely beyond description...

Exasperated with the banality of prose, he resorted to verse to describe the island:

> Twas on the Christian's day of rest,
> While men on shore their faith confessed
> In many a song of praise;

The gallant knight of the western star
Described thy headlands from afar,
And traced thy shadowy bays.

Clouds and mists were over thee flung,
And the rainbow on thy rock was hung,
And hauled the wind thy vales among,
And the mountain torrents roared;
But soon thou wast mounted o'er with smiles,
When the sunbeam broke thos' thy deep defiles,
And s'er the lovelist of the isles,
Beauty and grace were poured....

The parent of three hundred rill,
Asleep amidst thy ravined hills,
A fathomless lake was found;
And high around thy mountains rose,
But never wore the wreath of snows,
For they were forest crowned....

Then hail, the holy, happy day,
When all their chains were cast away
And freedom spread her general sway
O'er the islands of the west-
Thy verdant hills shall flow with peace,
Thy vales with plenty shall increase,
Thy notes of discord all shall cease,
Fair Dominique that blest.

One gets the feeling that Bishop Gurney, with his focus on free trade, doth protest too much methinks. But other visitors to the island, without the agenda of Gurney, no less resorted to poetry to describe the island. Lucy Larcom, another visitor at the turn of the twentieth century wrote:

> Dominica's fire-cleft summits
> Rose from bluest of blue oceans;
> Dominica's palms and plaintains
> Fuel the trade wind' mighty motions;
> Swaying with impetuous stress,
> The West-Indian wilderness.....

The most famous visitor of the nineteenth century however, was Anthony Froude whose observations were published in his 1888, **The English in the West Indies**. The ostensible purpose was to acquaint himself with the conditions of the West-Indies, but his central argument was clear. The English had neglected the West Indies. They had been derelict in their responsibilities to their Caribbean possessions and had to jettison all misguided notions of self government and assume, as in India, direct control of their West –Indian possessions.

The magnitude of imperial neglect, according to Froude, was nowhere more evident than in Dominica. He was unrestrained in use of language in portraying the grandeau of the island:

> Here was all this profusion of nature, lavish beyond all examples, and the enterprising youth of England were neglecting a colony which might yield them beyond the treasures of the old sugar plantations , going to Florida, to Texas, to South America,. bearing Dominica, which might be the

> garden of the world, a precious emerald set in the ring of their own Antilles, enriched by the sacred memories of glorious English achievements, as if such a place had no existence.

Oh! The pity of it!, Froude lamented:

> It was startling to see such insolent beauty displaying itself indifferently in the heart of the wilderness with no human eye to look at it unless of some passing black or wandering Caribs.

Where are thou, O true Englishman?, he implored:

> The poor black was a faithful servant as long as he was a slave. As a freeman he is conscious of his inferiority at the bottom of his heart, and would attach himself to a
> notional white employer with at least as much fidelity as a spaniel.

Any Englishman would suffice to preserve the English presence on the island, he stated, "even a Sancho Panza would do". With the help of a "few intelligent persons who understand the cultivation of soils and the management of men, in half a score of years, Dominica would be the brightest gem of the Antilles".

Froude invokes Homer's **Odyssey**, to magnify the imperial neglect of the island:

> Woman! no mortal o'er the widespread earth
> Can find a fault in thee; thy good report,

Doth reach the widespread heaven, as of some prince
Who, in the likeness of a god, doth rule
O'er subjects stout of heart and strong of hand;
And men speak greatly of him, and his land
Bears wheat and rye, his orchard bend with fruit,
His flocks breed surely, the sea yields her fish,
Because he guides his folk with wisdom...

THE TWENTIETH CENTURY

Dominica's 'good report', did not quite reach heaven, as Froude envisioned, but it nevertheless reached the attention of a number of Americans and Englishmen in the twentieth century. The author has chronicled the persons who were attracted to the island in the book, **Distant Voices**. For myriad reasons, including a desire for solitude, an antidote to the frenzy of cosmopolitan life, financial adversity and a Wordsworthan desire to be closer to nature, many settled on the island and led a tranquil and serene life. Some like Andrew Green, John Archbold, John Knowlton and the English painter Stephen Hawies, established "model planations" where they cultivated exotic plants and wildlife. Others, like Elma Napier and her compatriot, Hawies, engaged in creative activity and in the case of Napier, wrote books about the island. The titles of her two books, **Duets in Discord and Flying**

Fish Whispered, are unavailable while that of Stephen Hawies, the 1968 **Mount Joy**, is still available in print.

The presence of these persons on the island, engaged in their individual pursuits, fostered the reputation that Dominica was inhabited by a collection of "eccentric misfits." This reputation became an attraction to visitors who sought out the island during their travels. Indeed, the best impression of the island has been left by American writer Alec Waugh who visited the island periodically in the first half of the twentieth century.

In a 1929 story written, entitled "The Judge", Waugh highlights the excruciating loneliness of a retired judge who pined for civilized company at his timbered bungalow near Colihaut. In a 1938 story entitled "The Beachcomber", he focused on another eccentric misfit, one Max Weston, who had squandered his fortune after being misdiagnosed. Given one year to live, he spent his fortune on "a succession of house parties." When he had finally spent his fortune, he suddenly got well again. His doctors had been wrong. He was not stricken with a fatal disease. Dominica became his refuge.

In Waugh's 1948 "Typical Dominica," he highlights the sense of despondency which accompanied every effort to develop the island. Natural disasters such as hurricanes, mismanagement, an incompleted Imperial Road. The sense of futility which pervaded any effort or attempt at productive activity on the island.

The isolation. The despair. The eccentric things which happened in Dominica. Waugh commented that three of the expatriates he met on this trip committed suicide.

Waugh's main contribution to the island is his novel, **The Fatal Gift**. It is the story of Raymond Peronne, the debonair second son of an English aristocrat who chooses the island over his ancestral home.

His decision takes a heavy toll on the family. His wife returns to England and divorces Raymond who falls in love with a sixteen year old local beauty. A local character places a spell on him preventing him from ever leaving the island. Undaunted, he lives serenely on his island estate, very much like his real life counterparts.

Waugh's novel highlights a theme which emerges in the accounts of expatriate life on the island. The physical and social isolation, the umbilical ties to England and the perennial fear of interaction with the local population confined the whites to a social reservation.

Two incidents in the novel illustrate this. Raymond's wife, before boredom sent her packing to England, complained about "the same people in the club in January as…in June, the same talk; gossip about G.H, about AG's capacity or incapacity for rum." On another occasion, she allows her daughter to run carnival. To her horror, her daughter ends up in a deserted alley with a local masquerader. "I should have been on my guard", she uttered. "Thank God we've been warned in time, and we can get her back to a cold climate".

THE GENESIS OF AN INDIGENOUS LITERATURE

Raymond wife's actions in ferreting her daughter out of Dominica is a metaphor for the separation of the races in Dominica during the early twentieth century. The local characters were as invisible in the expatriate literature as they were at the Dominica Club during the period.

And yet by the 1920s, there was an incipient awakening of the consciousness of Dominicans. In the U.S. , the Harlem Renaissance had generated a flowering of literature not only by African Americans but by West Indian writers such as Claude MacKay and Eric Walrond. Marcus Garvey had rejected the premise of W.E.B. Dubois that salvation of the black race rested on the shoulders of the "talented tenth" and had initiated a mass movement with millions of adherents in the United States, England and the Caribbean.

Within Dominica, Garveyism battled ferociously with the proponents of Afrosaxonism, or those locals who advocated close ties with the mother country. J. R. Ralph Casimir, educator, book binder, lawclerk and poet, challenged this thesis head on and in the process caused a **Bildungsroman**, or growth in consciousness on the island.

Fired by C.E.A. Rawle for his Garveyite philosophy, Casimir established a Dominica chapter of Garvey's Universal Negroes Improvement Association (UNIA) in 1920 and soon branches of UNIA had sprung up in Pointe Michel, Soufriere, Grandbay and Marigot.

Garveyism had an ameliorating effect on indigenous creative activity on the island. At UNIA's inaugural meeting on August 1, 1920, hundreds of Dominicans at the Liberty Hall in Roseau listened to songs, farces and recitations. A similar function in Soufriere on August 31, 1920 featured a speech by C. Morancie, known as the patois orator.

Casimir initiated a literary society on the island which was a forerunner of many similar organizations in later decades. Noted Dominican educators, such as Henckell Christian, played significant roles in the Literacy Club Movement in the 1930s. This proliferation of literary clubs coincided with the establishment of over 28 village councils, the growth of trade unionism primarily through the efforts of Emmanuel LoBlack, and the development of grass roots political awareness culminating in the founding of the Dominica Labour Party in 1956. In 1937, Ralph Casimir arranged the visit of Marcus

Garvey to the island and his October address to a huge gathering at the Coronation Hall.

Between 1940 and 1948, Casimir edited four volumes of poetry. The poems were written by a disparate set of individuals including educators Roy Dublin, Albert Lawrence and Alexander Nicolas, agriculturist Edward Leblanc, retired Dr. Daniel Thaly and then medical student Philip Griffin. The groundwork for the interest in the written word was laid in the 1920s and 1930s. In 1941, a gala literary festival was held in Grandbay featuring representatives from 12 literary clubs from villages all over the island.

This writing was different from that written about the island by colonial apologists or by any *eccentric misfit*. The beauty of the island was described not as a means to highlight imperial neglect. The local population was portrayed not as a propagandist ploy to incorporate the island into some mercantile arrangement. It was art for the island's sake, and it marked the genesis of a Dominican aesthetic in creative writing:

In a poem, **Sunrise In The Tropics,** Cynthia M. Leblanc writes:

>Struggling o'er the hill-tops
>To bathe the earth in splendour
>Beams the golden sun,
>Caressingly sweet in grandeur,
>Through misty haze and palms entune;
>Sweet-smelling flow'rs and herbs are thine

To smile on...

In a poem, **Be Real**, Rupert Casimer scolds his AfroSaxon contemporaries:

> West Indians prate about the winter's snow
> And speak of snowballs, skates and skis
> That people ride in pictures they have seen.
>
> You sing of foreign stuff, of lovely scenes
> You cannot lead me to, but only heard about.
> You do not praise your better beauty spots,
> Your friendly clime, and hospitable lands...

Daniel Thaly sings the beauty of the island in **Les Iles**:

> Qui dera les charmes des iles,
> Oasis que borde d'azur
> Le disert des andes mobiles?
> Qui chantera leur soleil pur?...
>
> Ile ardente du Pacifique
> Stevensornne t'ame pas mieux
> Que je n'aime ma Dominique,
> Ma belle ile auz oiseaux heureux.

Creatively speaking, the indigenous Dominican had found a voice. Granted that to many locals, these were not only distant but barely audible. To the vast majority of Dominicans, they were not heard at all. In the travelogues of the period, the local population was portrayed primarily as porters, or indigent hewers of wood and carriers of water. When they were heard, it was, as one writer described a scene in the Roseau market, speaking indecipherable words, such as **mandez this, mandez that**.

VOICES FROM ABROAD

But this incipient awakening was not confined to the island's shores. Migration historically has acted as a safety value for the island's population. From the late nineteenth century, to the early twentieth century, Dominican workers had traveled to the Panama Canal, Cuba, the Dominican Republic and the Netherland Antilles for employment. The white expatriate or creole sector had gravitated to England or North America for education or employment opportunities. Jean Rhys and then Phylis Shand Allfrey had followed the well beaten path in 1906 and 1927 respectively.

Elizabeth Paravisini- Gebert in her 1996, **Phyllis Shand Allfrey, A Caribbean Life**, gives a marvelous account of Allfrey's sojourns in New York, the United Kingdom and her life after returning to Dominica in 1955. In the 1930s, Allfrey became immersed in the London Fabian Socialist Movement and ultimately the British Labour Party. She also came into contact with Rhys, other members of the expatriate white Dominican society and or few coloureds such as Edward Scobie.

Allfrey's immersion in the radicalism of the period was not unusual. The 1930s marked the emergence of the West Indian intellectual with both Eric Williams and C.L.R. James migrating to England in 1932. James had recently published his now classic, **The Case for West-Indian Self Government**. William would subsequently blaze a trail at Oxford University while James, along with other West-Indian radicals most notably, George Padmore, would become a leading theoretician in the Communist International.

It was not unusual for Allfrey, the Fabian Socialist or political activist, to have had a simultaneous interest in creative writing. These differing modes of expression augmented each other. James, the quintessential Renaissance Man, would publish his **World Revolution** in 1937, the brilliant 1938 study of the **Haitian Revolution, The Black Jacobins** and **Minty Alley**, a novel of yard life in Trinidad. Of James, a contemporary noted that "politics was his religion, Marx his god, literature his passion, Shakepeare his prince among writers and cricket his beloved activity."

Allfrey's **beloved activity** was undoubtedly her poetry. ParaVisini- Gebert describes the 1940s as her most productive. Numerous poems written within that decade would be published in her 1950, **Palm and Oak**. In one poem, **Expatriates**, Allfrey deals with migrants in Britain:

> Living in sunless reaches under rain
> how do the exiles from enchanted isles
> tend and sustain their rich nostalgic blaze?
>
> Those who are crazed and lone ignite in pain,
> but some stoke inner fires with golden riches
> and some feed sparsely on rare labent days.

In "**True-Born Villager**" she writes:

> The true born villager will thatch a village deep in metropolis. He draws a line round the arena of his daily trudging and shocks pedestrians with bright good marrows; shrewd as a fieldmouse weaves his one track way through the great wheatfields of the rusting crowds with a whoa, whoa, the grey sheep backs the woollen coats of shoppers…

Allfrey was not alone among Dominican migrates who, on lonely nights, **beat poems…out of stored tropic heat on brumal nights**. Others, confronted by the harsh living conditions, the alien environment and the racial prejudice, would undergo a type of psychological deconstruction and reeducation.

Gillis Simon, a Dominican migrant who arrived in England in 1955, exemplifies this individual. An accomplished musician who played the piano, saxophone, clarinet and organ, he wrote a poem, **In the Fifties Bye and Bye**:

In the pub in Ledbury Road, off Powis Square,
near Portobello Road
With Julie Vandterpool,
Memories of my schooldays unwound.
The colonial school met its autumn
Shed its leaves in the winter
Of a painful disenchantment…
Fill like rags in the gutters of

Kensal Rise, Goldbourne Road and Royal Oak
And in the shedding, new births,
New springs, new buildings on the dung heap,
Self and radical assessment,
New responsibilities, political
Sociological and otherwise,
Re evaluating of norms,
Repairs to the eyes of the mind…

These *repairs* give him a clairvoyance hitherto unimaginable:

Ledbury Road and Powis Square
Will be remembered by lots of us…
A horrid slum of houses then
Damp bricks and broken men
Broken women, crippled children,
Stunted, crippled in the mind
Black soles that suggested to arrive
The crippling damnation gnawing
At the gates of their beaten-up minds,
Danced with misery
In the frost filled world…
Until she smiled with icy teeth
In the cold cold world.

The smiles did not possess the enchanting enigma of a Mona Lisa. Simon continues:

> There were the dullest Whites who saw
> Themselves a thousand cuts above
> Any nimble witted-wise Black
>
> A misplaced enigma, sure, sure,
> But why? Did they think that because
> We are full of laughter and songs
>
> We would be impervious to pain?
> Or did they think that we were made for pain
> And the bites of grey beard prejudice?

THE ORCHID HOUSE

In her novel, Allfrey rejects the invisible status relegated to the black population in works such as Waugh's **The Fatal Gift**. Largely autobiographical in that, according to Paravisini-Gebert, it recreates her own family history, the novel nevertheless chronicles the island's history at the time it was written. It prefigures Allfrey's founding of the Dominica Labour Party with Emmanuel Loblack and the development of an incipient workers' consciousness in the 1950s.

More significantly, Alllfrey portrays the changing of the social order in Dominica in **The Orchid House**. The white population is slowly declining and is being superseded by the coloured middle class. One character laments that nothing changes, except that the coloured merchants grow richer and the white people poorer. The whites are aware of their diminished status. Some, like Marse Rufus, achieves an accommodation with the coloreds. Others exhibit a type of resignation to their inexorable decline.

The novel however, is significant since it reflects the ascendancy of those whose voices had hitherto been muted or unheard in the literature of the island. It is narrated by Lally, a servant of the white family. She regards herself as a book taught English speaking Negress, not a patois speaking one as some of her counterparts. She is disdainful of the alliance between Miss. Joan, the novel's central figure and Baptiste, whose real life counterpart was Emmanuel Loblack. She dismisses the locals as "a great horde of those worthless, no work labourers…"

Allfrey's subtle distinctions within the local population makes **The Orchid House** more than a mere tale of her family's relative loss of status on the island. It reflects an awakening, a realistic portrayal of the local population which neither sentimentalizes nor sanitizes them. Lally represents a whole generation of local servants whose disdain for their own kind was second only to that of their employers. Although there is a growth in consciousness in the local population, many are resistant to the change in the community.

JEAN RHYS' WIDE SARGASSO SEA

Jean Rhys' life and works have been dissected by a significant number of scholars who have waged a virtual Battle Royale over her literature. She has been claimed by some feminists and spurned by others. To some, she is an anticolonialist while to others, her portrayal of the local population makes her a colonial apologist. Others regard her as making an artistic statement on the Caribbean white expatriate who, torn between an identification with England and the local environment, exhibits a "terrified consciousness".

The contours of her life are well known. Rhys was born in 1890, her mother from a Creole family, her father a Welsh doctor who had come to Dominica in the 1880s. Her father lacked the class contempt towards the blacks as the resident white creole population and exhibits more of a paternalistic attitude towards them.

But Dominica in the 1890s was not a hotbed of social democracy where the races interacted freely. The young Rhys was discreetly kept away, from the **others**. Rhys' writings, including her partial autobiography, **Smile Please**, is replete with examples of this separation. She secretly longs to be part of the spontaneous exuberant world of the black children but was intentionally excluded from it. When she attempted to befriend a black girl Tia, she was painfully rejected.

Relations between the races were no better. Froude's **The English in the West Indies**, resulted in the attempt to reestablish Crown colony in Dominica during the 1890s. There was a virtual race war between the wealthy colored merchants and planters and the white expatriate society. Politically and socially, the local black population did not appear on the radar screen of either combatant. The island's population numbered 40,000 in the 1890s with only 613 registered voters.

The young Rhys remained in Dominica until she was sixteen and migrated to England. Her father died four years later and Rhys was subsequently thrown into an emotional and financial tailspin which plagued her for the rest of her life. Work as a choirine and a number of failed relationships, failed to ameliorate her condition and only her growing reputation as an important writer gave her a modicum of respect.

Following her publication of the acclaimed **Wide Sargasso Sea** in 1966, she received the Royal Society of Literature Award and the W.H. Smith Award in 1966. In 1978, a year prior to her death, she received a CBE from the British Government.

Her writing career started with the 1927 publication of a set of stories, entitled **The Left Bank**. Collectively, they deal with a theme which recurs in Rhys life and writings. An unmitigating rootlessness and dependency of her female characters on their male paramours. Her literary landscape is as bare and arid as a Dali painting.

In her other novels, **Quartet, After Leaving Mr. Mackenzie, Voyage in the Dark** and **Good Morning Midnight**, there are variations of the same theme. The heroines in all four, Mary Zelli, Julia Marten, Sasha Jensen and Anna Morgan, have difficult subservient relationships with the men in their lives. New relationships merely herald a repetition of the old. Always there is loss; of relationships; of a child, of money and of stability.

Her third novel, **Voyage in the Dark**, is different from the others written in the 1930s since there are direct references to Dominica. Anna Morgan suffers flashbacks of her childhood life in Dominica. She is most descriptive and alive when she recalls her childhood. They provide an internal sanctuary from the haggard and cruel lights of England where everything is cold and sad.

The local population is seen, not heard. Anna not only recalls the masquerade on the island but her ironic separation from it. She recalls not only the family's black servant, but the family's efforts to resist any influence which her presence had on the young Rhys. The black population is regarded as a contagion to be guarded against by the resident white population.

Wide Sargasso Sea marks a departure from earlier Rhys novels in some respects in that it is based in the West-Indies. The drama between Antoinette and her husband unfolds in the post Emancipation period when the wounds inflicted by slavery had not completely healed and when an uneasy truce existed between the social groups.

Both Antoinette and her husband have been scarred by history. The husband is the second son of a member of the English landed gentry. Because of the rule of the primogeniture, he is cut-off from inheriting the family's ancestral home and the perks which undoubtedly go with it. His father arranges the marriage to Antoinette whose major attribute is her inheritance which includes a "little estate in the Windward Islands."

The husband's economic compulsion to get married is matched only by Antoinette's need for emotional comfort. Antoinette's mother had succumbed to madness but not before her home had been torched by former slaves. Antoinette's attempts to befriend a local girl had been painfully rebuffed. She had a number of coloured relatives but her uncle's "lectures" had made her "shy" about them. She had established a "close" relationship with one of them but in the race conscious period when the story unfolds, marriage between a white creole and coloured was unthinkable.

Antoinette is therefore trapped by circumstances to marry this stranger. She had a strong emotional attachment to the West-Indies. On the other hand, he regards it as malignant and alien. Antoinette is caught between the two worlds; that of the white planter class and that of the exuberant, spontaneous black population but belongs to neither. As she laments, "I often wonder who I am and where is my country and where do I belong and why was I ever born at all."

In this atmosphere of uncertainty, the husband receives letters from Daniel, one of Antoinette's coloured relatives. He informs her that Antoinette's parents were mad and her mother became the play thing of the blacks. Furthermore, he tells the husband that he is not the first to kiss her pretty face. Indeed, she had had an affair with Sandi, a coloured man.

Thereafter, the marriage is doomed. Antoinette's husband resorts to having an affair with Amelie, the "half caste servant," of the family. Sensing his withdrawal, Antoinette seeks a love potion from her servant, Christophene, to repair the marriage, despite being warned that the potion "too strong for béké." There is a dramatic verbal confrontation between the husband and Christophene. He eventually takes the seemingly mad Antoinette bound for England and locks her up in Thornfield Hall.

He had no choice, he rationalised. He could not endure the hostility, the conceit the envy and deceit. Besides, if he remained, he'd "be gossiped about, sung about (but they make up songs about everything, everybody) you should hear the one about the Governor's wife."

Alas! The reader is not privy to that song. But a reading of **Wide Sargasso Sea** evokes a popular 1960s calypso, which theme deals with the near tragic consequences which a clash of cultures can trigger in a marriage:

> Pardon, Pardon, Mousieur Majestwa
> Un fanm Canada, qui faît tout sâ
> E'pasa lavé, E passa passé
> Mai e cay payé, pou hadi es li
> (Sorry, Sorry, mister Magistrate
> A Canadian woman did all this
> She cannot wash; She cannot iron
> But she will pay for her rudeness)

Perhaps the most poignant moment in **Wide Sargasso Sea** is Christophene's verbal confrontation of Antoinette's husband. That Christophene, a black servant from Martinique; the type frowned upon by Lally in Allfrey's **The Orchid House**, would confront the husband is unprecedented. In one of her letters,

Rhys' explained that Christophene had regular contact with the white creoles and hence her ability to confront the Englishman.

Christophene is the voice of the voiceless majority in the Dominican community. She articulates the historical revulsion of those whose lives had been aborted by the rapacity of the colonizer. She gives vent to the accumulated resentment of those who had watched silently as the island's resources were ravaged by foreign interlopers. Written when Edward Leblanc was in the throes of initiating a cultural revolution on the island, Christophene's actions represent one of the most significant moments in the literature of the island.

For example, the Englishman asks her what she'd done to Antoinette after his rejection of her. He describes her response:

> "Your wife! She said. You make me laugh. I don't know all you did but I have know some. Everybody know that you marry her for her money and you take it all. And then you want to break her up, because you jealous of her. She is more better than you, she have better blood in her and she don't care for money" ... You young but already you hard..."

The husband is surprised by Christophene's outburst. "And then, she went on in her judge's voice," he notes. He then accuses Chistophene of trying to poison him.

She couldn't wait to respond:

> "Poison you? But look me trouble, the man crazy! She come to me and ask me for something to make you love her again and I tell her no I don't meddle in that for béké…"

He accuses her of getting Antoinette drunk:

> "You are a damn hard man for a young man," she flung at him:

He hypocritically blames Christophene for what had happened to Antoinette. At this point;

> She drew herself up tall and straight and put her hands on her hips. Who you to tell me to go? This house belong to Miss. Antoinette's mother, now it belong to her. Who you to tell me to go?"

With this declaration, she proves herself his superior. She puts him on notice that he had no right to tell her to leave the island. Her attitude can be summarised in the Creole which he abhorred so much:

> ***Ou Djab ma hadie kamem, pou dit mwen pou kite ési.***
> (You are very rude to tell me to leave this place)

"I will have the police up, I warn you," he threatens her with a stiff upper lip.

And then she utters what may well be the most important statement in the novel:

> No police here... No chain gang, no tread machine, no dark jail either. This is free country and I am free woman.

It is no accident that Rhys makes Chistophene the obeah woman from Martinique. She is not afraid of the obeah of the colonial interloper. She is not aspiring to be accepted by the white family. Rather, she is *one* Josephine or Christophene Dubois who without fanfare, is the moral center of the novel.

THE ROAD TOWARDS POLITICAL INDEPENDENCE

With the advent of party politics in the 1950s, the development of ministerial self-government and the West-Indies Federation in 1958, Dominicans assumed a direct stake in self government. This assertiveness was evident not only in politics but in other spheres of life on the island.

In 1951, a number of Dominica Grammar School graduates formed the Dawbiney Literary Club. The club's purpose was to encourage debate and discussion on contemporary issues and to extend "the literary faculties of its members along the lines of public expression".

This club was different from its predecessors in that the best and brightest of the community became involved in it at some time or the other. In the late 1950s, women were allowed to become members and early members including former school principals Kay Clarendon and Olive Harris and Joan Sorhaindo.

By the 1960s, the club had developed as a crucible for future leaders on the island. Its membership included future politicians Jenner and Ronald Armour, Charles Maynard, Sportswriter R. St. H. Shillingford, future University of the West Indies professor Randolph Williams and island president, C.A. Sorhaindo. As its ranks were decimated by migration in the 1960s, new members included future editor, poet and writer Alick Lazare, teacher Alfred Leevy, lawyer S.P. Richards, economist Michael White and Frank Watty and mass communication specialist, Jefferson Charles.

The club's magazine, **Dawnlit**, served as a training ground for budding writers. Lazare's early poems and at least two stories would later be published in his 1974, **Native Laughter**. Until its demise in 1967, the club produced five editions of **Dawnlit,** the final edition being published in 1965. The demise of the club was partly due to the migration of prominent members such as Lazare and the immersion of others in politics.

The growth of creative writing also has its etiology in the political and social developments of the 1960s. The decade marked the ascendancy of the island's first Premier E.O. Leblanc and the cultural transformation which he initiated. Folk expression, such as indigenous dance, the island's oral traditions, the government's sponsorship of a publication, **Dies Dominica**, which featured creative writing, were all promoted in this decade.

The emphasis on indigenous expressions also led to the use of creole, as a legitimate form of expression. **Dies Dominica** featured "patois proverbs," Jean Harris's Siffleur Montagne Chorale featured creole songs while Cynthia Watt, one of the Dominican poets featured by Ralph Casimir in the 1940s, wrote stories in the island's newspaper about " Ma Titine." The process of legitimization was cemented with annual belaire, caudrille, and story telling competitions.

These changes were not achieved without resistance. The traditional middleclass which had superseded the white expatriate creole sector, was largely unsympathetic to Leblanc's egalitarian reforms and waged a rearguard action against what they perceived to be a debasement of the island's values.

The conflict between the upwardly mobile working class and the middleclass is captured in a poem by economist Frank Watty entitled, **Marshand Poisson**:

> "Gros coulihou frais! Gros coulihou frais!
> Mi moi ici, qu'on criez moi?"
> She bustles with pride,
> Along the roadside,
> Past the middle-class porticoes, her voice echoes inside.
>
> "Comment coulihou, Vio?" "Trois pour cinq g'ros
> C'est a ce 'ment yo sortie bord la mer."

"Oh! Sorry I'm sorry my dear,
They're too expensive I fear,
I think I'll have a codfish and avocado pear,"

"Ah! Mais zor maichastais; zor par vlé moi manger;
Et garçon moi école il obige aller",
"That's hardly my concern,
and why should your boy learn
to outstrip my son Godfrey, and his position to spurn."

Dites tout ca 'ous vle, ces temps la cay changer,
S'il ni Bon Dieu en ciel ca garder nous",
"I adjure your invocation,
I'm not subject to trepidation,
Remain reconciled with your own humble station."

"Tend ca moi ca dis bon, moi meilleur jeter les poisson,
Zor mulatre! Eh bien mi monde qui cheap."
So she replaces her load,
Her cry awakens the road,
Her faith in the future by none understood.

"Gros coulihou frais! Gros coulihou frais!
Si personne vlé, veni hacer,
Veni vite avant moi aller."

Political conflict also fueled creative writing within the decade. By 1966, the Dominica Labour Party had become firmly ensconced in power. Opposition to the DLP emanated from the

D.U.P.P., the Dominica United Peoples Party, and from Phyllis Allfrey who had been expelled from the DLP in 1961. Another voice of dissent was Edward Scobie who, in his sojourn in England two decades earlier, had met Allfrey.

Their medium of writing was the weekly newspapers, **The Star** and **The Herald**. Allfrey had unsuccessfully run for office in 1966 and following a brief sojourn as editor for **The Herald**, had founded **The Star**. Both papers would carry stories from writers such as Ralph Casimer, and Cynthia Watt (nee Leblanc) and works from Scobie and Allfrey.

Allfrey's poems reflected her political allegiances within the period. Disillusioned with the DLP., she castigated what she perceived as the shortcomings of the labour government.

In a poem, **Sunday Dinner,** she wrote:

> My fadda bought de beef
> costin a whole day pay,
> just for our family
> to eat one meal dis day
>
> The balance of de week
> is dasheen dat we eat;
> sometime a little fish,
> Only on Sunday, meal.

In another; she mocked the drive towards political independence:

> Oh, a dose of independence is superb;
> but prepare a notice PLEASE DO NOT DISTURB
> you may find your state much sicker
> from consumption of its dregs;
> so do test your head and legs
> before you drain that Independence liquor…

THE LITERATURE OF THE 1970s

SEEDS OF CONFLICT

The attainment of internal self-government in 1967 should have paved the way for the coming together of the competing interests within the community. However, the seeds of social transformation sown by Edward Leblanc in the 1960s, sprouted saplings of dissension within the community. Indeed, towards the end of the decade, the contending political forces had consolidated their support into rival camps and within a year of the attainment of Statehood, were massed against each other on opposite sides of the political spectrum.

By July 1968, the Leblanc government fired the opening salvo against its detractors. It sought to enact the Seditious and Undesirable Publications' Act to emasculate the voices of dissension primarily at **The Star** and **The Herald.** The public opposition to the passage of the statute gave birth to the Dominica

Freedom Party, of DFP, which leaders included Scobie, Allfrey, Loblack and then political neophyte, Mary Eugenia Charles.

Even with a schism in the Labour Party, the DFP was unable to stem the tide of a massive Leblanc triumph at the polls in 1970. Emboldened, Leblanc tried in 1971 to neutralize the opposition forces now ensconced in the Roseau Town Council. He attempted to do this by legislation which aim was the dissolution of the council. In a massive public demonstration on December 16, 1971, the Court house and House of Assembly were stormed and the public actions effectively prevented passage of the proposed legislation.

By then, the tenor for the decade was set. Industrial action, legislation enacted to curtail the right of citizens, social unrest and political chicanery all blossomed in the 1970s as exuberantly as the island's lush vegetation. Social unrest engendered by the twin forces of the Black Power Movement and the rise of the Dread Movement added to the sense of chaos and by the mid 1970s, there was almost universal consensus that Dominica was teetering at the edge of a social and political abyss.

Paradoxically, it is within the context of social and political unrest exacerbated by repressive legislation, racial tension and wanton acts of violence, that an effervescence of creative activity occurred within the community. A number of factors explain that. Creative expression, particularly calypso, had historically between a convenient medium of social commentary and criticism of political forces. As repressive measures enacted by the Labour government in the 1970s persisted, there was an increasing need for a medium of dissension which did not carry it in its wake, the political retribution wreaked by the government in the 1970s. Furthermore, the political radicalism of the period induced a degree of introspection and concern for the future which found a natural expression in creative writing. This was fuelled by the drive for political independence which possibilities captured the imagination of a large segment of the population and ultimately led to the publication of a large number of booklets of poetry.

In music, theatre and creative writing, Dominicans not only narrated their experiences as Lally in **The Orchid House** but in the manner of Rhys' Christophene, voiced their opposition and condemnation of their leaders. In music, the **Gay Lords Power Union** burst onto the music scene in the late 1960s with a number of popular songs including "Pray for the Black Man." In the early 1970s, Dominicans bands such as **De Boys an Dem**, **Every Mothers Child**, **Liquid Ice**, **Belles Combo**, **Gramacks**, the inimitable **Exile One**, sprouted as if from nowhere and with their distinctive Cadence sounds, gave the island a degree of visibility in the French islands which superseded its growing notoriety as an unstable small island.

Exile One in particular, and the **Gramacks** to a lesser extent, best epitomised the possibilities of the island's creative potential. The showmanship of lead singer, Gordon Henderson, the charisma of pianist, Fitzroy Williams, the musical dexterity of guitarist Julie Mourillon and the unflappable, Vivian Wallace created a synthesis of sound which was virtually unparalleled in the French music world in the 1970s. Indeed, the albums of **Exile One** and **Gramacks**, **Face Au Public** and **La Vie Disco** respectively, stand as enduring testaments to the musical brilliance of the 1970s.

And yet superlatives come tumbling down with a review of the music of the **Midnight Groovers**. If **Exile One** exemplified the urban, sophisticated sound of Dominica's upwardly mobile, that of the Midnight Grovers exemplified its underground currents. Grandbay had been the cradle of the radicalism within the decade. It had borne the brunt of the Dread onslaught by the Dominica Defence Force. The concentration of arable land in the hands of a few and the inequitable system of justice had all being exposed in the case of **Her Majesty versus Phillip Mark,** A.K.A. Chubby, when he was convicted and jailed for the theft of a lonely coconut.

The **Midnight Groovers** therefore represented a kind of existential movement within the period. More than any other contemporary sound, their music seemed to have been forged from the suffering, depression, and the cruelty just as it represented an existentialist triumph over adversity within the period.

The **Groovers'** lead singer exemplified this duality. Mark was incarcerated in an era when the Prohibited and Unlawful Associations Act granted state sanctioned impunity for the killing of any Dread. He transformed his ordeal into a song "Coco Sec" or dry coconut, which became a metaphor for the political bankruptcy of the period. Social commentary in music reached its apogee in the music of the **Midnight Groovers**. In three albums, the **Midnight Groovers**, in a number of songs produced by Mark, featured hard hitting themes ranging from the increased Amercanisation in **Talon Haut,** prostitution as in **Anita,** state repression as in **Coco Sec** and family values as in **Pas Negliger Maman Ou.**

In the spheres of drama and theatre, a similar phenomena occurred. Alwin Bully had emerged in the 1960s as a budding poet and play wright and following a three year sojourn at the University of the West-Indies, had resumed playwriting. He formed a theatre company, the Peoples Action Theatre, P.A.T. and with Daniel Cauderion, teacher turned radio personality, staged a number of plays to mass audiences in the early 1970s. Cauderion's **Speak Brother, Speak,** and **Bully's Streak** and **Ruler of Hiroona,** gave Dominicans, cowed into silence by repressive state legislation and by the States' Security forces, an opportunity to reflect on the barren social and political landscape of the period. Lesser known artists, such as Clement Richards and Michington Isreal, under the banner, Aquarian Expression, also produced plays, most notably the 1978 production called **Mirrors**, which parodied the current political leadership on the island.

Similarly in dance, Raymond Lawrence founded the Waitukubuli Dance group which combined traditional folk dance in their repertoire. In 1978, Lawrence produced **Papa Toussaint**, a portrayal of the exploits of Toussaint L'ouverture and the attainment of Haitian independence. On a deeper level however, **Papa Toussaint** dealt with black liberation, identity and the Dominican peoples' quest for political independence.

Creative writing within the period originated from three sources. The first could be roughly catergorised as the traditionalists, foremost among whom were Phyllis Allfrey and J.R. Ralph Casmir. In 1973, Allfrey published **Palm and Oak II** which explored the duality in her indentity and her intense feelings for the island. In 1971, Casmir published **Farewell** and another volume in 1978 with an Introduction by Allfrey. In it, Allfrey distinguished the poetry written by the traditionalists from that by the younger generation of writers:

> Some of the new young Dominican poets...will ramble on with their "free verse" without knowing the meaning

of the words, lyric, assonance, blank verse, sonnet, scansion and so forth...

Others who come within that genre were Alfred Leevy, and Alick Lazare, both of whom were members of the Dawbiney Literary Club in the 1960s. In 1973, Leevy published a small volume entitled, **The Mountains Sing**, while Lazare edited the 1972 edition of the Government publication, **Dies Dominica**.

In this publication, another loosely defined group of writers emerged. Many of these such as Emanuel Joseph, the 1971 Island Scholar, had published works in the **New Clarion**, the magazine of the Dominica Grammar School. Others, like Raymond Lawrence, had similarly been active at the St. Mary's Academy, while others like Lennox Honey Church, who in 1974 would first present **The Dominica Story** in serialized form on radio, had a short story published in **Dies Dominica**.

In the 1970s, this loose group of young writers would be fed, like a gushing stream, from the Theatre movement and on the eve of independence in 1978, writers such as Mark Sylvestre, Lennox Honeychurch, Anthony Lockhart, Arundell Thomas, Giftus John, all of whom had been associated with Alwin Bully, published volumes of short stories and poems. As political conflict intensified in the 1970s, these voices coalesced and rose to a new crescendo by the eve of political independence in 1978.

In addition to being the artistic director of the Peoples Action Theatre, Bully also founded and edited a literary magazine, called **Wahseen**. The magazine included poems, short stories, book reviews from writers including Bully, Cauderion and W. O. M. Pond and from budding poets, Steinberg Henry and Minchington Isreal.

In 1974, the Arts Council of Dominica, which purpose was the promotion of indigenous art forms, published a two volume magazine, entitled **Dominica Short Stories.** The stimulus for the stories was the annual Short Story Competition and also a radio program, **From the Green Antilles,** initiated by Cauderion and then manager of the Dominica Broadcasting Corporation , Jeff Charles. Perhaps the most notable, Lockhart's short story, **Man In The Hills,** dealt with the dark violent underside of the dread phenomenon, an unfortunate legacy of the Black Power rhetoric of the period.

Between 1976 and 1978, a number of works would be produced by members of this group of writers. Lockhart and Thomas jointly published **Two Heads**, a booklet of short stories and poems. Mark Sylvester published a small volume of poems **When I Awake,** Giftus John released **The Dawn** while Lennox Honeychurch published a small volume of poems entitled, **Green Triangles.**

All the works dealt with displacement, disfunction, despair and impending doom. Lockhart's stories focus on the educated though alienated individual, Dr. Honeychurch appeals for racial harmony in his title poem, Thomas's poems dwell on the serenity of communal life while in Sylvester's poems, premonitions of society's impending breakdown abound. John longs for a new reality amidst the selfishness and greed which his persona beholds. Collectively however, the works portrayed a society being torn apart by social political racial and economic divisions even while being seduced by the siren of self-determination and political independence.

The third group of poets is that generated by the radical intelligentsia within the period. The Activists in the 1970s did not form a monolithic group since there were as many distinctions, orientations and factions within their ranks as within the established political parties. Some agitated for Black Power, others were Marxist Leninists, others were labeled Trotskyists or Maoists while a few espoused an amalgam of all four **orientations**.

The ideological infighting and the interminable conflicts within the Leftist movement of the 1970s need not concern us here. Neither its corrosive effect on many youth within the decade who abandoned legitimate pursuits such as higher education for a life as dreads on the island. The kidnap and murder of farmer Ted Honey Church, the murder of a Canadian couple at Pond Casse in November 1974, the activities of Tomba and then Pokosion, all had their genesis in the radical activism within the decade.

The radical movement however, spawned a cadre of literary works within the period. Their early organizational umbrella, the Movement for A New Dominica, the MND, published a number of magazines such as **Flambeau, Twavay** and **MND Speaks.** The proliferation of street publications with a circulation numbering a few hundreds led to other publications by groups dispersed in the island. Cadre I, a socialist study group in Roseau, published a monthly newsletter, **The Vanguard**, while in Portsmouth, writers Aurendell Thomas, Anthony Lockhart and Reginald Royer started a literary magazine, **Seine La.**

If the radical movement, spearheaded by Rosie Douglas and the Popular Independence Committees he established in the late 1970s, was the main catalyst for the attainment of political independence, creative writing may prove to be its second, most meaningful legacy. Allfrey spoke disparagingly of the growth of these new poets and their seeming ignorance of the traditional tools of the poet. This obliviousness to poetic form is more apparent than real. The radical poets did not eshew form and structure but focused on the shortcomings of life on the island. Indeed, in so doing, they were harking to the nineteenth century opinion of English poet Coleridge that poets are 'unacknowledged" legislators.

Nowhere was this more apparent than in the radical poetry of the late 1970s and 1980s. Poet Ras Mo introduced performance poetry in the island in a 1981 presentation **Levé Domichen,** accompanied by the Grandbay based Southern Liberation Dancers. In **Peasants Encounter**, he captured the cynicism and emptiness of the Independence promises:

> The scornful eyes of Civil Servants
> cause the peasant to reminisence
> of pre-election promises.
>
> Telephones ring in alien tones
> The clock constantly ticks
> While typewriters click
> And thimble heeled shoes tock.
> It is almost one o'clock
> The bus is leaving soon.

In another, **Dear Sonny**, he laments the disappearance of the Dominican landscape by using colloqualism:

> Remember the big breadfruit tree,
> That was in the yard
> The town council cut it down you see
> That make me feel so sad
> Remember down here is sikwi where we
> Used to swim
> There polluted with sewage wi

Another representative of the radical school has moved the bar for creative writing even further. Gregory Rabess had been involved in the radical movement and in the indigenous movement for Carib living space or **lebensraum.** After the dispersal of the radical forces following the 1980 elections, Rabess became immersed in organizations such as SPAT and the Konmiti Pou Eted Kweyol, the KEK, which sought to preserve the island's oral traditions. In the 1980s, the KEK established a Creole newsletter, **Kon Lanbi,** featuring works written in Creole. Rabess was also involved in the 1989 Kweyol Journal and a publication of Dominican folk tales, **Twa Kont Donmnik.**

Rabess continued the traditional of protest and social commentary in his 1992 Dub CD Album, **Woch La,** or The Rock. The albums marks the successful consummation of the marriage between poetry, song and Creole which courtship on the island began with Ras Mo's **Leve Dominchen.** In **Woch La,** Rabess deals with a number of themes including the island heroes, dependency and the increasing materialism of the island's people.

Another poet who is a member of the radical orientation is transplanted Trinidadian Harry Sealey. Sealey is part of the Frontline Movement, a cooperative bookstore established by youth radicals, Gabriel Christian, Eddie Toulon, Sonny Felix, Bobby Lewis and Rastafarian poet, Albert Williams. Ironically dubbed the **Frontline poets,** the group produced two volumes of poetry entitled **Rampart I** and **Rampart II**. Much of the works in the two volumes are weighted down by social commentary. One exception is a poem, **Ma Cherie**, written by Christobel La Ronde, who later published a volume of works, entitled **Llesywé Fanm**. The poem deals with the island's hold on the sensibility of a young girl in a manner reminiscent of Jean Rhys' flashbacks of Dominica **Voyage in the Dark**.

Sealey's works in Rampart I exemplifies the new writing. In an unpublished volume, **Is So We Is**, Sealy dwells on the human suffering occasioned by the new freedom:

> I does feel ah how
> meh eyes does start to water
> whenever I see them eating
> from garbage bins
> or drinking water from the gutter
> and sleeping in front of stores
> no bed to rest a weary head
> no home to call their own...

A number of initiatives in the post 1980 period ensured that creative writing on the island would have a vibrancy and vitality of its own. The period witnessed the dispersal of many radical voices of the previous decade. Some ultimately gravitated to creative writing. Sobers Esprit for example, took a sojourn from politics and became editor of **Wahseen**, while Gregory Rabess became involved in the Small Projects Assistance Team

(S.P.A.T) which provided funding for myriad projects including a tourist video on the island and his own **Woch La.**

Furthermore, a number of writers including Sobers Esprit, Rabess, Ian Jackson Ras Albert Williams and Ras Mo, formed the Dominica Writers Guild (DWG) in 1983. The Guild has promoted creative writing by hosting a number of activities such as poetry festivals, workshops and book fairs. At one point, it hosted monthly sessions entitled, **Word, Sound and Power** where poets read from their works. The DWG also hosted presentations called the **Voice of Poets** while in 1996, it launched a shortlived radio programme entitled, **Poets Corner.**

Successive Dominican governments have also fostered creative writing since the publishing of **Dies Dominica**. Either through the Ministry of Culture or Education, periodic government publications have featured prize winning poems or short stories. A 1999 publication, **Dominican Expressions**, features works of noted short story writer Jenaud Jacob, poets Harry Sealy, Ian Jackson and Arundele Thomas and lesser known writers such as Desmond Dublin, Carla Armour, Emmanuel Prince, Algernan Ducreay, and Albert Panman Bellot, among others.

The most recent literary magazine, **Building Bridges**, is published and edited by Roman Catholic Priest Fr. Clement Jolly. He has followed in the tradition of Catholic priests such as

Fathers Breton, de Rochefort and Prosemans who since the fifteenth century, recorded the experiences of the Dominican people. The magazines periodically contains short stories and poems by noted Dominicans as well as contributions from the editor himself. Easily the most recent prolific of the Dominican writers, Father Jolly's recent publication, the 2002 novel, **Children of the Sunset,** affords a vision of the island from a theological perspective.

In 1995, Irving André published **Distant Voices, the Genesis of An Indigenous Literature in Dominica.** The book sought to delineate the literary rites of passage of the Dominican people and analyzes the social, political and economic factors which shaped the development of an indigenous literature. The initial publication was well received and in 1999, André published a revised edition which provided more detailed analysis of creative writing on the island within an historical context.

THE DOMINICAN NOVEL

The works of Jean Rhys, Phyllis Shand Allfrey and Alec Waugh have, to a large extent focused on the fate of the white contingent on the island as it grappled to establish and preserve a sense of identity. Novels by other writers have shifted this focus and have sought to imbue members of the local population, with a similar sense of purpose. Father Jolly's novel **Rainbow Man,** deals with a successful lawyer who undertakes a journey into the island's interior for a sense of purpose and meaning in his life. Raglan Riviere's **Rumpunch and Prejudice** focuses on the transformation of an Englishman, Bruce Knowles, whose radical prejudices dissipate under the influence of the very people he abhors. Anthony Lockharts's incomplete novel, **Midlife**, like Jolly's **Rainbow Man**, explores the professional paralysis of a noveau riche family who undergo a period of soul searching with the death of their father.

Irving André's **The Island Within** and **Jumbie Wedding**, have a different focus. The first deals with an immigrant community who is victimized by the son of a member of the small close knit community. The criminal act induces a period of soul searching and forces the father of the offender to finally accept that his obsession to return to the island has taken a heavy toll on his son and family.

Jumbie Wedding is set in the town of Portsmouth during the 1960s. The local and lonely magistrate, becomes "friendly" with his young maid and her pregnancy throws the close knit community into a frenzy of gossip. A confrontation between the young girl and her local lover ends in near tragedy but in the end, her long suffering admirer succeeds in winning her affections.

The Island Within and **Jumbie Wedding** employ colloquialism and Creole to maintain a greater fidelity to the real life experiences of the Dominican people. The third person narrative in the former shifts from standard English to colloquialism which in turn gives way to Creole. Thematically, the language patterns in **The Island Within** underscore the characters' adherence to the norms and values of their island of origin.

SHORT STORIES

The island's rich tradition of story telling has led to a rich body of short stories written by Dominicans. In the 1960s, writers such as Edward Scobie, Michael White, and Alfred Leevy wrote stories which dealt with rootedness and the search for local identity. In the 1970s, Raymond Lawrence, Emmanuel Joseph and Anthony Lockhart expanded on these themes and particularly in the case of Lockhart, explored the psychological struggle of their characters as they searched for meaning in their lives. In the last two decades of the twentieth century, other writers would build on this tradition, exploring themes quintessentially Dominican.

In 1985, Alick Lazare published **Native Laughter** a collection of short stories and poems. Collectively, the stories are a satirical portrayal of the island community. Lazare satirizes issues which appear to be taboo in his community. These include alcoholism, the obsession towards material acquisition in a community which can ill afford material luxuries, the reverence accorded to the colour white in a black community and the deeply embedded superstition in a seemingly religious society. These stories are all very funny and hence dilute any backlash which his candid portrayal of his compatriots may provoke.

Lazare published another volume of short stories in the 1990s' entitled **Caribs** with "the same satirical sketches as... in **Native Laughter**" In some stories however, Lazare expresses nostalgia for the richness of a past life while in at least three others, he dwells on the atavistic violence of the Dread era of the 1970s.

Gabriel Christian, published a book of short stories in 1999, entitled, **Rain On A Tin Roof.** Written in the early 1980s, the stories recreated an edenic period when youth were nurtured in a tranquil environment which was not being besieged by drug use, violence or divisive forces. A protean innocence underscores his description of his various rites of passage from youth to adolescence. Whether he is describing trips to the cinema, the fastidious combing of his hair to conform to middleclass respectability, the untrammeled excitement of carnival, Christian superbly interweaves imagery with an appeal to the senses.

Other writers have written prize winning short stories. Local columnist Helena Durand has written a number of stories which affirm the values breathed from one generation of Dominicans to the next. Her stories are reminiscent of **Aesop's Fables** in that they convey a message or moral. The community reprimands or reproaches any deviations from its values and ensures that it is not negatively impacted by negative influences.

Perrennial winner of the Dominica Independence Day Short Story Competition, Jenaud Jacob, has published his short stories in publications entitled **Ghetto Prisons** and **Columbus Come Third**. His stories invariably focus on the richness of village life particularly its dance, folklore and story telling traditions. The writings are suffused with references to traditional beliefs, historical events, and local customs. Jacob possesses an amazing ability to reproduce local speech rhythms and customs in his writings.

He does not sentimentalize his community. Poverty is not only strangling the aspirations of many youth but drives his characters into a life of criminality which deals the final blow to their chances of escaping the ghetto which holds them prisoner. The characters however, are not passive players in a hostile environment but choose a course of destructive behavior.

THE POETRY OF REDEMPTION

In the 1970s, creative writing was fuelled by intense social and political conflict. Writing became a form of catharsis, giving voice to individuals who otherwise lacked an outlet for voicing their concerns at the signs of impending breakdown within the community. In later decades, political activism, although lacking the violence of the 1970s, was just as intense, particularly following the emergence of the United Workers Party in 1988. By the 1990s, the island had become divided into political camps with a great deal of antipathy between supporters of the UWP and the DFP.

The only area which remained largely impervious to these divisive forces was the writing community. The traditionalists, including Allfrey and Casmir, were as much critical of the community's shortcomings as members of the radical school of poetry. Lazare, who in **Native Laughter**, describes the breakdown of legitimate authority under the DLP in the 1970s, mourns the demise of Rosie Douglas in **Nature Island Verses**, his most recent volume:

> But when the day ran past two thousand years
> The sun came out shedding a million tears;

And from the blue another shepherd brave
Come striding forth the stricken land to save
Brief though his reign, full unity he brought
To right the wrongs the earlier times had wrought
Hope and relief survived a brighter day
That swept injustice and despair away...

Similarly Dr. Kay Polydore, whose four volumes of poetry, **Reflect and Chuckle, The Facetious and the Sublime, Pause to Ponder** and **For Mirth** and **Meditation,** poke fun at the shortcomings of her community, nevertheless deals with serious issues affecting her community's survival. In a poem in **Pause To Ponder,** she deals with the fall of the Russian Communist regime. In two memorable lines, she deadpans:

Communist lasse westay faim
L'air boudin capitalist plain
(The communists remain hungry
While the capitalists' stomachs are filled)

In another, she grieves the poverty on the island:

Astaphan's twin gables, Karam's mansion
With the longest verandah in the Caribbean
Pond flats trying to reach over Karam's roof
Alas! The rusty roofs covering more dilapidation
Cannot be a source of inspiration

In yet another, she castigates the disciples of globalization and international aid to the island:

> You improvident islands,...
> Why do you hasten to woo
> These implacable men of finance,...
> Why do you hold trysts
> With these intractable merciless financiers
> Who speak glibly of structural adjustments,
> Which is just a euphemism for misery,..

Similarly, Ian Jackson, one of the most accomplished of the **new** poets, does not feel constrained either by his language or themes in his poetry. An accomplished songwriter, he recently released a dub recording entitled **Soucouyant** which continues in the humor tradition of Lazare and Dr. Polydore. In **Broken Images**, his more serious publication however, he writes of the reality which the youthful Rhys was shielded from:

> I know of the cruelty and pain
> But Antoinette suffers no more
> No more do I am scream to see
> The glitter of white teeth
> Bathed in tropical sun

In another, he laments:

> Teenagers belly a grow
> An' who is de fadah no one know...

Albert Bellot's **Nest of Life**, is a scathing indictment of life on the island. Indeed Dr. Polydore cautions in her Foreword that the poems constitute material for serious reflection. In one poem he writes:

> Is now de new enslavement
> of we brother
> and we sister
> by we own colour

He complains that the old spirit of protest has been emasculated by the new forces of subjugation:

> Gagged, we shout no more
> Crippled, we march no more
> Betrayed, we uprise no more

We no longer do any of that since, according to Lockhart, yesterday's rebels are trapped in a crisis of **Mid Life**. They have become victims of their own vices as in Fr. Jolly's **Rainbow Man**. They now, as in Ras Mo's, **Peasants Encounter**, "finger files of black and white"... or worse, they have become, as in Father Jolly's **Song of the Dove**:

> ...Like birds of prey,
> They mouth their squealing epithets,
> Sing their chilling song,
> Dripping the rabble...

"Where are those?" Anthony Toulon asks, in his splendid volume, **The Gardens of Attainea, "who heard"** the island's **"song of life"**:

> The ripping cadence
> The soundless plunge
> Of stillborn waters
> Trickling from some lonesome mountain brook

To hidden vales
In distant timeborn meadows.

Where are those, who will reach, in the words of poet Gerald La Touche's, **Our Renaissance**:

> Across the Wide Sargasso Sea
> the Orchid House of
> Arawaks, Carib, Blacks
> weaved in a basketry of culture
> painted on a whiteboard of time
> drink of this concoction
> taste the nectar of our land

Where are those who will, in the manner of Arundell Thomas's persona, in his prize winning 1981 poem, **Transcending:**

> ...Let the "tim-tim BWA chess"
> of felt hatted men
> in khaki clothes
> reverberate the mirth, foolery and
> frolic
> of Compere Lapin and Compere Tigre
> amidst rippling faces of cheering people.

Alas! most are concentrated in the island's creative community. As Bertrand Riviere writes in his poem, **A Moment With Sandra**:

> Pastoral, Satirical and Didactic
> All forms are contained in your Rhymes, ...

Their rhymes have pointed out the follies of the island's leadership but the poets remain unacknowledged legislators. The voices cry out as the island's prospects fade under the harsh glare of globalization, free trade, dwindling returns from exports and the insidious effects of drugs.

Whether it is the pastoral poetry of an Arundell Thomas, or Anthony Toulon, the satirical works of Lazare or Dr. Polydore, the didactic works of Albert Williams, Christabel La Ronde or Fr. Clement Jolly, the indictment of Ian Jackson, Albert Bellott or Gerald La Touche or the patriotism of Augustus Colaire in his **Voices from The Mansion of My Soul**, Dominican poets have collectively offered a vision of a temporal salvation for the island. They have relied on imagery, experiences and folklore to show the possibilities of an island where all can work harmoniously for the common good of everyone. It is a vision where, in the words of Giftus John's 2001 volume of poems, **The Island Man Sings His Song**:

>The gentle night breeze
>Sweeps over the small sandy village
>While the strums of a guitar
>Resound somewhere as
>Young voices in discordant notes
>Chant a local folk song.
>
>Flickers from kerosene lamps
>Sip lazily through
>Curtained windows and doors

Softly kissing the glistening branches
Of the palm leaves
Growing tall and strong.
On the shore the sea
Sings herself a song ….

RENDEZVOUS WITH HISTORY. THE ATTEMPTS AT REGIONAL INTEGRATION.

Irving André

The current attempt at regional integration is as much an attempt to escape the tyranny of geography and history as was the failed attempt at a West-Indies Federation in 1958-1962. The history of the islands shares commonalties of race, culture, language and history. These unifying factors however, have been superseded in the past by insular nationalities which have forced the region's inhabitants to identify with their islands rather than with the region as a whole.

During the short-lived West-Indies Federation between 1958-1962, the debilitating effects of insular nationalism within the region manifested itself in two ways, both of which proved fatal to the West-Indies Federation. Between 1955 and 1959, net migration to Trinidad and Tobago from the other islands of the Federation increased from minus 286 to 6284.[1] In 1960, concern over the deleterious effects of intra-regional migration on the economy of the island forced Premier Eric Williams to deport

---

[1] E. Williams, "Statement of Government's Immigration Policy", **Trinidad Guardian**, March 19, 1960, Page 7.

some of these immigrants, much to the chagrin of the other islands.

Conflicting opinions about the form of the Federation account for these deportations. In his 1959 book, **The Economics of Nationhood,** Williams presented a case for a strong and viable Federation where the Federal government would have complete jurisdiction over economic development. The Federal government would have full authority over the twin issues of freedom of movement and freedom of trade. Premier Williams anticipated that a custom union would ultimately provide a regional market for Trinidad's food and textile industries where real output had increased from $8.5m in 1951 to $21.1m in 1958.[2] This regional market would ultimately generate employment for the West-Indian migrants who were coming to the island.

In contrast to the Williams' model, the Federal Constitutions of 1953 and then 1956 drawn up by Britain placed control of the movement of goods and persons largely in the respective legislatures of the ten islands comprising the Federation. This arrangement was supported by Jamaica which leadership feared that a customs union would prove detrimental to the island's incipient manufacturing industry. Business interests in Jamaica feared that a custom union would inundate the island

---

[2] Frank Rampersad, "Growth and Structural Change in the Economy of Trinidad and Tobago, 1951-1961" (**ISER** N.D.), pages 11-17

with Trinidadian products.[3] While Jamaica nominally supported the idea of a customs union, it felt that there should be a hard core of industries existing outside of a customs union.[4]

An intergovernmental Conference in 1959 failed to adopt the Williams' model of Federal government. Instead, the Conference agreed to establish Working Committees to study the different proposals for a Federal Constitution. In the interim, there would be no customs union but persons would continue to migrate to Trinidad and Tobago with virtual impunity.

The Trinidad leader's dissatisfaction with this situation manifested itself in the deportation of West-Indians from the island. Williams refused to accept this influx of immigrants when the island legislatures particularly Jamaica, steadfastly opposed the creation of a Federal Customs Union. He reasoned in his book, **The Economics of Nationhood** that:

> Freedom of movement of persons must proceed pari-passu with freedom of movement of goods. If there is to be delay in the establishment of a strong Federation…in which the burdens and the advantage will be equally shared, it is manifest that Trinidad and Tobago cannot reasonably be expected to shoulder premature one of the heaviest burdens to us of Federation without any assurance of any of the concomitant
> advantages.

---

[3] G.H. Flanz, "The West-Indies", in M. Frank ed. **Why Federations Fail**, (New York University Press 1968), Page 109.
[4] John Mordecai, **The British Caribbean, From the Decline of Colonialism to the End of Federation**, (Toronto, 1977), Page 159.

In the case of both Jamaica and Trinidad and Tobago, preservation of the insular economy superseded the desire for a West-Indies Federation with the inevitable result that the Federation collapsed in 1962. As noted by Franklin Knight, *Federal nationalism ran headlong into unit nationalism and lost.*[5] Gordon K. Lewis has argued that preoccupation with the form of the federation resulted in its demise.[6] However such preoccupation was merely a manifestation of the desire of Jamaica and Trinidad to protect their respective economies.

The other factor explaining the genesis of the West-Indies Federation and its inevitable failure lies in the proffered justification for its existence. The need for a Federation did not arise from the islands of the West-Indies. There was no indigenous consciousness clamoring for such a union neither was there any conscious attempt to gain that support for the union. Federation was a political contraption clamped on the islands to achieve administrative economics for Britain. It was not, as one scholar has suggested, a union *made in the West-Indies by West-Indians.*[7]

This argument ignores the fact that since the nineteenth century, the British had assiduously attempted to create a union of its West-Indian territories to facilitate their

---

[5] Franklin Knight, **The Caribbean**, (Baltimore, MD 1978), Page 206.
[6] Gordon K. Lewis, **The Growth of the Modern West-Indies**, (New York, 1968).
[7] E. Wallace, **The British Caribbean**, Page 216.

administration.[8] Indeed, ridding itself of the expense of duplicating the colonial bureaucracy in each island, according to Proctor, was the *oldest and most persistent of the reasons for the British's desire for a West-Indies Federation.*[9]

The expense of this bureaucracy was quite formidable. As one observer noted in exasperation:[10]

> There are attorneys general, solicitors general and inspectors general of departments, and registers general, and inspectors general of education, and so forth, for each of the eight general governments, all of them with the costly appendages of separate great department of state, as if each of these colonies were large widely distant rich and powerful communities that had nothing in common and could never be amalgamated...

The combined salaries of all the Governors of the British West-Indian islands in 1946 amounted to $108,208.[11] In contrast, five states in the U.S. with annual revenues more than 20 times that of the West-Indian islands paid their governors a combined salary of only $76,000.[12] According to a contemporary observer:

---

[8] J.H. Proctor Jr. "Britain's Pro-Federation Policy in the Caribbean – An Enquiry into Motivation" **The Canadian Journal of Economics and Political Science**, V.22,#3 (1956)319. E. Williams "The Historical Background of British West-Indian Federation, Select Documents", **Caribbean Historical Review**, *Pages 13-68.*

[9] J. Proctor Jr., "Britain's Pro Federation Policy", Page 319.

[10] C.S. Salmon, **The Caribbean Confederation. A Plan for the Union of the Fifteen British West-Indian Colonies**. (London, N.D.) Pages 137-138.

[11] **Quarterly Digest of Statistics**, No.5 (1948) Jamaica: Central Bureau of Statistics, (1949) Page 31.

> By simply pooling all executive salaries there would be enough and to spare from this source alone to take care of the entire operational costs of the new political enterprise.[13]

If Britain regarded the Federation as merely the most expedient way of administering its colonies, it had the tacit approval of the West-Indian leadership in so doing. With few exceptions, most notably Dr. Eric Williams of Trinidad, the region's leadership viewed federation as anything but a break with the economic ties to Britain.[14] In 1961-1962 for example, 47% of Dominica's leadership opposed political independence and favored an indefinite colonial rule while 26% favored independence in varying degrees but only in the distant future.[15] The remaining 27%, the lowest amount in the five island sample, favored independence immediately.[16] The vast majority of the regions leadership including 13 of 15 Dominicans leaders, favored aligning the Federation with traditional Western nations.[17]

---

[12] A.H. Maloney, **After England – We** (Boston: Meador Publishing Co. Publishers, (1949), Page 156.
[13] As in Footnote No.22, Page 153.
[14] C.L.R. James, **Spheres of Existence** (Allison & Busby Ltd. 1980), Page 138.
[15] Wendell Bell, ed. **The Democratic Revolution in the West-Indies**, (Cambridge, Massachusetts, 1967), Page 55.
[16] Bell, **The Democratic Revolution**, page 55. The other four islands surveyed were Jamaica, Trinidad, Grenada and Barbados.
[17] Bell, **The Democratic Tradition**, Page 89.

The absence of major divisive forces appear to guarantee the success of the renewed attempts at integration among Dominica, St. Vincent, St. Lucia and Grenada. None of the islands has a sufficiently advanced industrial sector which would precipitate a mass exodus of persons to that island as happened in the West-Indies Federation. Absent any major economic disparities among units of the proposed union, the strength of the insular nationalism within each island will be a powerful force inhibiting mass migration from one island to another.

In any event, the powerful concerns manifested in Trinidad over intra-regional migration are not manifested among the islands of the proposed union. Following the deportation of Grenadians from Trinidad in 1960, the Barbados Minister of Trade, Labour and Industry sent a delegation to Dominica to decide whether Barbadian migrants could travel there instead of Trinidad. The delegation examined a 700 acre proposed settlement site in the Calibishie / Hampstead area and a 1,200 acre site in La Plaine. The Dominica government agreed to accept 10, 000 - 15,000 Barbadian migrants but lacked the resources to provide the social amenities to accommodate the influx of Barbadians.

The dissolution of the West-Indies Federation gave rise to two unconnected though divergent political alternatives in the 1960s. Jamaica and Trinidad quickly shed their aspirations towards political union and following the Federation's demise, attained political independence from Britain.

Left to their own devices, the remaining eight islands, now known as **The Little Eight**, opted for a truncated union in the belief that political independence for each was nigh unattainable. For Dominica, the goal appeared unapproachable. Although the island was the largest among the eight, its population of 60,000 mocked the very notion of independence which Jamaica and Trinidad had so quickly embraced.

It was therefore with a great sense of optimism, that the islands' political leaders convened in Barbados on February 26, 1962 to forge a Federal Constitution. Animated by the belief that there was no other alternative than Federation, the leaders agreed on a political structure which gave the island legislatures the authority to protect their economies and invested the Federal government with the sole authority over defence and foreign policy. By March 14, 1962, the leaders sent a dispatch to the British Secretary of State with their proposals for a new Federation.

The response by the Secretary of State stoked the fires of dissent which ultimately consumed this new initiative to form a Federation. In April 1962, the Secretary of State urged a stronger central government than that envisioned by the islands. Britain always sought a structure wherein it would deal with one representative body, not a host of little legislatures cluttered in the Caribbean. More significantly however, the Secretary of State served notice that the British government was *unlikely to be able to assist the West-Indies on a greater scale than has so far been envisaged.*

Even then the island leaders, motivated in part by the efforts of Sir Arthur Lewis, the most noted economist of the region, sought to forge ahead with the Federation. A London conference from May 9-24, 1962 agreed on the proposals made in Barbados and proclaimed that the new union would be known as *The West-Indies Federation,* with its capital in Barbados. The leaders contemplated the Federation coming into being on May 31, 1962.

The British did not envision the birth of the Federation so soon, given its concomitant obligation to fund the new political entity. Rather, it proposed to publish a White Paper on Federation for discussion among the island legislatures, and the local population.[18] This would be followed by another Conference with input from her Majesty's Opposition in each island. Only if there was a consensus on the form of the new Federation, would the Draft Order in Council, ushering the birth of the new Federation, be tabled in the British Parliament. In the

---

[18] The British government appointed a Commission to ascertain the financial needs of the region and in October 1962, appointed the University of the West-Indies, Institute of Social and Economic Research to research this issue.

interim, the island governments established a Regional Council of Ministers, consisting of the Chief Minister of each island and the Governor of Barbados, to deal with issues pertaining to the Federation.

This laborious route towards formal political union did not address the fragility of island solidarity in the region. Each island, some more than others, continued to view political union through the myopic eyes of self interest, not as a relinquishment of certain interests for the greater good of the new entity. The intense parochialism of the island leaders, rather than any solidarity for a regional political entity, was the bedrock on which the drive towards the Federation was initiated and ultimately shattered.

The first manifestation of this was in August 1962 when Herbert Blaize supplanted Eric Gairey in Grenada as the island's Chief Minister. Blaize favoured a political union with Trinidad and Tobago which would formalize the symbiotic ties between the two islands since the nineteenth century. He immediately opted out of the Regional Council of Ministers. In 1965, Antigua's Vere Bird announced that the island would no longer be involved in the attempt at political union while contiguous Montserrat quickly followed suit.

With the original eight now reduced to The Little Five, differences became accentuated to a point which provided an excuse for withdrawal from the political union. St. Lucia's John Compton and Barbados' Errol Barrow were soon at odds over the disposal of revenues collected by the Federal government. Compton agitated for a single state among St. Lucia, Grenada, St. Vincent, and Dominica, as a counterweight against the smaller though wealthier and more populous Barbados.

At the tenth meeting of the Regional Council of Ministers in 1965, the die was cast. The Barbados delegation expressed its' concerns over the viability of the proposed union, much to the chagrin of the St. Lucian delegation, which reiterated its desire for a union among the Windward Islands. The Barbados Premier angrily withdrew from the meeting. The next day the St. Lucian delegation failed to appear, thereby prompting Dominica, its sister island, to follow suit. On April 29, 1965, deliberations for the establishment of a new Federation effectively ceased.

Henceforth the islands plodded towards a political destiny divorced from their island neighbours. Barbados gained independence in November 1966 while the others, with the exception of Montserrat, settled for the intermediate stage of Associated Statehood. Dominica became an Associated State in March 1967 and in November 1978, became an independent country.

The 1970s witnessed another futile attempt at political union. In July 1971, E.O. Leblanc joined with St. Kitts, Nevis,

Anguilla and his Windward Island counterparts to form another political union. This culminated in the signing of the Grenada Declaration in which each signatory committed his respective island to forming a new Caribbean State. The other islands however, were indifferent to the idea of a new political union. Grenada and St. Lucia withdrew from the proposed union and it was ultimately shelved.

There were two further half hearted attempts at regional unity in the decade that Dominica attained political independence. In 1972, the Heads of Government of Grenada, St. Lucia and St. Vincent met in the latter island to discuss areas of cooperation. They agreed to ensure freedom of movement of nationals among the three countries but subsequently failed to live up to their agreement. Five years later in Grenada, the governments of Dominica, St. Lucia and Grenada proclaimed an era of greater collaboration and unity among the islands. With the advent of Dame Eugenia Charles in 1980, and her antipathy towards the Bishop regime in Grenada, this initiative fell by the wayside.

THE LATEST ATTEMPT AT POLITICAL UNION

The drive to regularize what was hitherto an informal relationship usually carries dissension and acrimony in its wake.

This principle is as equally applicable to conjugal relationships as it is to political unions. In 1981, the islands of the Windward islands established the Organization of Eastern Caribbean States (OECS) which provided a regional forum for intergovernmental dialogue. In economics, the Eastern Caribbean States Central Bank served the financial interests of the member islands while organizations such as Windban provided a clearing house for information on the banana industry in the member islands. In 1995, the islands established Wibdeco and together purchased the assets of Geest. In the sphere of justice, the region is served by the Organization of Eastern Caribbean States Court of Appeal. These regional institutions functioned smoothly and efficiently since they did not intrude on the exercise of political authority in the individual islands.

The attempt at political union sought to advance these areas of regional co-operation to their logical conclusion. The initial proposal arose at a meeting of the OECS in May 1987, when St. Vincent Prime Minister James Mitchell recommended a political union among the islands to his colleagues. The euphoria following the announcement soon dissipated as the insular nationalities within the region began to assert themselves. The leadership of some of the islands could not rid themselves of the old colonial divisions. The islands constituting the Leeward Islands, Antigua and Barbuda, St. Kitts, Nevis and Montserrat opted to maintain their colonial nomenclature rather than be integrated with the Windward Islands.

The four remaining islands soon established a 44 member Regional Constituent Assembly (RCA). The Assembly had the task of determining the form of the proposed political union. It initially convened in January 1991, where there was a consensus of opinion that a political union was necessary for the region. The task ahead, according to the Assembly's report, *was to devise a form and structure which would meet that need.*

Since its' initial meeting, the RCA met on three other occasions, the most recent being on January 20, 1992. At its second meeting in St. Lucia in April 1991, government and opposition delegates discussed the form of the new union. The opposition favored a Constitution in which the role of its central government would be subject to that of the government on each island. The prevalent view however, sought a strong central government with total responsibility for governing the islands.

In the RCA's third meeting held in Roseau during the first week of September 1991, the delegates focused on the structure of the union government. The government delegates favored an executive president elected by universal suffrage. The president would preside over a bicameral legislature which lower house or House of Assembly would be comprised of elected representatives. The Upper House or Senate would be based on proportional representation. The House Speaker would be elected by the House of Assembly from outside the Parliament.

The Report of the Third Meeting of the RCA stressed that the proposed union should be federal and not unitary in nature. This meant that the units would reserve legislative authority to help them preserve the identity of each island. The precise allocation of areas for the exercise of federal and unitary jurisdiction remained unresolved until the Fourth Meeting of the RCA in January 1992.

The Fourth Assembly adopted a report from political scientist Patrick Emmanuel on the role of the federal government. The federal government would have jurisdiction over defence and national security, foreign affairs, judicial affairs, currency and social services. By implication, the unitary governments would have jurisdiction over matters of culture, economic development and labour relations, amongst others. Areas of conflict and overlap would be resolved presumably through the courts or through negotiation between the federal and unitary governments.

PROBLEMS OF POLITICAL UNION

One of the reasons for the failure of the West-Indies Federation was the inability of the leadership to generate sufficient indigenous interest to give the desirability of a Federation a life of its own. The region's citizenry was apathetic at best to the idea of a Federation. In the case of Trinidad, public opinion was hostile at the prospect of competing with hordes of small islanders descending to take the jobs of locals.

The new attempt at political union has sought to overcome these problems. Prime Minister Charles initiated an island wide campaign in 1987 to educate the public on the advantages of political union. In 1990, Charles appointed a Minister with responsibility for OECS unity and established a board based consultative committee to encourage public discussions on unification. Similar initiatives were taken by the political leadership in the other islands.

Despite these efforts, a mother lode of apathy and even hostility to political union can easily be found on the island. Much of this is undoubtedly political. For example, the Dominica opposition party boycotted the first meeting of the RCA and refused to join with Dame Eugenia Charles government in 1987 in the drive to educate the public on the issue of OECS unity. In the August 31, 1991 edition of the **New Chronicle**, historian Dr. Lennox Honeychurch lamented that the government's public awareness programme in furtherance of OECS unity failed miserably to heighten public interest. The following week's editorial concurred that *there really is no evidence that the*

Ministry of OECS unity has made any headway in attracting public attention to the importance of this RCA and the value of the people's role as keen students of the unity process.

There still does not appear to be any discernible interest for OECS unity. That may be attributed to the fact that the public is more concerned with matters such as the fate of the banana industry and the economics of daily life as opposed to the economies attendant on political union. The recent guarantee of free movement of goods and labour has not as yet, had any significant effects on employment and trade within the island.

Another problem appears to be the precise division of powers between the federal authority and the units. Matters such as foreign affairs, defence, general economics and monetary policy fall under federal authority. However, matters of a merely local or private nature such as labour legislation and occupational health and safety will likely fall under unitary jurisdiction. That may inevitably lead to four different regimes in each island affording various degrees of protection to workers. The likely result of such a scenario would be the spectacle of foreign investors gravitating towards the unit which offers the least protection to workers.

A further difficulty arises in the unitary government's ability to pursue its own policies of generating economic activity on the island. Throughout the 1980s and 1990s, Dominica offered a number of concessions to foreign and local enterprises to foster economic growth on the island. It may be problematic however, whether such concessions are compatible with the establishment of a customs unions in the new entity. Do these concessions constitute a subsidy to industry and as such, amount to unfair trade practices within the new state? To what extent can each unit protect its incipient agro industry within the framework of a union predicated on the free movement of goods?

Political union will be further frustrated since the islands produce competitive rather than complementary products. If every unit continues to produce the same goods as each other, then this duplication of effort would mitigate any synergy which a union would create. On the other hand, designating certain islands to produce certain products may initially lead to retrenchment and in effect resentment at the new order. While such changes may be regarded as inevitable in any new entity, their effects will be more than merely trifling in nature to those who will experience their deleterious effects.

Similar problems arise with the free movement of persons within the four units. Any union guaranteeing free movement of persons would necessarily involve the relinquishment of the right to exclude convicts from the three other units. It would also mean giving up its ability to protect the local labour force from competition in the islands. Finally, it would entail amending legislation so that any restrictions on ownership of land by aliens do not apply to citizens of the new state.

The changes wrought by free movement of goods and persons may not be insurmountable. However, they represent the concerns which the average citizen would have on the advent of the proposed union. Such concerns are inevitable given that the historical experience of the region has fostered an identification between citizens and island rather than citizen and region.

The form of the union agreed to at the third and fourth meetings of the Regional Constituent Assembly merely exacerbates the insular nationalism among the islands. The four units possess legislative authority which in essence enables them to retain their respective identities. Retaining the Dominican identity will inevitably involve imposing restrictions on land ownership and enacting legislation to protect indigenous industries. This scenario creates the anomalous situation where citizens of the new union may be prevented from establishing themselves in some of the units of the new country.

This less than ideal result can best be explained by the fundamentally ambivalent attitude towards OECS unity in the region. On one hand, there is virtual unanimity of opinion among the intellectual elite that political union is not only desirable but necessary. However, no island wishes to completely give up the things which distinguish it from the others. Neither will they relinquish the legislative means to maintain those differences. Their reluctance to do so stems from the fact that each island wants to be assured that if political union fails, no one will be any worse off economically than prior to the union. It is this very ambivalence however, which will ultimately pose the greatest challenge to the viability of a new union.

The attempt at political union in the late 1980s failed since the region's leaders viewed union through the jaundiced eyes of national self-interest. Only initiatives which did not encroach on the political turf of the respective leaders were undertaken. These included the abolition of most tariffs in 1988 and travel without a passport after January 1st, 1990. Any initiative which did not directly benefit or worse, placed the island in a disadvantageous position vis-à-vis the others, was regarded as sacrilege. According to Janet Higbie, Mary Eugenia *Charles approached the regional issues of the 1980s and 1990s with one concern in mind: the direct benefit to Dominica.*[19]

This approach did not change with the Edison James government. In December 1995, the Dominican government enacted legislation allowing CARICOM nationals with degrees from regional universities to live and work in the island without restrictions. This was extended in 1996 to include cultural artists, sportsmen and women. In July 2001, the Heads of the

---

[19] Janet Higbie, **Eugenia – The Caribbean's Iron Lady**, The Macmillan Press Ltd., (1993), Page 271.

Organization of Eastern Caribbean States (OECS) constituted a sub committee comprised of the Prime Ministers of St. Lucia, St. Vincent and Dominica to create the political and legislative framework where ultimately, a single OECS passport would enable nationals of member states to enter any member island to work, live and even purchase property.

The proliferation of trading enclaves in North America and Europe, unemployment and persistent economic problems will undoubtedly force the islands to establish closer relationships. In July 1997, the 14 member states which comprise CARICOM met in Montego Bay to attempt to establish a free trade zone in the region. The Jamaican Prime Minister, P.J. Patterson, announced the collective intent *to embark on the most far-reaching cluster of trade and economic co-operation arrangements in which our nations have ever been engaged.* If successful, the leaders would establish a single market with a single economy and currency by 1999. In 2002, that goal still remains elusive.

The stark reality is that in the foreseeable future, attempts at integration will fall short of political union. The insular nationalism is too firmly entrenched; the localization of politics too intense for the island politicians to relinquish the possibility of being Prime Minister for the relative anonymity of a seat in a regional governing body. In the 1950s, for example, Phyllis

Shand Allfrey, co-founder of the DLP, accepted a Cabinet appointment in the West-Indies Federation, and divorced from her support base, was ignominiously expelled from her party in 1961. Regional leaders such as Eric Williams and Alexander Bustamante shied away from a seat in the Federal Parliament, partly to avoid a similar fate. The Federation may be dead, but like Banquo's ghost, it will haunt the political landscape of the islands for years to come.

TOWARDS A NEW POLITICAL CONFIGURATION

Not all Dominican leaders have accepted the view that the island's best interests are served through closer economic relations with the rest of the Caribbean. A few months after being sworn in as Prime Minister of Dominica, Rosie Douglas stunned his regional counterparts by announcing that he would seek closer association with the European Union. Douglas reasoned that *since Dominica is situated between the two French departments of Guadeloupe and Martinique and given the trading links that currently exist between these countries, Dominica stands to benefit if it holds its independence and become a department of France.*

Many regional leaders immediately dismissed Douglas's announcement as a pathetic attempt to bring back colonialism in the region. Yet Douglas's proposal has a certain degree of logical clarity. The European union, with a collective population of over 300,000,000, has more to offer than any economic union within the Caribbean. Strong historical ties exist between the island and the nearby French Departments of Martinique and Guadeloupe. Dominica's agricultural products find a ready market in the two islands and Dominican workers have made significant contributions to both islands. Commonalities of culture, geographical contiguity and the fact that Dominica has historically proven to be a haven for French nationals fleeing political upheaval, made Douglas's proposal quite persuasive.

Indeed by June 2000, the Dominica Association of Industry and Commerce (DAIC) and its Guadeloupe counterpart, the Union DES Enterprises De La Region Guadeloupe (UDE) executed an economic partnership accord. The accord provided for joint promotion of economic cooperation programmes supported by the European Union and to lobby for the removal of visa restrictions which inhibit joint business initiatives. Douglas's untimely death however, has placed a damper on the development of closer political ties with the European Union.

It is unclear whether Douglas's successor can advance this initiative to its logical conclusion. The economic reprieve recently received by the island's banana industry, the imposition of visa requirements by the Canadian authorities, the recent blacklisting of the island by the United States of America because of the 1996 Offshore Banking Act and its proven link to money laundering, all add a greater urgency to Douglas's bold initiative.

Paradoxically however, Prime Minister Pierre Charles' preoccupation with dousing the political fires set by the James government's economic citizenship and offshore banking programmes may spell the doom of the Dominica/France *rapprochement*. Thrown back on its own resources, the island will prove to be singularly incapable of dealing with the harsh economic realities which confront it in the new millennium.

RETURN OF THE PRODIGAL: DOMINICAN MIGRATION AND ITS AFTERMATH

Irving André

A. OVERVIEW OF DOMINICAN MIGRATION

An examination of the history of Dominican migration reveals two distinct forms of migration. The first is international migration to the United Kingdom, the United States of America and Canada and to a lesser extent, Europe.

This migration for the most part is permanent in that migrants reside in their displaced Dominican communities although expressing the hope of returning to Dominica at some unspecified time in the future. This migration has continued unabated since the early twentieth century. Periodically, certain conditions within the host country has stimulated the exodus of Dominicans. These include the prospect of employment in the U.S. in the early decades of the twentieth century and in labor starved Britain during the 1950s and 1970s. Just as predictably however, legislation such as the 1924 *Walter McCarran Act* in the U.S. and similar legislation in the U.K. in 1962, significantly closed the portals to immigrants from the Caribbean.

Alongside this chain of migration has been the movement of agricultural labour to Canada and the U.S. under the Caribbean

Agricultural Workers Programme[1] and the recently ended H-2 Programme.[2] Under the H-2 programme, the U.S. Department of Labor allowed Florida cane growers to contract 8, 500 workers annually to harvest cane while Immigration Canada allows farmers to do the same in South Western Ontario. Between 1980 and 1991, 2,135 Dominican workers migrated to the U.S and Canada as farm workers. Of these, 126 workers failed to return to Dominica as they were contractually obligated to do.

The other distinct pattern is intra-regional migration. This migration is more permanently rooted in the island than migration to international destinations. Accurate estimates of the number of such migrants are unavailable but the salient features of this migration are well known.

Throughout the late nineteenth and early twentieth centuries, labor recruiters from Panama, Cuba, the Dominican Republic, the U.S. Virgin islands and the Dutch colonies of Curacao and Aruba have plied waters of the eastern Caribbean to recruit labor. The need for such labor may have differed from island to island; - to build the Panama Canal between 1885 and 1920; to harvest cane in Cuba and the Dominican Republic

---

[1] Irving Andre, "The Genesis and Persistence of the Commonwealth Caribbean Seasonal Agricultural Workers Program in Canada,"**Osgoode Hall Law Journal** (1990) V.28 No. 2, pages 244-301.
[2] H.M. Semler, "Aliens in the Orchard: The Admission of Foreign Contract Labourers for Temporary Work in U.S. Agriculture."(1983), **Yale Law Review.**

between 1900 and 1930 or to work in the oil industry in either Trinidad or Curacao between 1945 and 1960. However, the basic attractiveness of such labor remained the same to all potential employers. Through a contract of employment, the migrant laborer could be controlled to a much greater degree than his native counterpart. Working hours and conditions could be tailored to suit the needs of the employer; labor supply during the critical harvest would be guaranteed and labor could not be weaned away by a rival farmer's promise of higher wages. Most important however, the laborers could be repatriated when they were no longer needed. To add a degree of finality to the process, legislation could be enacted to restrict the number of future laborers to suit the exigencies of the moment.

Intra-regional migration from Dominica followed this pattern with little variation. Regional recruiters regarded migrant labor not as persons with rights pursuant to a contract of employment but primarily as expendable labor to be discarded when the need for such labor abated. Protection of these workers was limited to legislation ensuring registration of labor recruiters in the islands and monetary deposits to ensure repatriation of workers without expense to the colony. Limited provision was also made for the families of migrant workers during the latter's absence from their home colony. However, legislation ensuring basic housing conditions or amenities for the migrant workers was virtually non-existent since any expense which encroached on profit was avoided by their employers.

THE EXPORT OF EXPENDABLE LABOUR IN DOMINICA AFTER 1834

University of the West-Indies Historian Dr. Patrick Bryan noted that the British adopted a policy of exporting blacks in the twentieth century; such a policy being the converse of the slave trade policy of the seventeenth to nineteenth centuries.[3] In fact, the policy of exporting blacks commenced in the early nineteenth century following the abolition of the slave trade in 1807. In 1811, commerce involving slaves as items of property was declared to be a felony except that slaves could be legally transported under licence from one British colony to another. This lacunae in the law resulted in the movement of slaves from Dominica, Antigua and Barbados to needy colonies such as Trinidad and what was then British Guiana. Between 1808 and 1830, 3,356 slaves were exported from Dominica to other West-Indian colonies.[4] Furthermore, of 3,800 slaves sent to Trinidad

---

[3] Patrick Bryan, "The Question of Labor in the Sugar Industry of the Dominican Republic in the Late Nineteenth and Early Twentieth Century." **Social and Economic Studies** V. 29 No. 3, pages 280.

[4] D. Ellis, "The Traffic in Slaves between the British West – Indian Colonies, 1807 – 1833." **Economic History Review** (1972) #25 page 58, Table I.

from other West –Indian islands within the same period, 1,100 originated from Dominica.[5]

The continuation of the slave trade in this fashion was not a clandestine operation conducted by colonial malcontents. In Dominica for example, an active participant was A. Hobson, puisne judge and former speaker of the House of Assembly. In 1829, Hobson departed Dominica with nine slaves bound for Trinidad *where their value, considered as articles of traffic, was immediately doubled and where the motives to retain them in slavery were strengthened and the price of freedom was increased exactly in the same proportion.*[6]

The *Emancipation Act* of 1834 formally put an end to intercolonial movement of slaves in the region. Theoretically, the slaves were now freed men and had the privilege of deciding whether to travel to other islands in search of a better life. However, conditions in Dominica at the time appeared to conspire against any wholesale exodus of free blacks. Never a major recipient of slaves and only a marginal producer of sugar, the island was under populated with over 70,000 acres of Crown land in the interior. In 1837, the island's population was 20,000, the vast majority living along the east and west coasts. The freed

---

[5] Eric Williams, "The British West – Indian Slave Trade After Its Abolition in 1807. **Journal of Negro History**, (1942), page 178.
[6] IBID, pages 181-182.

men could therefore settle within the interior and hence avoid the ordeal of travelling to another island.

Settlement in the interior however, remained largely unattractive to the freed slaves. Much of the land comprised thin soil over sheet rock. Production of cash crops such as cocoa and then limes was impossible because of heavy rainfall, transportation problems and the unavailability of start-up capital. Only two settlements had been established in the interior by the end of the nineteenth century. Land on the coast was virtually unobtainable and by 1920, only the Berricoa Estate in Grandbay had been divided up into lots and sold to peasants. The result of this, as noted by the Imperial Department of Agriculture's Report of 1920, was that Grandbay was the most productive area in Dominica since it was better supplied with labor than the rest of the island.

The failure to institute a land settlement scheme and the unattractiveness of life in the interior conspired to force the ex-slaves to settle along coastal districts of the island. A report of the local Department of Agriculture in the 1920s concluded that the absence of any assistance to the peasants in the form of financial aid, a comprehensive land settlement scheme and co-operative factories as had been freely given to small growers in Grenada, St. Vincent and St. Lucia, ensured the existence of a large labor pool on the island.

ADVENT OF LABOUR MIGRATION

What appeared to be an abundant supply of labor to the estate owners in Dominica however, soon dissipated with the advent of labor migration. The estates could only offer employment during the sugar harvest, between June and December. Wages were generally unattractive, given what could be realized in the larger islands. Juxtaposed to these limitations on local employment was the evidence of better wages overseas where the migrant laborer returned *with a flashy cap, a flashy shirt and suitcase....* If land deprivation was intended by the planters to create a labor pool for the local labor market, such deprivation paved the way for the exodus of the ex-slaves in search of employment.

Colonial neglect and the promise of higher wages therefore, made the departure of persons inevitable. Poverty transformed what should have been a matter of choice into a matter of the most urgent necessity. The signs of poverty rampant throughout the eastern Caribbean in the nineteenth century and early twentieth century were even more evident in Dominica. One visitor noted in 1860 that *it is impossible to conceive of a more depressing sight. Every house is in a state of decadence. There are no shops that can properly be so called. The people wander about, idle, chattering, listless.... Everything seems to speak of desolation, apathy, ruin.* Author Jean Rhys recalls how, as a child in the 1890s her father required her, *on certain mornings, to hand out a loaf of bread and small sum, to a procession of indigent men from Roseau.*[7] A member of the Royal Institute of Great Britain summed up the situation in 1899 by noting that *her majesty's black subjects in the West-Indies... have to chose between death from starvation in their native lands and suffering ill-treatment in St. Dominigo....*[8]

Economic adversity and the need for agricultural labor, made Dominica the happy hunting ground for regional labor recruiters. Dominican workers were solicited with contracts of employment for work in Panama, the Dominican Republic and Cuba. Workers were taken to St. Thomas where they would travel to their respective destinations after signing their contracts of employment. Inevitably however, onerous working conditions in their new environment conspired to make the journey less than worthwhile for the migrant worker. The absence of any viable alternative however, ensured that labor recruiters continued to travel to Dominica in search of expendable labor.

The precise number of Dominicans who left in the late nineteenth and early twentieth centuries is uncertain. However, out of a population of 28,000 in 1900, 7,000 laborers were

---

[7] Jean Rhys, **Smile Please**.
[8] Bryan, "The Sugar Industry", page 281.

contracted to work on the Panama canal between 1880 and 1920. A less impressive number travelled to the Dominican Republic, Cuba, Trinidad and British Guiana. Migration to regional destinations such as Curacao and the Dominican Republic continued unabated until 1930 when economic downturns forced migrants to return home.

MIGRATION FROM 1930 TO 1950

From 1930 to 1946, the movement of migrant workers to regional destinations was reduced significantly. This was due to the embargo placed on foreign migrant workers in the United States, Cuba, and Puerto Rico. Furthermore, by the 1930s, the government of Panama started repatriating indigent laborers at their own expense. Travel during the Second World War was also restricted with the threat of German naval activity in the region. Migration to Guadeloupe was limited by the ascendancy of the Vichy regime in France which prompted French nationals to seek refuge in Dominica during this period.

The building of a string of military bases by the U.S. from Guantanamo, Cuba, in the north to Aruba in the south, resulted in the hiring of thousands of migrant workers in these countries.[9]

Two regional developments stimulated the movement of workers in the 1940s and 1950s. Under the auspices of the British, the U.S. contracted 116,000 workers from the British West-Indies between 1943 and 1946 as contract labor.[10] Alongside this movement was a less formal migration to Trinidad and Tobago, engendered by the West-Indies Federation between 1958 and 1962. Migration from the East Caribbean islands constituting the West-Indies Federation to Trinidad increased from approximately 1,900 in 1957 to 4,900 in 1958 and 6,300 in 1959. However, the representation of Dominican workers in that regional labor force was quite small. In the case of Trinidad, the vast majority were contracted from more contiguous islands such as Barbados, Grenada and St. Vincent.

---

[9] See C.R. Otley, **East and West-Indian Rescue, Trinidad**. (Trinidad: Crusoe Publishing House, 1975).
[10] Mary Proudfoot, **Britain and the United States in the Caribbean**, (New York, Pragger, 1953), page 318.

MIGRATION FROM 1950 ONWARDS

Migration increased in the 1950s, particularly from 1955 to 1961. Within the decade, Dominicans travelled to Guadeloupe to work in the sugar and banana industries. Between 1952 and 1958, 550 workers travelled annually to Guadeloupe while in 1955, 103 workers were recruited for employment in the U.S. In the seven year period ending in 1961, over 6,000 Dominicans migrated to the United Kingdom, 2,300 of these being women. (See Table I)

A detailed study of these migrants may well reveal that international and intra- regional migration within this period were not mutually exclusive in that those who laboured in Guadeloupe moved later on to the United Kingdom. The figures indicate that more persons travelled to the U.K. in 1962. Dominicans joined their island counterparts in migrating to Trinidad between 1955 to 1961 although the actual number who did so remains unclear.

Table I   Dominican Migration 1955 – 1960

Year	United Kingdom Men	Women	Guadeloupe
1955	668	117	500
1956	725	401	500
1967	520	383	667

1958	300	260	360
1959	505	360	N.A.
1960	1,222	850	N.A.

Source: Great Britain. Colonial Office. **Annual Report on Dominica**, 1955 to 1962.

Regional developments and natural disasters after 1960 merely perpetuated the migration of Dominicans. These include public works program in the U.S. Virgin islands between 1963 and 1964 and the 1965 construction of the Hess Oil and Harvey Alumina industrial complexes in St. Croix.[11] In August 1964, Hurricane Cleo left 10,000 homeless in Guadeloupe and the ensuing reconstruction created employment opportunities for Dominicans. Internationally, the Domestic Programme in Canada resulted in the migration of a number of Dominican women. According to Basil Cracknell, some 6,069 Dominicans migrated to various destinations between 1960 and 1970.[12]

This figure would undoubtedly have been higher were it not for a number of local construction projects undertaken during that decade. These included a road connecting Soufriere and Pointe Michel, the extension of the Rosalie and Castle Bruce Roads, the

---

[11] Klaus de Albuguergue and Jerome L. McElroy, "West-Indian Migration to the United States Virgin Islands: Demographic Impacts and Socioeconomic Consequences", **International Migration Review**, v. 16, No. 1, page 61 at 67.
[12] Cracknell, Basil, **Dominica**, Harriburg V.A. (1968).

building of the government Printery, the Melville Hall Airport Terminal and five primary schools. The Dominica Grammar School and the Fort Young Hotel were completed in 1963 and 1964 respectively. Migration however, was not severely impacted by this local demand for manual labor since legislative measures in Canada for example, made it easier for educated Dominicans to migrate. Correspondingly, many Dominican emigrants in the 1960s and early 1970s were better educated than their counterparts in an earlier period.

As long as the need for immigrant labor existed, Dominican laborers migrated and were indeed welcomed in the host countries. Once the emergency which necessitated the importation of laborers dissipated, legislation was enacted to repatriate what had then become superfluous labor. The timing of such legislation was usually determined by economic down turns and local backlash against the presence of *small islanders, nigger locusts*[13] *and Domnichen.*[14] In Guadeloupe and Martinique, there is a persistent sentiment that, *Domnichen mal casse, Domnichen volaire, Nous pas vlai Domnichen ici.* (Dominicans are ill-mannered, Dominicans are thieves; we do not want Dominicans here.) In these two islands, cultural xenophobia or the desire to

---

[13] Term mirroring the perception of hordes of immigrants overrunnig their intended destinations.
[14] Pejorative term used in the neighbouring French islands of Guadeloupe and Martinique.

preserve all things French periodically leads to random acts of violence against Dominicans. These developments usually climax in the almost ritualistic purging of the population through well publicized deportations and other legal means.

In the other islands, the Dominican presence is no less evident. Jamaica Kincaid's **The Autobiography of My Mother** illustrates how deeply entrenched is the Dominican presence on the island of Antigua where 20,000 Dominicans reportedly live. This presence has some historical antecedents since villages such as Marigot and Wesley were reportedly populated in the late nineteenth century by immigrants from Antigua and Montserrat. Similarly, a casual stroll in the duty free shopping areas of St. Marten, St. Thomas and St. Croix and at the hotels of Tortola will inevitably be rewarded by the Creole banter of Dominican migrants conversing among themselves.

TRANSPORTATION AND MIGRATION

Migration in the twentieth century has been achieved primarily through sea travel. In the first decades of the twentieth century, Dominica was connected to the United States, Canada, England and Europe by a number of steamships lines providing regular travel service to the island. For example, the Canadian

National Steamships Limited company maintained a regular service to Dominica every two weeks. Later, other steamship lines such as the Royal Mail Lines and Messers Van Geest Ltd. would provide transportation to Britain while the American Defence Line and the Dooth American Shipping Corporation would link the island to the United States of America. Steamship lines from Europe which listed Dominica as a port of call included the Compagnie General Transatlantique Ltd., the Combined Grimaldi and Sissa Line and the Royal Netherlands Steamships Ltd. company.

Air travel in the first half of the century was virtually non-existent. In the early 1950s, the St. Vincent Government operated a Grumman Goose aircraft, connecting the island to St. Vincent and Barbados. In 1958, the Leeward Islands Air Transport Company (LIAT) commenced operations between Antigua, Dominica and Barbados twice weekly, following completion of a 2,500 feet runway at the Melville Hall Airport. Air travel has since overtaken sea travel as the most popular means of migration.

In the nineteenth and twentieth centuries, labor recruiters arranged the transportation of laborers to their respective destinations. Alongside this organized movement however, was a less formal movement in which sea-faring Dominicans travelled to neighbouring islands. One visitor in the 1880s described how, in travelling from Guadeloupe to Dominica, *along the ship, countless canoes... tossed on the great waves. In each craft were two darkies.*

Sea travel became firmly entrenched in the psychology of Dominicans with the development of inter-colonial shipping. By 1954, there were 61 regionally owned vessels and about 80 sailboats registered in the British West-Indies.[15] Vessels ranged from a few feet to 50 feet in length while schooners ranged from 50-120 feet with gross tonnage between 40 to 150 tons. Rates of travel were normally a matter of negotiation between the parties.[16]

Dominica's involvement in inter-colonial commerce ensured that the movement of persons from its shores would continue unabated. In the 1930s and 1940s, sloops and schooners plied the Caribbean Sea transporting goods and persons from one island to another. Sloops such as the Una captained by Captain Veve and the Octavia C owned by prominent Portsmouth merchant Robert Garraway were involved in the movement of goods and persons among the islands.

Other *foreign* owned sloops became well known to Dominicans because of the regularity of their presence. One guided by Captain Gumbs from Anguilla and another by Captain Bramble from Monteserrat brought cattle and donkeys to the

---

[15] Caribbean Commission, **Caribbean Economic Review**, V. 6 (December 1954) (The Hague: Ten Hague N.V.), p.133.
[16] IBID, page 115.

island and returned with bananas, ground provisions and persons. Others such as the Concorda from St. Thomas purchased coconuts from St. Lucia, Dominica and St. Vincent for eventual sale in St. Thomas. Larger ships involved in the carrying trade included the War Spite which carried persons from Barbados to Dominica during World War II and the Caroline under the stewardship of Captain Joseph from the Grenadines. Lady Noel, captained by Captain Noel from the Grenadines, carried firewood and ground provisions from Dominica. During the same period, the steel hulled ship, the Mermaid, plied the waters between Dominica and Barbados but later switched to carrying asphalt from Trinidad to Dominica.

Inter-colonial travel received a strong impetus in 1961 with the Canadian government's gift of two ships, the Federal Palm and Federal Maple to the now defunct West-Indies Federation. Each ship possessed a gross tonnage of 3,200 and provided accommodation for 50 cabin and 200 deck passengers. These ships soon added a degree of regularity to the carrying trade in the region. They made round trips between Jamaica and Trinidad every four weeks and were legally bound to visit each of the ten islands constituting the Federation twice monthly. The presence of these ships altered intercolonial travel in that it attracted a more privileged type of traveller than the sloops and schooner favoured by previous voyagers.

The persistence of trade between Dominica and its neighbouring islands has also perpetuated movement of persons outwards. Vessels depart Portsmouth weekly and fortnightly bound for Antigua and St. Marten. Others depart Roseau weekly bound for Guadeloupe. Until recently, a large vessel, the M.V. Stella, with a 350 ton capacity, travelled fortnightly from Roseau to St. Lucia and Barbados. The ships all carry bananas, lime juice, bay rum, passion fruit and inevitably a few persons remain in the port of call.

Ease of travel, geographical propinquity and limited employment opportunities, conspire to overcome virtually all impediments, legal or otherwise, to intra-regional migration. The possession of valid travel documents is not a prerequisite for the hardiest of travellers. As an exasperated yachtsman complained in a February 1989 letter to the **New Chronicle**:

> One is constantly harassed by young men demanding rides to "anywhere" even though they have no visas or passports to show that they are not travelling illegally.

This compulsion has engendered an even more informal form of travel than that involving sloops and schooners. Itinerant traders and prospective migrants usually embark on a canoe, 24 feet long and 7 feet wide, for the short journey to the French island of Marie Galante where they hope to travel to Guadeloupe. The ease of travel to Marie Galante and the low transportation cost makes this an increasingly popular if not hazardous route to the French islands. Largely unregulated, the perils of this journey are constantly brought to the public's attention with the drowning deaths of hucksters and travellers. Recently, one survivor explained that he had tried unsuccessfully to get a French visa and failing that had resorted to using the *back door way* to get to Guadeloupe.

Dominica's limited resources have earned it the dubious distinction of being a visa economy. On one hand, the island and many of its citizens are clothed in the borrowed robes of creditors, both local and international. Secondly, outward travel is increasingly difficult given that, with the exception of travel to Caricom countries, visa requirements restrict travel to virtually every other destination.

For example, Dominicans desirous of traveling to the French islands must pay onerous fees, ranging from $26.24 EC. for intransit visitors, $66.14 EC for those seeking to remain for up to 30 days, $79.39 EC for those seeking to stay between 31 – 90 days and $132.28 EC for the visitor intending to stay for one year, to the French Consular Agency in Dominica.

The justification for the visa and fee policy is simple. In St. Lucia for example, visa requirements to the French territories were relaxed in March, 2000. Within one year, 20,000 St. Lucians, or more than 1/8 of that island's population, traveled to the French islands, 2,000 of whom remained illegally. Of those who did so, over 600 were charged with criminal offences.

The French fear a similar problem emanating from Dominica. Already in Guadeloupe, certain residential areas around Pointe-A-Pitre, such as Chemin Fer, Bourg Grossier, Carenage, L'Assainimat and La Croix, are known as crime infested areas largely because of the presence of Dominicans. Many of the Dominican residents of these areas have been subjected to particularly harsh treatment from the French authorities.

The French's egregious treatment of Dominicans transcend any scrupulous anxiety over the alleged high incidence of criminal activity amongst Dominicans in the French islands. Those seeking a visa from the French Consular Agency in Roseau must continue to wait lengthy periods to be served by the agency, continue to be the last to be processed upon arrival in the French territories and continue to be treated with ill concealed contempt by the French authorities. In the meantime, French nationals continue to travel to the island without a passport, and can even be found selling Dominican souvenirs on the bay front to their vacationing compatriots.

MIGRATION FROM LEBANON

Lebanon, the international crossroads of the historical trade routes that linked Africa, Asia and Europe, came to prominence as the living space of the early Phoenicians or Canaanites, extraordinary tradesmen who plied their wares along the river Nile, the Black Sea and ultimately Spain. Their city states were conquered by Alexander the Great in 335 BC and thereafter, Lebanon was subjected to Hellenic culture. Subsequently, Lebanon would be ruled by various conquerors and would become part of the Byzantine and the Islamic Empires.

By the mid nineteenth century, Lebanon was part of the Ottoman Empire, with Istanbul as its political, economic and religious centre. The Islamic presence was enforced by local Bashas or governors or by local princes or Emirs. The country was then populated by two broad religious groupings, Christians and Muslims. Among the former, the Maronite Christians, a strain of Roman Catholicism, dominated the two other significant sects, the Melkites and the Greek Orthodox.[17] In addition, a bewildering number of subsects, such as the Syrian Orthodox, Syrian Catholics, Nestorians, Chaldeans and Latin Catholics, coexisted, not always peacefully, with their Christian brethren. Since the French declared the Maronites as part of the French

---

[17] See Andra Mackey, **Lebanon, Death of A Nation**, (Doubleday) 1989, page 31. The following section has been summarised from this book source.

nation in the Seventh Century, the Maronites, through the proselytizing activities of Jesuit priests, and later French imperialists, lived under the protective custody of the French.

Arrayed against this broad Christian grouping, were the Muslims of Lebanon. They were splintered into Sunnis, Shiites and Druze, the former being the dominant sect in Lebanon in the nineteenth century with the latter being the minority. What the Druze lacked in numbers however, they made up in a strong sense of identity. They occupied part of Northern Lebanon, known as the Shuff Mountains while the Maronites occupied the contigous area to the north, known as The Mountain.

For generations, the Druze and Maronite Christians warred against each other. In 1860, the Druze and their historical enemies, fought so viciously against each other that in the Maronite town of Dayr al Qamar, the Druze slaughtered 12,000 Christians in six hours. Alarmed over the carnage, the French came to the rescue of their historical allies and under threat of laying seize to Islamic Beiruit, declared The Mountain as an autonomous province within the Ottoman Empire in 1861.

These two incidents provided the initial impetus for the migration of Maronite Christians to French territories and ultimately to Dominica. During the First World War, the Ottoman Empire joined the Axis powers and the reigning Sultan imposed the brutal administration of Jamal Pasha in The

Mountain. Between 1914 and 1917, some 100,000 Lebanese died of starvation, disease and execution,[18] the majority between Maronite Christians. The end of the War resulted in the dismemberment of the Ottoman Empire and the establishment of Greater Lebanon under French control. Henceforth, the fate of many Maronite Christians would be inextricably entwined with that of their French benefactors.

The fear of being overrun by the Muslims in Lebanon and the opportunity of migration to various parts of the French Empire precipitated an exodus of Maronite Christians in the Twentieth Century. The first known Lebanese migrant to the Caribbean was Jacob Debs, a Maronite Christian who came from a village in The Mountain called Bazhoun[19]. He migrated to French Guiana in the late nineteenth century and then moved to Guadeloupe.

Debs subsequently encouraged numerous family members in Bazhoun and in a nearby village called Niha, to travel to Guadeloupe. Many of these early migrants ultimately traveled to Australia, Africa, Latin America, Surinam and French Guiana. Others traveled to other islands including Antigua, St. Kitts and Martinique.

Dominica became a favoured destination for a number of reasons. Land was relatively cheap, the island's

---

[18] Mackey, **Lebanon**, supra, page 106.
[19] From the notes of Antoine Raffoul.

population was relatively sparse and the island had none of the Maronites' historical enemies. Additionally, there was a miniscule commercial sector and therefore ample opportunities for motivated immigrants. Furthermore, there were little travel restrictions between Guadeloupe and Dominica.

The first Lebanese migrant to the island was Ayoub Dib, who arrived in the 1920s. During the Vichy administration, Lebanese residents in the French territories followed their French compatriots to Dominica. Dib sponsored his brother George Dib from Columbia while Antoine Karam, Antoine Gabriel, Miriam Younis and their respective families arrived from Guadeloupe.

Others soon followed suit. Elias Nassief and his family arrived from Surinam after the end of the Second World War. He subsequently sponsored his brother-in-law Antoine Astaphan, who arrived in the late 1940s.

The creation of the State of Israel in 1948 added another impetus to the movement. Palestinian refugees moved to the Caribbean, with one of them, Joseph Azouz, ultimately arriving in Dominica. In the 1950s, a few Syrians, M. George and Joseph Azar travelled to Dominica, while in 1961, the last of the men of Bazhoun, Hanna Raffoul and his son Antoine, followed by six other family members in 1963, arrived in Dominica.

Many of the early migrants established themselves as itinerant tradesmen, plying their wares in the towns and villages which dotted the island. They exhibited what would later become the hallmarks of their commercial success - low prices, accessibility and high turnover of goods.

The progeny of these early migrants became assimilated by attending local schools. The names of some would be Anglicized to dilute social ostracism. For example, Antoine Astaphan Georgy Chaia would be shortened to Antoine Astaphan while Elias Nassief would shed El Barswe, the family name in Bazhoun.

As the fortunes of the Lebanese immigrants grew, strategic political alliances would be forged, most notably, between Wadi Astaphan and the Dominica Labour Party in the 1970s. In that decade, Elias Nassief encountered sustained attack over his ownership of Geneva Estate in Grandbay, and the economic stranglehold which the estate held over the village.

Since then however, a new generation of the men from Bazhoun, such as Senior Counsel Anthony Astaphan and McGill graduate Ivor Nassief, have emerged. The old values which have yielded considerable economic benefits, continue to be manifested in businesses identified simply as Nassief, Astaphan, Raffoul and Issa Trading. In the interim, new social and conjugal relationships have been forged between the descendants of the Maronite Christians and the Dominican population to an extent unimaginable by the original immigrants.

AREAS MOST AFFECTED BY MIGRATION

Dominican migrants come from virtually every town or village on the island. Some coastal areas however, are more heavily affected than those in the interior. Grandbay for example, has suffered a steady loss of its people due to a number of reasons. Its proximity to Martinique has historically made it the first port of call for French refugees as early as the eighteenth century. Economic factors such as the relative unavailability of arable land, have deprived residents of the means of providing for their families. Individual ownership of the Geneva Estate has historically thwarted the ability of Grandbay residents to achieve anything more than a marginal way of life and this has been a primary cause for the steady exodus of Grandbay residents to foreign destinations.

The town of Portsmouth to the north however, is perhaps more closely identified with migration than any other part of Dominica.[20] It is nestled in Prince Rupert's Bay, the only natural harbour on the island. Historically, the harbour existed as a way station for boats plying the Caribbean. As early as 1857, the U.S.

---

[20] The town is reported to have the highest density of professional hucksters in the island. See Michel-Rolph Trouillot's **Peasants and Capital. Dominica in the World Economy**, (Johns Hopkins University Press, Baltimore, MD, 1988) page 38.

published Blunt's **American Coast Pilot** noted that *fleets destined to other parts of the West-Indies commonly come to anchor in this bay, for the purpose of supplying themselves with wood and water, for which there are excellent conveniences.* Residents can still recall the town being used a training ground for German battle cruisers prior to the Second World War and a port of call for American submarines later. During the War, the town served as the primary landing area for refugees from Guadeloupe fleeing the Vichy regime in France.

The attractiveness of Portsmouth to seafarers also led to boat building, an activity ubiquitous to the area. Along with the steeple of the Roman Catholic Church and the twin peaks of Forts Rupert and Shirley, the incomplete schooner, reposing either on the shores of Lagoon to the north or Glanvilla to the south, has been the most distinguishing feature of Portsmouth.

For boat owners seeking a respite from the monotony of travel, or from the hurricane season, or those merely desirous of effecting repairs to their sloops or schooners, the Indian River, separating the town of Portsmouth from the village of Glanvillia, provided a natural docking area for that purpose. While grounded, supplies could be bought and later sold in Antigua, St. Martin, St. Kitts and Nevis. Relationships could also be forged as the groundwork for a more sedentary life is laid. Many of the seafarers who visited the area later returned and settled in the town and in some cases, continued to ply their trade from the area. Names such as Captain Mitchell, Captain Joseph, Captain McLawrence, Kenzie and Wickham have all been etched in the fabric depicting the town's colourful history.

ECONOMIC REASONS FOR MIGRATION

Economic factors conspire against a favourable population density to provide the primary justification for migration of Dominicans.[22] The rugged interior contains land which is largely uncultivable. While banana production is the mainstay of the economy, production is limited to 6 - 7 tonnes per acre compared to 25 tonnes in neighbouring Guadeloupe.

The crop is also susceptible to hurricanes. Indeed in 1979, 1980, 1989, and 1995, Hurricanes David, Allen, Hugo and Luis, respectively devastated the industry and reduced export earnings from the crop by as much as 80%.

Unemployment and underemployment have historically been a major factor in migration of Dominicans. Economic destitution in the nineteenth century cemented the process of migration commenced between 1807 and 1834. A short-lived prosperity in the second decade of the twentieth century when the

---

[22] See B. Walsh, "Population Density and Emigration in Dominica", **The Geographical Journal,** V. 134 (Part 2), (June 1968), page 229

island became the world's largest lime producer stanched the exodus. However, the demise of that industry in the 1920s revived the flow of Dominicans outward.

The lack of viable alternatives to migration kept the sea lanes open for migrants. Indeed a report of the Imperial Department of Agriculture on Dominica for the years 1919 – 1920 concluded that *labourers are leaving the island owing to low wages and lack of regular employment. It would appear that the less work done on estates, the larger will be the exodus of able-bodied manhood, and matters in this respect, bad enough now, will become worse.*

NEED FOR FOREIGN LABOUR

Ironically, emigration from Dominica in search of employment gave rise to its converse – the need for cheap immigrant labor to sustain the island's agriculture. While Dominican laborers moved elsewhere within the region in the early twentieth century, they were replaced by laborers from St. Kitts, Montserrat, and Antigua. The development of the sugar and cotton industries in these islands quickly reduced this flow to a mere trickle and alternative sources of labor had to be found. By the 1920s, the colonial government was considering land settlement schemes involving laborers from Barbados and from India to supplement the labor force in Dominica. However, a report of the Imperial College of Agriculture in 1920 concluded that, *even if immigration is again permitted, the conditions likely to be imposed and the responsibilities to be undertaken will probably be such as to make them impossible of acceptance by Colonial Governments with very small resources.*

The migration of laborers, the resultant shortage of local labor and the singular inability of the island government to augment the dwindling local labor force due to financial constraints, are recurring themes in the history of Dominican agriculture. A 1960 plan to have 10,000 to 15,000 Barbadian laborers settle on a 700 acre site in the Calibishie / Hampstead area and on a 1,200 acre site in La Plaine foundered since the colonial government lacked the financial resources to fund the proposed settlement. Furthermore, a July 1991 Public Sector Task Force concluded that Dominica required an influx of foreign labor, preferably from Taiwan, to mitigate the weekly shortage of 150 persons in the local agricultural sector. However, such schemes for the importation of foreign labour will likely remain a chimera since low wages, the primary cause of labor migration on the island, will likely conspire to prevent foreign laborers from travelling to the island.

DOMINICA AS A HAVEN FOR IMMIGRANTS

Despite its general inability to attract agricultural labor, the island has a tradition of being the destination of persons fleeing political upheaval. During the French Revolution, loyalists fearful of Madame Guillotine which was holding court in Pointe-a-Pitre, Guadeloupe, sought refuge in villages such as Vieille Casse and Penville while their counterparts in Martinique fled to Grandbay and nearby villages. After the Emancipation of Slavery in 1834, several hundred slaves from Guadeloupe escaped to Dominica.[18A] Following the eruption of Morne Pelée in 1902, a number of French citizens, including the paternal forbears of former University of the West Indies professor Ashton Delauney, traveled to Dominica and settled in Pointe Michelle. During the Second World War, French nationals on the two islands sought refuge from the Vichy regime on Dominica.

This process was not only confined to French nationals. Following the abolition of slavery in 1834, the English population on the island slowly dwindled with the result that by the end of the nineteenth century, colonial apologists viewed this decline with great trepidation. In 1887, James Anthony Froude in his

---

[18A] Joseph John Gurney, **A Winter In the West-Indies**, (London:1840) page 70.

book, **The English in the West-Indies**, cautioned that the *white is relatively disappearing, the black is growing; this is the fact with which we have to deal with.*

The necessity to deal with the white population's decline arose because of the assumption that the white presence on the island was critical to the advancement of the Negro population. In 1899, W.R. Livingstone in his book, **Black Jamaica**, put it succinctly by noting that *the advancement of the Negro is contingent on his association with the white race and on the character of that race. Without the stimulus of that factor, he cannot better himself.*

That perception formed the basis for a scheme in the early 1900s to attract *gentlemen farmers* from England to the island. Between 1904 and 1905, 30 such families migrated to Dominica and endowed with grants of land from the colonial government, endeavored to replicate England in what was a very unEnglish environment. The harshness of the interior, the difficulties attendant on cultivating what in many cases was virgin forest, conspired with the onset of World War One to put an end to this influx of Englishmen. The trepidation experienced by many of these pioneers is captured by Jean Rhys in stories such as *Pioneers Oh Pioneers!* Indeed one of Rhys' character in her 1934 novel, **Voyage in the Dark**, notes that these individuals ran the risk of *never seeing a white face from one week's end to the other and growing up like a nigger every day.*

Political turmoil or the threat of it continues to have repercussions on the island. On one hand, it has given rise to a new advent of economic refugees as in the influx of economic citizens. In 1994, there was an aborted plan to grant temporary asylum to 1,000 Haitians fleeing the brutal Cedras regime. In both situations however, the justification was the same. Dwindling returns from banana production, the vagaries of the tourist industry, the need to obtain capital either from wealthy foreign investors or largesse from the U.S. government, either created a need for immigrants or justified the offer of temporary sanctuary to some. Economic pragmatism, not humanitarian zeal, best explains the contemplated advent of these newcomers to the shores of Dominica.

THE LEGACY OF MIGRATION

In assessing the legacy of migration on West-Indian societies, sociologist David Lowenthal has noted that *some West-Indian societies adjust to migration as the norm, others endure it as trauma.* Dominica likely falls within the former category since the island has developed a dependency on migration as one of the central factors guaranteeing its economic viability.

A number of factors explain this. In the post-emancipation era and indeed throughout much of the nineteenth century, the island depended on grants and subventions from the colonial government merely to meet its current government expenditures. This state of dependency persisted throughout the twentieth century to a point when in 1976, the government had to seek a loan from the British to pay its workers. Revenues have never kept pace with expenditures. This condition, inevitable in a small island with few natural resources, has led to the conclusion by economist Carleen O'Loughlin that Dominica, along with other Windward and Leeward islands, are *non-viable* economies.

This assessment is less true today than in the 1960s when it was made. A burgeoning tourist industry, retrenchment in the public sector and most importantly, remittances from Dominicans abroad, all combine to ensure that the island's future is not as bleak as had been previously anticipated. The steady exodus has relieved pressures on the island's social services and job creating capabilities. Remittances have further lessened the need for foreign exchange and have given resident Dominicans greater flexibility in education, social mobility and overall standard of living.

Financial assistance is not limited to contributions made by migrants to their families who remained on the island. A host of organizations contribute through financial aid, the expertise of their membership and fraternal organizations to worthy causes in Dominica. In England for example, the **Dominica Overseas Nationals Association** (DONA) has a mandate to create U.K. markets for Dominican products and in the aftermath of Hurricane David in 1979, sent 17 nurses equipped with medical supplies to the island. In New York, the **Dominican Association** (DARDA), the **Dominica Benevolent Society** and the **Dominica Patriots of New York** make regular financial donations to institutions such as health care and educational facilities along with their counterpart in Boston, the **Sisserou Cultural Association of Boston.** Similarly in Washington DC, the Dominica Association has contributed medical and education supplies to the island for over twenty years. Further north in Canada, the **Commonwealth of Dominica Association** in Scarborough and Hamilton, the **Sisserou Cultural Club Inc.**, **Le Club du Social du Quebec** and the **Dominican Association of Vancouver**, among others, make regular contributions to the island and its citizenry.

The contributions of these organizations cannot be overemphasized. Their efforts further reveal that the patriotic zeal which motivated such contributions, can be harnessed and then channeled into activities which will ultimately inure to the benefit of the island. These activities transform what had hitherto been the loss of the island's more enterprising and educated citizens, into a foreign-based resource which can be tapped in time of need.

However, migration is a double- edged sword in that while it relieves population pressures and increases foreign exchange earnings through remittances, it steals manpower and reinforces the knot of dependency.[23] Migration fosters dependency in that remittances and *remigrants* alter the indigenous value systems. Communal sharing therefore gives way to western style consumerism. Inexorably, visions of New York, Toronto and London become the biggest impediments towards the fostering of an indigenous lifestyle which reflects the realities of life on the island.

POPULATION SIZE

The most visible effect of migration and probably the most quantifiable, is population size. From 1891 to 1981, the island's population increased except for the ten year period prior to 1891. (See Table II)

---

[23] Payne & Sutton, eds., **Dependency Under Challenge**, (1984)

Table II

Dominica Population 1871-1991

Year	Population
1871	27, 178
1881	28, 211
1891	26, 041
1901	28, 894
1911	33, 863
1921	37, 059
1946	47, 624
1960	59, 916
1970	69, 548
1981	74, 625
1991	71, 797
2001	71,727*

Source: **Statistical Digest # 7,** 1992. Central Statistical Office, Ministry of Finance, Government of Dominica.
* 2001 Population and Housing Census preliminary report.

The most recent census figures however, indicate that net migration of Dominicans is greater than the natural increase in population. Preliminary reports indicate that between 1991 and 2000, the natural increase in population was 9,322 while 9,968 nationals migrated within the same period. Records from the Ministry of Health indicate that the natural increase in population between 1981 and 1991 was 12,600. Absent any migration, the island's population in 1991 should have been 87,225. Assuming that the population figure for 1981 is accurate, it appears that the net annual migration from Dominica in the 1980s was 1,260. Similar figures for 1970 to 1981 indicate that without migration, the 1981 population should have been approximately 86,650 persons instead of the actual figure of 74,625. This would suggest that 1,200 persons migrated annually from Dominica in the 1970s.

The above figures are significant for a number of reasons. The fact that more persons migrated from Dominica in the 1980s than in the 1970s is surprising since most economic indicators suggest that the decade witnessed a great deal of economic activity. That migration would increase even in periods of economic growth suggest just how deeply rooted it is on the island.

Secondly, the much vaunted perception that Dominica will soon be inundated by expatriates wishing to resettle on the island is not supported by the figures presently available. An undetermined number of expatriates have presently settled on the island. As noted by a commentary in the July 13, 1990, edition of the **New Chronicle**, *the returning expatriates and their offspring will be richer and more sophisticated people than those who left these shores in the 1950s and 1960s.* Indeed, the influence of these replanted Dominicans are already being felt in business, the professions and various charitable organizations.

THE CRISIS OF THE DOMINICAN *REMIGRANT*

The repercussions of this return migration on Dominica may be of some concern in the future. Already, some consequences such as the rise of land prices, the cost of construction, the increased demand for health care services given that a significant number of the *remigrants* are retirees and the displacement of some workers, are being felt. These potentially harmful effects however, may be more than compensated for by the job creating ventures which many of the *remigrants* are prepared to initiate.

For many remigrants, Dominica has become a land of shattered dreams. Many have had to abandon incomplete edifices and return to their adopted land. Anecdotal information suggests that a disproportionate number of those whose dreams have either been deferred or dashed, originate in England.

A number of factors explain this. Mass migration to England in the 1950s preceded that to North America. Dominican migrants to England for the most part, have returned less frequently to Dominica than their North American counterparts. As a result, they have clung to an edenic view of the island and its citizens to a greater extent than other migrants. Correspondingly, English remigrants have been less prepared to deal with the local labourers' cavalier approach to work; his casual disdain for contractual obligations and the graft which accompanies a significant number of housing projects on the island. All too late, the English remigrant learns that **cost overruns** are as ubiquitous as the unrelenting sunshine and exasperated and despondent, he inevitably retreats to his adopted land.

Those who return and remain in the island may well be surprised at the less than cordial welcome they may receive from those who remained behind. A 1993 calypso succinctly captured the perception of many Dominicans towards this new immigration phenomenon: *I hear that some are / coming home to roost / Overseas recession / See them coming / To cause division.* A commonly expressed view is that the *remigrants* left the *good ship* of Dominica for greener pastures and are only returning now that the ship is sailing in calm waters. Indeed, many Dominicans regard the *remigrants* as merely seeking refuge from the harsh economic realities of life in their adopted countries and their return motivated less by patriotism than by economic pragmatism.

The attitude of Dominicans towards the *remigrants* may not be the only factor limiting the number of Dominicans wishing to end their days on the island. By all accounts, many experience difficulty re-adjusting to the slower pace of life. They return to the island with unrealistic expectations about local life. Those who do envision a life of pastoral splendour as the just reward for difficulties experienced in the metropole.

This desire to compensate for former hardship often translates into a compulsion to build huge edifices with all the accoutrements of a genteel lifestyle. Many *remigrants* are also plagued by a desire to eschew their humble beginnings and to put as much distance between themselves and their social antecedents. Inevitably, the village becomes too muddy; the people too coarse and inquisitive and the life too slow and unfulfilling.

The effect of this perceived snobbery and ostentation on the local population, is not entirely unexpected. Many *remigrants* become the target of every hoodlum in the town or village. Inexorably, it is not the *dewy morn* which obstructs the view of the breathtaking landscape but the ubiquitous burglar bars which have transformed many an island palace into a prison.

Socially, many *remigrants* fare no better. Their prolonged absence has divorced them from the circles of the growing local middle class. Other than occasional family reunions or gatherings with fellow *remigrants*, social interaction is limited. Night-life on the island, except for Fridays and Saturdays, is virtually nonexistent. The breaking waves, the splendour of the setting sun and the lush landscape quickly lose their luster when viewed from a deserted porch, verandah or burglar-barred window. Inexorably, there is a realization that the idyllic Dominican landscape which had occupied so central a place in the *remigrant's* consciousness, is really a figment of his imagination.

Another problem besets many *remigrants*. Anecdotal information confirms that it is the male member of the family who is more desirous of return to the island. Invariably, the wives stay behind, intent on remaining as close to the children and grandchildren in the metropole. The result is that the *remigrant* becomes torn between a desire to remain in his native land and to be reunited with the family he left behind. In many instances, it becomes an impossible situation which inevitably leads to marriage breakdown. Depressed, the *remigrant* succumbs to the lethargy of local life and its myriad consequences.

Even where both spouses return to the island, they may find it difficult to relinquish the ties that bind them to the adopted land. The weekly pilgrimage to the shopping mall; the Friday night bingo; the Saturday garage sale; libation in a compatriot's basement is never as endearing as when one is divorced from it. Life on the island ultimately becomes an interminable comparison between the new reality and that which was left behind. Many overcome the seductive memories but others fail, and inevitably return to the metropole.

Government efforts to ameliorate difficulties experienced by *remigrants* are virtually nonexistent. Assistance is limited to tariff concessions on personal and household items. Initiatives evident on other islands, such as the establishment of a Facilitation Unit in Jamaica and Barbados, are noticeably absent. A few enterprising locals have established companies to provide services for the prodigals. However, the *remigrants* are largely left to their own devices or the assistance of friends and family, to cope with the new island reality.

To counteract some of these problems, many *remigrants* have banded together to provide mutual support to mitigate some of the adverse effects of returning to the island. They recently established Expat-Dominica, an organization which main objective is to preserve the fellowship and solidarity among Dominicans who have returned from abroad. While Expat-Dominica and similar groups may well offer the *remigrants* a sense of well-being, they may further increase the perceived distance between themselves and the rest of the island's population.

The difficulties attendant on resettlement will likely dissipate with the passage of time and an appreciation of the benefits wrought by the *remigrants*. Inevitably, most will see that return migration is less the end result of Dominicans seeking refuge in their own country than the logical end result of the exodus of Dominicans from time immemorial. In the interim, the reception accorded to many returning migrants will continue to be reminiscent of that accorded the biblical prodigal son by his brother. This time however, family and friends will feast the return of the prodigal but many onlookers will be frowning.

THE RISE AND FALL OF THE UNITED WORKERS PARTY

Irving André

The inauspicious beginnings of the United Workers Party (UWP) on July 3, 1988 could not foretell the tremendous success the party would enjoy in the 1990 and 1995 general elections. In its first news release, the UWP noted that its founding members were *deeply concerned about the erosion of basic democratic rights, the high handed approach to the business of the State, the state of fear in the nation, the organized victimization of the workers and the need for a creditable alternative government.*

The 35 to 40 persons who attended the Party's initial meeting at the Layou River Hotel formed a Steering Committee chaired by Edison James, former Manager of the Dominica Banana Marketing Corporation. The Committee had the responsibility of carrying on the business of the Party and recruiting new members until its first Annual Convention. The fact that the UWP held its first annual convention within four months on October 23, 1998 underscored the urgency with which it set about its business.

While the founding members of the UWP envisaged the new party as a viable political party, the DFP and DLP did not share that optimistic view. Prime Minister Charles expected that any third party would help her party at the expense of the Dominica Labour Party. Then Opposition Leader, Michael Douglas, dismissed the party as a group of disenchanted members of the ruling Freedom Party.

The Steering Committee of UWP represented a cross section of the society. Its leader, an agronomist by profession, had an intimate knowledge of the banana industry and a natural political base in the banana belt encompassing the villages of Marigot, Wesley and Woodfordhill. The Deputy Chairman, Julius Timothy, was a parliamentarian and businessman while the General Secretary and agricultural economist, Norris Prevost, had been involved in the garment and construction industries since the 1970s. The other members originated from the labour movement and the rural communities.

For the most part however, the UWP's leadership is comprised of upwardly mobile Dominicans nurtured in the radical chic of the late 1960s and 1970s. Whether through business or professional endeavors, they reaped the economic rewards which resulted from the social and educational policies of successive Labour Party governments in the 1960s and 1970s. Their foray into politics reflected a desire to seek political power commensurate with the economic clout they collectively yielded.

RELATIONS BETWEEN THE UWP AND DFP

Despite the animosity between the UWP and DFP, they have strong ideological affinities and their difference is only one of degree. They both recognized the crucial role of banana production in the economy although the UWP advocated greater government control over the marketing of the crop. Both parties also supported the goals of crop diversification, promoting Ecotourism and regional integration.

The primary difference between the leadership of the DFP and the UWP lay not so much in their respective economic policies but in their social composition. The leadership of the DFP for the most part, is thought to represent old money and its myriad interests. This is more apparent than real but on the islands, old perceptions do not dissipate easily. The DFP is thought to possess a more identifiable social pedigree than the UWP. The quickly vanishing old guard of the DFP can trace their political lineage to the 1950s and 1960s whereas the UWP's leadership is of a more recent political vintage. Lacking the social and political pedigree of the DFP, the UWP's leadership compensate for this seeming deficiency by priding themselves as being *self made men*, without having benefited from the economic tailwind generated by the wealth of their forbears.

The simmering resentment between the two parties results from the natural antipathy between these two loosely defined social groupings of similar economic standing, with one trying to usurp the other. The UWP resents the DFP and views it as a relic of the island's elitist past. The DFP on the other hand, dismisses its rival as an agglomeration of persons motivated by self-interest. The animosity between the parties was fuelled in the early 1990s, by the UWP's belief that its supporters were harassed or terminated from employment in the island's civil service. In a society where who wins office determines questions as mundane as who gets invited to the next cocktail party, the antipathy between the UWP and DFP will likely endure for the foreseeable future.

RELATIONS BETWEEN THE UWP AND DLP

The UWP shares with the DLP a base of support which is largely derived from the rural areas of the island. More than the DLP however, the party's original bastion of support was concentrated in the island's main banana belt comprising the villages of Marigot, Wesley and Woodfordhill. By the 1995 general elections however, the party's electoral base had broadened significantly, thereby enabling the UWP to gain 34.36% of the popular vote on the island.

That the UWP was able to broaden its appeal was due to some extent, to its ability to wean away key individuals from the DLP. These included former DLP strategists Dennis Joseph, Ferdinand Frampton, and former Prime Minister Minister Patrick John. They were able to attract individuals such as Sobers Esprit, Francisco Esprit, Ron Green and barrister Julian Prevost, many of whom had been in the vanguard of the anticolonial movement in the 1970s and in a few cases, had suffered from the repressive measures of the John administration. These defections weakened the DLP in the mid 1990s and gave the UWP a competitive edge over the DFP.

From its inception, the UWP proved to be quite skillful and adept at exploiting tensions within the two traditional parties and bolstering its support at the expense of its competitors. A case in point was the defection of former Prime Minister Patrick John. In his hey day in the 1970s, John's main challenger for the leadership of the DLP was Michael Douglas, the deceased brother of Rosie Douglas, leader of the DLP in the 1990s. Much of John's antipathy towards Michael Douglas was transferred to his brother who initially had been a supporter of John in the drive towards independence. This support dissipated after John had become tired of Rosie Douglas' socialist rhetoric in the late 1970s.

The UWP, particularly in the post 1995 period, was able to exploit another constant in the island's politics-a pervasive sense of ideological fluidity within the political community. Since the 1960s, the party in power has generally manipulated the granting of government jobs, contracts and statutory appointments to its respective supporters. Opposition to the government has historically been a costly proposition for even the most qualified professional and failure to support a party in power may confine an individual to oblivion for as long as the party remains in power.

This was true of Labour Party and Freedom Party administrations in the past, albeit to varying degrees. The unprecedented degree to which the UWP adhered to this constant in the post 1995 period had two consequences on the island. It caused defections from the party's two political rivals and bolstered the ranks of the party's support base, particularly in the four vote rich constituencies which comprise the island's capital. However, the cronyism and favouritism exhibited by the James administration after 1995 and the blurring of the lines between personal and public interest triggered a simmering resentment in the population which ultimately developed into a groundswell of opposition in the late 1990s.

THE ROAD TO ELECTORAL VICTORY

The UWP held its first public convention on October 23, 1988. Before an impressive and appreciative crowd, the leadership reiterated the reasons for the party and its policies. The policies included amending the Constitution to limit the tenure of the Prime Minister to two terms, and encouraging economic development based on private sector growth and national planning. In foreign affairs, the party declared its support for regional integration and the international community's condemnation of apartheid in South Africa. It also declared its support for crop diversification and the operation of a marketing organization which would purchase the produce of farmers. In assessing the party's successful first convention, one analyst noted that *"the so-called third force has rolled off the starter's mark in grand style with the joyful sound of a clear public blessing."*[1]

In the months following its first annual convention, the UWP pursued a vigorous policy of recruiting members and meeting various sector groups in the community. In early 1989, it met with the Christian Council of Churches for guidance on issues including drugs, casino gambling and corruption in high places. In April 1989, the party met with the trade union

---

[1] **New Chronicle**, November 2, 1998, page 62.

leadership for guidance on industrial issues. Later in June 1989, its leaders met with representatives from the Dominica Association of Industry and Commerce (DAIC) and the Media Workers Association for their respective input into the party's policies and programmes.

The initiatives taken by the UWP in 1989 to propagate their policies bore fruit in the 1990 general elections. The party gained six seats in the 21 seat Legislature, compared to 11 for the DFP and 4 for the DLP. That the UWP would displace the DLP as the main opposition party partly reflected the party's success in gaining the confidence of the electorate. It further indicated that while the public was grateful to the Dominica Freedom Party for the improvement in the quality of life in the 1980s, it had become somewhat resentful at the self-assuredness bordering on aloofness of the DFP. The vote for the UWP also confirmed the belief that the DLP was then little more than a spent force in the politics of the island.

The electoral success of the UWP on May 28, 1990, moved the party from the periphery of political life to become the principal player in opposition to the Freedom Party Government. Hitherto dismissed as political upstarts, the party seized the initiative as being the legitimate opposition voice in the Legislature and indeed pretender to the throne. In November 1990, the party's Third Conference of Delegates mandated its leader to move a motion of no confidence against the government. The reasons for the motion included Dame Charles' alleged refusal to broadcast the proceedings of Parliament, her alleged high handed manner in handling affairs of State and her alleged financial irresponsibility in appointing an eleven member Cabinet, the largest in the OECS.

The government's slim majority ensured the defeat of the motion. While the debate enabled the government to list its achievements since 1980, the motion forced the public to focus on the fate of the DFP government and the party which may have precipitated that fate.

Between 1990 and 1995, there was a war of attrition between the Dominica Freedom Party and the United Workers Party with the Labour Party acting as cheerleader for the UWP while savoring its potential role as king maker in 1995. The antipathy between the DFP and UWP was heightened by allegations of bugging of the UWP headquarters and personal attacks which form part of the fabric of political discourse on the island. Inevitably, the animosity trickled down to the supporters to a point where there were periodic clashes between the two political groups.

The party established itself as a legitimate alternative to the Freedom Party government between 1991 and 1995. A resolution adopted at the party's Fourth Delegate Conference in

November 1991, called on Government to assist Windban to become involved in shipping, ripening and marketing of bananas sold in the U.K. and Europe. Another resolution called for the withholding of voting rights to economic citizens for at least seven years, while another contemplated reserving certain areas of economic activity to Dominicans.

These resolutions were aimed at assuaging the alienation engendered by the Charles' government's attempts to attract foreign investment on the island. They further reflected the apprehension of members of the agricultural sector that their interests were subordinated to government efforts to encourage industrial activity on the island. They also capitalized on fears in the business community over the spectre of newly minted citizens from Taiwan or Hong Kong depriving them of economic opportunities.

THE 1995 GENERAL ELECTIONS

With the approach of general elections in 1995, the UWP was poised to assume the reigns of government. The party's economic policies had placed it on the right of the political spectrum. Socially however, the party's composition endeared it to the public since its key players had a long history of involvement in the banana industry and in business. While not populists in the manner of former Premier Edward Leblanc or Prime Minister Patrick John, they nevertheless had a closer identification with the electorate than the ruling Freedom Party.

Two developments favoured the UWP prior to 1995 and greatly accounted for its success at the polls in that year. In the years preceding 1995, many members of the Labour Party gravitated to the UWP. They did this for myriad reasons including disillusionment with the DLP's leadership; the return of former Prime Minister John, the absence of a populist leader, and various enticements from the UWP. Not only did these DLP stalwarts join the UWP but they also weaned a significant portion of the electorate away from their old party.

Even more significantly, the party capitalized on the public's disillusionment with the DFP by 1995. During the 1980s, the DFP had made significant economic progress evidenced by a burgeoning tourist industry, increased employment in the island's service industry and despite natural disasters, steady returns in the banana industry. This was achieved against a backdrop of a relatively stable industrial and political climate.

By the 1990s, much of this had changed. Economic growth dwindled to 2% per annum. Foreign investment failed to live up to its promise of a high level of job creation. Assistance from the U.S. to the region decreased from $226 million in 1985 to $22 million in 1995. Grandiose investment schemes such as the Guinness Project never got off the ground. The banana industry suffered from fluctuating prices and the resultant hardship created a motherlode of discontent in the banana belt of the island.

The main problem faced by the DFP by 1995 however, revolved around its leader. Dame Mary Eugenia Charles had rescued the island from the abyss into which it had sunk following 1979. Her role in the 1983 Grenada invasion had given the island a degree of visibility hitherto thought unimaginable. She was garlanded with accolades for her firm leadership and for the economic benefits her party bestowed upon the island.

Much of this goodwill however, evaporated prior to the 1995 elections. Economic downturns in the banana industry, retrenchment in the public sector, conflict with the island's main union, the Civil Service Association, eroded the DFP's support among the electorate. Dame Charles was criticized for cultivating a cult of leadership. Her failure to appoint a deputy leader and impatience with dissension within the party merely exacerbated the party's difficulties in the eyes of the public. In the 1980s, Charles' strong leadership, which earned her the moniker, *"Mamo"*, was a source of pride since it seemed a strong bulwark against the forces of radicalism on the island. By the 1990s however, her intransigence on issues such as power sharing, appeared self-centered and a source of irritation.

The 1995 election results reflected the public's disillusionment with the Charles government. The UWP captured eleven of the twenty-one available seats with the remaining ten being divided equally between the DFP and DLP. The party held on to the six seats won in 1990 and wrested five seats from the DFP. In 1996, the UWP captured an additional seat when Brian Alleyne, the new leader of the DFP resigned after accepting a judicial appointment. Two of the four new seats of the UWP were captured in Roseau, a DFP fortress for the last fifteen years.

ECONOMIC POLICIES OF THE JAMES ADMINISTRATION

The triumph of the United Workers' Party in the island's general elections in June 1995, did not herald a change in the island's economic fortunes. The government came into being when the ill-fated buyout of Geest had already begun, the preferential treatment of the region's bananas was already under siege and when international agencies, particularly the International Monetary Fund, demanded painful structural adjustment with its consequent retrenchment as a condition precedent to extending loans to the island.

The James government's economic policies can best be described as a relentless pursuit of foreign capital euphemistically termed the Mobilization of Capital for National Development. While in opposition, the UWP had presented itself as economic nationalists intent on protecting local interests from foreign investors. This approach was completely reversed following the UWP's ascension of power in 1995. Nationalist pride predicated on a desire to protect the island from foreign interests became sacrificed on the altar of economic exigency.

From 1995 to 2000, no sector would be immune from the UWP's solicitation of foreign capital. The island's Economic Citizenship Programme, land ownership, banking and the energy sectors all fell prey to policies which gave foreign interests a major financial stake on the island.

In 1996 for example, the government prepared a White Paper on the Economic Citizenship Programme. The Paper advocated a revision of the program from its avowed policy of facilitating foreign investment in private business to mobilizing capital for national development. The policy shift reflected a desire by the UWP government to become the direct recipient of foreign capital rather than having a portion of it filter back to government through taxes, excise duties or other government levies.

The reconstituted Programme provided two avenues for capital mobilization. A prospective immigrant could purchase Redeemable Bonds for fifteen years with a nominal value of $75,000 US at 2% interest annually, the principal amount to be redeemed on maturity. Alternatively, a prospective immigrant, under the Direct Investment Contribution Option, could merely purchase economic citizenship status for the applicant, spouse and two children under 18 years of age.

By late 1999, some 48 agents in Europe, North America and within the island, were authorized to seek Dominican passports for virtually any price, on condition that the agent remit $50, 000 US to the government for each passport sold. Between 1996 and 1999, 480 passports were issued under the Economic Citizenship Programme, generating $29,801,586 (E.C.) in total revenue for the island.

In 1996, the government enacted the *Mines and Minerals Act* which divested all landowners of all interest in or control of any rights to minerals contained on or beneath the surface of their lands. Such property was irrevocably deemed to be and always to have been vested in the State. The *Act* also prohibited any prospecting or mining unless in accordance with its provisions. Any contravention of the new legislation garnered a maximum fine of $10,000 or one year imprisonment in the case of an individual and a maximum fine of $20,000 in the case of a corporation. No lands were exempt from the new legislation including National Parks or cemeteries.

An Australian company, Broken Hill Proprietary Ltd. (BHP), received a licence to perform soil and water tests to assess any concentration of copper in an area comprised of 15% of the total land area of the island. Had the company and the government tested the waters of public opinion however, they would have avoided the avalanche of public criticism which followed. As it turned out, the Dominica Conservation Association, supported by 20 other organizations, spearheaded widespread opposition to the proposed explorations and effectively halted the plan.

The James government's need for cash to fill the island's coffers explains a number of other initiatives. In 1996 it aborted a plan by the United Kingdom to deport Dr. Muhammad al Masari, a Saudi Arabian dissident, to Dominica, because of public opposition. At stake was some $20 billion of arms trade between Saudi Arabia and Britain if the latter gave political sanctuary to the Saudi dissident. Increased aid and a guaranteed preferential trade in bananas was the *quid pro quo* for the Dominican government's humanitarian gesture.

Similar imperatives best explain other UWP initiatives. These included the 1996 passage of the *Offshore Banking Act*, to establish offshore banking; duty free shopping areas, and the recent sale of 73% of the state owned Dominica Electricity Services Limited (Domlec). This divestment seemed at odds with the purchase of the assets of Geest in 1995 but the justification remained the same – a desire to gain access to ready or liquid capital to meet its financial obligations.

The Colonial Development Corporation (CDC) seemed an unlikely suitor for the island's electricity programme. It arrived on the island in 1949 and thirty years later had failed to provide electricity to a string of villages in the north and northeastern parts of the island. Following the devastation of Hurricane David in 1978, CDC had had enough. It refused to rehabilitate the island's electricity services and ignominiously left the island.

In 1997, the prospect of easy financial pickings forced CDC to succumb to the advances of the Dominican government. The company agreed to pay $21,000,000 (E.C.) for Domlec which net value stood at $60,000,000 (E.C.). As consideration, CDC received exclusive rights to sell electricity in Dominica for 54 years, while enjoying a number of tax free and duty free concessions, in addition to a minimum return on investment of 15% annually. For good measure, the company also gained the right to increase electricity rates by 19% over the first two years of the agreement. If this increase failed to garner the benchmark 15% return on investment, CDC was granted the right to increase rates in excess of 19% between 1997 and 1999.

The UWP's slavish pandering to foreign interests triggered significant opposition from political and non-political sources. Its five year tenure was wracked by unrelenting criticism from the island's main newspaper, industrial strife among policemen, civil servants, and teachers, and unrelenting opposition primarily from the Dominica Labour Party. The government also faced strong allegations of corruption and the blurring of the line between public service and personal gain which appeared to be a distinct legacy of the UWP government.

Exacerbating the growing discontent with the James government was the worsening economic situation facing the island as it approached the new Millennium. The deprivation of the preferential treatment accorded the island's bananas in Europe, the failure of tourism to generate sufficient revenues, the demands of the IMF to reduce recurrent expenditure as a condition precedent to the granting of International Aid, placed a great deal of pressure on the UWP. Indeed by the end of the decade, the government's buzz words had shifted from *economic mobilization* to *retrenchment, structural adjustment, user fees* and *divestment*.

PROFILE OF AN ELECTORAL DEFEAT.
THE JANUARY 2000 GENERAL ELECTIONS

At the dawn of the new millennium, and amidst a multitude of Dominicans holding candles and staring wistfully into the firmament, Edison James invoked biblical imagery, patriotic zeal and political platitudes, to announce the dissolution of Parliament on January 3, 2000 as a prelude to holding general elections on January 31, 2000.

The announcement could not have been more exquisitely timed. The UWP had basked in the afterglow generated by the visit of thousands of Dominicans in November 1999, for the island's twenty- first anniversary celebrations. Its elections warchest was filled to the brim, polls showed that the party was endeared by the public and its economic policies appeared to be bearing fruit. This euphoria extended into the national celebrations marking the dawn of the new millennium. The first rays of sunlight in the east, were greeted by thousands of fireworks bursting in the star studded sky. As if in awe, the leader, with the halo of fireworks as a backdrop, announced the dawn of a new Age on the island. The faithful gasped and then cheered wildly. James reciprocated in his Millennium Address To the Nation by promising an end to the banana crisis, construction of an international airport later that year, universal secondary education by the year 2003 and youth employment enhanced through new government initiatives. He rhetorically asked the faithful:

- Does the team have the attitude to work, the maturity and the sense of responsibility to take on the daunting challenges of the new millennium?
- To what extent is the team genuinely capable of being tolerant of others, and allowing all views to contend as enshrined in our constitution…?
- What is the track record of the team in the places where they have worked, if anywhere.
- What is the track record of the captain of the team?

THE CAMPAIGN

Within the first two weeks of the 2000 campaign, events seemed to unravel in accordance with the script written by the UWP. One early poll by the regional based Caribbean Opinion Poll and Marketing Association, gave the UWP an approval rate of 39.5%, compared to 34.7% for the DLP and 9% for the DFP. One week later, another poll by the Association showed the UWP extending its leader to 45.64%, compared to 36.49% for the DLP and 7.84%, for the DFP.

On the campaign trail, the UWP appeared to be holding its ground and then gaining some. A smooth election campaign with a glossy paged manifesto, the ubiquitous blue shirts for its supporters, and a popular calypso from calypsonian De Brakes whipped up the party's supporters into an electoral frenzy during its rallies around the island. These were augmented by gifts such as televisions in constituencies such as Wesley and Roseau Central when it appeared that the opposition was gaining ground. The party also benefited from its incumbency status, profiting from its use of government resources and the power of the state to bolster its pronouncements. Furthermore, history appeared to be on the side of the UWP since prior administrations had served more than one term in office with the DLP governing from 1961 to 1979 and the DFP from 1980 to 1995.

POLITICAL ACCOMODATION

Ironically, the widespread perception that the UWP would have triumphed at the polls united the opposition in their common effort to unseat the UWP government. On January 14, 2000, Charles Savarin, leader of the DFP, talked about an *accommodation...in government* with the DLP despite the fact that historically, both parties had been at opposite ends of the ideological spectrum. Savarin announced that the DFP would field only 14 candidates, leaving the DLP to have a head on confrontation with the UWP in Petit Savanne, Salybia, LaPlaine and Wesley. The DLP later reciprocated by withdrawing its candidate in Savarin's constituency which the DFP leader ultimately won by a mere 5 votes.

This political understanding between the DFP and DLP was confined to select constituencies since both parties aspired to obtain a majority number of seats in the island's legislature. Indeed, in two constituencies, Castle Bruce and Mahaut, the parties' failure to field only one candidate may have paved the way for a UWP victory. In Castle Bruce for example, the successful UWP candidate polled 727 votes while both opposition candidates polled 747 votes. Similarly in Mahaut, Barrister Julien Prevost, the UWP candidate, polled 1399 votes while his two rivals jointly polled 1954 votes.

PROFESSIONAL SUPPORT

Ultimately, two precipitating issues derailed the UWP's plans to seek reelection. In December 1999, a letter allegedly written by a deported Chinese national warned of certain government ministers having sex with a female Chinese immigrant in exchange for business concessions.

A political response by Prime Minister indicating an intention to establish an Inquiry to investigate the allegations, may well have sufficed to defuse the matter. Rather, James stonewalled when confronted with the allegations. He challenged his political foes to prove the allegations. These allegations, along with old accusations of cronyism and the misappropriation of government funds by UWP members, forged an alliance between opponents of the UWP which transcended party lines. In so doing, James succeeded in bringing the DFP and DLP together, for only the third time in almost forty years.[2]

One other issue galvanized popular opposition to the UWP government and paved the way for its defeat on January 31, 2000. In November 1999, eleven Chinese nationals, in possession of legitimate Dominican passports, arrived at the Lester B. Pearson International Airport, in Toronto, Canada. The Canadian Immigration Authorities subsequently detained them on the grounds that they were trying to illegally gain entry into the United States via Canada.

The evidence for this was irrefutable. Many had spent only a few days in Dominica. Others couldn't sign their own names while virtually all were woefully ignorant of even the most basic information about the island. Their contention that they had come to enjoy the sights and sounds of Canada after spending only a couple of days in their adopted land sounded ludicrous to the Canadian authorities. Faced with a deportation order, all

---

[2] In 1995 both parties agreed to alternate the Leadership of the Opposition.

agreed to depart voluntarily without a hearing to determine their true status.

By then, the damage had been done. The Canadian authorities were alarmed over numerous incidents of smuggling of Chinese nationals into Canada within the past year and were wary of a new circuitous route, through Dominica, used by illegal immigrants from mainland China. An article in the Toronto **Globe and Mail**, the newspaper with the largest circulation in Canada, warned on November 20, 1999, that the *tiny Caribbean island of Dominica, which sells citizenship for US $50,000 is causing a huge problem for Canadian immigration authorities.*

Patriotic zeal, political activism and the new cyberspace technology combined to present the DLP and DFP with an important issue with which to scale the rampants of the UWP. Within Canada, Dominicans discussed the issue on the internet and soundly criticized the UWP for the passport fiasco. E-mails outpaced the humble envelope in relaying messages to the island about the status of these newly minted Dominicans.

Within Dominica, the opposition parties, particularly the DLP, seized the momentum. Erstwhile political leaders, including the venerable Dame Eugenia Charles, attorneys Anthony Astaphan and Alex Boyd-Knight and retired economist Dr. Bernard Yankee, campaigned on behalf of the DLP. The Dominica Association of Industry and Commerce, (D.A.I.C.)

lamented in the Cyberspace Edition of **The Independent** newspaper, that *there is the inherent loss of confidence by our friends in North America for the integrity of the administration of our economic citizenship and offshore investment programs.* It also cautioned that *arbitrary appointments of persons to national boards without due regard for civil society undermines Dominican's ability to develop the capacity of its civic organizations to play their rightful role in nation building.*

Others used cyberspace to voice their concerns about the UWP government. The Cyberspace edition of **The Independent** featured an article in which biblical prophecy was used to decry the policies of the government.

Reverend Father Clement Jolly, a Catholic priest and prolific writer, ignored his Bishop's admonition about getting involved in partisan politics and condemned electoral irregularities perpetrated by the UWP government in an article entitled, *Cry Beloved Country*. **The Chronicle**'s feature column *Nabes & I*, a thorn in the side of James' government since 1995, bluntly stated on January 7, 2000 that:

> *A vote for Eddie and he plunderin predators be a vote for Helen of Troy* (a reference to the Chinese businesswoman who allegedly exchanged sex for business favours) *and prostitution and money launderin and wheelin and deelin wif we sovereignty, for Russian mafia, for VAT, for high hospital fees, for ministas self-aggrandisement, for all de nasty fings*

> *dat have been de hall-marks of de 4 1/2 years of bluebug control.*

THE CONFESSIONS OF TWO CYBERSPACE CORRESPONDENTS

Within Cyberspace, Dominican nationals residing abroad flailed at each other on **Cakafete** and **Delphis** Message Boards. Names such as *Rags, Brian Phinass, P. Victor, Last Dog, CeCe, Erasmus, County and Paul Alexander* provided an anonymity wherein nationals, sometimes in a derogatory manner, decried the alleged strengths and shortcomings of the three political parties. An even larger number of Dominicans, diligently visited these Websites for updates on the elections and to peruse the conflicting views expressed by the cyberspace combatants.

Within Dominica, a few resourceful persons sent regular election bulletins to family members and friends in Europe and North America. In Canada and the U.S., these bulletins were closely scrutinized for news which would signal any gains made by the UWP or DLP in the electoral race. A pastache of these *hotmail messages* sent by a Labour and Freedom Party supporter captured the emotional highs and lows of the elections campaign:

> U.W.P. start wif a bang. Everywhere you turn is blue, blue, blue. Labour and Freedom doh know what to do.
> *January 7, 2000, 12000:4:30 p.m., Election Bulletin #3*

There was a leaders' debate last night. Charles according to most, won the day. But what effect will that have on the final outcome? We can all wait and pray.
January 12, 2000, 11:09 p.m., Election Bulletin #21

Hi folks. I'll try to capture the scene for you guys. In town today it was like Carnival. Much more tomorrow!!! There must have been about 50 vehicles around the place with loudspeakers blasting out "The Brakes" Calypso for the UWP.
January 28, 2000, 1:47 p.m., Election Bulletin #23

Everywhere you pass its' people wearing UWP t-shirts, blue headties and anything blue. It can really make the opposition blue. One gets tired of this constant refrain of the Workers' calypso and retreats home. You turn on the radio and there it is again. Ok try the TV instead and its' there too.
January 29, 2000, 8:18 p.m., Election Bulletin #24

We mus win! All de big shots talking on our platforms. I hope Rosie doh make dem *kyonney* him. If we win dey will have a big fete in Dierriere Laosine.
January 29, 2000, 11:03 a.m., Election Bulletin #25

Well guys it's almost hysteria out here now...The loud speakers are getting bigger, the music louder...The tension is increasing and the predictions changing by the minute. The P.M's Moonie charge did not seem to have any effect except to convince people that it was an act of desperation...The 'war' is on but in the midst of all this, one marvels at what has been really an absence of any mentionable violence. Thank God for that.
January 27, 2000, 4:36 p.m., Election Bulletin #22

What a cohesive intense campaign they have waged! UWP cannot be faulted for planning, organization and strategy. People are less confident of a Labour victory. My gut feeling is the Government may hold on. The polls could well be right. But just when you are beginning to doubt, you meet someone who assures you they are out. It is difficult to imagine a party, with such visible demonstrated support losing! But there is good support on the other side as well.
January 29, 2001 4:47 p.m. Election Bulletin #26

Hi Folks. We deserve a break from all this tension so I'll just try to lighten things up with a bit of some election tit-bits. Do you all know of "Pappy" Baptiste? He is a guy who surfaces each election time with his "Progressive Liberal Party." He has parked his vehicle in Lagon outside PM James' shop just outside the Lawrence's house on Hillsborough Street.

Pappy has a big blue marlin fish on top of his van with hooks in the mouth and he keeps saying as the cars and people pass, "I ketch Edison!!!" In the van he also has a red Santa Claus and he says "This is Rosie!!!"

On Dyer's withdrawal from the race he had this to say: "His name is Dyer so he Die already."
January 30, 2000 10:03 a.m. Election Bulletin No. 27

I cast my vote for Freedom in Goodwill. Alas! I feel it is a lost cause. I will await the official results in a few hours time. *January 31, 2000 10:39 a.m. Election Bulletin No. 27*

Your bayche!! We win! Labor 10, UWP 9 and Freedom 2. Look fete. All I want now is a glass of labset!!
January 31, 2000 11:39p.m. Election Bulletin #31

THE ELECTION RESULTS

On January 31, 2000, 35,650 voters, an amount 1537 less than the total votes cast by the electorate in 1995, cast their votes in the island's General Elections. Of this, the UWP accounted for 43.28% of total votes cast compared to 43.09% for the DLP and 13.64% for the DFP. However, these percentages translated into 10 seats for the DLP, 9 for the UWP and 2 for the DFP. Three seats won by the UWP in 1995; that of Vieille Case, St. Joseph and Salybia, all went to the DLP. In 1995, the UWP had amassed a 649 votes and 21 votes margin of victory over its DLP rival in St. Joseph and Vielle Case respectively while in 2000, the DLP won these same seats by margins of 143 and 256 respectively over the UWP. Similarly, in 1995, the UWP's Salybia candidate defeated his DLP counterpart by a mere 61 votes while in the year 2000, the DLP candidate outpointed its UWP counterpart by 281 votes.

In terms of sheer numbers, the biggest loser in the 2000 elections was the DFP. Its share of the total votes cast decreased from 13,317 in 1995 to a mere 4,862. The number of seats held by the DFP declined from 14 in 1995 to 2. In four constituencies, that of Castle Bruce, Grandbay, Paix Bouche and Vieille Case, the DFP accounted for less than 10% of total votes cast in each constituency. In its winning constituency of Soufriere, the DFP's support shrunk from 60.76% in 1995 to 50.62% in the year 2000. In 1995, the DFP triumphed in Roseau Central with only 47% of the votes compared to 35.55% for the UWP 16.68% for the DLP. The party proved more fortunate in the recent elections following the withdrawal of the Labour party candidate in that constituency.

SIGNIFICANCE OF THE RESULTS

Ironically, the UWP's share of the total votes cast increased from 34.36% in 1995 to 43.28% or from 12,777 votes to 15,428 votes. That increase however, failed to match a similar increase for the DLP, from 11,064 or 29.75% of the votes cast in 1995 to 15,360, or 43.09% in the year 2000. Indeed, the UWP received the largest number of votes cast in the recent elections although it only won 9 of the 21 constituencies.

The numbers obviously do not tell the story of the island's most recent general elections. The UWP's loss of power is unprecedented for a number of reasons. The party became the first single term government on the island. The short-lived Committee for National Salvation which governed the island from 1979 to 1980 comprised a number of individuals, organizations and political parties and therefore cannot claim the dubious distinction of being the island's sole single term party.

Furthermore, the UWP lost the elections despite the advantage which any incumbent party has in choosing the date of the elections, exploiting events such as the World Creole Festival and the Twenty-First Birthday celebrations, to its own advantage. There is also the historical disinclination among the electorate to vote against the incumbent government particularly when one's financial future is dependent on largess from the party in power. That fear is even greater when the outcome, and indeed one's fate following the elections, is uncertain.

Additionally, the UWP failed to retain the government despite a well financed campaign and the distribution of free items to prospective supporters. The party reportedly outspent the DLP and DFP by a ratio of 4 to 1. It further distributed free items including television sets and other items to supporters in a number of key constituencies, most notably in Roseau Central and Wesley. Added to that were promises including duty free concessions, jobs and the usual platter of programs to various constituencies.

REASONS FOR THE UWP DEFEAT

The UWP suffered defeat largely because of the cumulative effects of a number of self inflicted wounds during its tenure in government. These injuries were precipitated by the party's departure or abandonment of some of its declared policies while in opposition from 1990 to 1995.

During its formative days, the UWP presented itself as a viable alternative to Dame Charles' government. It promised to establish a consultative government, to rescue the island's banana industry, restrict the scope of the Economic citizenship programme, and to end victimization within the island's Civil Service.

Those promises buckled under the cumulative weight imposed by the need to reward its supporters, a desire for retribution against the former DFP government, declining revenues from the banana industry and in some cases, a desire for personal financial gain. One of the central criticisms of the James' government was the appointment of supporters to all government boards, tribunals and financial institutions regardless of qualifications. Another widespread criticism was the granting of contracts without resort to a tendering process and the granting of jobs to party supporters without consideration of qualifications or merit. The doling out of rewards to the party faithful did not commence with the James government but what appeared reprehensible, in the eyes of the government's detractors, was the extent to which the UWP government engaged in such practices.

If in opposition, the UWP adopted the posture of economic nationalists, in government its economic policies were completely reversed. The sale of Dominican passports by agents strategically located in Europe and North America, filled the State coffers but effectively removed any checks or screening on those who qualified for those passports. Dominican passports provided entry into 94 countries without the requirement of a visa and inevitably has become a cherished commodity in the hands of someone seeking sanctuary from criminal proceedings or passage to the North American mainland. This policy would come back to haunt the Dominican people since in December 2001, the Canadian government imposed visa requirements on Dominica and Grenada.

Other policies of the James government catered slavishly to foreign economic interests to an extent unprecedented since the final days of the Patrick John government in the late 1970s. The 1996 *Mines and Minerals Act* wrested ownership of any rights to minerals beneath the surface from landowners. The government subsequently granted a licence to an Australian Company to perform soil and water tests to assess any concentration of copper in those lands. Similarly, the UWP government sold 73% of the national owned Domlec to CDC, a multinational from England, with exclusive rights to sell electricity on the island for 54 years. Finally, the rights to excavate huge concentration of sand deposits accumulated at the mouth of the Layou River were given to a French company over the objections of local interests.

The James government also suffered from intense criticism following the removal of the preferential duties which had hitherto given the island's bananas a competitive edge over its Latin American counterpart. Following the U.S. government's successful challenge of the reigon's preferential status in the European market, the number of banana growers on the island fell from 7000 in 1995 to 3000 in 1999. Banana prices also fell 38 cents a pound in 1995 to 16 cents a pound in 1999.

The political fallout from declining banana production was exacerbated when the government purchased lands from farmers in Wesley for its international airport project. This led to a demonstration of growers in the island's capital and created antipathy among some of the UWP's staunchest supporters.

The precipitating factor for the government's downfall however, was the one-two punch caused by the passport scandal in November 1999 and the anonymous letter hinting at corruption by some of government ministers. The government's response to these problems merely added fuel to the opposition's charge that it was insensitive to the spectre of corruption.

Edison James' response to charges of corruption was to deny its existence. His Finance Minister's response to the Chinese passport scandal was that the Programme had brought in $12M (E.C.) to the island's coffers since 1996. James also opined that the Canadian government would not impose visa requirements on the island's citizens.

Every indication is that the UWP underestimated the repercussions of these charges and their effects in galvanizing the opposition. Talk of an *accommodation* between the DFP and DLP resulted in each party campaigning jointly to unseat the government. Prominent individuals started appearing on opposition platforms, criticizing the James government and the need to dispense with it. Suddenly, the two parties which had been at loggerheads for almost forty years were united in their common antipathy towards the UWP government.

One significant development preceding the elections made it possible for supporters of the DFP and DLP to support each other's candidates in areas where the main opposition was the UWP. After the UWP assumed power in 1995, it actively courted the island's first Prime Minister, Patrick Roland John. It did this for myriad reasons including a need to wean support away from the DLP and to shore up its support in the Roseau North constituency where John was still popular in working class areas such as *Pound* and *Fond Cole*. John's involvement in the UWP was not as unseemly as it appeared since in the 1970s, his import substitution polices had enabled two key members of the UWP, Norris Prevost and Sheridan Gregoire, to create a financially successful, garment manufacturing company, By Trinee Ltd.

Allegations of corruption and the presence of John among the ranks of the UWP, made it more palatable for DFP supporters to vote for Labour candidates. John's actions in the late 1970s had created an enduring enmity between the DFP and DLP. The repressive legislation in the 1970s, the 1981 attempt to invade the island and John's complicity in the planned invasion not only resulted in his imprisonment but his condemnation by the DFP. Indeed, attempts in 1999 by the government owned radio station, the DBS, to include John in a pantheon of 100 Great Dominicans were strongly condemned by Dame European Charles and DFP supporters.

With its open support of John, the UWP unwittingly made an accommodation between the DFP and DLP more palatable. The union may have assisted the UWP's Julius Timothy in winning John's former constituency but elsewhere on the island, John's newfound allegiance did not translate into votes for the UWP. On the contrary, the insinuations of corruption which rose to a crescendo during the last weeks of the elections, may have been bolstered by the association between the UWP government and the island's first Prime Minister.

The single most significant factor which accounts for the fall of the James' government was the passport scandal of November 1999. The charge of corruption directed at the UWP was not a new phenomena but the spectre of foreigners abusing the island's citizenship laws struck a raw nerve on the island.

Historically, migration has provided the key to educational opportunities and upward social mobility to generations of Dominicans. The relative ease of travel, symbolized by the island's passport, has provided the means to seek greener pastures outside of the island. That the UWP would seek to jeopardize those avenues by selling passports to foreigners appeared as an affront to many Dominicans and it is this anger, fuelled by rhetoric from the DFP and DLP which engendered a groundswell of opposition to the James' government.

This is not to say however, that the triumph of the DLP was merely a protest vote against the UWP government. The DLP had been in the political wilderness for twenty years. Since 1980, many of the party's old guard had left. In the interim, Rosie Douglas, along with other members like Pierre Charles, had laboriously retooled the DLP with a delicate balance between experienced persons like F. O. Riviere , Athie Martin, and Ambrose George and youthful leaders such as Lloyd Pascal and Kelly Graneau.

Both indogenous and exogenous factors account for the acceptance of the Douglas led DLP by the electorate. The John factor no longer plagued the DLP, time had dimmed the memory of the excesses of the DLP in the 1970s and a new cadre of individuals with a greater commitment to the community had emerged in the 1990s. Douglas had jettisoned his socialist rhetoric to adopt a more pragmatic approach to nation building and in the process, allayed the fears of the business elite. The buzz words of the 1970s such as *nationalization, land redistribution,* and *imperialism,* gave way to slogans such as crop *diversification, entrepreneurship* and *free enterprise in the 1990s.*

Other programs advocated by the DLP such as a commitment to affordable housing, free secondary education and the democratization of all public institutions, all harkened back to the ideological roots which had sprouted in the 1970s. However, the ebbing of the tide of communism in the region and elsewhere made the acceptance of an erstwhile socialist acceptable to the electorate. In the 1980s, Dame Eugenia Charles had successfully invoked the communist threat to keep the opposition DLP at bay. In the 1990s, both the DFP and UWP governments exorcised the ghost of communism and openly received technical assistance and scholarships from the Cuban government. In so doing, they diffused any opposition to Rosie Douglas on ideological grounds.

More significantly, Douglas appeared to be the antithesis of the James-led UWP government. Allegations of corruption had plagued the government while in power. Party hacks and supporters were publicly scorned because of what appeared to be an insatiable appetite for self- aggrandizement. At the time, James was never personally implicated in any allegations of corruption but his unwillingness to investigate those allegations seriously hurt his government.

Douglas' political shortcomings paled in comparison with his UWP counterpart. Douglas explained his penchant for travel as efforts to muster support for the island's ailing banana industry. Douglas was also criticized for never having been gainfully employed, a fact which worked in his favour since there was no suggestion that he was tainted by government handouts. Furthermore, the DLP leader had shown a general disinterest in material acquisition in contradistinction to a few members of the James' government.

In a final act of desperation, James made a radio address to the nation on January 21, 2000, accusing Douglas of inviting the Unification Church, a religious sect banned from many Caribbean islands, to the island. This accusation was blunted with the revelation that a government's representative had met the head of the sect in Washington D.C. the previous year. Furthermore, James offered no proof in support of his allegation and seriously undermined his own credibility in the eyes of the electorate.

CONCLUSION

In the end, the UWP's defeat was less the result of a desire for a DLP government as a need to remove the incumbent government. The government was undone not merely by allegations of corruption but what appeared to be its unwillingness to deal with those charges. Whether the electorate's decision marks a new intolerance for perceived corruption or a need for accountability and transparency in government remains to be seen. It does appear however, that it is not the mere presence of impropriety which repulsed the electorate but the aloofness, bordering on conceit, with which the UWP government responded to those allegations.

The lessons of Elections 2000 will not be lost on the Freelab coalition which succeeded the UWP. Douglas immediately emphasized transparency in government and sought the publication of the assets of each minister in his new government. Furthermore, he suspended the Economic Citizenship programme under which passports were sold by individuals who were little more than commission agents.

It is a matter of conjecture whether Douglas's successors will adhere to these principles. Whether the DLP will buckle under the weight of expectations from its supporters, or the precarious economic situation faced by the island, remains to be seen. One thing is clear however. Being the major beneficiary of the electorate's dissatisfaction with the UWP administration, the DLP will be loath to repeat the mistakes of the Edison James' administration.

ROSIE DOUGLAS. A DOMINICAN TITAN.

Gabriel J. Christian

FOREWORD

This work is not a comprehensive history of the period that Roosevelt "Rosie" Douglas spent in politics. That work is yet to be done. It is part personal memoir, by one who was engaged in the national liberation struggle alongside Douglas while still at high school, and in the early years of Dominica's independence and who later shared many moments with him toward the end of his life. It is also part reflection on the successes and failures he confronted and the legacy that he leaves behind. None of the events described can come close to capturing the spirit of a man who inspired our young, met great crises and whose death transfixed a nation. Yet, I hope that this effort will indicate an appreciation of the new opportunities he provided in education, his unyielding quest for justice and the imperishable memory he left behind.

A PASSING

In October, the leaves are turning color, from green to brilliant reds, and oranges as they prepare to fall off the trees in the Washington, D.C. area. And the breeze which wafts through open windows can bring a chill to an otherwise bright morning. Falling leaves, the changes in temperature, all evince a passage from one season, to the next. So it was, on Sunday, October 1, 2000, as my wife and I were readying our children, Samora and Makonnen, for worship at the nearby St. Mary's Catholic Church in Upper Marlboro, Maryland. Suddenly, at about 9:10 a.m., Ronald Isidore called from Dominica. Immediately, before he could get a word in, I began querying the status of the Dominica Cadet Corp in its preparation for the upcoming November 3, 2000 Independence Parade. The Cadet Corp program, a youth leadership training effort fervently supported by Prime Minister Douglas, had earned my support and that of many others in Dominica and the Diaspora. Many had complained about the errant ways of our young. Some had been determined to make a difference. The Education Minister under the United Workers Party (UWP) government, Ron Green, had begun the process of resuscitating the Cadet program, but it had not reached fruition by the time of that party's departure from office. Others kept the flame of hope for its revival burning. Captain Francis Richards, Lieutenant Ackroyd Birmingham, Police Commissioner Mathias

Lestrade, Assistant Superintendent of Police, Nicholas George, Police Inspector David Andrew, Dominica Grammar School Principal Alicia Jean-Jacque, Security Advisor Rayburn Blackmore and the Cadet Corp Committee were constantly on my mind, as they were leaders in that quest to provide guidance to Dominican youth and prepare them for nation building.

"Had the drills started yet?" I asked Isidore. His reply was, "*Garçon*, I not calling you about Cadets." A committed Dominican mathematician and management specialist trained at Iona College in New York , Isidore had volunteered to lend his skills in human resource development to the Corp.. Energetic, with a perpetual smile, Isidore's voice was not affected. Nothing betrayed the weighty news he was about to convey. Perhaps his earlier inclination toward a life in the priesthood, before he changed career paths, afforded him an emotional discipline above the ordinary. "Rosie die..," he said. "They found him on the floor of his home in Portsmouth this morning[1]." he went on.

I was stunned. Unable to say anything. Outside the bay window of my kitchen, a light breeze, scattered the dead leaves which had formed on the backyard lawn. And my mind raced

---

[1] . The Honourable Prime Minister, Roosevelt "Rosie" Douglas, born October 15, 1941, was discovered by his assistant, Judith Honore at about 8:00 a.m. "in a recumbent position on the floor of his home," on Sunday, October 1, 2000. He had arrived from a series of overseas meetings the previous afternoon. ***Post Mortem Examination Report*** of Dr. H. Daisley, Professor of Pathology, University of the West Indies, October 4, 2000.

backwards: To that night in 1976, outside Hilarian Dejean's home when my brother Samuel and I first met Rosie, after he had delivered a blistering attack on colonialism from the steps of the Dominica Trade Union Hall in Lagon, Roseau. Then, he had called for independence from Britain:

> Today we are dependent on Britain for everything. After hundreds of years of colonialism we have only eight local doctors...our bananas are not ours. The banks are not ours. The telephone company is not ours. The electric company is not ours. Colonialism is like a corbeau[2] which feasts on the blood of the peoples...brothers and sisters, we cannot even seek assistance from friendly countries, for we have no control over our foreign affairs....we need independence. We have no science, no technology. They take our cocoa, refine it and sell it back to us as Milo[3], brothers and sisters...we need independence....not tomorrow, not next year, we need independence now![4]

---

[2] Local vulture.
[3] A powdered chocolate product manufactured by the transnational Nestle and sold in most stores on the island.
[4] Notes of Cadre Number 1; The Roseau Branch of the Popular Independence Committee 1976-1981. There are several written sources for matters which are being related in quotes; the minutes and notes from the Notebook of Cadre No. 1. The 1978 Notebook given by the Cuban Revolution to the Dominican delegates to the 11th World Festival of Youth and Students which I have used to chronicle political and personal events over twenty four years and my personal diaries and memoranda from the period.

Independence now! So that was Rosie Douglas? We had heard of him. In the early days of the black power movement, adherents would talk of: When Brother Rosie comes. That he was a radical, was the common perception. A black power militant from a rich family which owned plenty land, a supermarket and a cinema. That his ambitious father had sent him to study agricultural engineering in Canada, but that he had gone astray in the white man's country and made trouble for himself there[5]. It was rumored that, instead of focusing on his books, he had led a revolt among black students in Canada, burnt a computer center. Had been jailed. Deported. A troublemaker. A bad man. He would poison our minds, some old folk warned. A communist, to be feared. But to the enraptured audience of workers, students, civil servants and the unemployed, his words resounded: Independence Now! And the thunderous applause which greeted his message had washed over many of us. In particular those of us who had followed the Movement for a New Dominica (MND), which had popularized black nationalist thought in the 1970s.

---

[5]. See generally **Let the Niggers Burn-The Sir George Williams University Affair and its Caribbean Aftermath,** (Black Rose Press-Our Generation Press Montreal, 1971) edited by Dennis Forsythe. It is chronicled that Douglas had, by 1968, become a prominent human rights activist in Canada. Douglas was a leader among the Sir George students who led a rebellion against a racist biology professor. The students were assaulted by riot police while attending a sit-in at a computer center on campus. The facility sustained major damage during the police operation. The students were blamed and some were tried and jailed, including Douglas. In the words of Forsythe it became a highly charged episode which shook the West Indies and boomeranged black consciousness towards a consolidation called "Peoplehood."

After the meeting, a throng had followed Douglas westward on Queen Mary Street, across Kennedy Avenue, over the Old Bridge which spanned the Roseau River and into the Pottersville suburb of Roseau, to the home of Black Power activist Hilarian Dejean. There, next to the steps which led into Dejean's modest home, Douglas expounded on the need for Popular Independence Committees to be formed. A tight knot of onlookers listened, hanging on his every word. Staring at the tall, Afro wearing guy in thick rimmed glasses who wore a black shirt with a Nehru collar, many of the bystanders had questions:

- Could we trust PJ?[6]
- Wasn't PJ the same guy who had passed the notorious *Dread Act*[7] and victimized those who sought a radical overturn of Dominica's colonial society?
- Could we afford this independence?
- Dominica is a poor country, where are we going to get money to pay civil servant salaries?

---

[6]. Then Dominican Premier and Dominica Labour Party leader, Patrick Roland John.

[7]. The Dread Act (The Prohibited and Unlawful Society Act-1974) was the Patrick John regime's response to the uprising in black power militancy and Rastafarianism in 1970's Dominica. It was the government's belief that lawlessness was the trademark of that uprising and many crimes of crop theft ad murder were blamed on so-called "dreads" or those who wore their hair in locks fashion. It protected any civilian who killed or injured any member of such an unlawful association found at day or night inside a dwelling house, from any civil or criminal liability. See Irving Andre's *Prelude to Disaster, Legislation and Repression*, Gabriel J. Christian & Irving W. Andre, **In Search of Eden, Dominica-The Travails of a Caribbean Mini-State** (Pond Casse Press, 1992, 1st Edition) at pages 63-70.

- Wasn't England our mother country?
- Shouldn't we have a referendum on the matter, to see if Dominicans really want independence?

The questions came fast. Some were furious and disagreed with him. Douglas, eloquently answered all questioners. Quoting Ghana's Kwame Nkrumah, he stressed that we should seek the political kingdom and all would follow-meaning that political self-determination was the first step toward nationhood. The Popular Independence Committees (PIC), in his words, would support and spur the independence movement and be ready to take the lead to ensure that independence meant social justice. That the government needed to be supported on independence, even if its leadership on other issues might be questionable. That we had to ally with forces who could help get us freedom, even where we would have to part ways with them later on issues of principle and the strategic objective: a state swept clean of the exploitation of man by man. That social justice demanded independence. That was our right, to be masters in our own homes. That to have justice, meant we must build socialism and maintain control of our own affairs. And that we did not want, *flag independence,* where the Union Jack came down to be replaced by Dominica's own banner, but everything remained the same with imperial control of our energy, banking, industry, and land.

Those listeners who agreed with Rosie, signed up for the cause. Then the independence struggles followed. The rise of a new student movement, and the birth of the Dominica Federation of Students from the womb of the older United Student Council. The founding of the Dominica Cuba Friendship Society. The open embrace of the Cuban Revolution by the local independence movement. The fabricated Communist Plot of January 1978, which led to Premier Patrick John's dismissal of Labour cabinet members Michael Douglas and Ferdinand Parillon. Independence at midnight, November 3, 1978 and Popular Independence Committee cadres looking on, from the outside. Not invited to share in the new day which they had helped give birth to, while Princess Margaret looked down on the masses from her perch on the stage at the Windsor Park where the flag raising celebration was held. Thereafter, the island-wide mobilizations over the Leafspot Crisis and Freeport Crisis. The March 13, 1979, overthrow of Grenada's Eric Gairy by Maurice Bishop's New Jewel Movement and the PIC slogan popularized island-wide: ***Gairy Gone-PJ Next! Alliance is the Answer!*** Thereafter, the link-up with the Dominica Federation of Students, Popular Independence Committee, Dominica Freedom Party and an insurgent Dominica Farmers Union led Athie Martin, Alvin Armantrading,[8] Edward "Ted" Honeychurch[9] and others. The

---

[8]. Alvin Armantrading (1918-1991) was a well to do was a banana planter from the village of St. Joseph, whose genteel ways and eloquent manner of

South African Plot disclosed by the British Broadcasting Corporation's Panorama program to use Dominica as a base to use Dominica as a base to circumvent the anti-apartheid oil embargo by the Organization of Oil Producing Countries (OPEC). The attempt by the errant regime to impose anti-union and anti-press legislation which raised the anger of an increasingly incensed populace. The May 29, 1979 riot and the deaths, injuries and disorder which ensued[10]. The coming together of the dispersed left forces of the PIC and Dr. William "Para" Riviere's

---

speech conjured up images of the "Gentleman Planter" of the colonial era. A leader in the Dominica Farmers Union and a black Dominican, he was an early Dominica Freedom Party (DFP) supporter and election candidate. In 1978 he ran under the DFP banner, unsuccessfully, for the St. Joseph seat.

[9]. Edward 'Ted" Honeychurch (1923-1981) was a white Dominican planter, village council leader at Giraudel, and the father of Dominican historian Dr. Lennox Honeychurch. A vocal opponent of what he considered government mis-management of the banana industry, he served on the leadership of the Dominica Farmers Union and was a significant player in the 1978 Leaf Spot Crisis mobilization which threatened the vitality of the banana sector. He was killed during a kidnaping by a group of errant Dreads led by Leroy "Pokosion" Etienne, on February 12, 1981, in what was seen as a reprisal attack against the Dominica Freedom Party government then determined to clear the mountains of such groups. His son Lennox Honeychuch then served as Government Press Secretary. See Lennox Honeychurch's, **The Dominica Story** (The Dominica Institute, 1985) at page 216.

[10]. On May 29, 1979, ten demonstrators were shot and wounded in the vicinity of the Government Headquarters in Roseau when the riot squad of the Dominica Defence Force opened fired on a crowd estimated at 15,000 which had been blocking entrance to the parliament to prevent passage of amendments to the Industrial Relations Act and the Libel and Slander Act. Ten were wounded, and two killed: Phillip Timothy was slain by a soldier's bullet and a newly born baby girl was suffocated by tear gas. See *A Rain of Stones, The May 29th, Riot and Aftermath* at Page 119 of **In Search of Eden-Dominica The Travails of a Caribbean Mini-State**, 1st Edition, by Irving W. Andre and Gabriel J. Christian (Pond Casse Press, 1992).

Peoples Democratic Party (PDP) under the umbrella of the newly named Dominica Liberation Movement (DLM) on August 30, 1979. The popular uprising which followed and the burning of the courthouse. Hurricane David of August 29, 1979, and Rosie's aid missions to Cuba, Grenada, Guadeloupe which secured millions in assistance for the island. The petty divisions among the political left which helped the Freedom Party Victory in 1980. His role (after being alerted of the mercenary plot by Black Power activist Algie Maffie) in aborting the attempted 1981 mercenary invasion by Mike Perdue and the US Ku Klux Klan and Nazi Party. Then, after a lifetime in what seemed the political wilderness, the Labour Victory of 2000. My mind reeled backwards to glimpse a past time. Brother Rosie had come. And now, brother Rosie was gone!

    I dropped the phone and ran upstairs to break the news to my wife. She was shocked. It was unbelievable. Little Samora remembered "Uncle" Rosie and the visit to our home in May 2000 and that the presence of all these men in black suits who stood around the house, talking into tiny communication devices. The US Secret Service, traveling in a tight security motorcade, gave Prime Minister Douglas close security. Emergency lights flashing, they had staked out the house and blocked off the lane. Personally, Prime Minister Douglas, Brother Rosie, or "Comrade" as many of us called him, did not seem to care about all the fuss and protocol attendant to his office. He felt awkward with all this security and on his last visit had dispensed with it, preferring the close company of vehicles driven by Dominican friends. So it was at his last visit at Georgetown University, where Gillian-Gunn Clissold's Caribbean project had invited him to give a major policy speech. Thereafter, he waved off the official chauffeur driven limousine provided by Georgetown University and crammed into the tight confines of my Acura sedan with Portsmouth Town Council leader Irving Knight, Dominican Diaspora activist Claudette Loblack, former Mayor of Portsmouth Renwick "Super Dude" JeanPierre. Driving through the bright lights of Georgetown, he relaxed the group, some of whom voiced concerns about his grueling travel schedule, its impact on management issues, stress and his need for rest, with jokes from his college years in Canada and his plans for Dominica. He was too busy to stop for a drink as he had to meet with planners at the Marriott Hotel in Reston, to put finishing touches to his presentation at the Million Family March. It was on that day, October 16, 2000, he would address the largest gathering of African Americans by a black foreign leader and map out a plan for the coming together of the African Diaspora. It was his position that, Dominica, the Caribbean, Africa, would benefit when all her far-flung sons and daughters worked in unison, for development. Never one to forget Dominica's tourism product, he asked us:

> What could Dominica do with 100,000 African American visitors, a year? What if I told them at the march, they were all honorary Dominicans? We wouldn't have to sell them passports....but we could benefit from their investment, their presence...we have less than 1,000 hotel rooms and still have an occupancy problem. What do you all think?[11]

We agreed. A brilliant idea well in line with Rosie's Pan Africanist philosophy and a practical economic option free of tarnish. The sale of passports by the Dominica Freedom Party and the United Workers Party governments had been controversial. The issue is now widely seen as the reason why many in the Diaspora campaigned against the UWP, especially over the internet, during the 2000 elections. Douglas had promised to end the passport sales once he got into office. Now he was gone. And Samora, who had surprised him by blowing a note on one of the trumpets soon to be donated to the Cadet Corp during his May visit, was too young to grasp the enormity his passing. Amidst the dark moment our boy, Makonnen, who had sat upon a playful Rosie's lap, kept right-on looking at the bright colors of his *Blue's Clues* program. A lover of children, he would not have had it any different. He would not have wanted too much fussing over him. Yet, the shock rang out like a fire bell in the night.

---

[11] . September 22, 2000 discussion with Rosie Douglas, Washington, D.C.

Soon I was off the phone. And then more calls, swaddled in grief, came pouring in.

Rosie Douglas' death was followed by an outpouring of grief, not seen before in Dominica's history. The laudatory words in support of a man who had been once reviled as a radical troublemaker was heard from church pulpits across the land that day, and in the weeks to come. His farewell started with a dignified lying in state on October 12, 2000, at the former British Governor's mansion, now the State House of an independent Dominica. There, he was viewed by thousands of mourners who streamed by his Canadian oak casket which was attended to by solemn police sentries with US M16's, and the newly outfitted Cadets[12] who provided a splendid honor guard. On October 13, 2000, Grandbay, the birthplace of 1970s left, said goodbye with a stirring rally at Ma Tutu's Park. There, Pastor Peter Augustine, President of the Dominica Evangelical Council, rocked the crowd with heartfelt words:

> Rosie is not dead, he lives! If he were to come back today, he would not come back as a politician. He would come back preaching the Gospel ....he was a man who stood for the least among us....it was he who, as a mere boy, told

---

[12] . In an effort to ensure a Cadet presence at the farewell, the new Cadets from the Dominica Grammar School were issued their uniforms by Capt. Richards and, Inspector David Andrew at the Police Training School, Morne Bruce the evening before the lying in state, October 1, 2000. On the morning of the lying in state, October 12, 2000 they were taught their basic drills by former Cadet, Claudette Loblack, one hour before they assumed their positions.

thirsty workers on his father's estate to drink the jelly nuts to quench their thirst...and if the foreman asked who gave it to them, say it is "I, Rosie Douglas who give it to you..."[13]

Thereafter, the motorcade traveled the length of the island, from Grandbay to Portsmouth, flowers tossed atop the hearse from many a hillside. His funeral on October 14, 2000, was a victory march and a spiritual triumph for those who had made common cause with the National Liberation principles for which he stood. From the British Labour Party and Northern Island's Sinn Fein, to El Salvador's FMLN, from the U.S., Taiwan, France, Canada, Venezuela and Cuba, more foreign delegations, and overseas Dominican representatives attended his farewell than at independence celebrations twenty two years earlier. That his ideas were not deemed as radical and troubling at death, as at the start of his political career in Dominica, was a vindication of his efforts in education which opened the doors of opportunity to many. To many in the establishment and private sector, he had mellowed and was now a fervent promoter of private enterprise and investment. Though born of privilege, he was a champion of the working class and rural poor. His style was not one of vanity or arrogance and he had a profound distaste for materialism. Frequently, he dismissed his security detail and

---

[13] . The tale of Rosie Douglas feeding thirsty workers jelly coconuts off his father's estate is one of the many legends of his generosity of action and kindness of spirit which now populate the mass consciousness in Dominica.

would often drive himself. He never occupied the official Prime Minister's residence at Morne Bruce which overlooked the island's capital. One of the most fitting tributes paid to Douglas came from the *Nyabingi*[14], the representative arm of Dominica's Rastafarian community. In their words:

> Rosie was a friend of Rasta,
> A true son of Africa and a liberation fighter.
> He was not a grabilacious politician....

He was not a ***grabilacious*** politician! Though it may not be found in Webster's or Oxford dictionaries, the word ***grabilacious***, needs no explanation when placed in context. In a time when the pursuit of political office is too often viewed as an opportunity to grab the perks of office and line pockets, no more honorable statement could be made about Douglas, at his passing.

A friendly man, with a warm and welcoming style which gained him many friends, Douglas died alone, unattended by the masses he loved. And the masses mobbed his home that day, weeping bitterly that their hero had suddenly departed. Reports reveal that a spontaneous procession led by a tearful Portsmouth Mayor Brewster followed the hearse which removed the body,

---

[14]. The term came from the early Rastafarian movement followers of Jamaica who called themselves *Nya* men-linking their ideas to the anti-colonial movement of Kigezi, Uganda - *Nyabingi* - which called for "Death to the Black and White Oppressors." Horace **Campbell's Rasta and Resistance - From Marcus Garvey to Walter Rodney** (Africa World Press, 1992) at page 72.

before it was whipped into a patriotic fervor by Attorney General Bernard Wiltshire who, like thousands of others, had rushed to the scene upon hearing the news. Wiltshire seized the moment to rally the dejected crowd and urged them to continue the struggle for National Liberation, in Rosie's memory.

Great controversy surrounded his death and burial. Suspicion was rife that his detractors in the Labour Party were colluding to oust him and had held a secret meeting in his absence to further that plan. An editorial by Dominica's **Tropical Star** on October 11, 2000, stated:

> Already questions are being asked about the circumstances which led to the passing of one who appeared so robust, flamboyant, cheerful, charismatic and healthy. One of Mr. Douglas' sons made a public statement concerning what kind of post mortem he wished for his father, and requested that independent pathologists be employed for that purpose. Rumours of a planned palace coup while Mr. Douglas was away are getting stronger, and the reported behavior of some of Mr. Douglas' colleagues, confirmed by statements they themselves made, fuel some of these rumours. Just as in the United States of America the question "Who killed John F. Kennedy?" is still being asked today, in Dominica for a long time to come, the question "Who killed Rosie Douglas?" will continue to be asked. The pathologists have given a scientific answer, but Dominicans will not rest until they are satisfied with a plausible answer to their question as to what precipitated that fatal event.

Many felt Douglas died of overwork, as he had been engaged in an almost frantic series of overseas tours, seeking development assistance, private investment and addressing Dominica's far-flung Diaspora to seek its support for the island. As alluded to in the **Tropical Star** editorial, others felt he died of a broken heart, unappreciated by those who should have been closest to him. Rosie's younger brother, Adenauer "Washway" Douglas felt that such lack of appreciation and dark muttering by critics, did not "help" Rosie and added to his burdens. His sturdy mother and matriarch of the Douglas family Bernadette, well into her mid-80s and reeling from the sudden blow of her beloved son's passing, hinted that "Mike die, now Rosie. But the way he die not too straight at all, at all. Something happen there, what happen to Rosie too shaky for me."

However, according to the first autopsy on Prime Minister Douglas conducted on October 4, 2000, by Dominican pathologist Dr. Peter Bellot and Dr. Hubert Daisley, Professor of Pathology, Faculty of Medicine, University of the West Indies (UWI):

> The cause of death was very easy to discover...He suffered a massive aortic dissection [which led to] a massive cardiac tamponade..[15]

---

[15]. See *Douglas Had a Giant Heart*, **The Sun**, Wednesday, October 11, 2000 at page 3.

Dr. Bellot went on to state that the Prime Minister's heart weighed 600 grams, while a normal person's heart weighs about 150 grams. The pathologist further stated Douglas was hypertensive and had been for some time and that he died instantly when large vein which carried blood away from the heart ruptured.[16]

Not satisfied, some in the family-in particular Rosie's Canadian born sons, Tiyani Behanzin (Robert Douglas) a law professor in England and Cabral Douglas sought a second autopsy. His daughter, attorney Debbie Douglas, also felt he was the victim of evil hands and supported further inquiry. Many of his comrades joined in the chorus and called on the Cuban Revolution to intervene. Ironically, the island's health minister Dr. John Toussaint, was a Cuban trained Veterinarian, who had benefited from one of the Cuban scholarships offered as part of Cuba's 1979 Hurricane David Relief Plan for Dominica. It is of note that the first medical doctor on the scene, was Dr. Gregorio Pinera Monterrey, a Cuban medical doctor who formed part of the Revolution's medical assistance program to the island and who was stationed at Portsmouth. It was he who pronounced the Prime Minister dead.

Upon the request of Health Minister, Dr. Toussaint, The Revolution dispatched some of its best scientists and investigators from the Cuban Ministry of Public Health, Institute of Legal

---

[16] . Id.

Medicine. Using state of the art DNA sampling and other processes, their report, by Dr. Othon Torres Figueroa, Dr. Signo Pou Palvi, Dr. Pilar Soto Pardeiro, Lic. Fermin Amaro Suarez and Tec. Carlos Grenet Oribe, confirmed the earlier findings of the UWI autopsy, that the Prime Minister's death was due to natural causes; i.e cardiac tamponade, rupture of the aorta. There are no findings in the Cuban report for trace elements of any poison in the tissue samples presented them. However, a January 15, 2001 letter by Dr. Daisley, to Dr. Ettienne, Dominica's Chief Medical Officer, refers to presence of the drug ***phenylpropanolamin*e** in the Prime Minister's circulation. He presumed that it came from cold medication or weight reduction medication and opines that:

> This drug, as you are aware propagates hypertensive episodes and can have disastrous effects in the uncontrolled hypertensive patient. I am almost certain the FDA had recalled all the medication with this agent in November 2000.

The investigative studies claim that the Prime Minister had complained of a cold and had been observed coughing. However, nothing is said as to whether any of the medicines found in the Prime Minister's residence by his sister in law Mrs. Olivia Douglas[17] were ever examined and/or subjected to rigorous

---

[17]. A Jamaican born, British-trained nurse, Olivia Douglas was then the Principal of Dominica Nursing School and former Senior Nurse at the Portsmouth General Hospital. She was the widow of Rosie's older brother,

testing to determine whether the drug noted above formed part of their ingredients. While the UWI study shows a low concentration of the substance noted above in the tissue samples examined, one is unsure as to the role its presence played in the Prime Minister's death. Absent appropriate focus on the source of the substance, the autopsy reports may well be of limited value.

When someone with Douglas' political history dies suddenly, it is reasonable to view his actions and utterances, and analyze who they might have taken offense to them. In the September 14, 2000 issue of the Nation of Islam's **Final Call**, Douglas had appeared on the front cover between Minister Louis Farrakhan and Libyan leader, Colonel Muammar Gadhafi, at the 3rd Congress of World Mathaba held in Sirte, Libya. There, he delivered remarks alongside, Sam Nujoma of Namibia, Robert Mugabe of Zimbabwe, and former Nicaraguan President, Daniel Ortega. At that time he praised the steadfastness of Libya in the face of its enemies and spoke in favor of an International Bank owned by developing countries, as a means to escape the strangulation of weaker nations by the powerful under the guise of *globalization*.[18] As an Executive member of World Mathaba

---

former Dominica Labour Party leader and Minister of Finance in the interim government, Michael "Mike" Douglas, who died in April of 1992 after taking ill with cancer.

[18] . See **The Final Call**, *World Mathaba of Libya, Which Supported Liberation Movements, Plans Its Future-* September 14, 2000.

headquartered in Tripoli Libya, he enjoyed a closed relationship to National Liberation leaders such as Hugo Chavez of Venezuela, South Africa's Winnie Mandela, and Gary Adams of Northern Ireland's Sinn Fein. In his speech at Georgetown, he departed from his text and riveted the audience with his various daring missions on behalf of World Mathaba, in particular his role in assisting the African National Congress (ANC) after the collapse of the Soviet Union, which had been one of its important allies. Later, when news of his death reached them, some veteran Caribbean nationalists like Jamaican born Leo Edwards who had been in the audience claimed he was "foolish" to have revealed so much of his involvement in anti-colonial activity, while in Washington, D.C.

Nonetheless, Douglas was fearless and felt that he had to speak his mind, no matter what the consequences. In that vein, he saw the African American Community as a key ally in his quest to link the African Diaspora to that continent for technical assistance and economic development. Premised on Garveyite self-reliance principles, he felt that if Africans abroad did not rally to the cause of self-uplift, it was all for nought. To that end, he had invited Martin Luther King III to the first seating of the new parliament in April 2000, and had appointed the Nation of Islam's International Secretary, African American Akbar Mohammed, as Dominica's Special Envoy to Africa. Despite that focus, Douglas spent part of his last visit to Washington conferring with US officials and with the well-connected law firm of Hogan & Hartson, lobbying on behalf of Ross University, a U.S. owned and accredited medical school based in his constituency of Portsmouth which faced challenges to its Federal student loan program and related accreditation issues on Capitol Hill.[19] The school was a major income earner for Dominica and the economic mainstay of Portsmouth. At all times, Douglas avoided any overt criticism of US policy and promised Washington continued cooperation in all spheres, to include joint US/Dominica anti-money laundering and anti-drug initiatives. In his view, the U.S. was often misinformed about the Caribbean and could be a strategic ally in the quest for developing Dominica's eco-tourism market. Thus, efforts at mutually beneficial partnerships which led to the training of Dominicans, as with U.S. universities like the University of New Orleans, offered a departure from prior dependence on U.S. State Department sanctioned aid programs. However, some later felt

---

[19] . Ross University, which started as the University of Dominica Medical School in 1976, had a student body of close to 1,000 students in 2000 and, as of the date of this publication, is the island's major foreign investor, making academic tourism Dominica's second largest source of income. The vast majority of the students are US citizens or residents, who study for two years in Dominica and then proceed to US mainland hospitals for internships and residency programs. As of 2000, no Dominican had graduated from the school, though four students are scheduled to do so in 2003. Meanwhile, the Cuban scholarship program had graduated at least twenty five Dominican physicians by 2000, with one hundred more in training.

that the hand of friendship he extended had not been enough to quell the malice of those who stood against his success.

On October 16, 2000, Douglas was scheduled to deliver the opening address at the Million Family March in Washington, DC where he would be introduced by Minister Farrakhan. Douglas intended to use the event to boost relations with the African American community and invite marchers to visit Dominica. Upon his death, his sons Cabral and, Tiyani along with his nephew Sean Douglas, were invited by the Nation of Islam to deliver greetings to the huge rally on October 16, 2000. There they shared the podium with, and was introduced by, Minister Louis Farrakhan, who was deeply moved by the death of Rosie, who he considered a brother. Later, the families gathered held a moment of silence for the departed Prime Minister Douglas on the Mall in downtown Washington, D.C..

While it is the view of many that his work in the liberation struggles in the Caribbean, North America and Africa made him an enemy of imperialism and a possible target for assassination, there are others who felt his death was part of a natural chain of events. Perhaps brought on by his spirit of sacrifice which, often times, robbed him of rest and much needed sleep. Unmarried, Douglas was known to accommodate visitors to his home at odd hours, offering them the hospitality of his couch, if the discussion carried on past bedtime. On many occasions, his trusted Special Assistant Emmanuel "Mano" Nanthan tried to preserve some quiet "down" time for him; guarding him against over-encroachment by hovering supporters. Yet, too often, he would call on friends and government colleagues at midnight and into the early hours of the morning to discuss ideas, projects, or other matters of state, robbing himself of rest. A keen sportsman, he was possessed of great energy on which he may have over-relied to pull him through the challenges of office.

The Prime Minister was succeeded by Pierre Charles, a former President of the National Youth Council and one of his trusted cadres; a man who had stayed in country, when many activists of the early years of the struggle had departed. Charles had worked as a farmer, community organizer and small businessman in his community of Grandbay, solidifying his leadership in the party along the way. Indeed, he had been one of the Labour Party stalwarts who held a sure seat in Grandbay. Over three general elections, he had won the seat for Labour by a wide margin. Now, he had the unenviable task of filling the shoes of a man who now assumed legendary stature in the popular mind. Unfairly, many have compared Pierre Charles to Rosie Douglas, and he has come in for much scrutiny. As with Lyndon Johnson who assumed the U.S. Presidency after the death of Kennedy, Prime Minister Charles may find it, at times, discomfiting that the shadow of his departed mentor looms large. He showed genuine grief at the death and he has promised to fulfill Douglas' vision. However, the problems he faces are no different than that confronted by leaders of small island states: How is one to advance the cause of national development, in the absence of adequate financial and human resources with which to do so? It was the same problem-set which compelled Douglas to undertake numerous trips, in his last days. Many of these trips promised success, with few delivering immediate results. Many Dominicans at home, and in the new Diaspora upsurge have rallied to the cause of duty to country. Prime Minister Charles may yet benefit the country, and ensure his own legacy if he can complete the mission upon which Douglas embarked.

As with most legends Douglas' stature grew in death and his human flaws are often overlooked. However, those who know some of that history of struggle owe it to posterity to engage an assessment of Rosie Douglas' legacy. His years of sacrifice, and his sudden passing, should compel similar reflection and positive action by every conscious person, who love freedom and justice, whatever their station.

THE POLITICS OF NATIONAL LIBERATION

Ideas motivate men and women to form organizations to propagate and enthrone their political principles. In many newly formed nations, organization and political philosophy are often times ill defined and mobilization sometimes reside in the ability of a charismatic leader to woo a crowd and spur a movement. In a colonial and former slave society, Douglas on his return met with no state legitimacy other than that conveyed by his social class. Though black, he was definitely of rural bourgeois origin; his large family, arguably, being one of the wealthiest on the island. Despite that fact, Douglas always related that his parents Robert and Bernadette were thrifty, saved their money, gave much to charity and insisted on modesty. In that context Douglas did not live a pampered life. Instead his family's estate and commercial activities brought him into very close contact with farmers and the urban working class, in a way which gave him an acute appreciation for their difficulties at an early age. It also helped his social intercourse that he grew up in Portsmouth and surrounding rural areas, which were not as socially stratified as Roseau, the capital. Having been born in the second town of Portsmouth on October 15, 1941, he was sheltered by his family's prominence in the town. As a result he escaped the caste system that typified Roseau in the 1940s and 1950s, allowing him the language and the humility of manner, to move easily among the dispossessed. Such style prefaced a substance in things political, which eased the acceptance of his principles of independence, socialism and support for the Cuban Revolution, despite the crude anti-communist feelings of the time. Aside from Douglas' friendly manner, it is important to consider the role of race pride and Cold War politics of the time, as it colored the degree to which he was able to gather political support over time.

The Universal Negro Improvement Association (UNIA) black pride and self reliance movement and, the socialism of Dominica Labour Party founders, Emmanuel Loblack and Phyllis Shand Allfrey were distant memories by the time Douglas returned to Dominica in 1976. However, it can be argued that the existence of early black nationalist and working class politicization, may have created a perfect incubator for the politics of National Liberation espoused by Douglas. National Liberation, as espoused then, was a mix of Marxist Leninist principles, from the viewpoint of ideologues at Moscow's Progress Publishers and black nationalist writing with which Douglas had become familiar during his studies in Canada. Only partially digested, the Marxist Leninist ideology on Dominica had currency only where it related to Cuba and its Revolution under the leadership of Fidel Castro. Cuba was a Caribbean country which, in 1976, was battling the hated south African army in Angola, while assisting the ZAPU[20] and ZANU'[21]s fight against the racist settler regime in Rhodesia under Prime Minister Ian Smith. Cuba had been involved with liberation leaders and

---

[20]. Zimbabwe African Peoples Union led then by veteran Zimbabwean nationalist Joshua Nkomo.

[21]. Zimbabwe African National Union led then by Robert Mugabe (later Prime Minister).

movements such as Amilcar Cabral and the PAIGC in Guinea Bissau, as well as SWAPO freedom fighters in Namibia, all of which endeared it to the Pan African community in 1970s Dominica. The victory of the MPLA[22] and Cuban armies over the invading South African apartheid army, led to the 1976 Soweto student uprising, an event now commonly accepted as the beginning of the end for the apartheid regime.

That relationship between Cuba and black Africans eased acceptance of Douglas' approach in building a following for relations with Cuba. By 1977 a Dominica Cuba Friendship Society was formed and Cadres of the Popular Independence Committees (PIC) had met with senior Cuban diplomat Osvaldo Cardenas, a special emissary of the Cuban Revolution. Shortly thereafter, the Friendship Society sent the first mission to Cuba which included the wife of Premier John, Desiree, and noted playwright Alwin Bully[23]. With **Granma** articles touting the combat prowess of the Cuban Revolutionary Army in its battles against mercenaries and South African commandos, their was little hindrance to the popularity of the Cuban Revolution among students and large segments of the intellectual class.

---

[22] . Popular Movement for the Liberation of Angola then led by Dr. Agostinho Neto.

[23] The founder of the Peoples Action Theater and English teacher at the Dominica Grammar School, Bully was sympathetic to left wing causes. A skilled artist, his design of the new Dominica flag was accepted by the Labour Government in 1978. Not commonly mentioned now is the fact that the central area of red in the flag was designated to represent Socialism.

The United States of America, though culturally popular as an English speaking country with a large black population, was viewed as mired in racial prejudice and acting in concert with the South African invaders and swashbuckling mercenaries who looted and raped their way across 1960s Congo and Angola in 1975. As the prime exponent of a brand of Cold War anti-communism which often sponsored Latin American dictators, the political ideology emanating from Washington was seen as unacceptable to most self respecting Dominican intellectuals and students. Its support of Apartheid and the brutal dictatorships such as Haiti's Francois "Papa Doc" Duvalier, Nicaragua's Anastasio Somoza and other military leaders in Argentina, Peru, El Salvador, Guatemala and Chile who had *disappeared* tens of thousands of their own citizens was unappealing. The Central Intelligence Agency and U.S. Secretary of State Henry Kissinger were widely viewed as instigators of the overthrow of popularly elected Chilean leader Salvador Allende. Allende had infuriated the Washington political elite when he sought land reform, and nationalized U.S. owned multinational companies that dominated Chilean copper mining and commerce. Allende's murder on September 11, 1973, by U.S. backed coup plotter General Augusto Pinochet and his co-conspirators further soured many Dominican observers of world events to the abuses heaped on small states which sought to extricate their economies from the stranglehold of domination by multinational corporations.

Further resentment against neo-colonial rule grew, once the blatant efforts by Washington to stifle Jamaican tourism and disrupt foreign investment escalated, after Prime Minister Michael Manley attempted to impose a bauxite levy on the U.S. owned firms which dominated that island's industry.[24] Dominica, with a banana industry dominated by the multinational Geest, was seen as much a victim, lacking control over its economic lifeblood as Jamaica was. And to escape that victimization, it was the preference of National Liberation ideologues like Douglas, that Dominica join the Non-aligned Movement to make common cause with allies in the developing world.

While those who were avowed Marxist sought closer links to the Soviet Union it held little attraction and was more distant in cultural mores and history, than Cuba. Thus, the Cuban Revolution came to be yardstick by which Dominicans judged revolutionary consciousness. The record reveals there to have been no relationship with Cuba and the Dominican nationalists, prior to the return to Dominica of Rosie Douglas. In essence, his return opened Dominica to an internationalization of its local politics in a manner, hitherto unknown.

---

[24] . On May 15, 1974 the Jamaican government imposed bauxite levies on the US and Canadian firms ALCOA and ALCAN which dominated that industry. The levy, or tax, was used by the government of Jamaica to finance projects geared to internal industrialization, and to transform subsistence agriculture into larger and more productive enterprises. See **The Social Origins of Democratic Socialism in Jamaica**, Nelson W. Keith and Novella V. Keith (Temple University Press, 1992).

The Dominica Federation of Students became a member of the International Union of Students based in Prague Czechoslovakia in 1978, following the return of its delegates Steve John, Debbie Douglas, Agnes Esprit and Gabriel Christian, to the 11th World Festival of Youth and Students in Cuba. The National Youth Council under Pierre Charles became an affiliate of the World Federation of Democratic Youth, headquartered in Bulgaria and links were established with Guyana's People's National Congress, Jamaica's Peoples National Party, and the Workers Party of Korea led by the Kim Il Sung. In addition, Douglas established friendly relations between the PIC and the communist parties in Guadeloupe and Martinique, as well as the independence movement in both countries. Later, Douglas built links with Socialist International, in an endeavor to broaden links with parties such as Britain's Labour party and the Socialist Party in France. In a dramatic indication of his efforts to foster those links, Douglas led a delegation to Martinique within two days of his election to office and negotiated a grant of 1 million French francs which would be made available to assist fishermen who lost property due to Hurricane Lenny[25]. Those links continue to this day and made for the delegations to Douglas' funeral from

---

[25]. See **Tropical Star**, PM Douglas Visits Martinique, Wednesday, February 9, 2000 at page 2. British Labour Party (BLP) Member of Parliament Bernie Grant was a close ally of Rosie and led an inner party support group which printed the Dominica Labour Party manifesto for the 2000 election. Tragically, Grant died on April 10, 2000 of a heart attack, to be followed by Rosie.

the French islands alone to number close to two hundred persons, with Marie Galante Mayor Jean Girard giving the most impassioned speech to the thousands gathered at the October 13, 2000 solidarity rally, at which time he likened Douglas' role in the struggle of black people to that of a giant.

Such a nexus between the politics of National Liberation and being able to provide substantive assistance eventually diminished opposition to Douglas. In that regard, its biggest impact was in the area of education.

EDUCATION, CUBAN SCHOLARSHIPS & OTHER DEVELOPMENT PROGRAMS

Rosie Douglas' focus on education was rooted in the manner of political organization he led. The early PIC adherents were organized on the basis of study groups. Their objective was to promote the cause of independence and plan an economic path forward, which would rid the island of all vestiges of colonialism. Groups like Lechelle and Pillier of Grandbay, Caco Café, The Northern Farmers Fruit Canning Cooperative, the Mahaut cell grouped around Francisco "Tinko" Esprit and Cadre No I, were all expected to have a study program. The founding July 28, 1977, charter of Cadre No. I relates:

> ...a Cadre bent on the study of Marxist Leninist principles, its relevance to our situation and our firm decision to carry out the National Liberation Revolution, along with other inevitable phases, to a successful socialist conclusion[26].

The literary diet among cadres ranged from K.N. Brutents on **National Liberation Revolutions Today,** Black Panther leaders Huey Newton's **Revolutionary Suicide** and Bobby Seale's **Seize the Time,** to Frantz Fanon, **The Wretched of the Earth, Black Face, White Mask** and **A Dying Colonialism**. The main storehouse for radical literature was at the Grandbay library run by the Dominica Literacy Project (DOMAL) that had carried out the most vigorous literacy program in the village in recent times. By that period the library run by the Movement for a New Dominica at Canal Lane in Goodwill, had closed. At times, UWI Extra Mural Tutor, Bernard Wiltshire, supplemented the books Douglas had brought down from Canada, with his own collection. The cadres were intent on abolishing illiteracy, as it was seen as an inhibition to the building of scientific socialism, which required a keen sense of history, science, economics and technology. All the while copies of the Cuban newspaper **Granma** were eagerly exchanged, especially during the period when the Cubans were engaged in fighting off the South African

---

[26]. Minutes of Cadre No I founding meeting, July 28, 1977.

invaders during the Angolan war. Cadres were required to study, keep regular meetings, with minutes reviewed, amended, approved and seconded. On occasion, Douglas attended meetings and reported on a foreign trip, gave a lecture or suggested some new organizational tactic or line of march. Criticism and self criticism was encouraged among group members, and every effort was made by cadres to join as many different organizations as possible to persuade them to support independence and socialism. Prior to public meetings at the Parish Hall or other major public forums, cadres would meet under the leadership of Douglas, Pierre Charles and Francisco "Tinko" Esprit and plot strategy to include sitting arrangements which would maximize the impact of the leftist contingent at the meeting. In one notable debate on the draft independence constitution held during a August 1977 meeting at the Goodwill Parish Hall, six requests were made for the "right to work" to be enshrined in the constitution. Every speaker making the request was a cadre, but they wore different hats: United Student Council, Gutter United Football Club, Sisserou Youth Movement (the public name for Cadre No. I), the Dominica Federation of Students, the National Youth Council, or the St, Alphonsus Youth Group. To further spread the independence message youth groups such as the Young Freedom Movement, St, Alphonsus Youth Group, the Methodist Youth Group, were contacted, debated and/or joined.

Douglas' relations with foreign left wing causes and the Cuban Revolution had a material impact on island life, as evidenced by the 800 scholarships granted by Cuba to Dominica over twenty years; the highest number of scholarships ever granted to Dominicans by another country. Prior to the founding of the Dominica Cuba Friendship Society in 1976, there had been no opening to Cuba, far less a scholarship program. For a period between 1980-1984, the Cubans directed the scholarships through the Dominica Liberation Movement (DLM), as they had been encouraged to do so by Grenada's Bernard Coard who had unilaterally appointed himself Czar of revolutionary purity in the Eastern Caribbean. Douglas and the PIC had split off from the DLM and supported Oliver Seraphine's Democratic Labour Party in the 1980 election, in a move seen by the DLM and its New Jewel Movement (NJM) backers as opportunistic and lacking in leftist loyalty. Many in the DLM leadership, along with Coard and the Cuban Ambassador to Grenada Torres Rizo, distrusted Dominica's interim Prime Minister Oliver Seraphine, They felt his offer of Dominica as a US submarine base went against the principles of non-alignment. After a sober reassessment of Coard's role in the collapse of the Grenadian Revolution in 1983 and the imperative of progressive alliance politics in the Caribbean, the Cubans resumed their relations with Douglas and continued the scholarship program. The defeat of the Grenada Revolution represented the ugly face of ultra leftism and the

Cubans would have none of it. Thereafter, they sought to enhance links with Douglas, who along with his brother Michael, Pierre Charles and others now formed Dominica's Labour Party as the official opposition in parliament. To Douglas' credit, he did not enforce any rigidly partisan litmus test to those who sought to access the scholarship program. All he expected was that beneficiaries would make their contribution toward national development. While the early Cuban graduates faced discrimination and suspicion under the Freedom Party regime, popular acceptance of their training grew in time. Today, the Cuban trained scholars are an intrinsic part of the island's intellectual establishment, several of them like Forestry Engineer Lloyd Pascal, Dr. Albert Severin, Dr. Damian Dublin, Rock Bruno, barrister and UWP MP for Mahaut Julian Prevost, Dr. Jonathan Prevost, Dr. John Toussaint, architect Severin McKenzie and Dr. Griffin Benjamin serving in prominent public sector positions or running their individual professional practices.

Douglas efforts went beyond Cuba. Through Socialist Iternational member parties, like the Austrian Socialist Party of Chancellor Bruno Kreisky, scholarships were obtained. Dr. Steve John graduated with a Doctorate in Chemical Engineering via such a link from the University of Vienna. Prominent telecommunications specialist, Sylvester Cadette, studied in Kiev, Ukraine, while others studied in Leningrad, Russia and Libya. The first Caribs, in any number, to attend university were beneficiaries of the Cuban Scholars Program, to include former Labour Party Member of Parliament Worrell Sanford. Sanford was also the first Carib doctor of the modern era. Douglas also played a role in linking Caribs with other indigenous movements worldwide such as the Movement of Indigenous Peoples, and sent a Carib delegation to China to explore their Asian roots. In addition, Douglas obtained technical assistance training for PIC and Labour Party cadres in Guyana, and Guadeloupe. Members of Parliament Reginald Austrie and Mathew Walter having attended College in Guyana as a result of such efforts. Both Walter and Austrie, as of mid-2002, serve as Ministers of Communications and Works and Community Development respectively. If one were to count cabinet or former cabinet members Lloyd Pascal, Dr. John Toussaint, Reginald Austrie and Mathew Walter, Douglas had a hand in the education of almost a third of his cabinet.

The impact of the education efforts led by Douglas can be felt to this day, where 65% of Dominican doctors and 50% of local dentists obtained their education through the Cuban and other programs initiated by Douglas. Such is an imprint left on Dominica's social landscape that few, in any country, can match. However, a question mark hangs over the program as the unyielding U.S. blockade of Cuba and the squalid unwillingness of some Dominican parents to subsidize their children's free education places it under much strain. In addition, Douglas shared some concerns with this author in February 2000:

> The Cubans are complaining...some of these students have dollars.
> They like to party and hang out by the hotels,...it's not like the cadres who went to Cuba in the early days, who were patriots and sacrificed for a cause..some of those students are now only looking for a good time..I can see that breeding problems down the road

Sadly, the self reliance which the scholarship program was supposed to spur is sorely lacking in some areas and many Cuban graduates have not maximized their impact by building health care and other enterprises on the island, upon their return. Others have resisted a prominent role in the non governmental and Diaspora organizations, in disregard of the fact that it was such community activism by Douglas and others which opened doors of opportunity for them, in the first place. Aside, from private practice, Douglas lamented that the Cuban trained doctors were yet to unite and build a facility comparable to Harlsboro Clinic which was built by the post World War II medical graduates such as Drs. Winston, McIntyre and Sorhaindo. While it is true many of the Cuban medical graduates are from humble origin and without the capital formation of the early wave of Dominican physicians who came from the upper classes, it was Douglas' hope that their entrepreneurial energy would soon come to the fore and bear fruit.

Upon attaining office, Douglas continued on his education focus. One of his key areas of approach was the formation of a Dominica State College. To that end, he worked closely with Harvard trained educator Dr. Hilroy Thomas and Dr. Donald Peters who, as Dean of Student Affairs at the University of Mississippi and State University of New York at Plattsburgh, facilitated many scholarships for Dominican students at schools where he served. In the words of Peters:

> The State College will be able to provide students with the first two years of their education at a local institution, thus rendering the additional two years at an international university more affordable. ..the college will create jobs for university graduates, and will allow professionals currently in the work force to go back to college through adult education programs...the benefit of the local college to a small nation is limitless, and has the potential of improving the quality of life of the entire nation. It is my hope that the state college will be operational in the Fall of 2003 and begin offering 4 year degrees by 2010. The Dominica State College, a dream of our late Prime Minister Rosie Douglas, is an idea whose time has come.[27]

---

[27] . **The Dominica State College-From Vision to Reality** by Donald C. Peters, Ph.D, at page 58. **Waitukubuli** Vol. II-*A Collection of Papers Presented at the Dominica Diaspora Symposium-Rosie Douglas Foundation,* New York December 8, 2001.

To promote the college Douglas sought partnerships with major overseas educational institutions. His first trip to the US mainland after taking office was to New Orleans, Louisiana. There, on March 27, 2000, he was warmly received by Chancellor Gregory O'Brien of the University of New Orleans (UNO). A Government of Dominica (GoD) UNO Technical Assistance Protocol was signed by Prime Minister Douglas and Chancellor O'Brien, due to the efforts of UNO Foundation Washington, D.C. representative Roy Morgan. Morgan had teamed up with

Nature Island, Inc., a non-profit founded in 1999 by Chapin Wilson, Janice Jackson and this author to spur eco-tourism development and marketing for Dominica. The UNO protocol resulted in 300 Dominicans benefitting from training in eco-tourism and hospitality management seminars held on the island and taught by UNO faculty in 2000. Upon Douglas death, he was posthumously made a member of the UNO faculty. In Fall 2001, the first young Dominican, Farrah Laronde, was admitted to a full four year scholarship in what will, hopefully, be an ongoing partnership. Similar partnerships were developed between York University, Canada and Middlesex University in England. The primary strategic objective for Prime Minister Douglas' pursuit of such relationships was to encourage as many foreign universities to set-up shop in Dominica and partner them with the local university he intended to have built. It was his vision that such partnerships would allow the local university to quickly acquire much needed technical assistance and surmount the dearth of credibility attendant to the formation of any new institute of higher learning. At times, thinking simply of the Ross Medical School-model, he relished the income from rental property, support services and related spin-offs such academic tourism could bring. To that end, he offered UNO government land on which to build a world class eco-tourism training center. He envisioned Dominicans and others interested in the blend of environmental protection and tourism considering Dominica-the *Nature Isle-* as a leader in those fields. But always, he was keenly interested in education for Dominican students, something on which he placed a premium and which had gained him a cherished place in the hearts of many a Dominican parent.

Douglas' success in the 2000 election had its tap root in the National Liberation ideology which had distinct international links to like-minded political movements. Where those movements held state power, Douglas embarked on personal visits to seek assistance, long before he assumed political power. As a result, he was the first and only Dominican leader to this date to have carried out diplomatic missions while in the political opposition, which accrued benefit in the form of scholarships or medical and other material assistance for supporters on the ground. Even in private industry, Douglas was able to open the Cuban market to the sale of soap by Dominica Coconut Products

(DCP). Former Cuban scholar Clarkston Thomas, now Dominican Honorary Consul in Cuba, led that effort with Douglas to bring industrialist Philip Nassief to Cuba to promote trade.

The Dominica Liberation Movement and later the Dominica Labour Party were able to have independent scholarship programs because of the outreach pioneered by Douglas. The donation of a trawler by Forbes Burnham to the PIC is a case in point. An effort aimed at teaching deep sea fishing to PIC cadres, the trawler sunk mysteriously off Woodbridge Bay shortly after the Freedom Party's ascension to power in 1980. Such substantive provision of opportunities, especially to the young, assisted the revival of the Labour Party and its eventual return to power.

OPPORTUNIST OR MASTER TACTICIAN?

The Dominica Labour Party won the January 31, 2000 election after Douglas had made common cause with the Dominica Freedom Party, its former arch enemy. Some staunch Labour supporters, including former Prime Minister Patrick John, abandoned the party at that time in favor of the United Workers Party (UWP). As a result, the charge of political opportunism was launched against Douglas, as it had been in the past. Clearly the irony may have been lost on John, that his presence in Labour

Party, in which Rosie Douglas played a role, underlined Douglas' willingness to forgive John's past political missteps in dealing with shady investors, South Africa and racist mercenaries. Despite those mistakes, Douglas was cognizant of John's working class leadership credentials and that it served national unity to return him to the fold. When he felt the UWP, was proceeding along an anti-national path in its pursuit of the passport sales program, he made common cause with the Freedom Party. By that time the conservative Freedom Party was bereft of any solid ideological moorings, yet retained support in many areas. Thus, to Douglas, an alliance with the DFP would avoid a splitting of the electoral vote. He was right in that analysis. Had the DLP and DFP not united, the UWP would have won the 2000 election.

His detractors in the old black power movement had long complained of Douglas as an opportunist, with no fixed ideological address other than that of enlightened self interest. They felt his critical support for Premier Patrick John's Labour government on the independence issue, was self serving and done at the behest of his brother Michael who was then Labour's Minister of Communication and Works and later Agriculture. However, none of these leaders were able to articulate a way forward outside the Labour Party which garnered any measurable support amongst the population. All their efforts at political office failed, with the exception of Ron Green who won as a UWP candidate in the 1990s-*not as a member of an insurgent left wing*. The DLM became defunct shortly after the 1980 election. Martin, Wiltshire, Riviere and many other leaders of the left departed from the country. It was left to Michael Douglas, Rosie, Pierre Charles, Irving Knight and other leaders of the left to rebuild the movement amidst the embrace of Labour's receptive remnants. Patrick John, once released, for his involvement in coup plotting, rejoined the party and maintained a relatively level relationship with the Douglas brothers, Mike and Rosie, and left cadres like Erickson Romaine, youth leader Cecil Joseph and Pierre Charles. A man of charm and inclusion, Rosie worked hard at rebuilding a once faltering party and successfully retained Labour's rank and file, and stalwarts such as Flossie Joseph, Elford Henry, Elkin Henry, Austel Anselm, Vena McDougal, Marie Dyer, O.J. Seraphine and Julian Giraud.

By the late 1990s, with the departure of Dame Eugenia Charles, Douglas was able to build good relations with Charles Savarin, Herbert Sabroache, and other Freedom Party stalwarts who favored functional unity. The end of the Cold War removed much of the ideological rationale behind the Labour/Freedom schism, especially as the Freedom Party sought the allegiance of the new middle class born of Labour's 1960s revolution. The taint of the Freedom Party being a refuge for the reactionary rich had eased some, and issues of good governance, environmental protection, export promotion, information technology, gained in relevance over who was a "Cuban agent" or a "running dog of imperialism." Douglas, sounded more like a responsible elder statesman and such helped his ability to rally people.

In that mode, he contested the 2000 general election with almost a new team, only one of whom-Grandbay MP Pierre Charles[28]-held any national leadership role in the 1970s left. Among the other candidates, Lloyd Pascal stood out as a Cadre No I, PIC veteran of many mobilizations and some clandestine action, who served on the 1979 Committee for National Salvation, and obtained a master's degree in Forestry Engineering from the University of Pinar Del Rio, Cuba under the Revolution's generous scholarship program. Labour's general election candidates, Reginald Austrie, Kelly Graneau, Mathew Walter, Osborne Riviere, David Bruney, Jacqueline Theodore, Roosevelt Skerritt, Eugenia Maffie, Urban Baron, Dr. John Toussaint, Benjamin Shillingford, Vince Henderson, Terry James, Brian Louis, Ian Pinard, Rayburn Blackmore, Alfred Rolle and Ambrose George were part of a rejuvenated Labour Party with limited, or no, involvement in the 1970s National Liberation struggle. Most if not, all were to credit Rosie with having persuaded them to come aboard and cast their lot with a party which, after 1979, most had considered dead.

---

[28]. Pierre Charles had been President of the National Youth Council.

How was Douglas able to breathe life into the left? How was he able to blend the old left and Labourites after the divisive 1970s conflicts? It was no easy task and it is a work which his successors must continue in order to succeed. To understand Douglas' success, one must appreciate that style can have substance where it motivates one to act, to commit, to contribute. Douglas rebuilt Labour and attracted new blood, because enough people believed him sincere. In that way, he persuaded many to act, by committing themselves to the cause of a Labour victory and contributing their time and money to that end. That, where victory was quite doubtful in January 2000. It must be noted that no Dominican political party had been rejected after only one term. Further, the UWP, which included seasoned campaigners and business people like Julius Timothy and Norris Prevost, along with community activists such as former DLM leader Ron Green, looked impregnable in 1999. In his quest to win in 2000, Douglas was ably served by party leaders, such as Pierre Charles, Ambrose George, Mathew Walters, Urban Baron, David Bruney, Reggie Austrie and others. Emmanuel "Mano" Nanthan, Ian Douglas,[29] Erickson Romaine, Cecil Joseph and others rebuilt the Labour Youth Organization, in a manner which ensured a solid

---

[29] . Ian Douglas, the barrister son of former Labour leader Michael Douglas, went on to win a resounding victory in the Portsmouth by-election of December 11, 2001. The by-election was to fill the seat left vacant by his departed uncle, Rosie Douglas. Ian Douglas gained 80% of the vote. See *Douglas Whips Opponents,* **The Chronicle**, December 15, 2000.

youth bloc for Labour's many Election 2000 rallies and motorcades.

In a society where education is the primary pathway for social mobility, Douglas' focus on securing scholarships for the children of the masses consolidated his position of leadership in the society. It must always be remembered that all of this work was done when Douglas was not yet in office. Truly, had he waited to secure office, *before acting on behalf of the needy*, his legacy would have been negligible. He saw his brand of politics as serving the people, not some brand of self-focused political theater. His efforts to secure advanced health care for ill Dominicans among his more wealthy leftist counterparts in the powerful socialist and communist parties in Guadeloupe and Martinique, earned him affection and unyielding loyalty among many. It was the depth of that affection, which created an emotional earthquake on the island which had grown men and women weeping in public upon hearing the news of his death. It was his international reach and respect in the Diaspora, which caused a collapse of the island's state-of-the-art telephone system on October 1, 2000 when distraught islanders and supporters of Rosie overloaded the circuits when they sought to inform and comfort each other at his passing. Clearly, his personal kindness and integrity in substantively meeting real needs, defeated any claim that he was a dishonest opportunist in the public mind.

To assume power, Douglas first had to show an ability to change with the times, while preserving key values of justice, equitable development and independence. The record reveals that where the political left has risen to political power in the Caribbean, it is by being flexible, while adopting the tactics of alliance with pre-existing working class organizations and evincing an ability to meet real needs. The victories of Dr. Ken Anthony's St. Lucia Labour Party and Dr. Ralph Gonsalves United Labour Party in St. Vincent confirms that analysis. In countries where a majority of the population reside within an English-speaking cultural framework deeply soaked in British and U.S. cultural mores, simple Marxist-Leninist dogma is without a political future. What has worked is an amalgam of nationalist thought, rooted in the anti-slavery resistance of the Caribbean people, coupled with Pan Africanism, and an appreciation of the democratization wrought by principles of socialism, where it is shown to work. It is the same formula which has made for the survival of the Cuban Revolution, a decade after the collapse of the Soviet Union. Had Fidel Castro not maintained the essential links to the nationalist spirit of Jose Marti[30] and Antonio Maceo[31], while fighting to spread the benefits of the Revolution, the

---

[30]. Jose Marti (1853-1895) the father of Cuban independence and revered by the Cuban Revolution as the fount of its nationalistic creed.
[31]. General Antonio Maceo (1845-1896) the pre-eminent military leader and hero of the Cuban independence war against Spanish rule. A black Cuban, Maceo's vision for racial equality and military prowess during the independence war has become legendary.

process would have collapsed. Douglas, continuously paid homage to the legacy of Phyliss Shand Allfrey, Emmanuel Loblack and Edward Leblanc, in a similar marriage of his politics with the legacy of earlier Dominican nationalists. In fact he rebuilt the Labour Party's links with the British Labour Party (BLP), to the extent that Labour's 2000 manifesto was produced with BLP support, as was the case when Allfrey started the party after World War II.

While an ardent nationalist, Castro, like Douglas was an internationalist. Cuba's scholarship programs to students from the developing world and its military missions, is mirrored by Douglas role in World Mathaba of Libya which assisted Sinn Fein of Northen Ireland, SWAPO[32] and the ANC in its 1993 election. In a dramatic disclosure made while giving Douglas' euology, Tim Hector, leader of the Antigua Caribbean Liberation Movement (ACLM) who had attended university in Canada with Douglas during 1964-1967, noted:

> It is not so common knowledge that Libya has developed a new international (World Mathaba, ed. note) succeeding the four European Socialist Internationals. It embraces some 80 countries of Africa, the Caribbean, Asia and Latin America, including European countries too. ...besides

---

[32] . South West Africa Peoples Organization-SWAPO. Led by Sam Nujoma, the party now rules Namibia, with Nujoma as its President. Rosie worked with Nujoma in the last days of the liberation struggle in that country, and was Nujoma's personal guest at Namibia's independence celebrations.

Colonel Gaddafi, leader of the Libyan Revolution, Rosie is the best known international leader of this new international. Once again those of us who dared to visit Libya, dared to become members of the new international, the first such created in Africa, led by Africans, were demonised. This time not as communist, but as terrorist. Rosie scoffed at his critics and ridiculed them with his special brand of comic mockery....In the 1980's Rosie single handedly traveled thousands of miles between Libya, Tanzania and Zambia, meeting ANC leaders and fighters. He befriended the late Chris Hani[33] who would have succeeded Mandela, and who then headed South Africa's Army of Liberation. I have here to reveal a secret. Rosie in conjunction with Chris Hani had South African fighters trained in Libya, under the guise that they were Dominicans. Truth to tell, he used a few Dominicans as cover for this bold move. The South Africans so trained, distinguished themselves under the banner of the ANC, and South Africa and Libya proceeded to develop a unity of action, which Mandela himself has praised as decisive in securing South Africa's liberation, not from racism, but from racist rule. Rosie was the international catalyst.....

Rosie, the international catalyst! As catalyst, Douglas not only changed local politics, but made a positive contribution in international politics, be it in Canada, Africa or the Eastern

---

[33] . Chris Hani (1942-1993) was the brilliant leader of Umkhonto we Sizwe (The Spear of the Nation) the military wing of the African National Congress, and General Secretary of the South African Communist Party. The most popular South African leader after Nelson Mandela, he was murdered by a white racist prior to the South African election of 1993.

Caribbean. It was his leading role, which built that link between Cuba, Libya and South Africa for the left in many parts of the Caribbean. Even in far-off Australia he brought a delegation of Aborigines to Libya in the 1980s and saw to the publication of pamphlets popularizing their cause.

Like Castro, Douglas had been demonized and castigated as opportunistic. That Castro was no Soviet puppet, as claimed by his detractors in Miami and elsewhere, so too Douglas was no puppet of foreign interests. When Castro declared for socialism in 1961, as the answer to poverty, many of his early middle class supporters parted ways with him and considered him an unprincipled opportunist. In Castro's view, an alliance with the USSR, was the only way to obtain assistance and defend against unrelenting US hostility which had led to the failed Bay of Pigs invasion of April 17, 1961. Douglas saw his alliances in the same vein: linkages which would advance the cause of the Dominican people, not some narrow personal agenda. It was on that basis that he sought proposed Dominica becoming part of the European Union[34], as it is the only Caribbean island between two EU members (Guadeloupe and Martinique). Douglas had excellent relations with political forces in Guadeloupe and Martinique, who had assisted his rebuilding of the Labour Party. Many saw his

---

[34] . See *The Dream of Rosie Douglas, A Modern Technological Society*, By Tony Best in New York, **Tropical Star**, October 4, 2000 at page 3.

move toward the French as pro-colonial. However Douglas felt that such practical appreciation of what worked, allowed him and the Labour Party to escape the ideological blinders which relegated many left wing leaders and groups to that of fringe entities, far removed from the halls of power. By 2000, the Caribbean people can be said to have adopted the position of Castro and Douglas, that in areas of education and health care, public control, not privatization is the best means to achieving positive results in those areas. No credible opposition to that position exist, and even the IMF and World Bank now pay grudging respect to the successes of the Cuban Revolution in those areas.

In the area of business innovation and economic management, the left has been less successful. Initially seen as anti-business in his criticisms of the failure of capitalism to reverse centuries of poverty in Latin America and the Caribbean, Douglas saw a need to promote private enterprise and the spirit of scientific innovation. In that fashion he sought the development of a Dominica technology park, where Diaspora Dominicans, local businesses and foreign investors would work in unison to removed Dominica's dependence on bananas in exchange for a new prowess in information technology. His university partnerships and the proposed Dominica College was essential to that quest. In one of his last speeches, Douglas looked beyond the left-right schisms which had divided Dominicans:

> We live in a dynamic world and we as Dominicans have to open our eyes to the reality of the modern world. We are no longer in the Cold War. We cannot live in the Cold War. Our history is important, but we cannot live in our history. We have to be looking forward towards the dynamic situation in the world, take advantage of it and allow that advantage to redound to the benefit of the people of Dominica[35]

It was with such a view he sought the flexibility, which focused on what worked, as opposed to blind adherence to ideological tenets which left real human needs unmet.

A mixed economy, with solid state support and involvement where private investment fears to tread, or is unable to act, is the best guarantor of equitable development. That Douglas accepted that principle and forged alliances with elements of the business sector, is one of the reasons for Labour's final escape from the opposition benches. Of course, that is not to avoid the reality that perceived government corruption and the sale of passports to Canadian-bound Chinese and unsavory characters dealt the United Workers Party government a solid body blow in the election campaign of 1999-2000. Being in political power, so as to implement progressive public policy, was always Douglas' objective. His tactics worked, insofar as he was

---

[35] . Prime Minister Rosie Douglas, August 22, 2000. Courtesy of Frontline Cooperative Bookstore, postcard quotation of Prime Minister Douglas.

able to attain that goal by January 2000. In so doing, he was assisted by the likes of Athie Martin, who had supported the United Workers Party in its early stages, but who was separated from it over a copper mining deal which he feared would denude the island's precious forest cover. Attorneys Alix Boyd-Knight and Tony Astaphan, solar panel entrepreneur Michael Astaphan, and hotelier Yvor Nassief also took the government to task for a lack of transparency, further adding ammunition to the Labour charge that the UWP was engaged in unethical behavior. Despite its vehement denials, the interception of sixty Chinese bearing Dominican passports at a Canadian airport in mid 1999, dealt a blow to the image of the UWP, in particular among the Diaspora communities. It was felt that, soon, Dominican passports would be suspect in the major countries of the West, thus inhibiting travel by the island's far flung Diaspora. Douglas seized on the passport issue and promised the US and Canadian governments that he would end passport sales once he got to office. That position solidified support for him among Diaspora Dominicans who then urged their families in Dominica to vote Labour. Such adept politicking always kept the national interest in view, over and above narrow ideological inclinations.

In tactics, Douglas abhorred violence and was the philosophical midwife behind the Committee for National Salvation (CNS) which brought the 1979 uprising against the John regime to a soft landing. By leading an alliance of civic groups and political parties to the CNS conference and adopting consensus, over further street violence and loss of life, he secured a place in Dominican political history. Douglas, more than anyone, bridged the gap between the radicals who wanted a total revolution and the moderates, like Eugenia Charles, Charles Maynard, Brian Alleyne and Michael Douglas, who sought a constitutional compromise. During the turmoil he squelched a plan by some hotheads to ambush Patrick John's car, an event which he thought would shed more blood and open an unbridgeable chasm in the country. At the end, through pressure and threat, the Labour parliamentarians crossed the floor of parliament in 1979 and voted in Oliver J. Seraphine. No more lives were lost, except that of Phillip Timothy who had been shot on May 29th, 1979, and a still unnamed baby who had suffocated from tear gas hurled by Dominica Defence Force soldiers at rioters that fateful morning. Though many in the left called for an armed uprising thereafter, it must be said that Douglas was a hand of restraint. A patriot, he also gave critical support to the Eugenia Charles regime when it faced the mercenary invasion of 1981. He advised and encouraged former Black Power militant Algie Maffie to share the plot with the security forces, thus avoiding a bloodbath on the island. Such foresight, unclouded by political spite speaks well of someone who placed people over self aggrandizement.

The left, which had always been at odds with the church, was hobbled in past campaigns where it lacked a faith-based grounding. By 2000, Douglas had the support of many leaders in the Roman Catholic Church and the Evangelical movement. Leading Roman Catholic Cleric, Fr. Clement Jolly, C.S.S.R, lauded Douglas' life stating, *the genius of Mr. Douglas has been to attempt to review our political alliances and broaden the scope of Caribbean reach*[36]. So too he broadened his political reach, taking the faith based community into his warm embrace. The passionate support for Douglas by evangelical leaders such as Peter Augustine, have been alluded to earlier. In building a solid tie with the Christian and spiritual component of Dominica's population, he was able to escape the nagging criticism that the left was anti-religion or anti-God. His funeral service at the Portsmouth Catholic Church was a high mass presided over by the Bishop of Roseau with all the Catholic clergy on-island in attendance. Truly, it was the church and the others in the Christian community which finally came around to the view that by his works, he was a man of God; a follower of Christ. Though born of privilege, had he not dedicated his life to the needy? By his journey's end, the vast majority of his fellow Dominicans believed that he had done just that.

---

[36]. See *Death of A Statesman* by Father Clement Jolly, C.Ss.R. **The Independent** October 11, 2000 at page 4.

His critics blamed him for lacking managerial or business savvy. That he was too much of a traveler, a hands-off manager and one who left inefficiency in his wake. Such criticism has merit where some of the travel was clearly excessive and better handled by subordinates. As to inept management, at times, it would seem unfair a charge; as if Douglas could be expected to type his own letters and micro-manage his government. An unorthodox man, Douglas loathed the aimless chatter of some cabinet meetings and relished mingling with the people in the street. He was a man of action, who sought results. An indeed, in that quest he did not have all the skills one would want. But who does? Nonetheless, it is a truism that modern Prime Ministers, like captains of industry must have the discipline to sit still, focus, and ensure that tasks are accomplished in a timely manner. Such discipline was lacking on Douglas' part on many occasions.

The foregoing considered, it is of note that Mahatma Ghandi never ran an office, but his mark on modern India is monumental. Martin Luther, Jr, did not serve as a Mayor of Atlanta or as CEO to any major corporation, yet his role in the civil rights movement is revered. Winston Churchill inspired War-time Britons to defy the Nazi hordes, yet he was no managerial genius. In World War I, as First Lord of the Admiralty, his role in the failed attack on Turkey at Gallipoli, led to his resignation. After providing inspirational leadership to the

British people during World War II, Churchill lost the general election to Clement Atlee's Labour Party in 1945 before the embers of that war had cooled. Some leaders may provide vision, or access to opportunity, before leaving the scene. Others may be senior executives who may lack charisma or popular appeal, yet be superb managers. So for Douglas' critics, to expect him to have been possessed of every conceivable talent, is an unfair imposition designed to erase the respect that he is due for a life of service well lived. It is true, that he failed to adequately delegate, did not always put his plans to paper and did not always trust that he could share all his contacts. Organizational management was not his strong suit and building structures to train first and second echelon leadership sometimes eluded him. Many of his missions were shrouded in mystery. For that he was considered selfish by some, careful of security needs by others who knew of his involvement with clandestine work. It did not help that with a cabinet of dynamic young men like Vince Henderson, Ambrose George, and Roosevelt Skerrit, he needed to provide a firm hand on the wheel. Absent the firm hand, many went off on their own way, doing the best they could, they best way they knew how. Meanwhile, some senior civil servants stood back and waited for the inevitable slip-ups to occur and then to mutter under their breaths: *I told you so.*

Government aside, Douglas was able to reunite the political left after the petty divisions of the 1980s which had condemned it to the political margins of the society. He breathed life into political personages who never had a popular following, because he thought they had merit. He brought Athie Martin and Bernard Wiltshire back into the fold, despite their opposition to him during the 1980 election. Sadly, despite pleas that he not resign, Athie Martin abruptly departed his ministerial post in the Labour Unity government in July 2000, supposedly over Dominica's handling of the whaling issue at the International Whaling Conference held that year. Wiltshire was compelled to resign over mounting public controversy stirred by his perceived support for homosexual rights. In a conservative country, such advocacy of "gay" rights carried with it great political costs which the government seemed unwilling to bear. The same intolerance and lack of discretion which had bedeviled the political left in the 1980s was back at work in some *danse macabre* posing as principle. Soon words of splits and discord could be heard. To many, it seemed that factionalism among the left was alive and well again.

The pressure and disappointment felt by Douglas was enormous, and he imagined dark plots against him. He often times felt that all he had done and sacrificed was not appreciated. A man always willing to share the limelight and forgive others, was now the unforgiven. His belief that traveling to woo foreign investment and the Diaspora was not appreciated irked him. In the last days he reached out to the cadres he had known from the early days of the independence movement, urging them to play their parts, eager for their contribution. Never scornful of their separation from the homeland, and happy for their involvement where it occurred. In private he mourned the poverty of spirit and lack of commitment of those in his circle who sought the perks of position, personal material benefit and the pleasures of the flesh.

CONCLUSION

The return of Rosie Douglas changed the political landscape in Dominica, for the better. The ferment created by his presence compelled a new Dominican nationalism and linked it to a universal creed which sought freedom from colonial rule. His place of prominence in Caribbean history is widely acknowledged. In the words of the **Jamaican Observer** :

> Rosie Douglas helped also by his Canadian activities and his later actions at home to build a Caribbean nationalism that was part of the ferment of Black Power radicalism and socialism that swept the region in the 1970s.

Despite that, he had his critics. They are fewer today, but still exist. In their view, his was a discordant voice that Dominica could have done without. But what do they have to offer a people oppressed for five hundred years by colonialism? The perpetual silence of the vanquished? To such silence or imprisonment of the spirit, Douglas would never abide. He reached for the unity and development of Caribbean and African people so that we could take our rightful place among the family of nations. Though he fought racism, he never became embittered or racist and his funeral cortege was a rainbow nation of Libyan, Palestinian, Irish, British, South African, Salvadoran, Swedish, and Chinese mourners who had come to know and appreciate his humanity.

For the opportunities Douglas fostered and the pride he gave to the humble whose children had newly found intellectual capital, he made the island a better place. It is fitting that others have taken up his mantle of national development, with the same grace of spirit by which he abided. It can only hoped that those who formed the Rosie Douglas Foundation in his memory and organized the December 8, 2001 *Dominican Diaspora in the Development Process* Symposium in Brooklyn, New York will make common cause with their island folk, and rally together for self-reliant development. Such a coming together would be a fitting tribute to a man who sought unity for common uplift, at home and abroad.

THE RISE OF A NATIONAL DEVELOPMENT CONSCIOUSNESS AMONG DOMINICAN OVERSEAS COMMUNITIES.

Gabriel J. Christian, Esq.

INTRODUCTION

To understand the new dynamism in Diaspora Dominican involvement in development initiatives on the island, one must understand how tragedy can sometimes lead to unity of purpose. Many will trace that new spurt of energy in the overseas communities to the death of Prime Minister Rosie Douglas on October 1, 2000, barely eight months after he took office. Why his death led to an outpouring of soul searching and activism in the overseas communities had much to do with his life, which has been detailed elsewhere, and his dramatic outreach to major Dominican population centers overseas in his few months in office. However, its tap root could be said to comprise many strands: late 19th century economic depression which compelled the migration of Dominicans to the gold and oil fields of Cayenne, Venezuela, Trinidad and to participate in the building of the Panama Canal in the early 1900s; the great post World War II movement of young Dominican men and women to rebuild a shattered Britain; the outflow of Dominican talent to oil refineries and service industries in Curacao and Aruba, the U.S. Virgin Islands and Guadeloupe; the education reforms of the 1961-1979 Labour Administration; the upsurge of black nationalist and national liberation politics on island in the 1970s; the growth of the internet; the increased access to college education in the US by Dominicans in the 1980s; the advent of Dominica specific websites such as www.rosiedouglas.com,[1] www.thedominican.net,[2] ww.cakafete.com,[3] www.da-academy.org,[4] www.sensay.com,[5]

---

[1]. Founded by Dominican patriots and Douglas family members in March 2001, the **Rosie Douglas Foundation** is a non-profit organization named in honor of Prime Minister and Pan Africanist Hero Hon. Roosevelt B. Douglas, OM. It is focused on education programs and community development of Dominican communities at home and in the Diaspora. The Honorable Prime Minister Roosevelt Douglas was awarded the Order of Merit, posthumously, at the December 8, 2001 symposium.

[2]. **The Dominican**, founded in January 2001 by Dominican economist at the International Monetary Fund (IMF) Dr. Thomson Fontaine, is the most widely read Dominican electronic magazine. Focused on Dominican economic and social issues, as well as the role of the Diaspora in development, the site registers thousands of hits each day.

[3]. Founded by legendary Dominican radio engineer Fred White, O.M., **Cakafete** (means: How are you? In French creole) is a virtual Dominica website, informing the world of all facets of Dominican life. It has been a primary link for many Dominicans worldwide who seek to keep in touch with events on the island. Fred White was honored with the **Order of Merit** on December 8, 2001 at the RDF Sponsored symposium for his role in developing the website and a lifetime of service to Radio Dominica. He first came to prominence as the first person to alert the world, via his battery operated radio, to Dominica's Hurricane David disaster in 1979.

[4]. The **Dominica Academy of Arts and Sciences** led by agricultural scientist **Dr. Clayton Shillingford**, was founded by Canadian based Dominican, and former Hospital administrator **Raglan Riviere** and Washington, D.C. based attorney **Gabriel J. Christian**, in November 2000. Its primary mission is to gather the resources of overseas Dominicans in its skills directory, network its members with Dominicans at home and so promote specific research and development projects which benefit the island.

www.caribbeansupplies.com,[6] www.discoverdominica.com,, www.dsecinc.com, www.delphis.dm. These sites provide a virtual Dominica to the overseas Dominican at a click of the mouse and provide a variety of platforms from which the conscious Diasporan can make a positive contribution to the development of his or her country.

More than raising their flags or having a good time while at Brooklyn's Labour Day Carnival, Toronto's Caribana, or London's Notting Hill Carnival, the Dominican Diaspora in the early 21st Century seemed increasing fixated on:

- Good governance on the island
- Economic activity which favor local control
- The right to vote
- Integrity legislation to outlaw corruption in public office
- Increased investment by the Diaspora and government incentives to spur same
- Protection of Dominica's natural environment

---

[5]. **Sensay.com** promotes Dominican music, community and cultural events. It is the creation of New York based Dominican **Earl Lawrence**, a former leader in **DARDA** (Dominica American Relief and Development Association) of New York.

[6]. **Caribbeansupplies.com** is the brainchild of Dominican computer scientist, **Avonelle James-Christian**; a graduate of the Convent High School she built switches for Lucent Technology in Massachusetts, before investing in Dominica's first major e-commerce portal.

- And the building of a technologically advanced economy on island

The internet sites above, especially that of the Dominica Academy of Arts and Sciences, the Dominica Sustainable Energy Corporation and the Rosie Douglas Foundation focus on specific projects which advance the causes noted above. While some of these sites have been plagued by the idle purveyors of gossip or "Bef,"[7] they are now increasingly the spearhead of a new national pride, cultural identity, initiatives in education and business development, bent on self reliant national uplift. It was among that group of media and business savvy Dominicans that anger about the passport sales took hold in 1999. That, after 60 Chinese national showed up in Toronto, Canada in July 1999 bearing Dominican passports. The Canadian government immediately threatened to impose visas on Dominicans who, hitherto, needed only to purchase a ticket to travel to Canada.

Well traveled, the Diaspora community feared that - as Dominicans - they would now face increased and undue scrutiny from immigration agents at foreign borders. Possessed of a good reputation in most quarters overseas, the Diaspora Dominicans now feared a diminution in the respect formerly accorded holders of Dominican citizenship. That concern made itself felt in articles which condemned the passport sales program on Cakafete's

---

[7]. Dominican French patois term for wild gossip.

Casual Message Board prior to the 2000 election. Fearful that the mass sale of Dominican passports to those who could afford it would soon lead to the re-colonization of the island, many in the Diaspora opposed the re-election of the United Workers Party under whose administration the program had flourished, and have since condemned the Dominica Labour Party/Dominica Freedom Party Coalition for reneging on their campaign promises to shelve the sale of passports.

ROSIE'S OUTREACH 2000

The first Dominican head of state to have been active in high profile community development and international politics outside the country during his college years and after, Douglas was cognizant that Dominica's development was dependent on the Diaspora being engaged in a new partnership. He believed that offering the same concessions to Diaspora returnees as that offered to foreign investors would lure the financial and technical bounty of overseas Dominicans back to Dominica. In a whirlwind tour, Douglas visited the US Virgin Islands, Guadeloupe, Martinique, Miami, Washington, DC, New York, Boston, Toronto, London and other major Dominican overseas communities immediately after he was elected to office in February 2000. In his addresses to packed halls, he urged

Dominicans to return home to invest their talent and money. In his words:

> ...I know many of you visit home at Carnival, Easter and Christmas. You wearing your nice dan-dan[8], looking sweet...in your bags you make sure you have some gifts, cheap ones, you bought before. When you reach home, you eager for that bouden, ginger beer and sorrell. You having a good time. But sometimes you forget to see how the country's doing, and what you can do to make it better...[9]

In his affable manner Douglas delivered a serious message of duty and service to country, while peppering his speech with common slang and mirth. The above theme - ***And what you can do to make it better*** - would be repeated constantly at the meetings with the overseas Dominica communities. In his travels, Douglas was accompanied by free lance journalists Matt Peltier and Carlisle John Baptiste, and Desmond Augustine of the Government Information Service. These young Dominican journalists prepared regular newspaper articles, along with radio and television programs which chronicled the message to the Diaspora and spurred local interest in partnerships between the home based and overseas Dominicans.

He was Dominica's first head of state who, without

---

[8] Local slang for clothes.
[9] . Prime Minister Rosie Douglas to a May 5, 2000 meeting in New York's Dominican community.

equivocation, championed voting rights for overseas Dominicans. His new attitude of inclusion, followed on efforts launched in the past by the Dominica Freedom Party (DFP) and United Workers Party(UWP) administrations to reach out to overseas Dominicans. In 1988, the DFP organized a Reunion; a gathering inclined toward the festive and aimed at welcoming overseas Dominicans. A skills based directory of returnees which could have been developed as result, was not done. The UWP carried on the tradition of meeting visiting Dominicans to the local carnival. However, no Dominican head of state had gone much beyond rhetorical flourish about "Dominicans returning home" or launched such a concerted initiative as had Douglas. In that effort, he was ably assisted by a constellation of Dominican associations in the US Virgin islands, New York, Washington, D.C., London and elsewhere which - in the past - had plodded along with individual community projects for Dominica. He sought to unite these groups for the goal of self reliant national development initiatives. But in an instant, he was gone, and with his demise followed a muting of any talk of giving the vote to Diaspora Dominicans, or giving Diaspora investors and returnees the same concession and tax incentives offered foreigners.

THE HISTORY OF A NATIONALIST MOVEMENT: EDUCATION AND IDEOLOGY

The Dominican Diaspora has deep tap roots in North America, the Caribbean and Britain, born of the island's geographic location and history. Dominica is the island at midpoint in the Caribbean chain of islands which sweep from the Bahamas in the North to Trinidad off Venezuela's coast. With emancipation in 1834, the sugar industry in Dominica had lost any vitality it once had. As a result there was a degree of idleness and restlessness in the land. The Negro War of 1844, evinced a profound desire by the newly freed to strike out at a system of prejudice and economic disparity which continued to blight the lives of most Dominicans. The revolt, never certain of defeating a then powerful imperial Britain in its grip on the island, failed. With its failure, there existed a strata of islanders who were not resigned to living out their lives by squatting on government land, engaged in subsistence agriculture. They would form part of that nomadic proletariat, seeking economic sustenance beyond the shores of their island home.

Dominica was an island visited by US whalers which often sought resupply at Portsmouth. Local men would oftentimes obtain menial work aboard such ships and remain stateside once they returned to the US mainland. Several made their homes in major eastern port cities such as Baltimore, New

York and Boston. In addition, the ship building trade in Portsmouth and other small villages allowed Dominicans to interact with their neighbors in nearby French and Dutch dependencies such Martinique, Guadeloupe, St. Marteen, Marie Galante, etc. The cross-fertilization of ideas born of such commercial intercourse steadily created a sense of nationality and the opportunity for economic advancement.

Chroniclers of the Dominican community in New York City speak of meetings in the 19th century where Dominicans who had moved north met in Brooklyn and Manhattan brownstones and damp basements to plot the overthrow of British colonial rule. Dominican, George James Christian was one such Diasporan who went even further afield. The son of an Antiguan solicitor, he served as a schoolteacher in Dominica, and was admitted to Gray's Inn London in 1899. There he linked up with noted Pan Africanist lawyer, Trinidadian Henry Sylvester Williams. With Williams, Christian helped to organize the 1900 Pan African Conference in London. He addressed the conference on the theme *"Organized Plunder and Human Progress have made of Our Race Their Battlefield."* His speech was a scathing condemnation of colonialism and racism in Africa and elsewhere. He was called to the bar in 1902 and migrated to the Gold Coast (present day Ghana) and became a "concessions" lawyer, dealing in concession for goldfields. He served in the Gold Coast Legislative Council, served as Liberian Counsel in the Gold Coast and operated a successful practice in Sekondi. His house was called Dominica House and his son's home in Dominica was called Sekondi house. Along with Caribbean Diasporans such as George Padmore, and others who had settled in the Gold Coast early in the 20th Century, George James Christian played a key role in the development of an insurgent Ghanian and Pan African nationalist thinking[10]. His descendants, such as Dominica Department of Culture official Pearle Christian, Director of the Christian Musical Class Purcell Christian, BBC personality Moira Stuart, Dr. Samuel Christian, writer/publisher Margaret Busby, Estelle Appiah, Dr. Maude Meier-Christian, and Dr. Ferdinand Christian, continue to play a major role in Dominican and Ghanian public life. In time, the search for educational opportunity would bring prosperity to the Dominican Diaspora

---

[10] See Margaret D. Rouse Jones of the University of the West Indies, The University Libraries, **George James Christian of Dominica and the Gold Coast**, Conference on Henry Sylvester-Williams and Pan Africanism: A Retrospection and Projection, The University of the West Indies, St. Augustine, and Oberlin College, Ohio, USA, January 4-13, 2001. George James Christian was the uncle of Henckell L. Christian, MBE, Minister of Education in Dominica's first independence government and Lemuel M. Christian, MBE, author of the music to Dominica's national anthem **Isle of Beauty**. The First Reunion of the Dominican and Ghanian strands of George James Christian's family was organised by Joyce Christian, Joan Robinson-Christian and noted Ghanian author, publisher and playwright Margaret Busby (co-founder of Allison & Busby, Ltd.) on July 19-21, 2002 in Upper Marlboro Maryland. Also present at the gathering was his grand-daughter Moira Stuart, OBE, the leading newscaster of African descent on the BBC, as well the winner of the 1988 British TV and Radio Industries Club Award for "Best Newscaster of the Year."

and favor the transfer of resources to Dominica, even where such was modest.

The networking among the Diaspora led to a further diffusion of nationalist political philosophy, despite the barriers of distance. We now know that when West Indians Cyril Briggs and others formed the militant African Blood Brotherhood in 1915, they were followed by Messrs. Mongerie, Gardier, Casimir and others who formed a branch of that movement in Dominica in 1919. The Dominican group was the recipient of material and ideological nourishment from the small Dominican community in New York . Were they communicating? That we do not know for certain at this point. However, the fact that George James Christian then in Ghana and J.B. Charles collaborated on the 1932 West Indian Conference[11] held in Dominica from October 28, 1932 to November 4, 1932, says much about the networks of the day. Their sympathizers included J.B. Charles, an astute businessman, who corresponded with Marcus Garvey and sought to be the local agent of the Universal Negro Improvement Association (UNIA) **Black Star Line**.

---

[11] Chaired by Trinidad born Dominican Statesman, the dynamic barrister CEA Rawle, the West Indian Conference sought self government and a confederated state among the English speaking Caribbean islands. Attended by Caribbean leaders such as Capt. A. Cipriani of Trinidad, the UNIA representative at Dominica, J.R. Ralph Casimir served as Secretary at the gathering. See Lennox Honeychurch's **The Dominica Story** (MacMillan Education Ltd. 1995) at 163;

In the early 1900s when the newly formed Panama Canal Commission, needed English speaking, acclimatized and skilled labour for the job of building the canal, Dominicans answered the call, along with others islanders. Dominicans also traveled to the goldfields of British Guiana, and Cayenne to seek their fortunes. Others went to the oil fields of Venezuela, or the Dutch islands of Curacao and Aruba, where the rapidly expanding Royal Dutch Shell refineries needed carpenters, masons and maids. Dominicans were among the many islanders who filled the breach. In fact, the co-founder of Pond Casse Press, noted Dominican, writer, historian and senior defense counsel in Ontario, Canada, attorney Irving W. Andre, was born in Curacao of Dominican parentage. Such resourceful Diasporans, as Andre, and other Dominicans have constantly infused Dominica with energy, vision, skill and money to stave off economic, political and social implosion on many occasions.

When Raglan Riviere founded his personal website, *Sir Raglan Presents* in 1999, he did not know that it would be the incubator for the most dynamic overseas effort in Dominica's history to reverse the pernicious efforts of the brain drain. Initially, the former Royal Air Force officer and retired hospital administrator simply sought to display his country's beauty, his literary talents and the skills of fellow Dominicans. When the potential for a wider collaboration aimed at getting a skills directory of Dominicans at home and abroad presented itself,

Raglan and this author consulted, and the Dominica of Arts and Sciences was founded in November 2000. In Riviere's words:

> As we enter the 21st. century, small, developing states like Dominica must first come to term with the rapid re-organization of global economic structures around them. There is no way to avoid it. This irreversible rush toward trade liberalization in a world of unequal players - of developed, developing, less-developed and under-developed economies - is likely to drag us in every conceivable direction like bouncing balls at the whims and fancies of greedy, heartless, self-seeking, ruthless, developed nations. No longer can we plead poverty for preference. The law of survival of the fittest, in the face of modern civilization, now determines how the spoils of world economic growth will be allocated. So, what's new, you may ask? Don't the rich always get richer and the poor poorer? We must re-examine the old ways of doing things and seek more efficient ones. We must be prepared to abandon that which is unproductive and embark boldly on those which show promise for the future. Searching for these new mechanisms, this special niche, is the purpose of these web pages...

The website urged Dominicans to register on the skill directory and offer their talents to the task of nation building. The response, while not overwhelming, has been steady. Critics who mistook it as some elitist club for degree holders were informed that its founders meant no such intellectual snobbery. Since then students and skilled Dominicans of all stripes have joined the Academy. The DAAS was to be a leading exponent and co-sponsor of the Dominica Diaspora gathering held at Brooklyn's Marriott on December 8, 2001. As a service to the worldwide network Dominican Diaspora DAAS's webmaster, Raglan Riviere, set up free Home Pages for organizations such as CODA-Hamilton of Canada, The Dominica Association of Washington, D.C., Sweden-Dominica Friendship Association, Dominica Mid-Western US Association, Dominica United Kingdom Association (DUKA), Dominica Nationals Association (DONA), German Kalinago, e.V., which supports friendship between Germans and Dominica's Carib people, among others.

The information revolution made possible by the internet allowed the Dominican Diaspora new tools to create new links where none existed before. Such ferment led the Dominica Houston Association (DHA) in Texas and Dr. Thomson Fontaine to unite in common cause. Fontaine, founder of **The Dominican Magazine** was invited to address the DHA at their November 3, 2001 independence gathering organized by the Dominica Houston Association. His e-magazine had made its way to Houston. Impressed by his sense of national duty, he was called upon to address the Texas based Dominicans as the keynote speaker. His experience there spotlights how the Diasporan Dominicans have been able to preserve a sense of culture, national identity and purpose in foreign lands. Fontaine records in **The Dominican** of November 19, 2001:

> ....it was the cultural explosion that made one of the biggest impressions of the night Performing to drums, Jing Ping, music and other Dominica songs, members of the

> DHA's Kubuli Productions mesmerized their audience with dance, poetry, conte, songs and skit....

During the event he met a Dominican engineer, Carlton Dangleben, who works as a Protective Coating Specialist and project manager at BP Amoco's Yacheng 13 Gas Field in the China Sea. Dangleben, as with many Diasporan Dominicans still maintains a bank account in Dominica and supports the Houston Association, which in turn has donated much needed medical supplies to the national hospital system on the island. Such are the Diaspora organizational networks now forming which can assist Dominica's escape from its political and economic malaise.

When on December 8, 2001, five hundred Dominican scientists, students, entrepreneurs, lawyers, academics, teachers, political leaders, government leaders and community activists gathered in New York City's Brooklyn Marriott for the first ever **"Dominican Diaspora in the Development Process"** conference, they were continuing a noble tradition of spirited concern and contribution by Dominicans to their beloved homeland. The event was sponsored by the newly formed Rosie_Douglas Foundation (RDF) and Dominica Academy of Arts and Sciences (DAAS), in tribute to the legacy of the late Prime Minister whose greatest contribution to national development had been his leadership in the independence movement and his work in gaining access to university education for hundreds of underprivileged

Dominicans. To the audience and RDF organizers such as Shirley Allan, Sheba Robinson, Dawn Robinson, Neal Nixon, Cheryl Allan, Joan Robinson-Christian, Debbie Douglas, Dr. Clayton and Margaret Shillingford, Cartiann Allen-Lambert, Tracee Flowers, Roy Casey, Adenauer Douglas, Claudette Loblack, the moment was historic, in the words of RDF Executive Director Athenia Henry:

> ...December 8, 2001 will go down in Dominica's history as the Diaspora rallies its resources for the noble task of nation building, by gathering our intellectual capital and linking it to provide enterprise in banking, aviation, tourism, information technology, agriculture, and agro-processing, as we continue our quest for economic independence, self reliance and respect ...[and] take our rightful place among those who are working diligently to build a progressive Dominica worthy of our talent as a people.

With a welcome message from New York's Governor George Pataki and the presence of representatives of Brooklyn Congressman Major Owens and City Council member Una Clarke, the attendees were brimming with excitement and patriotic zeal. They listened intently to presentations from Dominicans who had traveled the world, attained academic excellence and a degree of personal success unparalleled in the history of the Diaspora, and who were now intent on making a contribution to the development of their island home. Commitments from songwriter Pat Aaron and poet Delmance

"Ras Mo "Moses to form a Dominica Musicians Association to protect and promote our cultural bounty were made. Captain Frankie Tonge of Marigot and his Trinidadian born partner pilot Bhagwerdinh Persad, operators of a small inter-island air charter and cargo airline, Nature Island Roots, sought Diaspora support for a much needed Air Dominica Project. Natural food entrepreneur John Robin, owner of Benjo's Seamoss, brought along cartons of his natural beverage produced from seaweed and bottled at his Canefield industrial site factory. The delicious and invigorating drink was snapped up in minutes, during the exhibition portion of the symposium. Buyers committed to ensuring that his product found space on Caribbean grocery stores shelves from Miami to Boston. Dominican architect, the Cuban trained Severin McKenzie of Mckenzie Architectural and Construction Services, Inc., handed out glossy brochures and provided video animation on his new initiative to build a new and affordable Dominican housing industry. Indiana based chemical engineer, Dorian Ettienne, displayed and sold cartons of his tastefully bottled barbeque sauce, chutney and salad dressing made from banana puree. In so doing he inspired those who have hope for a dynamic value-added, agro-processing industry in Dominica. Dominican workers such as Washington, D.C. tower crane operator Paul Carrette joined Dominican academics as Dr. Montgomery Douglas, Economists Eisenhower Douglas and Dr. Thomson Fontaine, lawyer Irving Andre, IT Consultant Dennis

Hermonstyne,[12] Dr. Edmund Tavernier, physicians Dr. Samuel Christian and Hospital Administrator, Margaret Greenaway-Chaplin, agriculturalist Osborne Baron, Environmental Advisor to Dominica's government Lloyd Pascal and medical advisor Dr. John Toussaint represented in their areas of expertise, Dr. Donald Peters, Planner James Abraham, Dentist/writer Dr. Emmanuel John-Finn, University of Chicago criminology Professor Dr. Peter St. Jean, as they networked with Dominican businesses/business owners such as Moka Production, Pond Casse Press, writer Giftus John, Screen Saver producer Lennox Royer, financial services consultant, Randy Corriette, Avonelle James-Christian's Caribbeansupplies.com. They all formed part of an awesome display of Dominican Diaspora, productivity and human resource wealth. It was welcomed that Dominica Minister of Education Roosevelt Skerritt and Minister of Agriculture Vince Henderson, presented summary positions on government's willingness to work with the Diaspora. Ambassador to the U.S., Swinburne Lestrade echoed a similar view. Yet, as of this writing no systematic effort has been devised by government to follow on the opportunities presented at the gathering.[13] The symposium's

---

[12] . Of Guyanese heritage Information Technology scientist and entrepreneur Dennis Hermonstyne presented a paper at the symposium. He is one of the many Caribbean Diasporans drawn to investment opportunities in Dominica as a result of the networking efforts of the Dominican Diaspora.

[13] . Minister of Communications & Works Reginald Austrie allowed DSEC a license to install the research turbine in January 2002, but the government is

keynote speaker, physicist and author Dr. Sherman Severin urged the speakers to use their *relationship capital* - or network of contacts-to bring development to Dominica and their communities[14]. Chancellor Gregory O'Brien of the University of New Orleans (UNO) addressed the luncheon gathering after receiving the well deserved *Order of Friendship* from the Roosevelt Douglas Foundation for his unswerving support for tourism management training of Dominicans and the establishment of relations between Dominica, UNO and Louisiana. He lauded the efforts of the event organizers and attendees in seeking to marshal resources to spur development on island. Aside from presenters and exhibitors, the newly minted RDF Medal of Honor and Friendship Medals were awarded to Dominicans/Dominican businesses and friends of Dominica who had contributed much to the island: sports hero Joffre Faustine, telecommunications whiz Fred White of **Cakafete.com**, Carib Territory health care worker Sylvie Warrington, Blow's Tea Processing, Dr. Donald Peters of Plattsburgh who facilitated

---

yet to fully embrace the Air Dominica project despite the absence of a national carrier.

[14]. Dr. Severin, winner of the 2001 Caribbean Excellence in Science Award for his work in developing the 80286-microprocessor has a Ph. D. and M.S. in Material Science and Solid State Physics from Iowa State University; MBA from Iona's Hagen School of Management, and a BS in Physics and Mathematics from Iona College. Serves as CEO of Pinchot & Co.-The Intrapraneurship Company. His expertise is in Creating & Implementing Alternative Scenarios-Vision to Action. He is the author of **In the Twinkle of an Eye-Corporation Extinction & Rebirth**, a book about personal and corporate rebirth during downsizing.

many scholarships to US colleges for Dominican students, Maurison and Kathy Thomas of MOKA Productions, a Dominican owned fashion boutique and community television company on Broadway, New York and Dr. Gregory O'Brien of the University of New Orleans, an institution with which the late Prime Minister signed a technical assistance program in March 2000 as a result of which 300 Dominicans became beneficiary of training in tourism industry management. A two volume symposium magazine to commemorate the event *Waitukubuli* (Karifuna/Carib language for: Tall is Her Body) was launched that day. As the energized attendees from Canada, the Caribbean, the US and other places far and wide dispersed, a new sense of commitment born of education and a philosophy of commitment and duty to country was born, where it was not revived.

In a frank assessment that a new path is needed, the **Brooklyn Declaration** issued at the symposium's requested:

- That Diaspora Dominican investing in Dominica be given the same pioneer status and benefits as is now given to foreign investors.
- That Diaspora Dominicans be given the right to vote in national elections, to include the next national poll. (We propose two open seats for the US, UK, and Canada; One seat each for St. Martin and USVI). That way we have our interest represented and respected at the highest level.
- That Dominica's government create an incentive package, similar to that created by the State of Florida to lure retirees, to attract the Diaspora's resources for development.

- Create the legislative basis for official recognition for the Dominica Academy of Arts and Sciences. While the product of private initiative, it would be right and proper that Dominica begins using its human resources gathered in the DAAS Directory or elsewhere in crafting public policy instead of continued reliance on external guidance-to the exclusion of native talent. Such a practice must be considered as a colonial relic which must be discontinued.
- Provide spirited government support to the intended Dominica State College and the Dominica Sustainable Energy Corporation, the Dominica Institute of Technology (DIT), PEC Shipping, Captain Frankie Tonge's Nature island Air. Such institutions are supported by the Diaspora and we are determined in our efforts that these entities be a reality within twelve months. The Diaspora affirms that the DIT will be a world class research and production laboratory for new products in information technology, sustainable energy, agro-industry, and compatible technology. The DAAS will be a primary resource base from which these entities will draw expertise.
- That govt. support creation of an indigenous energy sector, and moves to de-regulate the industry.
- That govt. support creation of an indigenous bank which has the primary goal of harnessing the financial resources of the Diaspora for local and Diaspora community development.
- That govt. support the creation of a Dominica Health Care Foundation as an ally in developing Health Tourism, maintaining and improving national health care standards, hi-tech medicine and an indigenous pharmaceutical industry.
- That government, support the creation of a

Dominica Cadet Corp Foundation as an ally in ensuring that the revived cadet corp has the resources, financial, technical and otherwise to fulfill the national development mandate envisioned by the late Prime Minister Rosie Douglas. One of the aims of the DCCF would be to partner with the different Diaspora communities to host an annual camp in Dominica that Dominican Diaspora children could attend. Immersed in the culture and homeland of their parents they will not be lost to Dominica as is now the case in most instances. The Jews have a similar program with Israel and it works to their advantage as it is now plain to see.

- That the DAAS/RDF commit to a Dominican owned Diaspora Center in Washington, DC, or Dominica within one (1) year. Staffed by a salaried officer, along with student interns, researchers and volunteers to ensure the achievement of the goals set by the 12/8/01. Without this serious, business like approach to this effort, we will not achieve the noble goals set. Such an office will be a solid incubator for our networking, development and business programs. We will then set up similar centers wherever a similar Dominican communities exist. The first office will be a template.

The **Brooklyn Declaration**, asks that government, private sector, and the grassroots, embrace their own and facilitate the objectives of national development sought. In that effort, civic education would have to be pursued at all levels and government bind its programs with that of Diaspora to enable success. In marketing, banking, medicine, technology, we now have the human resource capacity to be world leader in many areas. Hitherto, that capacity has been dispersed. The RDF has taken the initiative to support and partner with DAAS, DSEC, PEC Shipping[15], Benjo's Seamoss, Air Dominica, schools, the national hospital system.

OTHERS HAVE SHOWN THE WAY:

In the mid sixties, as a child, I passed by a glistening four rack rotisserie chicken display, well protected by iron bars from pedestrians on Hillsborough Street in Roseau. The fragrance of roasted chicken enticed pedestrians and the delicious rotisserie chicken was sold from a shop owned by a Diaspora returnee, who everybody called "Texas." Perhaps he was one of the Dominicans who worked in the oil industry in Houston and other areas of Texas. I never did find out. The chicken display is gone now, but represents an enduring memory from my childhood of Dominican enterprise started by Diasporans which enhanced the quality of life on the island. Sylvania Farms in which US Army veteran and journalist Joey Vanterpool was involved blazed a trail

---

[15] . Portsmouth based Dominica marine entrepreneur, Neville Wade, now owns three ships including a 700 ton roll-on, roll-off container vessel, the biggest ship ever owned by a local shipper. PEC Shipping, his company, is committed to networking with the Diaspora to facilitate niche marketing and the movement of goods shipped by the Diaspora.

in poultry farming. Norris Prevost, upon his return from studies set-up Buy-Trinee, the most popular clothing store for the "Hip" generation of the 1970s. His later ventures in lumber and cement commerce, employed many. Similar stories abound in every village of the house built, or the shop which was opened by a returning Dominican. However, we must strive to maximize the impact of such efforts in capital and skills transfer by encouraging more Dominicans overseas to replicate those efforts.

In the early 1990s radio engineer Governor "Guvie" Joseph returned to Dominica from Florida and built Kairi FM into the most popular local radio station, with the assistance of loyal expertise such as was provided by radio engineer George James and office administrator Eslie Florent. The station, as of 2001 was under the control of another Diaspora Dominican Frankie "Crazy Tee" Bellot. In July 2002 www.Kairifm.com was the most listened too Dominican radio station on the world wide web as Kairi's new owner Bellot challenged the IMF influenced austerity budget which threatened to further impoverish the island by its focus on taxes and cost cutting, without a similar emphasis on wealth creation.

Frontline Bookstore was founded in 1982, after the return of Diasporan Eddie "Izar" Toulon[16]. A Pan Africanist and

---

[16] Born on 9th May 1960 at the Princess Margaret Hospital in Dominica, Edmund "Eddie" "Izar" Toulon died suddenly on October 2, 2001. A national figure his shocking death at 41 from an asthma attack, had a similar impact on Dominicans as that of Rosie Douglas. A graduate of the Roseau Boys School

Dominican nationalist, Toulon united with Gabriel Christian, Alvin Bernard, Curtis Victor, Fred Mongerie, Dawen Daway, Peter Piper, and Bobby Lewis, Ras Albert Williams who came out of the 1970s student movement for social change and cultural identity. The bookstore spawned a new breed of writers and artist who strengthened Dominican culture. Zenith Jean Jacques and Harry Sealy, and the new Frontline board have committed to carrying forward the flag of Dominican cultural and artistic identity.

---

and Saint Mary's Academy, he attended college at the Hammersmith and West London College, where he studied business and black history studies. He returned to Dominica in 1981 to rejoin his family and set up a London based educational project program by establishing the Frontline bookshop cooperative, which opened in 1982. The focus of the store was the provision of inexpensive books for students and the reading public, which advanced the cause of national liberation, while promoting pride in African and Caribbean culture. Toulon held the position of General Manager of the bookshop, which shelved schoolbooks, Afro-Caribbean, Latin American, and Black Progressive Literature. The Cooperative, under Eddie's leadership, issued three volumes of *Ramparts* magazine, the literary expression of the nationalistic "Frontline School of Poets." The bookshop expanded it services in supplying photo development, music and souvenir items to its customers. During the period 1988 – 1992 Frontline was engaged in several promotions with regional and international acclaimed artists such as Gregory Isaacs, Culture, Burning Spear, Bunny Wailer, Dennis Brown, Chalkdust, Shadow, Maxi Priest among others. In 1998 Frontline accessed a grant from the *Program for Alternative Technology in Health (PATH)* of Washington, DC to perform a nationwide Reproductive Health Campaign in coordination with the Ministry of Health. Toulon was quick to note that AIDS and other threats to our nation required creative solution finding. As such he ensured that Frontline took a lead in efforts to protect our people, and the youth in particular. In 1991, he took on new duties and responsibilities as Executive Director of the newly established Dominica Festivals Commissions. In that role he was an avid promoter of Dominica's World Creole Music Festival.

In television media, another Diaspora Dominican led the way with Ronald Abraham's Marpin Telecoms. Having studied electronic engineering in England during the 1960s, Abraham returned to Dominica in the early 1980s and built the first local cable television company, Marpin Television. By 2000, Dominica became the first island to have an indigenously grown telecommunications company. By 1999, Marpin had successfully fought the British monopoly Cable Wireless all the way to the British privy council, over the issue of its monopoly of the local telephone services market. Having won, Marpin was then able to enter the cell phone, local and long distance phone market, an event which saw an immediate reduction in price per call to the local phone user. Prior to the IMF imposed conditions, which actually produced capital flight and worsened the economy, Marpin employed close to 800 employees. However, government support for such Diaspora ventures like Marpin have fallen victim to government neglect, where political differences have not engendered outright hostility. It has not yet dawned upon local policy makers that we must give preference to local industry and Diasporan Dominicans as they offer the best hope for the sustainable development on the island. Dominica Coconut Products gained such government protection and prospered. Yet, the lesson is yet to be learnt that no country can progress in the absence of home grown industry. No white knight riding a white horse is going to save the day for Dominica, yet local public policy makers and the bureaucracy continue to chase the illusion of development by foreign investment, in abject rejection of that offered by their own. The countless episodes of fly by night investors who prey on native ignorance have not yet sunk-in enough to stimulate a departure from business as usual. From Grace Tung[17], to the Paradise Group[18], many Dominican administrations have allowed themselves to be lulled by the siren song of dubious characters who promise much and delivers little more than derelict hotels rotting in the bush, law suits and embarrassment.

Vantil Fagan, a New York based Diasporan took over the faltering Bello Agro Products company in the mid 1990s. Together with his son Michael Fagan, he made great strides in seeking to broaden the company's market reach. Environmental activist Athie Martin, who spent many years overseas, returned with his wife Fae Martin to establish the Exotica Cottages in the southern heights of the island. On the hills overlooking Rockaway Beach, former Washington based Diasporan Jean

---

[17]. Grace Tung, an overseas Chinese, was invited to Dominica by the Eugenia Charles government in the 1990s to develop a resort at Layou. After several years of selling passports to raise funds, the proposed hotel site is being overtaken by jungle growth and calls by distinguished Dominican Talk Show host Lennox Linton for an investigation into corruption surrounding the deal, have gone unanswered where the excuses made have not been found wanting.

[18]. In July a group of Florida businessmen, called The Paradise Group threatened to sue Dominica's government over broken promises related to an aluminum plant shipped from Dubai. Nothing is known of any viability study which was done to show that such a scheme of aluminum processing, as proposed, could be supported by the island's anemic energy sector.

Finucane, runs Tamarind Inn. These are but some of the examples of Diaspora Dominicans who have made a real impact on wealth creation in the country.

OPERATION ENERGY EMANCIPATION

One area of sustained focus at the December 8, 2001 Diaspora in the Development Process Symposium, was Dominica's energy crisis. It was discovered that Dominica's energy cost was among the highest in the region and globally. In fact DOMLEC's electricity cost to the public is three times the average of the non-OECD countries.[19] In 2001 and 2002, Citizens Against High Utility Rates (CAHUR), a grouping of concerned Dominicans enraged at high electricity rates, demonstrated against CDC (the new owners of DOMLEC). Dominica is endowed with enough renewable energy resources to meet current and future electrical needs.[20] The preliminary assessment by Jamaican physicist Dr. Albert Binger, author of 2001 UNDP funded energy study, is that the most attractive

---

[19] The Potential of Renewable Energy Technologies for Diversification of Dominica's Energy Supply, Roseau, Dominica, August 10, 2001. Prepared by Professor A. Binger; R. Earl Sutherland of the University of the West Indies Center for Environment and Development (UWICED) at page 7.

[20] . Id at 23.

option for reducing energy services in the medium term is utilization of its wind energy resources. In consideration of the situation on the ground, and the need for Dominicans to take the lead in finding development options, a group of Dominican scientists, business persons and lawyers at home and abroad gathered to address the problem.

Under the leadership of electrical engineers Bevin Etienne, Adenauer Douglas, John Karam, Dexter Newton and Peter Bannis, computer programmers Gilbert Prevost and Janelle Prevost, Economist Dr. Thomson Fontaine, Mathematician Vincia Francis, Electricians Jerome Austrie and Brian Barry, Attorneys Alick Lawrence and Gabriel J. Christian and environmental scientist Mahala Shillingford, the Dominica Sustainable Energy Corporation (DSEC) seeks to be the prototype for a new Dominican business model. That is, a business which marries the talents and financial resources of local and Diaspora Dominicans in respectful partnership, focused on meeting energy needs on-island. On August 1, 2002, DSEC installed a Bergey's 1.5 wind turbine at Delices, on the island's wind affluent east coast. Code named: ***Operation Energy Emancipation***, the research effort is a bold response to Dominica's energy crisis spawned by high electricity rates and a rigid monopoly regime imposed by the British owned Colonial Development Corporation, later named Commonwealth Development Corporation. Located in a wind affluent area, the turbine is being undertaken as a pilot project under the auspices of the Ministry of Communications & Works, led by Reginald Austrie. Aside from wind, DSEC intends to engage in solar, tidal, geothermal, mini-hydro, fuel cell, bio gas and other of energy research, development and marketing, while educating Dominicans via its proposed Dominica Institute of Technology. The effort requires that Dominica's energy sector be de-regulated and that local resources and talent be used to reduce energy costs. Failing that it is the view of DSEC, that Dominica's economy will continue to be hobbled by prohibitive energy costs. Spending their own funds, the DSEC entrepreneurs are determined to embark on a new energy course for the island and so generate a new industrial base. To arrive at its objective, DSEC intends to work with students and youth organizations to change an inferiority complex which holds that Dominicans are not expected to do much more than complain. By their decisive action in building a competent institutional base, the DSEC team is poised to make a significant impact on Dominica's economy if they remain on track.

CONCLUSION:

Abject dependence on aid donors, foreign investors, or even friends in the so non-governmental sector cannot provide a solid path forward for Dominica. Dominicans at home and

Abject dependence on aid donors, foreign investors, or even friends in the so non-governmental sector cannot provide a solid path forward for Dominica. Dominicans at home and abroad have been and will be the primary means for advancing the country's education, society and economy. Unless we seek national collapse or the role of vassal state, sold to the highest bidder, strangers and tenants in our own land, old attitudes must perish. We must consign to the dustbin of history, the petty envy which frustrates returnees; the corruption of some public servants, who see their returning kith and kin as simply pockets to be pilfered; the raging political tribalism, which divides a small land and makes a mockery of commitment to nation over that of political party. As advocated by Dr. Emmanuel Finn and others, we must build a seamless nation, where the 150,000 Dominicans and their descendants overseas are considered part of the national family, even where they are non-resident. We must make a revolutionary departure from the smoldering embers of racial and class prejudice which compelled many in the original Diaspora to depart the deeply forested and hauntingly beautiful land of their birth. And we must be willing to volunteer our time and energy assist all things Dominican, where the cause is worthy.

When in 2002, my niece Trudy Christian, valedictorian of her 2001 class at the Convent High School told me that too many Dominicans still refer to others, in anger, as "black like tar," in scorn of their African heritage, it is no wonder we lag behind as a people. To engage in this new endeavor of nation building self hate must go, as Bob Marley admonished us in Redemption Song,

> Liberate yourself from mental slavery,
> only ourselves can free our minds...

Progress is not certain. But we make progress happen when we adopt the individual responsibility, such as staying up until 6 a.m. on a cold, New York or Maryland night to collect receipts at a dance by WCK or Serenade[21] so money can be raised for a Dominican school or hospital. Electronic engineer Fitzroy St. Rose, the only Dominican who we know to have perished in the World Trade Center tragedy of September 11, 2001 was a member of Exodus[22] and raised funds in that manner. One such dance co-sponsored by the Dominica Association of Washington, DC and Exodus raised funds which purchased a fetal monitor for the maternity ward of the Princess Margaret Hospital in 1998. On Labour Day 2001, St. Rose promised Diaspora activist and Dominica's goodwill ambassador in Washington, D.C., Claudette Loblack[23], that he would be at the October 27, 2001 symposium. He never made it and the symposium was rescheduled to December 8, 2001. Like Loblack, St. Rose is one of the

---

[21] . Dominican bands which travel to Diaspora communities worldwide.

[22] Founded by Fred "Judie" Symes, Paul Phillip, Irvin Guy, Georgie Karam and other New York based Dominicans, Exodus (Examples of Dominicans in the US), has sponsored many dances and raised funds for Dominica.

[23] Daughter of trade union legend Emmanuel Loblack.

thousands of Dominicans who have made a positive difference to his country.

A call to remember the fresh bouquet of her floral gardens, and the crystal clear waters have inspired much longing for those who seek a return to Dominica's fragrant shores. You see the emotion in the glittering eyes of dancers who are beyond their prime, long in the tooth and ample in the belly, who will leap from the seats they have warmed all night, to raise their hands in the air at the stirring rendition of the legendary carnival song "Solomon Roulez." At these Diaspora dances where such songs are played the overseas Dominicans will dance till dawn. However, the desire for the return is more than idle nostalgia. Rather it is a keen realization that we have the talent and resources to make Dominica the best island ever! That with planning and wise effort we can build a new and better life for ourselves in Dominica. That we not need be strangers in foreign lands forever. That Dominica is still relatively pristine, and retains a peace and gentility lacking in so many countries. To make Dominica live up to its potential we must makes changes. An excessive focus on parties and the festive, to the exclusion of serious wealth building endeavor must apply. We will have to purge ourselves of indolence, and be more daring in our effort to do so for self. Our ancestors did more with less, and we cannot backslide into failed state status now, as so many other countries have. We have the resilience and a tradition of overcoming the odds. And we must ensure, by dint of effort, that we exceed the gains of our parents.

We must embrace our own resources and cease such dependence on others, and commit to the sacrifices necessary to paddle our own canoe. For instance, dependence which prevent parents from understanding that they - not the cash strapped government - must support their children in Cuba, an embargoed country which has undertaken to educate our children free of charge, brings shame on those of us who first befriended that country. That failure by the parents to set up a foundation or similar mechanism to support their students, independent of government, means that we have forgotten **koudmen**[24]. Immersed in narcissism, consumerism and selfishness spawned by the new cable television culture, Dominicans must learn the art of discrimination and so avoid the poisoned chalice of vice offered during communion with the new electronic media. As the new Diaspora movement has used technology to unite many for development, so too we must abide. If we fail we will continue to witness our young devoured by the jails in Guadeloupe, the U.S., Canada and the United Kingdom as they seek an exit from their responsibility.

---

[24] . *Koudmen,* or community self help, was the primary means of collective survival for the newly freed slaves in Dominica who were never compensated for their unjust imprisonment and servitude after 1834. Squatting on government land they built their own villages by helping each other, the voluntary exchange of goods and labour being the only currency.

To inspire and train our young for the noble task of nation building all Dominicans must support the Dominica Cadet Corp, the Boy Scout and Girl Guides troupes, the youth groups, the student movement, and community development organizations. Without such youth leadership, there is no future for our country. Every teacher has duty to be a drum major for duty and a model of patriotic/civic endeavor. Teachers have a unique job and Dominicans teachers, who have taught well, must continue to raise a standard of "Of Can Do" as shown by Simeon Joseph, principal of the Marigot Secondary School[25], who with scant resources has produced one of the best organized and equipped schools in Dominica. A Diaspora, unbound, is committed to such schools and others and has already injected money, time and other resources in the efforts outlined here.[26]

The Diaspora is cognizant that it does not have all the answers. However, with Dominica hanging off its financial coat-tails, it is conscious of its role[27]. It is a role which cannot be disrespected, lest we court disaster. The call by the Diaspora to government and opposition to refrain from confrontation and

---

[25] Started by educator Martin Roberts, the school was initially a private venture.

[26] . In April 2001, a joint RDF/DAAS team comprised of DAAS President Dr. Clayton, Dr. Samuel Christian, Roy Casey, Ronald Isidore, and Alick Lawrence donated approximately $150,000 in computers, table saws, literature, medical supplies, copiers and money to schools, the Cadet Corp and local hospital system.

[27] . It is conservatively estimated that 45% of Dominica's foreign exchange income is derived from remittances from the Diaspora.

potential violence while striving for dialogue, following the austerity budget of July 2002, seemed, as of this writing, to have calmed passions. It must be understood by all and sundry that Dominica's failure to produce new wealth, is not amenable to resolution by street protest or endless talk radio chatter. That real solutions derive from reasoned discussion, partnerships across the political divide and the determination to implement the visions for better evolved therefrom.

All Dominican parties and organization must commit to giving the Diaspora the right to vote and the constitution be amended to allow same, where necessary. Such voting rights are a prerequisite to respectful recognition of the Diaspora's role. It would be an insult to continue to seek the Diaspora's economic support, while denying the overseas community its rightful role: That of equal partner in the nation building effort. The Diaspora, likewise, must curtail any arrogance or insensitivity in dealing with the home base and so avoid grievance.

In this moment we face the diminution of our gains, and the re-colonization of our country, if Dominicans do not act with all deliberate haste to secure the opportunity and promise of the **Brooklyn Declaration**. We have already lost some Diasporans who came, were rejected, and had to return to the often times cold and damp habitations of London, Boston and elsewhere. Our island is poorer for it when we lose the resources and know how of those who were suckled at its breast, and whose return implied a love for the homeland. If we succeed, we will serve as a model and a beacon for suffering humankind. Many developing countries, which have been punished by the brain drain await our example. The Diaspora Chinese, Jews and Koreans, have shown how effective conduits they are for technology, know-how and financial resources which have assisted their nations rise. If we fail, we betray our heritage and those who gave their lives for our freedom. Come now, let us unbound ourselves from the paupers' mentality which has us prostrate and in despair. With our native intelligence and God given faith, let us forward to victory for our people, over backwardness and inequity. This cause is just. Together, we do better and will win.

NATURE ISLAND FADING?

THE STRUGGLE TO PRESERVE DOMINICA'S NATURAL ENVIRONMENT

Gabriel Christian

Isle of beauty
Isle of splendour
Isle, to all so rich and rare

(Opening bars to Dominica's National Anthem, *Isle of Beauty*)
By W.O.M. Pond and L.M. Christian

INTRODUCTION:

A question mark hangs, like the sword of Damocles, over whether or not Dominica is, or will remain, the "Nature Island" advertised about in glossy tourist brochures; or the "isle of beauty", which reaps much blessings in the national anthem. Indeed, past and current Dominican governments, and ordinary Dominicans, were (and are) moved by a spirit of conservation long before it became politically popular to do so. But for that fact, much of the island's natural treasure would have been squandered a long time ago. However, current challenges to the island's ecology threaten disaster if they are not guarded against. Consider, the following:

Dominican elementary and secondary school geography classes of the 1960s and 1970s taught that the island measured some 305 square miles. Now, most publications refer to our island as measuring 289.5 square miles[1]. What happened to the other 16 or so miles? Was this change a result of more precise measurement? High altitude map calibration? Satellite technology perhaps? Or maybe, more disturbingly, 16 square miles vanished in the span of one or two decades due to poor sea defence management, along with unchecked beachfront sand and gravel mining for local construction? With regard to rivers, Dominicans at home and overseas are fond of referring to our 365 rivers; one for every day of the year. But, really, are they now talking of dry river beds, or stagnant creeks? What of the crawfish (or "kweebish" in local French Creole parlance), which were still plentiful in most of the local brooks and streams up, till the early 1970s? Have their stock been depleted (where not totally vanished) because of increasing agro-chemical run-off from the export-driven banana industry? Many are the Dominicans (both those who have remained, and those newly returned) and returning visitors who mourn the passing of such notable natural features of our island. Sad, but real, the foregoing points represent but a small sampling of the environmental problems confronting Dominica and

---

[1] See Dominica Environmental Profile, (Caribbean Conservation Association, 1991) at Page 20.

Dominicans at the beginning of the 21st Century. If humankind exist long enough, to allow us a backward glance at the 20th century, it may well be written that it represented the period when we committed the gravest crimes against our own interests. That crime of despoiling our habitat, or literally cutting from beneath our feet, the very land upon which our survival is sustained. But such a scenario need not be.

This essay does not wallow in any gloomy forecast. It is a warning and offers some solutions to the problem of environmental degradation. It is a call to heighten and broaden the struggle for the preservation of our common home. Such a struggle should not be a job solely of government, private enterprise, foreign environmental concerns, and individuals; rather every Dominican man, woman and child will have to enlist in the common effort. To speak about environmental protection, is to speak about Dominica's very survival. In time, if we are mindful of our duty to conserve, Dominica's unique natural features may well assume the role of a primary foreign exchange earner. Yes, that we have recognized (perhaps more than many others in the so-called third world) some of the problems and devised solutions thereto is commendable. However, the following will illustrate the depth and scope of the challenge, and some solutions thereto; solutions in which we will all have to play a part.

CHALLENGES TO THE NATURAL SETTING:

Situated in the middle of the Caribbean arc of islands, and among the Lesser Antilles, Dominica rises majestically out of the azure waters between the French dependencies of Guadeloupe and Martinique. Volcanic in origin, the series of mountains and valleys, which constitute the island's mass, plunge to sea level, separating the Atlantic Ocean to Dominica's east, from the Caribbean Sea to its west. From the shoreline, the land rises more than 4,000 ft, in some places: Morne Trois Piton, at 4,670 ft; Morne Diablotin at 4,747 ft. Chanced upon by Christopher Columbus on November 3rd, 1493, Dominica was to be opened-up to Western imposed chattel slavery, its defiant indigenous Carib people subdued and then relegated to a settlement on the island's northeast coast, now called the Carib Territory. The island, which had only known patterns of, primarily, subsistence agriculture prior to European colonization was now to be a base for export driven agricultural production. By 1700s the land was being cleared, forests burnt, for large scale cultivation of coffee and sugar for most of the 1800s, then vanilla, lime and (currently) banana production in the 1900s. With regard to colonial control Dominica had, by 1805, come under British rule. The influx of Europeans and Africans was to dwarf the early Carib population (which-by most estimates-numbered a few thousand) in size. The first post emancipation census of 1844 showed a population of

22,000; that figure more than doubling to 47,630 by 1946. By 1980, the population had again doubled to about 80,000. By 1991 migration had caused that figure to drop to about 75,000. At the beginning of the 21st Century the outward flow of Dominicans in search of opportunity kept the population steady at 77,000. With regard to the impact of that population, the "slash and burn" technique of clearing land, plus the growth of a small peasantry (following the emancipation of slavery in 1834) was to increase pressure on the environment; leading to soil erosion, noticeable receding of forests and a drop-off in river levels (to be detailed elsewhere). For most of the 20th Century Dominica's population had remained rural and wedded to agricultural production for sustenance. A dearth of flat land had prevented the growth of big plantation style agriculture, (as in, say, Jamaica or Barbados) delaying the environmental degradation that destroyed the original forests on most other Caribbean islands. However, the post World War II growth of the banana industry, along with 20th century trade, increased urbanization and US style consumerism, have all conspired to place a mounting burden on the fragile ecology of the island.

Enlightened leadership on the island (in association with like-minded foreign friends) made an early start in putting together an environmental protection structure. The base of that structure resides in the national park/reserved forest areas, presently under the jurisdiction of the Ministry of Environment's

Division of Forestry and Wildlife. It is in the thickly forested area of land over approximately 1,500 ft. that the Morne Trois Piton National Park and Northern Forest reserve are located. From that area drains most of the water used for agriculture, drinking, export to water-poor islands, and for energy generation. Literature on Dominica's ecology sometimes trace the original national park concept to the input of U.S. scientist David Lowenthal who visited the island in 1961.[2] Be that as it may, Dominica's agricultural division had always maintained a solid cadre of soil conservation officers and forest rangers, as far back as the 1940s (the Forestry Department being established in 1949) most of whom worked diligently at soil and forest conservation. Urged on by Chief Forestry officer (of the 1960s and early 1970s) Christopher Maximea and others, the government passed the National Parks and Protected Area Act in 1975, which formally established the park. That area of government oversight has continued to benefit from local leadership provided by the likes of Felix Gregoire, Collymore Christian, Arlington James (all of whom-as civil servants-are formally involved in environmental protection) among others[3]. However, despite such leadership, the

---

[2] R. Richard Wright Morne Trois Piton National Park in Dominica: A Case Study in Park Development in the Developing World (Ecology Law Weekly, 1985) at page 751.

[3] . On a non-governmental level, Dominica's environmental protection efforts is fortunate to have support from the Dominica Conservation Association (D.C.A.) US philanthropist John Archbold, the Smithsonian Institution,

pressures of export driven agriculture, poor land use management, natural disasters and commercial lumber operations have all posed (and continue to pose) threats to that verdant area of forest at Dominica's core.

> Dominica's forests are the most undisturbed in the entire Caribbean, and described as sheltering 50 species of resident birds, inclusive of the Sisserou parrot-Dominica's national bird. The island groups approximately a dozen forest types, from Mature Rain Forest at about 1,000 ft., to Fumarole Vegetation near areas of volcanic activity, to Montane Thicket and Elfin Woodland above 3,500 ft. These forests have always been important to the island: once a refuge for runaway slaves; the source of mythical island lore; the "Zion" or "Eden" sought after by local dread locks;, and always-the towering guardians of the Dominican citizenry who craved the cooling shade and barrier against fierce hurricane winds, provided by the stout centuries-old foliage and tree trunks.

When the disturbing news of an impending hurricane swept Dominica in the days immediately prior to August 29th, 1979, many dismissed the threat. With an almost natural reflex, many figured that Dominica's mountains would act as a sufficient barrier to the impending hurricane winds. Such faith in the island's mountains may not have been entirely misplaced. For, though lives and much of the tree cover was lost with David's

---

National Geographic Magazine, the Island Resources Foundation headed by Ed Towles, Lennox Honeychurch (whose efforts led to restoration of Fort Shirley at the Cabrits National Park), the Small Projects Assistance Team (S.P.A.T.) and many other individual Dominicans who have simply adhered to a conservation consciousness.

passage, the damage done paled in significance when compared to the losses sustained by the Haitian[4] people. There, loss of forest cover made the Haitian mountains prone to landslides, and the valleys susceptible to massive flash flooding. In Dominica the suffering was mitigated by the presence of forest cover which (though temporarily denuded by the fierce winds) acted as a brake to the flooding and landslides seen in the Haitian countryside. In essence, though there were many landslides around the island, much more of the topsoil was able to hold than would otherwise have been the case (if, for instance massive deforestation had, prior, taken place). Therein lies the lesson: That, though we may never preclude destructive acts of nature, wise forestry management offers insurance against the sort of damage visited on islands (e.g. Haiti) where massive deforestation has recently led even to desert-like landscapes.

Indeed, a correlation may be seen between the poorly managed cutting of lumber by local farmers and the Canadian firm Dom-Can Timbers (after it was granted a lumber concession in 1966) and the Roseau River flood of 1971. That flood (during which the Roseau River burst its banks when it rose-at times-in excess of 25 ft. above normal level) swept away a portion of the so-called "Old Bridge" which spanned the Roseau River; killing

---

[4] Hurricane David swept onto Haiti and the Dominican Republic, after ravaging Dominica on May 29th, 1979. Approximately 2,500 Haitians were said to have lost their lives, compared to about 60 on the island of Dominica.

one Dominica Fire Brigade officer Nicholas who had ventured out to rescue stranded pedestrians. The roiling mass of water, carrying huge trees, livestock and mounds of earth along, most likely found its tap-root (not just in the down pour which preceded it) but in an improper lumber harvesting regime. As recorded by an English survey team in the early days of Dom-Can's operations:

> No account had been taken of for the steepness of the land and the soil type...Dom-Can's promise to use the "best Canadian practices" were not necessarily the best for Dominica's sensitive tropical environment ...the practice of skidding logs to spar a tree is acceptable in the temperate forests of Canada, in Dominica it destroyed virtually every tree and sapling in the area and caused gully erosion and soil compaction in the skid path.[5]

As a result of the carelessness mentioned above tens of thousands of tons of precious topsoil washed away; never to be replaced. A decade after the rape visited on the land by Dom-Can had elapsed, recent evidence reveals that the lessons have not been learnt. Dominica Timbers Ltd. (DTL) is said to utilize the same skidder method[6]. As result lengthy furrows, or skidder tracks, have led to gully erosion. As of this writing it is questionable whether a land management plan proposed to DTL

---

[5] Wright's **Morne Trapiton** at page 753 of the Ecology Law Weekly *id.*

[6] See **Dominica Environmental Profile** at page 48-49.

is being fully utilized[7]. Degradation of the forests in that area, Morne Plaisance, is expected to result. Northeastern Timber Cooperative' (NET) use of a D6 tractor, along with its clear felling on steep slopes has also been criticized. Even though both groups (DTL and NET) allegedly engage in selective cutting, are they monitored for adherence to any national forestry plan? Who does the monitoring? Is reforestation taking place at the same pace, so as to ensure continued ground cover and minimize soil loss? Who is liable for any landslide damage, or substantive soil erosion that ensues? Are there certain established benchmarks (for damage to the flora and fauna) beyond which DTL and NET cannot go? Are the costs in environmental degradation, justified by the benefits garnered thus far? Or is the push for profitability going to overwhelm the interests of environmental protection and long-term survival? In essence, who are the ones asking questions; and is anyone listening while there is still time?

Dominica receives some of the highest rainfall per square inch on the planet. It is estimated that an average of 300-400 inches per year falls in the interior. Yet, with all that water, access to a reliable water supply, water pollution and water conservation are among the greatest challenges currently facing the country. The destruction of forests, or ground cover, inexorably leads to the death of rivers. In Dominica, the reality is

---

[7] Id.

chilling in the definite connection, observed by the most casual of onlookers, between improper harvesting of lumber or poor land use and the near death of the Roseau Massacre, Mahaut and St. Joseph Rivers (as with most other rivers on the island which have witnessed a steady drop-off in water levels). As recently as the early 1970s, both rivers allowed full-body submersion, swimming (and even diving in popular bathing areas like "Silver Lake", "Under Power", "Titou Gorge" and "Big Stone"). But with the advent of reckless lumber harvesting by foreign concerns, and poor land use management by locals, the rivers now wend their way lazily, almost stagnantly, through the major population areas they once served. That tragedy cannot be made to continue. The difficulties associated with dying rivers may have, also, negatively affected the provision of a reliable system of pipe borne water to the majority of the population. Even today, the population has to put up with erratic water supply, including frequent shortages. A 1989 US Army study on the issue found:

> Twenty one percent of the estimated 16,000 houses in Dominica had access to piped water; another 43 percent had access to piped water at a distance of less than 100 meters[8]; the remainder

---

[8] So called "stand pipes" (public water taps, usually with an enclosed concrete trough base); editors note.

(approximately 36 percent or 5,760 houses) had no acceptable or convenient access to water supplies.[9]

Indeed, most of the inadequacies cited above may have to do with poor human use management, antiquated[10] piping systems and overall underdevelopment of water resources, as opposed to the availability of water, or water catchment degradation. Yet, the marked drop in river levels is too visible to not be included in any assessment of water catchment destruction. Thus, water catchment areas must be given the highest priority and protected (either by legislation and/or economic incentives/disincentives). Further, the fact that 70% of the water catchment areas currently identified are within private hands should not be a bar to regulation of land usage. Though the entity responsible for Dominica's water supply, DOWASCO, intends moving further into the interior[11] for water catchment areas, that may not be feasible. In any case, one should not operate on the principle of avoiding the problem by seeking to move away from it. The limited area determined by Dominica's geography will

---

[9] Islands of the Commonwealth Caribbean, (Government Printing Office, for the U.S. Department of the Army, 1989) page 274

[10] A 1985 government report claimed that of the 8.25 million gallons per day produced by all of Dominica's water catchments, only 40% was actually consumed due to pipe leakage and consumer waste. See *Dominica Environmental Report* at page 92

[11] Id.

not allow for an "avoidance" approach to problem solving. In this instance, the concept of the "commons" (that the environment belongs to all in common, and must be protected for the general good) validates the regulation of land-use by the sovereign authority to further the public good[12]. Even the legal doctrine of "necessity" (one of the prime maxims of which holds: that the safety of the people is the supreme law) could provide the basis upon which to ensure the protection of that most crucial resource. Water that sustains life, agriculture, increasingly provides hydro-electric energy, and is now touted as a foreign exchange earner, belongs within the realm of the national patrimony[13]. Current moves toward privatization must be avoided, as the population that relies on a dependable source of that life-blood, could be held

---

[12] The **Crown Lands Ordinance** *(Cap. 169, 1960) and Crown lands regulations (SRO NOs. 49/1960, 28/1961)* govern the sale or lease of government land. Most of the remaining government land are in the heights, and fall within potential water catchment areas. It has been suggested that any sale or lease of land not in reserve or park status, should be strictly conditioned upon the preservation of water quality and soil stability. A view with which this author wholeheartedly concurs

[13] It has been noted that DOWASCO has proposed, under the *1989 Water and Sewage Act*, that all national water catchment areas be declared "Water Quality Control Areas". However, an efficient system of enforcement to prevent practices which degrade the water catchment is not in place. Under the **Stewart Hall Catchment Rules**, (1975), fines of Eastern Caribbean $10,000 may be imposed on those who breach catchment protection regulations. However, according to literature on the subject, not one person has been cited under the regulations. **Dominica Environment** at page 97.

hostage[14]. Thus, no conflict between private/public spheres of interests should penalize an entire nation because of the narrow interests of a few. It is therefore imperative that owners of private lands within water catchment areas be educated in land management which preserves the catchment. Compensation and other reasonable state support, should be provided as an incentive towards that end.

Another challenge is human waste disposal that poses more than a threat to the natural aesthetic; it is an issue of public health. Poor waste management once had the main road to Roseau (at Ravine Coque) abutted by a sprawling garbage dump. The dump was for a time moved to huge hole (measuring about a quarter a mile) which had been gorged-out of the earth just beneath the Government Live Stock Farm at lower Goodwill. That hole was created by the mining of rich seams of pumice for export to Puerto Rico. It is obvious that not much thought went into what was to be done once the mining operation ceased. Once the bulldozers had fallen silent, the area was to later become a bleak site of horrendous water and wind erosion, sometimes being filled with rain water which formed stagnant mosquito infested lakes. On the "brilliant" initiative of someone in waste

---

[14]. In April 2000, Bolivians revolted against water price hikes imposed by the US transnational corporation Bechtel. Seven people were killed in riots which followed the popular protest against such foreign control which disregarded local needs. Bechtel later lost the concession to control water distribution in Bolivia.

management, the hole was to be used for a time as the city garbage dump after the close-down of the Ravine Coque site near Fond Cole. However, such half-measures resulted in noxious fumes, and clouds of flies invading nearby homes and even the general hospital less than a mile away[15]. Community protests and sabotage of the dump's bulldozers (by young environmental activists) eventually saw the site moved to Palm Grove, next to a source of the Roseau River which served the bathing, drinking and washing needs of many homes down stream. The somewhat erratic selection of disposal sites, evinced a lack of long-term planning and thorough study. In 1986-1988 an effort was said to have been made to equip villages from Pointe Michel to Colihaut with garbage vehicles which would then transport waste to the Woodbridge Bay landfill (same general area of the earlier Ravine Coque facility). Nonetheless, little systematic effort could be seen in other areas such as Marigot, Grandbay, Castle Bruce, and La Plaine where solid waste disposal in the 1990s was said to "egregious"[16]. The implementation of an island-wide system of solid waste disposal, though under increased focus, remains an

---

[15] See **The New Chronicle**, July 1, 1978, at page 1. A photo on the front page show angry area residents demonstrating in front of the government headquarters with placards reading, "Protect Public Health', "Welcome to Stench" town etc.

[16] **Dominica Environmental Profile** at page 146

elusive objective. However, as of 2002 a sewage project was nearing completion for Roseau and its environs.

Any government effort to select an appropriate garbage site would need to be accompanied by a rise in the public consciousness about proper waste disposal (fostered by the appropriate public education) and adequate legislation via which to impose penalties for solid waste polluters. Any delay in that area would obviously undercut any serious attempts at attracting tourists interested in the island's natural beauty. While Dominica is rated as one of the top dive sites in the world, scuba divers who have to surface in the midst of floating human waste cannot be enticed to return. Such a problem requires immediate focus lest it undercuts valuable marketing efforts.

In some areas of waste disposal, movement is being seen. Commendable proposals have been voiced in recent times to build a modern sewage system for Dominica. The **New Chronicle** of November 16, 1990 mentions DOWASCO's manager Damian Shillingford as stating that his organization is "presently investigating and designing a sewage system for the Roseau" area[17]. That project is now in process. Yet as of 2001, it was reported that since 40% of the households were without satisfactory waste disposal facilities, water quality and coastal

---

[17] See **New Chronicle** of November 16, 1990 at page 5.

resources (i.e. fish, marine life etc.) remain under great threat from such inadequacies[18].

Below the parks and reserve areas export-driven banana cultivation (for the most part) has reigned supreme (even though some farming encroachment on the reserve areas have been noted). Dominica's, major export bananas has been referred to as the island's "green gold". The damage inflicted on the industry by the loss of a protected British market has reduced cultivation. However, we may yet realize that banana cultivation with the help of agro-chemicals may have introduced insidious toxic elements into our eco-system. Of late many Dominicans have been puzzled and are complaining of the increased incidence of cancer deaths[19]. Are there any relationships between the increased use of agro-chemicals over the past twenty or so years, and diverse forms of cancer affliction in the local population? No study has yet been done to disprove, what is now widely rumoured.

The benefits of agro-chemical utilization cannot mask its dark side. Toxic side effects in humans have been noted in areas where paraquat (a herbicide) has been used over time. Marketed in Dominica under the trade name gramoxone, paraquat has been

---

[18] **Dominica Environmental Profile** at page 107.

[19] In Dominica malignant neoplasms (cancer tumors) are currently said to be the second major cause of death. The rate of such tumors being 88/100,000 in 1986-87. **Dominica Environmental Profile** at page 159.

the suicide potion of choice for many a frustrated Dominican farmer or distraught lover[20]. Its fatal impact, once ingested, is well known. However, what about its percolation into the soil? What of gramaxone residue that may be leached into streams? On an island with one of the highest rainfall patterns in the world, we may have escaped the concentration of gramoxone necessary to cause harm within a short time frame. But what about prolonged exposure? Or exposure, via contaminated drinking water? Farmers are known to wash gramoxone receptacles in rivers, with deadly results: dead fish bobbing on the river surface soon afterwards. Also, it is common knowledge that empty gramoxone receptacles are frequently used in rural areas of Dominica to carry water to and from standpipes or rivers. Even discounting such direct use of contaminated containers for water transport, what of the pipe borne water? Has any study ever been done to check-on agro-chemical trace elements in the public drinking water system? It is known that the United States Environmental Protection Agency (E.P.A.) banned the use of paraquat more than a decade ago, since it was found to be a

---

[20] I focus on Gramoxone since it is the most widely used agro-chemical in Dominica with the most evident toxicity. In 1985, for instance, 42, 378 liters of the chemical was utilized in local agriculture. See table 1, Primary pesticides used in the Dominica Banana Industry, Dominica Banana Rehabilitation Project-Pesticide Assessment (Island Resources Foundation-Washington, D.C., January 30, 1987).

carcinogenic (i.e. cancer causing) substance[21]. Have Dominicans been made aware of the U.S. ban, so that they could take heed? The danger of such pollution to the future of Dominica's water-export enterprise cannot over emphasized? Has the government or Banana Growers Association engaged in a thoroughgoing education program (including use of television and/or radio) with farmers, housewives, students and others so as to educate the populace on the dangers inherent to agro-chemical use? Indeed, DDT, which was a much-heralded insecticide, used in the U.S. and elsewhere after World War II, was only later fingered as a culprit in causing negative side effects in humans, including cancer of the pancreas. In the early 1950s it was widely used in Dominica. In the words of Dominican physician, Dr. Derek Phillip:

> As a boy in Marigot in the early 1950s, the health inspectors would spray DDT into our homes; the white residue would get on our kitchen utensils, beds and our clothes. Cockroaches, rats, flies, mosquitoes, centipedes, they would all die soon after application. We would then sleep in the house, that same night.[22]

Later, DDT's former lavish use was restricted, where not banned outright. That such side effects took time to discover (in countries with a higher degree of technological development than

---

[21] **Islands of the Commonwealth Caribbean** at page 274
[22] . August 2002 interview with Dr. Derek Phillip in North Carolina.

Dominica) should jolt us out of any complacency on the matter. It would be to Dominica's credit if the Produce Chemistry Laboratory[23] of the Ministry of Agriculture, in coordination with the Princess Margaret Hospital Laboratory were to take the lead, and undertake such a study to rule-out any contamination of drinking water by agro-chemical trace elements. Later, trace elements absorbed by farmers in heavy-use areas could be tested for, and side effects (if any) determined. For now, however, simple habit changes (such as a ban on the washing of agro-chemical applicators and receptacles in rivers or the use of such receptacles to carry water) can certainly protect marine life, and the public water supply. Appropriate legislation to halt such negative traits may be fashioned, although a proper public education strategy focusing on the health risks might be sufficient. In addition, updated monitoring of studies by the relevant U.S. (e.g. E.P.A.) or British institutions should be maintained (inclusive of access by internet to their data-bases on agro-chemical side effects) to keep abreast of their own advanced studies. Chemical manufacturing giants like Imperial Chemicals Inc. (ICI) which have seen growth on the basis of sales to

---

[23] The Produce Chemistry Laboratory is said to be the best equipped in the Eastern Caribbean, and capable of doing pesticide residue analysis. Accordingly, the infra-structure may already exist to perform such an agro-chemical pollution study

countries like Dominica[24] should now be approached to assist that effort of data exchange. The knowledge of agricultural scientists and others on the newly created Dominica Academy of Arts and Sciences is a useful resource in this quest. By consistent exchange of data, electronically or otherwise, Dominicans can avoid the tragedy of being the last to have dumped upon them products outlawed elsewhere. That sort of "last-in-line" treatment has already been meted out to developing countries with unenlightened leaderships and/or complacent populations. With a population literacy rate approaching 95% in 2002[25], Dominicans cannot be accused of being illiterate. Individual responsibility requires that one seeks out relevant information and act accordingly, based on such intelligence. So, any failure by the

---

[24] Of the 42,378 liters of *Gramoxone* used in Dominica in 1985, 28,918 liters came from ICI. And that is merely one of ICI's products used in the banana industry. There are others, like Primicid, an insecticide. Other multinationals have a hand in servicing the agro-chemical regime in Dominica. The following companies provide the products listed below in 1985:

Trade Name	Company	Application	Amount Used
Benlate	Du Pont	Fungicide	3,960 kg
Calixin	BASF	Fungicide	6,000
Sigma	May & Baker	Fungicide	3,307
Mertect	Merck	Fungicide	Unknown
Spraytex	Texaco	Carrier	Unknown
Furadan	FM	Nematicide	Unknown
Vydate	Du Pont	Nematicide	4,671
Mocap	Mobil	Nematicide	8,310

Source: ***Dominica Banana Rehabilitation***
[25] ***Islands of the Commonwealth Caribbean*** at page 261

population to avail itself of such information would be negligent to say the least.

With increased travel, the explosion of cable television viewership and a general affection for U.S. style consumerism Dominicans now drive more cars, and have access to more "throw-away" consumables than ever before. With the number of automobiles approaching 10,000[26] on an area less than 300 square miles in circumference, problems such as exhaust pollution and waste oil disposal are increasing. There is even growing local use of fuel inefficient sports utility vehicles (SUV's) which are notorious polluters. Certainly, Dominica is not yet anywhere near the levels of air pollution found in Code Red[27] prone southern California, metropolitan Washington, D.C. or New York. But if national development is to find support in foreign exchange earnings gained from "eco-tourism", a national transportation policy favouring public transportation, and alternative transportation use must soon top the agenda. Not only would the island gain by conserving scarce foreign exchange for priorities in education, health and industry, but preservation of the

---

[26] **Dominica Environmental Profile** (at page 117) references a figure of 6,900 registered in 1988; current estimates range between 8,500 to 9,500 vehicles on the island in 2002

[27] . Code Red is a designation given to any day when the amount of pollutants in the air and other factors of air quality make it unhealthy for humans to remain in the open. In the Summer of 2002 the Washington, D.C. metropolitan area had in excess of twenty (20) Code Red days, the worst air quality Summer on record. Author's note.

natural environment and overall aesthetic (a lot of which have already disappeared in most other places on earth) would result. Citizens in developed nations such as Holland and France already make massive use of bicycles for transportation, whereas others (more mountainous) have utilized cable cars for a wide range of transportation services. A feasibility study on cable car use, as opposed to costly-to-maintain mountain roads, is one option aimed towards new modes of transportation. In the alternative, countries as diverse as Singapore and Bermuda have enacted legislation limiting automobile import to a set number per family so as to contain pollution, and limit congestion. In addition, so called "earth days" have been instituted to eliminate automobile use in major cities of the West on particular days of every month. Articles in early 1990s issues of the **New Chronicle** speak of traffic congestion becoming an increasing problem. However, not discussed is the associated problem of lead pollution in the atmosphere from leaded gasoline usage; such being the primary gasoline type on the island. Lead gasoline, once burnt results in lead particles being suspended in the atmosphere; inhalation of such particles (over time) lead to debilitating results. Studies in U.S. urban areas have pointed to brain damage, birth defects, and high blood pressure amongst urban dwellers from air pollution derivative of leaded gasoline use. Such adverse an impact on the public health of Dominicans can be avoided, if the relevant safeguards to arrest such congestion, waste disposal, and air pollution problems are erected.

With regard to oil-change waste, most local garages are not governed by any legislation that require environmentally sound oil disposal. Accordingly, oil is discharged directly into gutters, backyards, bushes, rivers, or the sea. Tires are also simply tossed into the bush, and the rusting carcases of derelict vehicles disfigure many beaches and roadsides. Again, an appreciation of the costly clean-up efforts faced by developed countries (most of which failed to arrest the automobile-waste disposal problem at an early stage) should move Dominicans to adopt corrective measures now. Since the plant and equipment investment required for recycling is prohibitive at this stage, collection areas for oil-waste could be set-up for later shipment to any nearby territory with the refinery or other capacity to recycle or utilize such waste. Any action taken now, would ensure future savings in clean-up and environmental costs, with regard to which there is no guarantee of 100% restoration of the former habitat.

No evaluation of environmental policy can be thorough without a focus on population control. Demographic instability is cited as one risk facing island developing countries (IDCs) such as Dominica.[28] Excessive population pressures could strain the

---

[28] See Dr. Courtney N. Blackman The Economic Management of Small Island Developing Countries, **Caribbean Affairs**, October-December, 1991 Vol. 4, No. 4

"carrying capacity" of countries with limited living space. Such strains would make the burden of housing, food and services provision unbearable. Accordingly, the efforts of government, Planned Parenthood and other non-government organizations are key to preventing such a population press. The Roman Catholic Church would, as well, have to adopt a more enlightened and constructive approach to family planning. Luckily, due to robust family planning campaigns and migration, Dominica's population pressures are minimal as of this writing. For that reason one can, often times, claim a degree of quiet and solitude along many beaches or riversides on a weekday afternoon.

One of the most short-sighted development proposals of late, relate to the Botanical Gardens at Roseau being chosen as the site for a new sports field. Protests from environmental concerns, and individual citizens may have delayed implementation of that idea for the time being. However education and continued vigilance in defence of the natural habitat is what will preserve the Gardens. Now over 100 years old (established in 1889), the Gardens are already home to the Chief Veterinary Office, the plant propagation unit of the Ministry of Agriculture, the Produce Chemistry Laboratory, and a new elementary school section of the St. Mary's Academy. Such physical plant intrusion, and irreverent pedestrian traffic has led to a degradation of plant life and general grounds upkeep. In reference to such degradation, and perhaps in a dramatic effort to stir his listeners to action, Dominica's President Sir Clarence Seignoret stated in a November 22, 1990 address to the Dominica Conservation Association, that he had terminated his walks through the Gardens since he did not like what he saw there[29]. Apart from being a refuge for those seeking quiet amidst the splendour of nature, the Gardens trees and plants act as a giant filter to cleanse and revitalize the air in the capital Roseau, now subject to increasing automobile exhaust pollution. Tree cover also has a cooling effect occasioned by photosynthesis, and the Botanical Gardens offers a cooling girdle for a town of tin and concrete now mostly bereft of trees. Preservation of this sole area of wholesome greenery within the bounds of Roseau will require every user of the facility to adopt a new attitude towards use of the facility. In that regard the Forestry Service; the Roseau City Council and Dominica Conservation Association have sought to impress upon users of the Gardens a new conservation consciousness. Only time will tell whether it takes hold. In the meantime, turnstiles, which open-up after the depositing of a small fee should be installed in certain areas of the national park system, where physically feasible. Perhaps the enforcement of a costs associated with facility use, will impose a new sense of respect for the importance of national park areas.

---

[29] The New Chronicle, November 28, 1990 at page 2

Mindless efforts at quick-cash have, at times, led to ill-considered proposals. A copper mining project, promoted by the United Workers Party regime in 1996-1997, foundered on the shoals of opposition from the Dominica Conservation Association led by Athie Martin. It was for such efforts that Martin was granted a $100,000 prize at the Clinton White House in 1998[30]. The copper mining plan would have led to massive deforestation and river basin decline. Further, the use of mining chemicals such as mercury may have poisoned off what is left of the islands once abundant river basin marine life. Considering the parlous state of world copper prices, Dominica's eco-system already diminished by agro-chemical run-off such as *gramoxone* would have seen further degradation, for very little in return. A plan for a tram to the area surrounding the Boiling Lake has drawn some protest. However, as of 2002, the tram project is inoperative and seems less likely to pose as great a threat to the forest as the copper mines would have.

Hard on the heels of the mining controversy, in what seemed a warning cry from Dominica's earth, a huge portion of the Layou Valley slid into the Layou River basin in 1998, causing a natural dam to form in the upper reaches of the river, flooding

---

[30]. Atherton Martin received the 1998 for **Goldman Environmental Prize for Island Nations** for spearheading the opposition to a large copper mining operation in Dominica.. The Australian mining company had been granted prospecting rights to one-tenth the area of the entire island, threatening the pristine rainforests that still cover this land known as "The Nature Isle."

Layou village, leading to major silt build-up and forever changing the face of Dominica's biggest and most famous river. As of 2002 the Layou River had returned to some semblance of normalcy, but much more abbreviated in its reach and depth.

As the detritus of 20th century living (oil waste, agro-chemicals, raw sewage) washes out to sea, so too it has negatively impacted upon Dominica's coral and other marine life. Fish caught within one mile of the coast may well return to the dinner tables of Dominicans, carrying back with them some of the untreated waste so-recently expunged. For centuries, waste was flushed straight into the Roseau bay, untreated. Prior, the small urban population meant that such a waste load could be rapidly, and naturally, broken-down and assimilated by the ecosystem. With the rapid rise in urbanization in the 1970s and 1980s, the load on the city sewage system may have brought with it greater problems for marine life. It is now reported that Dominica's few coral-growth areas in the Soufriere Pinnacle may have experienced the first signs of coral bleaching. Detergents and untreated sewage are blamed as the cause. Dominica Coconut Products (now owned by the U.S. firm Colgate-Palmolive), with its rum and soap manufacturing operations currently is pointed to as the biggest local waste generator; with rum generating the highest per production unit per year (i.e. dead yeast cells, slops).[31] As a major foreign exchange earner for the country (EC$24.3

---

[31] Dominica Environmental Profile at page 155.

million in 1988) there would be a reluctance to clamp "any polluter pays principle" onto DCP's production costs. Indeed any overly stringent pollution prevention protocol, would be a certain hindrance to its competitive edge in the short-term. I emphasize short term, because any ecologically-sound production techniques articulated by DCP will eventually be to its long term, competitive, advantage. Where Dominica's natural beauty promises to be a major foreign exchange earner (in an increasingly polluted world) one has to weigh the damaged caused by pollution to our waters, against the costs of controlling the particular polluting discharges. DCP aside, any idea of Dominica, as a source for cheap labour, or location for heavy-pollution industries (which seek to avoid strict regulations in their own countries), is a dead end. Countries like Taiwan, Malaysia, and Singapore have all realized the massive clean-up costs and overall damage to the quality of life in their respective countries as prohibitive (and which need not have been engaged in the first place) during their rush to modernize in the 1960s and 1970s. Accordingly, with regard to marine (and other) pollution, we should not blind ourselves to the mistreatment meted out to the environment in these countries, when we seek to emulate any economic model they may have followed.

Any rush to modernize must be measured alongside costs to the natural habitat. Such a balancing cannot be over-emphasized with regard to often-heralded plans for an international airport. This author having had a television set and other luggage forever "disappear" while in transit in Antigua (after seeing it off-loaded from an Eastern Airline aircraft in 1984) can readily appreciated the urgency with which many Dominicans view the need for such an airport. Currently, Dominica has two airports; Canefield near Roseau which accommodates small propeller aircraft in the 5 to 15 seat range; and Melville Hall in the north east, near Marigot, which accommodates mostly propeller driven 20 to 70 seat aircraft, as well as some recent jet aircraft flights. As of 2002, complaints by the travelling public ring-out against treatment received at regional transit points, the difficulties of overnight stay, the limits allegedly placed on the tourist trade, along with problems associated with delivery of airfreight felt most strongly by the commercial sector. All of the forgoing problems, however, may be solved without resort to a new airport. First, any debate on the new airport must be in public, and must be forever removed from the narrow confines of party politics. Rather, an objective reading of existing aircraft technologies, physical plant management capacity, the flight patterns of regional aviation, and (most important) the dangers such construction would pose to Dominica's environment must be part of such a debate.

The Freedom Party administration, to its credit, utilized its close links with the US government to obtain feasibility studies for such an airport project. A US armed service Atlantic

Command report noted that two on-site surveys by top US armed services experts were performed: Once, in January 1990, and again October 1991. An October 25th, 1992 review of both surveys revealed:

> The proposed undertaking is a massive endeavour. The Eden Estate (proposed airport site) is located at the extreme northeast of the island, two hours by passenger car from the capital Roseau... Four watercourses, the Eden River, Kraibo Gutter, and two unnamed streams must be culverted and covered. Depending on the final orientation an elevation of the runway there, 4.8 million cubic yards of earth would have to be cut fill (sic). The report proceeds to state that the area is "thickly covered with banana trees and forest, with some grazing land". The negative environmental impact of such a reworking of terrain cannot be minimized. In addition, the steady destruction of prime agricultural land for housing (which has already proceeded at an alarming pace!) will only be accelerated by this undertaking. Already slipping in domestic food production, especially in the area of livestock that lack grazing lands, Dominica's food security would be further threatened by this project.

Not withstanding the forgoing, the very same experts noted:

> Dominica has recently commenced 727-180 (cargo variant) flights into Melville Hall Airfield. The team was surprised by this unexpected capability which has been demonstrated [my emphasis]. Melville Hall has significant geographical restrictions---A river at one end of the runway, the

sea at the other, and approach departure obstructions on the landward side. But the operations of the 727 into the field, even with these restrictions [my emphasis] raises the possibility that something could be done to upgrade Melville Hall which would make it more attractive for passenger operations. This is beyond the scope of this assessment, but the observations are recorded here for information.

Why not explore the (perhaps) less expensive, less environment destructive option? It is clear that the US army experts themselves felt that Melville Hall could be refurbished and/or made amenable to regular jet aircraft traffic. Under the UWP a small fortune was spent to promote a new airport scheme, despite recent studies having indicated that such an airport would be an unprofitable undertaking.

An August 2002 check with the Amerijet Company of Miami, Florida (which operates the 727s mentioned above) revealed that it maintains a regular flight schedule to Melville Hall. In thirteen years of operation, the company's 727 aircraft have never sustained a crash or other mishap on the island having to do with short tarmac length. Current aircraft technology has grown to produce jet aircraft of the STOL (i.e. short-take-off-landing) variety. Thus airfields such as Melville Halls could accommodate such jet aircraft. Even if Melville Hall were never to be certified as adequate for aircraft of the Boeing 727 (or contemporary passenger jet) variety, it has not been shown that an efficient inter-island service (inclusive of night landings, and using STOL-type jet aircraft) could not solve the problem of commercial airfreight or regular passenger travel. All of the above is to say that we must fully explore the costs associated with levelling mountains, destroying hundreds of acres of original forests, covering rivers, blocking valleys, which would be associated with any "international" airport project at Eden or elsewhere. It would be better that the entire population be engaged in a mature debate on the costs and benefits of the issue surrounding such a scheme, as opposed to secretive, prestige, partisan or election campaign-spawned efforts which deny the ability of Dominicans to make a reasoned and measured choice. From the vantage point of fostering eco-tourism, the argument can well be made that a refurbished Melville Hall, with the latest in radar technology and night landing equipment, could allow access to STOL jet aircraft and would be a cheaper and less-environmentally destructive avenue to current air travel problems. In addition it would utilize an already existing physical plant (i.e. Melville Hall), and so maintain the novelty associated with Dominica's reputation as being unspoiled (while efficiently facilitating the movement of people, goods and services!). No amount of money could ever restore the destruction to the natural habitat that such an "international airport" (with its additional maintenance costs) would entail. Already Dominica finds it difficult to expand its fishing efforts, or maintain coast guard patrols because of the expenses involved. The already strained local tax base would be further burdened, if required to upkeep such a major facility *which may well be unable to generate sufficient funds itself* in the near future[32].

It is now evident that deregulation under President Reagan gutted the U.S. airline industry, leaving it in a shambles. Originally intended as a spur to competition in the industry, the current reality as of 2002 is that many U.S. carriers which once serviced the Caribbean area (e.g. Eastern, TWA, PanAm) are gone, some never to return. US Airways and United Airlines now face bankruptcy in mid 2002. A virtual monopoly on U.S. bound air travel is held by American Airlines at present. American Airlines is committed to the hub concept and services Dominica via the smaller turbo prop aircraft flown by its subsidiary, American Eagle. As of 2002, American's main Caribbean hub is at San Juan Puerto Rico and it directs smaller aircraft from there to islands like Dominica. Though this may change, there is no guarantee that Dominica's air traffic would ever rise to the level necessary to entice major carriers to use bigger aircraft on Dominica. And even if such change occurred, the current

---

[32] The report to the US Joint Chiefs of Staff stated that the proposed airport was at an impasse (as of 1991) because of negative economic forecast in an earlier British Overseas Development Corp study by the firm GIBB. That study estimated the proposed Dominica airport would be unable to generate a profit until the year 2010.

Melville Hall airfield could well be upgraded to accommodate that eventuality.

Further, by forcing such a major upheaval in the natural environment necessary to build a new airport (supposedly the lure associated with "eco-tourism") Dominica would be striking at what could in time be our greatest foreign exchange earner: the island's remoteness and natural beauty. According to former Minister for Tourism C.A. Maynard, Dominica promises "the ultimate in nature tourism[33]". Thus it is not posturing for any mass influx of casino and white-sand-beach-driven tourists, a la Jamaica, Bahamas etc., which would necessitate such a high-air traffic facility. Current official thinking seeks to cultivate an ecology conscious type tourist less prone to fluctuations in the economic climate in his/her home country, who seeks the best in natural beauty. To such a visitor, the novelty mentioned earlier would be crucial in maintaining Dominica's difference. Such a niche as Dominica offers is unique, and may well appeal to the high value vacationer eager to escape a world under assault by a certain crass modernity.

The old adage, "all that glitters, is not gold" still holds true, with regard to development projects. In that vein, it would be instructive to assess Grenada's international airport travails. It

---

[33] Discover Dominica (Warren Associates, Grenada in association with the Dominica National Development Corporation, Division of Tourism, 1990) at page 3.

is a good example of a project which brought much controversy, partially instigated a U.S. invasion and created regional political upheaval, only now to be used way-below expected capacity. That is not to say that Grenada's airport should never have been built. But Dominica would be perhaps better off, if we avoided the potential "white-elephant" that a new airport could be, along with the other noise and air pollution associated therewith. An airport is not made international merely by its size. If the equipment and facilities at Melville Hall are modernized and introduction of STOL technology takes place, the airport may well meet so-called "international" standards. Again, the rapid advance of technology has reduced tarmac length requirements which once confined Melville Hall's use to that of propeller-driven aircraft. Now, Dominica should first explore the fullest use of what is currently available, before gorging at the fragile ecology any further to construct what may not be necessary.

Such lack of early debate, or a proper environmental impact study may have seen mistakes made in Trafalgar Hydro Electric project. It is reported that the study for the Trafalgar Falls project that comprised hundreds of pages, contained only three (!) pages on environmental concerns[34]. Such attention to the environmental impact section of the study seems woefully scant, when the importance of the falls to Dominica is considered. Most

---

[34] Dominica Environmental Profile at page 121.

Dominicans view the falls as North Americans view Niagara Falls, or Yosemite National Park. Pictures of the falls grace every tourist brochure or travel article of significance that focus on the island. As well, considering the importance of hydro resources to Dominicans, it is amazing that the complete study was not published in the public media, or made available to secondary schools and colleges for discussion[35]. In that regard, there continues to be a practice of involving Dominicans in development plans *after* the fact, with such crucial information being under the select scrutiny of a few technocrats. Such a policy, sadly, will eventually breed distrust of government and frustrate development objectives; no matter of what political stripe such a government may be, or how well meaning its intentions. Already gems of the natural habitat, such as Titou Gorge, are said to have experienced increased sedimentation. A drop-off in the Trafalgar Waterfall has also been noticed. In a way, there always has to be some trade-off between development needs (in this case energy), especially where use of Dominica's hydro electric potential lessened the island's dependence on expensive foreign fossil fuels (in this case diesel). Nonetheless, vigilance should ensure that proper modulation of the dam intakes, and maintenance of ground cover in the water catchment

---

[35] It should be noted that considerable concerns were raised in 1989/1990 **New Chronicle** articles by local environmentalists who feared the destruction of the Trafalgar Falls.

area serving the Trafalgar Hydro Station be a priority. In that way, damage to the natural habitat may be mitigated.

CHALLENGES FROM THE OUTSIDE

In 1988, a garbage barge heaped with waste from New York state hospitals plied the Caribbean, seeking a dumping ground for its putrid waste. With a relatively ecology conscious government and enlightened people, the barge's captain was well advised to steer-clear of Dominica. For weeks, the barge was tracked sailing restlessly up and down Caribbean shipping routes, desperate for a port. To this date, it is uncertain whether or not the ship's captain found a dumping ground or whether his load may have been quietly tipped-over into the Caribbean sea at some point away from land, and beyond the reach of the islands weak coast guard services. With limited coast guard resources, Dominica is among many Caribbean islands which now face these new, perhaps more deadly, "garbage pirates". Cruise ships, ocean liners, oil tankers and other such vessels are said to regularly dump waste in Caribbean waters, in order to escape compliance with strict and readily enforced U.S. laws. Surveillance of vessels engaged in such practices would be an appropriate objective of the Regional Security System (RSS) set-up after the Grenada invasion of 1983. The U.S. coast guard could assist such a surveillance effort, since most of the vessels involved are moving to and from U.S. ports, or a U.S. owned. The risks to marine life, water quality and public health, posed by the pliers of such waste, are enormous. That problem can only adequately addressed on a regional level; with regard to which Irving Andre's article on Caribbean unity assumes even greater, and more immediate, significance.

On the international level, the twisted thinking of too many individuals, some associated with international institutions, behooves Dominicans to be ever vigilant. No one, local or foreign, should seek to dominate Dominica's environmental discourse for their own selfish ends. To succeed in this national effort for conservation requires a broad coalition of students, youth organizations, the church, farmers and the business sector. This coalition must be rooted in a respectful partnership even with those whose political views may differ from ones own. If the term "environmental activist" takes on a divisive and arrogant tonality, it may undo the work of years and undermine an otherwise noble cause. In that vein, it is important to note the view of someone who was fond of the island's natural attributes, but remained scornful of the locals. The British historian Thomas Carlyle wrote of Dominica in 1860s thus:

> Poor Dominica itself is described to me in a way to kindle a heroic young heart; look at Dominica for an instant. Hemispherical, they say, or in the shape of an inverted washbowl; rim of it, first twenty miles all around, starting from the sea, is flat alluvium, the fruitfulest in nature, fit for any

nobler spice or product, but unwholesome except for niggers held steadily to their work: ground then gradually rise,...now bears oak, woods, cereals, indian corn, English wheat,...salubrious and delightful for the European, - who might there spread and grow,... well fit to defend against all comers, and beneficently kept steadily to their work a million of niggers on the lower ranges.[36]

Language brimming with scorn, clearly, by one who coveted Dominica's natural attributes. That such wondrous prose did not extend to the inhabitants is evident: woe be upon those who were to work Dominica's fertile lands on behalf of their masters! And that is what passed for scholarly commentary in 1867; a full thirty three years after the formal abolition of slavery in the British West Indies, no less! Why then mention the above today, with all its squalid language? Keeping Carlyle's word *"washbowl"* (this time right side-up) in mind, the following tells why:

In a December 12, 1991 internal memorandum the World Bank's vice president and chief economist Lawrence Summers[37] argued.; "Should the World Bank encourage more migration of

---

[36] British Historians and the West Indies (Dr. Eric Williams, Africana Publishing Corporation, New York 1972) at page 85

[37] . After serving as Treasury Secretary in the Clinton administration, Summers went on to become President of Harvard University in March 2001. There he quickly became embroiled in a controversy with noted African American Academic, Harvard professor Cornel West, whose professional competence he had disparaged. In 2002, West departed for Princeton University in the wake of what he perceived to be unprovoked insults to his academic integrity.

dirty industries to the LDC's?" (i.e. Less developed countries in Africa and elsewhere). The memo reads as follows:

> "DATE: December 12, 1991 "TO: Distribution"FR: Lawrence H. Summers"Subject: GEP
>
> "'Dirty Industries: Just between you and me, shouldn't the World Bank be encouraging MORE migration of the dirty industries to the LDCs [Less Developed Countries]? I can think of three reasons:
>
> "1). The measurements of the costs of health impairing pollution depends on the foregone earnings from increased morbidity and mortality. From this point of view a given amount of health impairing pollution should be done in the country with the lowest cost, which will be the country with the lowest wages. I think the economic logic behind dumping a load of toxic waste in the lowest wage country is impeccable and we should face up to that...

The memo which fell into the hands of the international environmental protection group Greenpeace, stirred controversy worldwide, and shook confidence in the intentions of the bank. The insolence, disregard, and insult to the populations of the LDCs evident in the proposals by this World Bank official is mind boggling. Would he have suggested the same for Western Europe had it been made up of LDCs? Again, Africa, raped of its population, plundered of its resources, is now singled out as the prime "lowest-wage" "under-polluted" dumping ground for waste. But pause for one moment! If the repugnant behaviour of the garbage barge captain from New York who, in 1989, plied the Caribbean Sea be any guide, it might as well have been Dominica or some other LDC Summer's might have been talking about. Greenpeace condemned the memo as "crass, racist, and environmentally destructive". Brazil's then Minister of Environment Jose Lutzenberger, asked for Summers to be fired. He stated:

> Your reasoning is perfectly logical but totally insane... Your thoughts [provide] a concrete example of the unbelievable alienation, reductionist thinking, social ruthlessness and the arrogant ignorance of many conventional 'economists' concerning the nature of the world we live in... If the World Bank keeps you as vice president it will lose all credibility. To me it would confirm what I often said... the best thing that could happen would be for the Bank to disappear.

A world-wide outcry ensued, especially in view of the fact that the World Bank was charged with the responsibility to assist economic and social development in the so-called third world at the Summer, 1992 Earth Summit in Brazil.

In a January 14, 1992 rebuttal memo Summers' lamely argued that his ideas were only meant "as a sardonic counter-point, an effort to sharpen the analysis". A tepid February 6, 1992 World Bank memo responded to the worldwide outcry that "it deeply regretted the memo". That Summers could have the audacity to make such proposals or float such ideas, is a function of the mind set at the World Bank and the parameters within which he believed himself safe. The forgoing is instructive, and should serve as a warning to all those who would leave the protection of Dominica's habitat solely in hands of any so-called "international civil servant". Certainly, the ideas referenced above are not representative of other well-intentioned international experts who operate with the best of motives, including that of preserving the planet so all may share in its riches. However, the Summer's discharge is merely the flip-side of the racist and selfish coin traded-in by Carlyle a century or so ago. The trajectory of Summer's proposal is a stern warning that many individuals and organizations in this so-called "new world order" are still caught within the web of their colonial prejudices, and seem unable to escape it. Accordingly, we should welcome help from those who would, in good faith, seek to offer it. But popular local input, and oversight must never be far removed from any environmental impact study or development policy. We should always be wary of those who appreciate Dominica's natural attributes, without sparing a moment of concern for the development of their fellow humans, who form a part of that habitat.

In 2001 Mark Douglas, the brother of deceased Prime Minister Rosie Douglas led criticism of Athie Martin, who had resigned from the government over the vote of Environment Advisor Lloyd Pascal at the 2000 International Whaling Commission's (IWC) conference to allow for the resumption of limited whaling by nations such as Japan, and Norway. Douglas and Pascal's criticism of Martin painted him as a pawn of

Greenpeace and other international non-government organizations (NGOs) who cared little about the well being of Dominica or Dominicans. Douglas and Pascal took the view that to vote for limited whaling would not lead to the decimation of the world's whale stock. In addition, they were of the view that Dominica stood to gain from Japanese government sponsored development projects, such as a fishery complex that had been promised for Portsmouth and Marigot. The Japanese had already completed such a complex at the old Roseau wharf in the mid 1990s. They pointed out that Greenpeace, while vocal over the whaling issue, would have been better served by promoting Dominica as an eco-tourism destination, and so bolster the country's economy. Such protest by Greenpeace, without any meaningful contribution to the communities in the country they sought to serve, undermined their credibility. Greenpeace would have been in a stronger position if it had encouraged its associates to fill Dominica hotels, sign-up for whale watching tours, while providing technical assistance to island fishermen. Not so engaged, Greenpeace was marginalized, and deemed irrelevant to the every day struggle for survival by islanders. More so, when some supporters of Greenpeace and related NGOs threatened a boycott of the island's already struggling tourism industry over the matter. Martin's' reply to his critics was to lambaste the government, that he then served as Integrated Development Plan (IDP) advisor, for prostituting its values on environmental protection, in exchange for aid. Popular support for Martin's position was limited on the whaling issue; unlike the support he gained on the anti-copper mining campaign. The spirited whaling debate evinced a local concern that environmental policy is best handled with the national interest in mind, especially as limited whaling did not seem to threaten the wholesale slaughter of that species as Greenpeace and some of their supporters held. Usually well meaning, Greenpeace's behaviour during the whaling episode showed that even progressives and progressive organizations might fall victim to arrogance and insensitivity. In so doing, they victimize and malign the vulnerable that they claim to defend.

The above noted, we must never again allow foreign domination of the discourse concerning the welfare of our country's environment to the disregard of the need to build local leadership and competence on the subject of conservation. Overseas friends in the environmental movement can assist, but always on the basis of mutual respect, not *diktat*! With that in mind, it must be remembered that for years (and to this date, I dare say!) South Africa boasted the most splendid of game parks and natural reserves, while crushing its black population underfoot; condemning the majority population to a life of abject socio-economic misery.

In that vein, a very laudable statement, with regard to human concerns, was issued by Dr. Peter G.H. Evans, an Oxford University-based environmentalist who spoke at a Dominica

Association of Washington D.C./Smithsonian Visiting Scholars Program event, at the Georgetown University Law Center, in Washington D.C. on November 16, 1991. At that time, while championing the idea of a bird reserve in the south of Dominica, he cautioned his guests to always be mindful that when they viewed the splendour of Dominica's varied bird life, they see beyond. Beyond to the inhabitants so as to, in his words, "appreciate their difficulties, needs and aspirations". The humane character expressed by Evans and others, is what will build an indestructible bond between Dominican environmentalists and their foreign friends and allies. Simply put: to save the planet, old prejudices and practices will have to go. And, further, it is useless to speak of saving the whales, birds, or forests, if people are saddled by poverty and/or social injustice. Caught up in the maelstrom of a savage capitalism posing as Globalization, people are more prone to poison streams in their quest for gold, or deforest their lands in the quest to produce charcoal, as in Haiti and Somalia. However, where a government remains accountable to its people, spurring health, education, and social justice and sustainable and locally owned business development, conservation can thrive.

Cultural values that promote the shopping mall as the most desirable forum for human interaction may also be a threat where it disregards conservation. Economic models determine how best natural resources are used, and how sustainable growth can be or is. Economic models that measure an economy by the number of millionaires it produces, rather than its progress towards eliminating deprivation offers nothing to countries like Dominica. The current neoliberal economic dogma make us believe that so-called free markets, without governmental regulation or interference, result in the most efficient and socially optimal allocation of resources. Or that localities achieve economic success by abandoning goals of self sufficiency and aspiring to be internationally competitive in providing conditions that attract outside investors. That, even where such investment seeks to depress wages, and destroy local environmental laws.

The assumptions which underline current neoliberal ideological dogma pose the greatest human-driven threat to the future existence of the human species. Such pernicious assumptions include that:

> *Humans are motivated by self-interest, expressed primarily through the quest for financial gain;*
>
> *The action that yields the greatest financial return to the individual or firm is the one that is most beneficial to society;*
>
> *Competitive behaviour is more rational for the individual and the firm and more beneficial to society than cooperative behaviour;*
>
> *Human progress is best measured by increases in the value of what the members*

> *of society consume, and those who consume the most contribute the most to human progress;*[38]

Such a squalid focus on materialism and individualism challenges the empirical evidence that most human progress and creativity derived from the unselfish effort of visionaries and inventors who, at their outset, did not have corporate sponsorship or support. No wonder those assumptions have increased poverty and human despair to levels hitherto unseen in modern times! When one examines the ruinous state of society in post-Soviet Russia, or the economic collapse in Argentina, Peru, and Ecuador in 2002, to name a few countries, one can appreciate that free markets offer no panacea. Real incomes are lower in the developing world than they were in the thirty years immediately after World War II. Then, self-reliance and economic models seeking sustainable development were in vogue. With the neoliberal ascendancy, much independent thinking with regard to sustainable development was jettisoned. The new mantra was that privatization of government holdings, utilities, and deregulation, would solve all ills. Such limited vision has led many developing countries into failed state status. In Dominica, the sale of the electric utility which has been analyzed elsewhere

---

[38]. See **The Case Against the Global Economy, And for a Turn Toward the Local**, edited by Jerry Mander and Edward Goldsmith (Sierra Club Books 1996)

imposed a withering series of price increases on an increasingly burdened population. Popular protests have since ensued, leading to the formation of a citizen's group, Citizens Against High Utility Rates (CAHUR). Alternative energy models, driven by local initiatives, have since developed into a full-blown wind energy pilot project at Delices led by Diaspora and local engineers.

Environmental ruin usually follows hard on the heels of such failed state policies. State capitalism posing as socialism, with its authoritarianism and bureaucracy in the former Eastern bloc was often numbing of the human spirit and insensitive to the environment. Its replacement economic model has only done measurably better, where progressive local community interests have trumped the self-serving designs of transnational corporations.

In 2001, the world of international finance was confronted with the Enron and Worldcom scandals, in which senior executives of these US corporate giants had engaged in fraudulent accounting and other schemes to bilk profits from pension schemes and other investors. Clearly, the deregulation revolution of the Reagan era and the golden years of unbridled capitalism was coming undone, on the shoals of what is nothing less than grand larceny posing as economic efficiency. That experience shows Dominican governments and Dominicans to have acted at their wisest when bolstering government regulation of natural resource use on the island, or discouraging mining in our national parks, despite pressure from outside investors and "get-rich-quick" local politicians. Such unselfish wisdom which protects our island's natural bounty, will allow it to be a well watered oasis in an increasingly parched world, and a haven to visitors who seek communion with a pristine environment.

At this juncture in human history, only an unselfish cooperative spirit which rises above the imperialism and racism of old models, while taking the best in economic practice from the quest for human civilization, offers hope. Our eco-system will be sustained where we have an intelligent bonding with nature and realize that we have community of interest with the smallest living thing on the planet. And that economic efficiency must serve humankind and our ecosystem, not the other way round.

CONCLUSION

Not all the challenges to Dominica's natural habitat could be outlined. However, it is my hope that this review of local conditions and the problems we confront, will represent a clarion call for more Dominicans to assist government, and non-government efforts aimed at preserving Dominica's natural environment. With the island's once protected banana industry in the doldrums, we may well see a wise turn toward high-value, high-end organic farming. Linking eco-tourism to small farmers, who would run their own eco-inns, creates a new economic space born of local creativity and ownership not subject to the whims and fancies of some transnational corporate entity inimical to the welfare of locals. The demise of the banana industry provides Dominica with an opportunity to create an agriculture base that serves the regional market, to include hotels on St Martin, Barbados or nearby Guadeloupe. With our fertile soil, we could become the breadbasket of the Eastern Caribbean. That would require rejuvenation of the now-dormant Dominica Agricultural Center. The newly created Dominica Academy of Arts and Sciences (*DAAS*) led by noted agriculture scientist Dr. Clayton Shillingford, possesses the intellectual talent and experience to lead that charge. To succeed in its mission the *DAAS* would have to be embraced by the government and private sector, and become anchored in local legislation.

Such a renewed focus on agriculture, with new fruit, vegetable and others crops and best environmental practices, will enhance economic growth. In addition, the development of medicinal products from Dominica's unique ecosystem offers up yet another area of opportunity, which is yet to be engaged. It is the specific purpose of the *DAAS* to gather the human resource base that could develop that area as an income earner for the country. The efforts of the *Dominica Sustainable Energy Corporation* (*DSEC*), mentioned earlier are in a similar vein. An affiliate of the *DAAS*, *DSEC* seeks to build sustainable energy systems based on wind, hydro, wave-action, fuel cell and geothermal energy. Its installation of the island's first wind turbine at Delices in August 2002 has generated much interest on the island. As of September 2002, its CEO electro-mechanical engineer Bevin Etienne was busy at work on a prototype machine, powered by wind, which would be used by the local essential oil cooperative. Currently the cooperative, which uses wood fired boilers to distil bay oil, would save on fuel imports and cease their cutting of trees, once the prototype was shown to be effective.

But to exploit these opportunities requires mass participation spurred by the adoption, on an individual level, of a conservation consciousness. *Vwa Diablotin*, an insert to the *New Chronicle*, and published by Arlington James and M. Jones of the Forestry and Wildlife Division, is currently spreading such conservation and nature awareness concepts to the very young[39]. A grouping called The *Waitu Kubuli Foundation* gathered in 2000 at Springfield Guest House. With Mona George Dill, Bernard Wiltshire, Adenauer Douglas, "Blow's" Bellot and others in attendance, it sought to spur organic farming in the country.

---

[39] A **New Chronicle** article of March 27, 1992 pictured a bus christened "Sisserou Express, with rain forest murals painted on its exterior, and geared towards providing environmental education to the population. It represented a coordinated effort between Dominica's Forestry Division, the World Parrot Trust, RARE Center for Tropical Conservation, World Wildlife Fund, U.S. Fish and the World Wildlife Service, among others. See **New Chronicle** at page 12-13

Wiltshire meanwhile has sought to build interest and development in a system of trails in the national park system, as part of an eco-tourism thrust.

In 2000 the rejuvenated *Dominica Cadet Corp* was launched. Then Prime Minister Rosie Douglas, in a speech delivered at the Police Training School at Morne Bruce in June 2000, saw the student members of the Corp as pioneers in exploring the island's eco-system, while being protectors of the island's natural bounty. A *Youth Environmental Corp* was also proposed in 2001, though much has not been heard or seen of it since. In August local entrepreneur, Francis Richards[40] started *Nature Island Sports and Trail (NIST),* as an effort to boost hiking, camping and outdoor recreational activities to derive foreign exchange income from a renewed eco-tourism thrust. In that quest he allied himself with the new Diaspora movement as he saw it as a strategic ally in promoting Dominica in far-flung eco-tourism markets. Already, former Prime Minister Oliver Seraphine's *Floral Gardens,* Jean Finucane's *Hummingbird Inn,* Cuthbert and Ann John-Baptiste's *Papillote Wilderness Retreat,* Athie and Fae Martin's *Exotica* among others, represent a new breed of eco-inn facilities designed for the nature lover.

Dominica's popular tourist sites, such as the Emerald Pool and Trafalgar Falls are inundated by cruise ship visitors.

---

[40]. As of August 2002, Captain Francis Richards served as Commandant of the Dominica Cadet Corp.

Currently such visitors mostly take pictures, stroll by some sites and leave very little cash behind. If organized as refreshment, merchandising and educational reception points for cruise tourists, the eco-inns could well ensure that more foreign exchange is retained on island from such visitors.

Dominican Diaspora leaders Dr. Thomson Fontaine and Roy Casey, seek to build around the NIST concept a *Super Discount Store* that would service Dominica consumers with affordable consumables, while promoting a pro-national development and environmental consciousness. Such a marriage between wholesale/retail concepts and the environment is new for Dominica. It is the intent behind these efforts to give the environmental movement sturdy legs in enterprise, allowing local people to earn a decent living while protecting the natural habitat on the island. Mere protests at challenges to the environment will not suffice. The campaign must be broad, rooted in our spiritual values and supportive of the economic well being of the masses. These efforts reflect a positive beginning to the journey ahead for all Dominicans, indeed, humanity. In that regard, it is of essence, that we educate ourselves, make the relevant sacrifices where necessary and invest in substantial initiatives that develop our country, while protecting its fragile ecology. The time to act is now, and time is running out.

APPENDIX I

WHY A ROSIE DOUGLAS FOUNDATION?

The Importance of Symbolism and Substance in Memorializing Departed Leaders to the Building of a Durable Nation-State.

Gabriel J. Christian, Esq.

Introduction:

Roosevelt Bernard "Rosie" Douglas (hereinafter Rosie) died on October 1, 2001, after serving eight (8) months as Prime Minister of the Commonwealth of Dominica. The shock and national outpouring of grief which swept over the island, touched the hearts not only of resident Dominican nationals, but that of the overseas communities, Pan Africanist leaders worldwide, civil rights activists and politicians in the U.S., Canada, the United Kingdom and community and national leaders in the Caribbean, Latin America, Africa and other parts of the developing world. That such an outpouring led to more than 1,200 foreign leaders, activists and overseas Dominicans to attend his farewell ceremony had more to with his work prior to gaining office.

Immediately after the interment of Rosie's mortal remains, talk was heard of establishing a memorial in his memory. Conscious that national identity and dignity resided in respect for those who contributed much to the creation of our nation-state, patriots, friends of Rosie and members of the Douglas family agreed to the formation of a Rosie Douglas Foundation in November 2000. ***The foundation stated focus is aimed at improving Education, Health and Community Development in Dominican communities at home and abroad.***

A website was launched on December 4, 2000 to inform the world of its existence and a coordinating committee was formed.* On Saturday, March 10, 2001 meeting was held to set-up a structure and design a program for the foundation. The meeting was held at the Law office of attorney Gabriel J. Christian, former President of the Dominica Federation of Students in the 1970's and, later, the Dominica Association of Washington, D.C. Several resource people attended to lend their wisdom and support to this effort: Dr. Thompson Fontaine, a Dominican economist with the International Monetary Fund; Shirley Allan, a Dominican resident in the Washington, DC area involved in health care management; Athenia Henry, Industrial Development Specialist and resident of New Jersey, Neal Nixon resident in Alabama, an Internet Marketing Specialist and founder of "Buy Dominica" a bi-monthly magazine on the world wide web which promotes Dominican products; Michael Etienne student, entrepreneur and marketer of *Nature Island Gourmet* food products and a former community activist in Dominica's eastern District who worked alongside Rosie Douglas in the 1990's; and Dominica's Consul General in New York, Christine Parillon, who served as Dominica's official representative at the meeting. Not present, but instrumental to the launching of this initiative was Adenauer "Washway" Douglas, and Debbie Douglas, the brother and first child, respectively, of the departed leader

RATIONALE FOR THE FOUNDATION:

It must be understood that Dominica's history, as an island whose native population was subjugated and then developed with kidnapped African labour under brutal colonial conditions, bears a relationship to its current culture, ethnic composition, social mores and economic status. With so-called emancipation in 1834, the economic disparities between the majority African descended people and Caribs at the bottom of the social ladder, with the British plantocracy at the apex meant that little had changed.

except that there were more squatter communities on government owned land and most people of color could now walk around their country unhindered by slave catchers. Early in the 20th century education reform allowed for elementary school education for many of the formerly unschooled majority. Further, the acquisition of some seed capital by Dominicans who worked on the Panama Canal, or Dutch owned oil installations in Aruba and Curacao or goldfields in Cayenne, British Guiana, or Venezuela improved the lot of some of the formerly dispossessed majority who had traveled abroad to seek their fortunes. As a result a small middle class of shopkeepers, teachers, policemen and estate holders developed. It was from that strata that Rosie Douglas came, when he was born in 1941. His father Robert (RBD) Douglas, was a shopkeeper and estate holder who had traveled, worked overseas and then returned to invest his savings. RDB was also a politician, with a great degree of community involvement and charitable works, which his wife Bernadette shared. That basis shaped Rosie's life. In the late 1940's RBD bought the Hampstead Estate. In 1960 he assisted his son's travel to Canada to study agriculture, with the plan being that he would return to manage the family's estate. However, Rosie Douglas was to quickly involve himself in the freedom struggles sweeping the black community in North America.

Rosie involvement in Civil Rights struggles among Canada's black and native peoples, his Pan Africanist work with the African National Congress, and his friendship with the Cuban Revolution found resonance in Dominica's political life. Upon his return to Dominica after being deported from Canada in 1975 for his political activism, he founded the Popular Independence Committee (PIC), the Northern Development Agricultural Program (NDAP), the Dominica Cuba Friendship Society, and assisted the foundation of the Dominica Federation of Students, the Work Study Library project in Grandbay. Through his links he provided access to hundreds of Dominicans to study in Cuba, Guyana, the former USSR Libya, UK, France, Taiwan and Austria. Shortly before his death he enhanced his new administration enhanced its relations with the U.S. on a governmental and non-governmental level. To that end he formalized a technical assistance agreement with the University of New Orleans which led to short, on-island, training programs for stakeholders in the hotel and tourism industry. At last count two hundred resident Dominicans have benefited from such training. It was deceased Prime Minister's plan to partner with the University of New Orleans, York University of Canada and Middlesex University in the United Kingdom in his quest to develop a University of Dominica. While Rosie did not live to see that institution opened, his work in opening the door to educational opportunity is evident in some current statistics. Today 90% of our forestry engineers, 90% of our chemical engineers, 80% of our linguists and 60% of our physicians owe their education to his efforts. In the area of dentistry for instance, Dominica saw the presence of only one local trained in Britain, prior to independence in 1978: Dr. Williams. Today, thanks to the generosity of the Cuban revolution there are at least five (5) Dominican dentists working alongside their local colleagues who have studied in the U.S. or Britain. It is an indisputable fact that, prior to Rosie's return to Dominica, the local independence movement was anemic and had little-if any-link to the national liberation movements and progressive countries worldwide. His presence on the local scene spurred support for the Dominica Labour Party's move to independence. His interest in the youth of the country rejuvenated the National Youth Council and student movement via the Dominica Federation of Students and tilted the focus of many at that time away from the pursuit of selfish individual interests toward a collective quest for social justice and national development. In essence, Rosie was a nation builder who used his contacts to advance the interest of the poor and forsaken. Hitherto, only a tiny minority had been able to penetrate the thick walls of academic and professional opportunity. Today, due to the revolution he created in educational opportunity, access to university education is not an unattainable dream. Now the RDF seeks to link such education to productive activity, such as investment in local industry, with locals at the helm, which can enhance he lives of all our people.

SYMBOLS AND SUBSTANCE:

Symbols endure when they are substantive. Prussia's Otto Von Bismarck was so critical to the ascendancy of that state in the latter 1800s that his role left an indelible mark on its diplomacy, military power and economic development. The phrase that "A country has no permanent friends or permanent enemies, only permanent interests" is often ascribed to him. The roles of Winston Churchill in World War II Britain, Mohandas Ghandi and Jawaharlal Nehru in Pre-and Post Independence India, Kwame Nkrumah in Ghana and Abraham Lincoln during the US Civil War also led to the creation of symbols in their names which endure to this day. The late U.S. Democratic Party Leader John F. Kennedy fought and won a bitterly contested 1960 US presidential election against Republican Richard M. Nixon. At that time, the U.S. was fighting an internal battle over the real meaning of freedom as Black and progressive Americans led by Dr. Martin Luther King and others marched for human rights and against the tyranny of racism which trampled the rights of blacks. Three years later, President Kennedy was dead; assassinated on November 22, 1963. While Kennedy was no Dominican citizen, within one year Dominicans named a major street in Roseau in his honor: Kennedy Avenue on which the country's current government headquarters is located. Today, there is the Kennedy School of Government at Harvard associated with a distinguished library in his name. And in Washington, D.C., there is the world famous Kennedy Center for the performing arts. These living monuments to the slain U.S. President are open for the benefit of all and are not restricted to only Democrats, Republicans or those who ascribed to his ideology. It is important to recite the foregoing, as colonialism has robbed too many of us of the self-respect necessary to create institutions in our own image. Our history of denial shows a singular inclination to pay homage to heroes other than our own. In our capital city of Roseau, the profusion of streets named after Queen Mary, King George IV, Great Marlborough and Great George, are cases in point. However, we can all learn from such substantive rendering of homage to fallen heroes as exist in other lands. In a mature society it is understood that public service is to be revered, so as to encourage others to give of themselves. These symbols, through libraries, street names, holidays, works projects, museums, songs, poems, literature, schools, universities, ships, medals, awards, or scholarships named in honor of those who dedicated their lives to serving their fellow humans create dignity for a people, while ensuring the continuity of that tradition of sacrifice and civic duty. In essence, it allows a people to build self-respect for the ages. It is a sign of political and national maturity when there exist a national consensus on such symbolism born of a desire to build national unity and purpose.

The insidious presence of pro-colonial and self hating ideas frustrate attempts by new states to build stable and prosperous societies. Such self loathing leads to apathy, political tribalism, indolence, distraction and a lack of coherent national will, purpose or direction. The success of the newly industrialized and/or independent countries like Taiwan, Barbados, Cuba, Malaysia, Korea, and Singapore owe much to the bastions of self respect and national purpose grounded in the heroes they revere. The difficulties and failure of many states in Eastern Europe, Indonesia, South and Central America and Africa proceed from a lack of coherent national purpose and symbolism which binds.

It can thus be said, that Rosie's life showed a preference for substance over symbolism and sloganeering. His life was about national service. In his last years, he embraced his Christian roots and faith in a manner which rejected the materialistic component of his prior ideological leanings. He died a relatively poor man. He never stayed at the state house in the capital Roseau and died at his modest home in Portsmouth. In his absence we owe a duty to ourselves and country to memorialize him, via symbols which are substantive. In so doing we will strengthen our nation-state, enhance its political culture and the notion of non-partisan unity for national good. We can work through the RDF and other Dominican groups at home and abroad to spur development, reverse the so-called brain drain, and erode the barriers of racial and class prejudice. By our actions, we enhance respect for self-less public service. We will inspire our young to appreciate that an austere life of service to the people will not go unrewarded and unappreciated. In so doing we will smash the cynicism which prevents many from engaging politics as a tool for national development, not unjust personal enrichment. We can then build on a rock-solid national unity in which we respect our own.

The rationale of the RDF resides in national pride and love of and for our people, without which any development plan, environmental protection, campaign, foreign aid and talk of a knowledge-based economy will be meaningless. To that end we must commit to memorializing Rosie as a National Hero in the following manner:

1. A National Liberators Monument which honors him and others who have been notable in building our nation;

2. Creation of a Scholarship program for High School Students.

3. Creation of a annual book and technology fair in his honor;

4. The striking of a National Hero or National Service Medal in his honor;

5. The creation of sustainable agro-industry enterprises in his name and/or with our support, along with the promotion of trade and investment for the island.

6. A National Heroes day on August Monday to make it a time for Planning, Study, Community Service and focused on its roots in the emancipation proclamation, instead of the day being fete driven;

7. Creation of a University on-island with his name attached to the main campus;

8. The creation of a library system in rural areas in his name, with the RDF's support;

9. Investment in a ship bearing his name to spur inter-island trade and transport

10. Maintenance of publications, posters, symposia and other tributes in his memory and focused on national development priorities.

11. Building of durable links with Dominca's diaspora, to include granting that community the right to vote in national elections;

12. Building durable links with African and African American communities, as well as promoting the well-being of Dominica's indigenous Carib People;

The RDF is a platform geared toward national development and named for someone who gave his last full measure for that objective. It welcomes all Dominicans and friends of Dominica, without regard to race, national origin, class, creed, religion or political affiliation. If we can achieve but a fraction of the above noted objectives, we will be able to redeem the best hopes of our people, strengthen our spiritual fiber and ensure the progress of our country and its far flung sons and daughters for years to come.

The Struggles Continues!
With Faith, Our Victory is Certain!

Appendix II

SPEAKING NOTES FOR AN ADDRESS BY THE LATE HONOURABLE ROOSEVELT DOUGLAS PRIME MINISTER OF DOMINICA AND MINISTER FOR FOREIGN AFFAIRS AT GEORGETOWN UNIVERSITY, WASHINGTON, D.C.. SEPTEMBER 22, 2000

TITLE: CARIBBEAN DEVELOPMENT OPTIONS IN A GLOBALISED WORLD

INTRODUCTION

Firstly, let me say that when I speak of the Caribbean my most immediate observation is that we are survivors. Never conceived as entities that would ever attain a semblance of nationhood, we have been able to confound our colonial originators and other doubters. We strive to remain relevant to our survival as nation states. Despite the difficulties now imposed on us by the imperatives of structural adjustment and decreases in commodity prices for our exports, we remain resilient. While the onward march of a certain brand of craven globalisation seeks to have our economies be subject to the lowest common denominator, we make haste to carve out new options for our people. We remain committed to the rule of law, strong environmental regulations, workers rights, gender equality and dignity for our indigenous Carib people. We will not abide by prescriptions that diminish health care and education opportunities for our people. Such investments build hope for our future. And we will struggle to maintain the gains earned by our nation-states which are, particularly in the English speaking Caribbean, social democracies in their approach to public and private sector development.

Using my island, the Commonwealth of Dominica as an example, one immediately appreciates that the limitations of size, population, and natural resources need not be a death warrant. For the most part, the adherence to a democratic pattern of regular elections, unfettered by fraud has assisted our survival. We maintain a free press and abide by a system rooted in an equitable system of law. Due to the investment of our limited funds on education and health care, Dominicans now have a literacy rate of 97% and an average life expectancy of 82 years. The oldest living person on our planet, Elizabeth "Ma Pampo" Israel, born: January 27, 1875 is a Dominican who lives in my constituency of Portsmouth. To consider the time frame she has spanned, note that she lived in three centuries, and was born when US Civil War General Ulysses S. Grant was President of the United States.

Why is this vignette or piece of our social history important? Well, we are not unique, in that many other sister Caribbean states in the region have similar indices, despite our limitations. But it would be true to say that our gains are under attack. And it is also true to reflect that we do not always have the concern and consideration of our old allies. It is my hope, by this address, to dispel any notion that we intend to follow the conflict-ridden path of so many of the failed states that occupy the newspaper headlines and CNN. We are not pessimists or fatalists and we will strive to make our own history, as a region united by hope and faith in our own native abilities to find solutions to our problems. In that endeavour, we will continue to count on the support and understanding of our great friend and ally the United States, which itself is a Caribbean nation.

A CARIBBEAN OVERVIEW:

Over much of the last half-century, the small, vulnerable, developing countries of the Caribbean have seen the economic development options available to them either diminished or radically changed under the growing trends of liberalisation and globalisation. From import substitution policies and protectionism to preferential trade arrangements with former colonial masters, choices have been taken away from these countries.

Now on the threshold of the twenty-first century the Caribbean is facing along with the rest of the world a whole new era. Everything is changing fast. New rules for trade, commerce and production are being written as fast as technological and communication advancements can write them. While small developing countries have inherent disadvantages, which will be returned to later, the new world is offering up opportunities that if properly gotten hold of could transform the economies of our region.

This presentation shall first outline the main characteristics of the current globalized world. It will then deal with the implications for the countries of the Caribbean. Finally the development options, which are available to Caribbean countries, will be highlighted. Frankly, my position will be that we have the keys to our liberation if we depart from prior modes of conduct born of dependency. While we will need the assistance of our friends such as the United States and other more developed nations, we are more interested in mutually beneficial partnerships that provide us with the tools to attain our own creative means of capital formation and technology transfer.

GLOBALIZATION: FRIEND OR FOE?

Globalisation has been defined by one writer as simply the institutionalisation of the open world capitalist economy, under the impulse of technological change. Another writer has defined it as the multi-dimensional process in which national barriers to the international flows of goods, services, capital, money and information are being reduced or eliminated.

Advances in information technology and telecommunications and the fusion of these technologies have altered the landscape on which nations and firms operate. Firms are able to diffuse an ever-widening range of operations and functions to wherever labour is cheapest, the necessary infrastructure is available and the macro-economic policies are just right. Information diffusion causes nations to become increasingly borderless and more prone to external forces. Space and distance are now less important factors to be considered in how nations or private enterprise organize a bureaucracy or manage production.

Goods and services produced and exchanged within countries have to meet international standards, costs and tastes. Peter Drucker explains that, *'every business must become globally competitive, even if it manufactures and sells only within a local or regional market. The competition is not local anymore – in fact it knows no boundaries. Every company has to become transnational in the way it is run.'*

I have yet to mention the Internet and the growth of electronic commerce and how this new revolution will fundamentally affect the way economic activities will be conducted in financial services, telecommunications and others.

While advancements in information technology and communications have been the conduit through which globalisation has progressed, international institutions and organisations such as the International Monetary Fund (IMF) and the World Bank have formed the circuit board on which the conduits have been run. These organisations, or as some have put it, the **Washington Consensus**, have advocated and championed the new worldwide orthodoxy, whereby greater reliance is placed on market forces and private enterprise for development. The role of government is to be reduced through privatisation and deregulation. However, such cannot be done in a manner that destroys our gains in health, education and the environmental protection. Privatisation is no magic wand and must only be engaged where it injects capital into a bankrupt enterprise, enhances efficiency or imparts new technology. We must always engage a cost-benefit analysis when we contemplate privatisation to ensure it serves the greater good of the nation-state. Too often we cede control of a profitable state owned enterprise, as happened recently with Dominica's electric company, without full regard to the loss of income to the local treasury over the long term, or the decreased opportunity for locals to manage their own affairs.

Public sector management and planning fostered a healthy and educated population which sustains us and grants our people an opportunity for economic growth. Where a Caribbean country has prospered, you will find that the **public sector** was the driving force behind the creation of strong education and health care sectors. Frankly, the history of our private sector rooted in plantation economies, made it a poor engine for building health or education initiatives. Therefore, we cannot place blind faith in the dogma that market forces are best suited to deal with all societal needs. In the particular instance of health and education, we must ensure that strategic public policy ensures the constant advance of those areas.

The signing of the Uruguay Round and the creation of the World Trade Organisation (WTO) has all but cemented this ideology. One writer has stated that the Uruguay Round may be considered to be the institutional expression of the globalisation impulse. The WTO is thus the institution established to manage the transition to a liberalised world economy beyond trading blocs. However, the WTO cannot be allowed to express insensitivity to the social and economic gains made by small states that do not have the financial wherewithal to lobby the U.S. congress or powerful parliaments in the North. If we are forced to compete at the bottom of the barrel, restricted to providing cheap labour for the rich and powerful, compelled to suppress environmental and labour laws in the dash to secure investment, we can be assured of more inequity, social discord, and a polluted planet. In essence, we will witness the creation of more failed states that will, eventually, threaten the comfort and security of the rich and powerful.

Globalisation therefore, confronts us in the developing world with new problems and new opportunities. While it is true that economic forces are becoming more and more intractable, weak groups and countries are being marginalized, inequality is increasing, financial crises are being exacerbated as in the recent Asian financial crisis and global crime is on the increase, we have technology hitherto unknown. Viewed from the South, globalisation and increased trade liberalisation have had negative consequences on employment, wealth distribution, the environment and cultural diversity. Simply put, we in Dominica and in the wider region have not benefited much from increased trade liberalisation or the multilateral system. However, if we focus on educating our population for this information age, we can ensure a niche for ourselves. As the **Nature Island of the Caribbean Dominica** intends to link information technology to environmental protection and cement such a niche for itself as a world leader in eco-tourism education, bio-diversity management and the development of health care products from our forest.

The concept of globalisation as friend, rather than foe, guided my administration in cementing a new partnership with the University of New Orleans (UNO), Louisiana under the visionary leadership of its Chancellor, Gregory O'Brien. It is a partnership which will train Dominicans and others from the region in eco-tourism and ecology management, while allowing UNO and other mainland students to do research and development on a soon-to-be-established on-island campus of higher learning. The facilitator of that project, the Washington, D.C. based non-government organization (NGO) Nature Island, Inc. represents the "friendly" face of a more wholesome globalisation as cooperation *NOT* conquest. Nature Island, Inc. embraced a philosophy which recognized that to protect our gains our region needed new options and partners in light of the attack on the preferences once granted our banana industry by the European Economic Community (EU). In short partnerships with

US based institutions of higher learning are means to the end we seek: A skilled population, ready to navigate the rapids of the new world economy. My life, and the philosophical bent of the movement from which I come, have shown a dedication to such education partnerships to train our youth. Such partnerships will allow us to train our people for the knowledge-based economy we seek to build.

Frankly, we would appreciate such practical approach to cooperation between our countries and NGO's in the developed world that allow us the means for improved human resource development for the information age and capital formation. In particular, where such practical assistance takes precedence over a sterile activism that wallows in media attention yet educates or feeds none; is rich in flowery words, yet short on positive action.

The detractors of globalisation stress that unrestricted trade and capital mobility will lead to a movement of industries away from high wage regions to low wage regions leading to lower standards of living in the high wage regions. It is also argued that the global financial market takes way from the ability of sovereign nations to carry out independent economic policy and that poor nations are further marginalized.

However, we have the opportunity to utilize our educated populace and relatively advanced telecommunication systems in the region to build a knowledge based economy. By our consistent investment in upgrading the skills of our human resources, we may well have that comparative advantage to service the needs of major services industries in North America and, indeed, worldwide. Via internet systems and data transfer that occurs at the click of a mouse, we can link work centres in our region to global markets and so service pertinent needs. Our facility with English and other major language groups such as French and Spanish make our region well poised to compete in the service industries spawned by the information revolution. In that vein we seek not the status of sweatshop centre, but that of hi-tech centre. If we have the vision and drive, we will find the means to realize that objective. In so doing globalisation can be a friend which allows us an exit from abject dependence on one or two commodities, rather than a foe which slays any opportunity we may have to compete in the market place.

A NEW DIRECTION FOR CARIBBEAN COUNTRIES IN A GLOBALIZED WORLD: ISSUES TO BE CONSIDERED

Close examination of the Caribbean's political economic history will reveal that globalisation has not been a recent phenomenon for the Caribbean. The Caribbean has always been integrated into the world's economy through trade and investment. It will be seen that the region has always been responding to cyclical fluctuations in the international economy and has had to adjust its political and economic relationships to the challenges in the international environment for a long time.

However, the recent trends in trade liberalisation, privatisation, and deregulation of financial markets and the rapid advancements in communication and information technology has brought the implications of globalisation to sharp focus for the region. While the Caribbean has always been small and vulnerable, this characteristic is now of critical importance. The issue of sustainable development has become a serious concern. The post-colonial era of special relationships is coming to an end and the region is now experiencing severe demands on their resources to be represented and participate in negotiations, meetings and conferences at the bi-lateral and multilateral level.

SIZE AND VULNERABILITY

The issue of smallness and vulnerability and its implications for economic development has become one of the most fundamental and contentious issues in the globalized world. Some view the concept as having little bearing or effect on the ability of a country to effectively participate in the globalized world. Others on the other hand see it as a particular set of characteristics that pose special development challenges to those countries, which share in it. Being a part of the latter group obviously the Caribbean countries have fought to have the concept recognised in every international forum in which they participate from the WTO to the Free Trade Area of the Americas (FTAA) now being negotiated.

Small states are susceptible to natural disasters and environmental change such as hurricanes, volcanic eruptions and earthquakes, which typically affect the entire population and economy sometimes to disastrous ends. These countries have limited diversification, limited institutional capacity, limited access to external capital and high income volatility. While poverty levels tend to be higher in small states, the evidence shows that our indices, especially in the Organization of Eastern Caribbean States (OECS), Barbados, Trinidad and Tobago, place us in the range of middle income countries. So while it is true that most Caribbean states are small, we have managed, for the most part, to build working civil societies.

Again, despite our limited size, we remain societies with a sense of identity and community. We have a comparative advantage in that our culture is appreciated and welcomed in most parts of the world. Dominica has an annual Creole Festival which has generated income and garnered worldwide attention. Jamaica's Sunsplash Festival, Trinidad's world renowned carnival, St. Lucia's Jazz Festival, Barbados' Crop Over Festival are all examples of creative niche building which foster economic development. We are a welcoming people, friendly and kind. We abhor xenophobia and strive to bridge the divides of race, ethnicity and class which tear so many societies apart. Our record is not perfect as the region's history of slavery, class prejudice, ethnic discord in some states and the mistreatment of indigenous peoples have shown. But we have a track record of bridge building which strengthens our democracies and of which we can be proud.

If we harness our cultural treasures and mastery in calypso, reggae, zouk, cadance, salsa and meringue, we will attract overall investment. Health tourism, heritage tourism, academic tourism and eco-tourism are all new areas of economic activity under consideration by us. So we will continue to welcome humanity that seeks a respite from pollution, disorder and discord elsewhere. Thus, size need not be an inhibiting factor if we focus on keeping our region ecologically pristine, stable and being the best at what we do.

In short, we can dominate specific niche markets, despite our geographic and demographic limitations.

SUSTAINABLE DEVELOPMENT

There has been a growing awareness in the international arena of the impact on the environment of the socio-economic activities of a country and that the world may be reaching the limit to sustainable economic growth and development. Several international conferences have been held to discuss this issue including the UN Global Conference on Environment and Development in 1992 and a similar Conference for Small Island Economies in 1994.

The 1987 report of the Brundtland Commission, *Our Common Future* defined sustainable development as development that meets the needs of the present without compromising the ability of future generations to meet their own needs. This can be interpreted as stating that economic development activities of the present should not so deplete the assets used to for development that future generations are unable to ensure development themselves. In addition, sustainable development for Small Island Developing States means development within the constraints of the carrying capacity of island environments or ecosystems.

The island economies of the Caribbean are characterised by fragile ecological systems, which are easily affected by socio-economic activities. Risks, which arise from the demands made on the natural resource endowments of the region include, deforestation, desertification, soil erosion, water resource depletion and over fishing.

Given these factors, the question then becomes how can Caribbean countries accomplish the task of raising the income levels of their populations over a sustained period of time far into the future. There is no doubt that we should adopt sustainable development principles if we are to survive into the future. We are too small and vulnerable to do otherwise.

There is however a limit to which the environmental factor can be taken into consideration. One cannot expect Caribbean economies to accommodate environmental concerns at the expense of the pressing problems of unemployment and poverty which some would suggest that they do.

It should be very instructive to note that the overwhelming majority of world's environmental degradation originates in the wealthy developed nations. This tells us that environmental concerns were not and may not still have become a central part of their policy making framework.

I have already mentioned our partnerships with mainland universities which seek to deal with the issues of sustainable development and environmental protection and so I will not repeat my admonition that education, while a long term investment, is where we must focus.

LOSS OF 'SPECIAL RELATIONSHIPS' AND CONSIDERATION

The Caribbean's economic evolution has been based to a large extent on special relationships with Europe and the

Americas primarily characterised by preferential access to these markets and access to aid and other concessional financial resources. The prime example of this being the LOMÉ Agreement between the European Union and the African Caribbean Pacific countries.

In the globalized world Caribbean countries are finding that these development crutches are progressively being taken away. The pressure is on to remove all forms of barriers to trade and to allow the market forces to have supreme control over all economic activities.

In the most discussed trade dispute to date at the World Trade Organisation we have seen a clearest illustration of this. The banana case is a dispute between the United States along with three Latin American countries and Europe. While all have said the objective of the case has never been to take away the preferential access granted to ACP bananas the effect of it could be exactly that.

Since losing the case at the WTO the EU has been seeking to reform its regime to make it compatible with the WTO, while trying to meet Caribbean needs, and at the same time satisfy complainants like the United States. It has however been a very difficult process.

From a Caribbean perspective, the situation has now come to a point where the search for a solution has become rather desperate. We are fighting for a solution, which will maintain the tariff rate quota with licenses allocated on the basis of historical trade. This is the best way we believe for us to obtain secure access to the European market and to receive an adequate level of remuneration.

There is however, resistance to such a solution by the big fruit monopolies and their political agents. If a solution is not found along those lines there will be serious economic dislocation in the Caribbean. The Windward Islands rely exclusively on the

EU market as the sole outlet for their bananas. Banana production is a significant contributor to employment and export. Loss of the EU market would be a major economic blow. The US government must appreciate our deep concern in that regard. We urge that there not be any squandered opportunities as we seek to forge more reliable links with the US based on mutual interest and a sensitivity to our fragile position in the world economy.

In the coming decades after the finalisation of the FTAA and the new post LOMÉ Agreement it is likely that a new era of cooperation would have been ushered based on reciprocal relationships and access to aid with new forms of decentralised cooperation.

Another dimension to this is what has been termed the decline of the strategic importance of the English-speaking Caribbean to the Unites States and Europe. The region is no longer the supplier of critical raw materials. These materials are either available cheaper from other sources or technological advancements have allowed the development synthetic alternatives.

Security concerns have also changed in the post cold war era with new priorities emerging in the Middle East and Asia. Consequently less thought is being given to Latin America and the Caribbean. In addition to that the region is perceived as relatively well off compared to their developing countries.

Dominica has embarked on a new thrust to build strong links with the EU. Located as we are between two EU member entities, Guadeloupe and Martinique, we already share a special relationship. It is our determination to share any benefits of our new thrust with our sister states in the region. In that regard, we see ourselves as facilitators of new linkages for our region, above and beyond that which obtains at present. Our effort at consolidating links with the EU is an essential ingredient in our effort at expanding our special relationships. Therefore, in our relations with progressive African states, the Republic of China on Taiwan, Greece, Cyprus and Japan we will share with our OECS member states, any opportunity to open new markets which can serve our region.

With regard to our Caribbean Community (CARICOM) partners it is our continuing determination to form common cause on foreign policy issues. We also need to recognise that there is a growing diversity of perspectives on regional integration in the Caribbean. We, therefore, need to be flexible enough in this process. There are different strategies for economic development among the countries and different speeds of integration. A case in point was when I indicated that Dominica would seek a special relationship with France because of the strategic location of Dominica between Guadeloupe and Martinique. My CARICOM colleagues raised some concerns as to how that would affect Dominica's relationship with CARICOM. I had to point out that it should not negatively affect CARICOM. Other CARICOM countries had taken similar action. However, as much as is feasible the Caribbean diplomacy we pursue seeks a unified position.

As we cultivate our relationship with the US, we believe that where US assistance is given there should be a mix that favours the US Department of Agriculture and other civilian sectors of US government. Quite frankly, if we are allowed to share the bounty of agricultural know-how that has made the US the breadbasket of the world, we can deflect any tendency by farmers inclined to replace bananas with more profitable, yet illegal crops. Thus, while we are in accord with and support the US and other allies in drug interdiction efforts, we prefer a focus on the productive civilian cooperation that will lead to longer lasting results. Our distinct preference is for projects and programs like those run by Dr. Gillian Clissold of Georgetown University's Caribbean Project which seek to train farmer's in internet use, so as to better market their produce. It is only fitting and proper that US assistance should continue to our region, in more creative ways, as it more than doubles the return to the US economy in the resultant trade and development linkages created.

Building a knowledge-based economy is the objective of my government. It is the objective of most of our region. We do not seek to exchange banana dependency with narco-dependency. In that vein, the US Department of Energy is a desirable partner in our efforts at building new energy sources from our marine and land based eco-systems. The US Department of Agriculture should partner with our farmers to improve technique, to better feed our people, supply food products to our tourism industry, promote research and development of new crops and soil revitalization, encourage inter-regional trade and the export of specialty products to the US market. In particular, we would appreciate such cooperation where it focuses on the supply of Caribbean agricultural products to the 35 million strong Caribbean and Hispanic community that share a similar taste in food products.

Such an approach which institutionalises a relationship between the civilian sector of US government and the Caribbean aims at a long-term solution to illicit drug production, use and abuse. It would, out of necessity, involve a technical exchange that would derive mutual benefit. It would also include the US agro industry that could partner with our local private sector to engage areas of equipment and technique upgrade.

Once again, this new cooperation would require a departure from the remnants of any Cold War thinking that may still influence US policy toward the region. Truly, it would be a noble continuation of the special relationship long shared with our friend and neighbour.

THE DIPLOMACY OF THE CARIBBEAN AND THE LACK OF EFFECTIVE PARTICIPATION IN THE INTERNATIONAL SYSTEM

It has been said that no man is an island. To this may be added, no island is the world. In the formation of its strategies and policies, Dominica, and other Caribbean States, given their size and location, must position themselves within the context of the wider hemisphere, and the world at large.

Small developing states face numerous constraints in the manner in which they conduct their foreign policy. One of the most significant is with respect to overseas representation. Like other Caribbean States Dominica has few diplomatic missions. At present overseas offices exist in London, Washington, Ottawa, Rome, Brussels and New York, which serves the UN.

Compounding the problem of limited overseas representation is the fact that Ministries and missions do not have the capacity to deal with the numerous issues. Today the conduct of foreign policy including that of overseas missions has to contend with not only the established issues like representation abroad, trade and finance issues but also with new issues. These new issues include protection of the environment, drugs and money laundering.

In addition development issues are at the forefront of the foreign policies of small states. Diplomacy is likely to be directed to securing international finance, problems arising from loan schedules, restrictions to key exports, the promotion of regional cooperation and relations with major foreign powers.

Due to our limited diplomatic representation, the influence, which the Caribbean has been able to exert on the world's multilateral frameworks, has been somewhat limited over the years. At the UN and the World Trade Organisation for example the Caribbean has had to succumb to the rules that are being made without being able to effectively contribute to the making of these rules.

However, the OECS runs a joint mission in Washington, DC and shares the cost of investment promotion. As such, we have taken practical steps to overcome our limitations. Where we still lag behind, is in the area of effectively harnessing the potential of our overseas population in representation abroad. It is said there are more Jamaicans overseas than at home. Dominica now has approximately 25% of its population in the US, UK, Canada and neighbouring islands. However, few Caribbean governments have systematically approached trade and investment linkages with the Caribbean diaspora.

Economic data reflect that annual foreign exchange remittances to the region from overseas nationals range from 20% to 25% of total foreign exchange inflow assessed. In some of our smaller Caribbean states the rate of foreign exchange inflow from our overseas communities is even higher. Yet that overseas community is not given the right to vote in local elections, is not sought out for investment in a respectful and substantive manner, and is sometimes the object of ridicule, jealousy and governmental neglect upon return. That must change. We must put systems in place to court our overseas communities. We cannot ever achieve real development in the Caribbean region, until we deal with the effects of the brain and resource drain, by re-integrating our overseas communities as an essential part of economic planning. The role of the overseas Chinese in China, the overseas Jews in the creation and development of Israel, and the overseas Koreans in the rise of Korea, should be incentive enough to us to rise above our limited approach in that regard.

My government, and indeed the Caribbean governments, should extend special recognition to organizations such as the Institute of Caribbean Studies (ICS), the National Council of Caribbean Organisations (NCOCA) and others that seek to build the Caribbean nation. By linking with them, we can create that data base of Caribbean expertise on the World Wide Web that can be placed at the service of the Caribbean's public and private sector. We can encourage our transplanted nationals to invest their money and talent. And we should pursue them with even more zeal, as their commitment—once obtained—may well prove to be life long.

Further, we should intercede with the host governments, as a matter of policy, to facilitate a regulatory scheme whereby Caribbean nationals or those who invest in certain Caribbean Development Fund Instruments (CDFI's) should be allowed local tax breaks as an incentive.

DEVELOPMENT OPTIONS FOR THE CARIBBEAN

STRATEGIC GLOBAL REPOSITIONING

The first response, which Caribbean countries must make to the globalized world, is what Jamaican Ambassador to the U.S. Richard Bernal has termed Strategic Global Repositioning. Bernal has defined this process as the repositioning of the country in the global economy and world affairs by implementing a strategic medium to long term plan formulated from continuous dialogue of the public sector, private sector, academic community and the social sector. It involves a proactive structural and institutional transformation not just adjustment focused on improvement and diversification of exports and international economic and political relations.

We need to abandon the old and traditional ways of thinking and approaches of the past, while retaining what is useful. That means we must be willing to diligently seek out and accept new ideas. We need to be more innovative and more proactive.

We are living in an information age. We are in the heat of the information revolution. As Owen Arthur Prime Minister of Barbados stated information has replaced energy, commodities and natural resources as the basic raw materials in the production process. There are now a whole new range of knowledge based, skills intensive, service-oriented production possibilities, which can readily be exploited by all societies and we must position ourselves to take full advantage of these.

In order to do this we must plan. That leads to the next important phrase in the definition, which is "strategic medium to long-term plan". We need to stop continually fighting economic fires in the Caribbean. We need to stop continually dealing with one crisis after the other. We need to stop sit down and plan, and we need to plan strategically. We waste a huge amount or resources and energy when a lot of the time what we do is implement a series of stopgap measures which are short term in their effects. The result is a continuous cycle is created where the previous short-term measure contributes to the next crisis, which was not foreseen.

I believe that in order for Caribbean countries to ride the wave of technological advancements on the sea of globalisation we must strategically chart a course of development. We need to evaluate what we have, what we do not have. We need to set bench marks which set deadlines and project desired outcomes ten to twenty years from now.

Our governments cannot and should not plan by themselves. We need dialogue. This is the other important component of repositioning. In most of the Caribbean countries there is a marked absence of a mechanism of bringing all the stakeholders together where the only thing that matters is the future of the country. This has been to our disadvantage. There will always be disagreements and different points of views. But these have to be set aside when they get in the way of what each citizen of the country wants which is economic growth and development. Therefore, in setting up management committees and commissions for planning purposes, inclusion of opposition and NGO representatives enhances the process and fuels inclusion. As a result, national unity and cohesion is fostered and political and ethnic discord avoided.

Once this mechanism is put in place it needs to be a continuous one. It needs to form an integral part of the country's economic and political structure.

THE DEVELOPMENT OF THE SERVICE SECTOR

Of course an integral part of strategic global repositioning is export diversification by the development of new exports. In Dominica the development of the services sector forms a major part of our economic diversification thrust.

A major pillar of this thrust is the development of a competitive and well-regulated offshore sector. The international financial services sector offers the region one of the few areas in which we can have a competitive advantage over the developed world. We intend to capitalise on this opportunity as far as it will take us.

I mentioned the phrase well regulated because we are committed to ensuring that the sector does not provide support to the perpetrators of criminal activity. However I must voice my concern at a recent series of orchestrated activities by the G-7, through three organisations of its creation.

In a May 26, 2000 Report from the Financial Stability Forum created by the G7 several Caribbean jurisdictions with offshore financial centres were negatively categorised based on a unilateral evaluation of the quality of supervision of these jurisdictions, even as its report found that "Offshore Financial activities are not inimical to global stability."

In the June 22, 2000 Report of the Financial Action Task Force (FATF) Caribbean countries were listed as "non-cooperative jurisdictions" in the prevention of money laundering.

In the June 26, 2000 Report on 'Harmful Tax Competition: An Emerging Global Issue', the Organisation for Economic Cooperation and Development (OECD) listed Caribbean jurisdictions as tax havens because these countries have competitive tax regimes and have not agreed to bind themselves to the elimination of policies and practices which the OECD has unilaterally determined to be "harmful" to its members.

These activities are unilateral and inconsistent with international practice and are simply designed to impair the competitive capacity of Caribbean jurisdictions in the provision of global financial services. Each of these reports was based on incomplete information and on standards set singularly by these bodies. The objective can only be to taint the respective Caribbean countries in the eyes of the investment community and the international financial market. Such actions are contrary to the tenets of a global market economy that the G7 promotes.

International rules and practices must evolve from genuine consultative processes and in international forums in which all interests are represented. These rules must be made and applied democratically based on accepted principles and norms. No Caribbean country is a member of the OECD or any of its created organisations.

We are ready to address any concerns of the OECD in the appropriate multilateral forum, and are committed to fighting money laundering and all other forms of financial crime. We are in the process of introducing international best practices in our regulation of the financial sector and in strengthening legislation and enforcement machinery.

We have found an area in which we have a competitive advantage and with the appropriate legislative and regulatory frameworks we intend to make maximum use of it. It is just unfortunate that such a course of action was taken by the world's largest and most developed countries against some of the world's smallest and developing ones.

In Dominica we have been promoting investment in telecommunications. However, this had been hampered by the monopoly environment in which the telecommunications industry operated.

We have taken steps to addresses this. Just two weeks ago in the House of Assembly of Dominica a new Telecommunications Bill was enacted. The main purpose of the new Act is to move Dominica from a present position of monopoly, restrictive laws and licenses, exclusivity and limited availability of services to a position of liberalisation, which is in line with developments worldwide.

With the passage of this Act we are seeking to ensure that the demand for existing telecommunications services is met in order to support economic growth and diversification, provide a suitable environment for tourism, informatics and financial sectors, and satisfy the educational and social needs of the community.

A new national regulatory body will be created to coordinate, advise and harmonise broad policy directives for Dominica. The national body will work in tandem with an OECS sub-regional regulatory authority to ensure that the telecommunications sector is characterised by fair competition, consumer protection and investor confidence.

In addition to the Act we will be putting in place a comprehensive enabling framework. Clear, action-oriented policies that will provide a strategic framework within which Dominica can position itself to seize the opportunities that are being provided: Issues to be addressed include:

- The role of the education system in meeting the skill requirements of the information technology industry;

- The identification of the legal and regulatory changes required to support the new and emerging business modalities (e-commerce, e-government, electronic banking, etc.);
- Intellectual property rights;
- The role of information technology in international marketing and promotion of the local tourism and offshore industries and its impact on work processes and the work force; and
- The redefinition of our investment promotion strategy.
- The key role of the Dominican diaspora in capital and technology transfer
- The creation of strategic partnerships with overseas universities to foster the growth of our knowledge economy thrust

A multi-sectoral coordinating task force will be appointed with a mandate to develop these policy guidelines and a strategic plan of action.

THE NEED TO RESTRUCTURE THE AGRICULTURAL SECTOR

Repositioning also involves improving the competitiveness of and productivity in existing export sectors. Hence we need to restructure our agricultural sectors to be able to fit in the current globalized world and the world that will be twenty and thirty years from now. We need to bring competitiveness and productivity to new heights. We need to find new markets and new products. We need to invest in research and development to allow us to develop new uses for the fruits and vegetables that we have in abundance.

In Dominica the restructuring of the banana industry has been identified as a priority of government. The Dominica Banana Marketing Corporation is pursuing a long-term goal of being a farmer owned, commercial enterprise that is capable of competing on the world market with resilience to price competition. A programme of productivity and quality enhancement initiatives, a restructured marketing and distribution strategy and efforts to promote greater competition in the market for the supply of inputs will also be implemented.

A NEW FORM OF REGIONALISM

Regional integration is critical for the Caribbean. There is no doubt about that. As small, island developing states with very limited resources we need to pull our efforts together in areas of external economic relations and negotiations, foreign policy and functional cooperation. Each of us in the region cannot afford to be fully represented in Geneva at the WTO the way we need to be. We can't afford to attend all the meetings and conferences that are demanded of us from the various international and regional organisations such as the United Nations, Organisation of American States and the Commonwealth. In order for us to become integrated into the world trading system without too much damage to our domestic economies we have needed CARICOM to provide us with a means of gradually preparing our economies for trade liberalisation.

However, as one writer has put it regionalism needs to be reinvented in the region. We the policy makers need to undertake a thorough re-evaluation of CARICOM. We need to reassess its operation. We need to determine whether it is meeting the objectives, which have been set for it. We need to determine whether those objectives are realistic. We need to determine whether the ideas we have of CARICOM and regional integration in the region as a whole are economically and politically feasible. Some of these ideas include monetary union and a single currency and even political union.

We need to realise that the reasons and underlying thinking for the establishment of CARICOM in 1975 should not be the same reasons we have for maintaining the organisation in the twenty-first century. Regional integration, however, should now be a response to the dynamics of globalisations. The objective of regional integration should focus more on shared science and technology development, joint strategies in international relations and shared resources. We should seek the creation of regional economic space without any borders that is conducive to globally competitive economic activities where nationality of ownership is not a consideration.

Hence the creation of the CARICOM Single Market and Economy (CSME) should be accelerated. We have taken too long in getting to this point. While CARICOM has had a number of successes in the area of functional cooperation, the progress towards true regional economic integration has been rather slow. The nine Protocols for the creation of the CSME have been completed and signed by most of the member states. It is important that we implement these protocols particularly Protocol II which deals with movement of services, capital and rights of establishment.

CONCLUSION

The Caribbean in the twenty-first century faces a number of threats to its political as well as economic development. The increasing forces of globalisation have heightened the region's inherent disadvantages arising from its smallness. As a result the Caribbean is more vulnerable to risks and threats than it has ever been in the past.

The question of sustainable development has become of global concern and more particularly for Small Island Developing States. The pressure for development is sometimes at odds with the need to preserve the environment so that future generations will be able to survive.

We have met challenges before and vanquished them. We can continue to do so. Globalisation will be what we make of it. I say we must use it as an opportunity to build partnerships, not an excuse to institutionalise oppression under the guise of freedom. We have to be willing to utilize market forces where necessary, but not be dogmatic and blind to the limitations of the marketplace. We must seek efficiency and rid our state sector of numbing bureaucracy, yet be mindful to maintain processes that work. I am confident that if we embrace our native intelligence we can make it! If we enhance the education of our people, guard their health systems, protect our environment, build our links with our overseas nationals and those of Caribbean heritage, we can do it! Assured that we have the partnership and consideration of traditional allies such the United States of America, our efforts will blossom into new economic activity of mutual benefit. Finally, if we finesse our cultural bounty, nurture our comparative advantages, while ensuring that **social justice thrives** then we, in the words of Martin Luther King, Jr., shall overcome!

Thank You.

APPENDIX III

MS. OCTAVIA NORDE.

PROFILE OF A DOMINICAN MIGRANT TO CANADA

Irving André

It was March 2, 1996, and the three of us walked purposefully towards the unassuming brownstone condominium complex. The brisk wind added a greater urgency to our gait and instinctively, we clutched the folds of our padded jackets.

The black extra length jacket I wore carried the equipment I needed. A micro-cassette recorder, an automatic camera, pen, paper, and batteries. My two companions, Ferdinand Fortune and Jonathan Charles, set the pace and led the way from the cold streets of Toronto into the warm lobby of the condominium complex. As Fortune pressed the button for the arrival of the elevator, I mentally rehearsed my much anticipated meeting with Ms. Octavia Norde, a Dominican who was born in the village of Pointe Michel and who had lived continuously in Toronto since 1931.

I learned of her by sheer accident. Fortune, a fellow Dominican, himself a native of Pointe Michel, had found out about her through relatives who had moved from England to Canada. He subsequently visited her and soon his visits became a quest for knowledge. Speaking to her quenched his own deep seated thirst for knowledge about his village. Through her story, he was able to untangle much of the gordian knot which represented his own family ancestry.

Intrigued, I suggested meeting with the venerable Ms. Norde. Such a meeting, Fortune surmised, would have to be planned. Arrangements would have to be made. Ms. Norde herself would have to be consulted. She did not give kindly to strangers and would have to be reassured about my presence.

The cooperation of her caregiver would not be difficult but the "right time" had to be chosen.

"We must see her when she is in a talking mood," Fortune cautioned.

Not given to being reticent himself, I had waited two months while Fortune bided his time before advising me that the moment of truth had arrived.

And so we mounted the elevator for the short journey to the third-storey. To the casual observer, there was nothing unusual about the three of us. Fortune talking, glancing upwards, downwards, clutching two Bi-way bags in each hand. The curious would have hazarded a guess that this was perhaps a visit to an ailing relative and the contents of the bags being merely a gastronomic delight. He was partly right. We had taken the precaution of leaving no stone unturned in ensuring that our mission was successful.

Strangely enough, Jonathan seemed to sense our anticipation. Only fifteen, he had listened to his uncle Fortune talk about Ms. Norde. He had frequently accompanied him to Ms. Norde's house. She was well-known to him and vice-versa. On previous visits however, he had contented himself with "chilling" with his two cousins, Camille and Marissa, the daughters of Fortune. Today, the girls had been left behind and he felt that he was part of the great quest. In preparation, he had taken his own recorder to have his own record of Ms. Norde's history. His own journey into his mother's past would be conducted independently of Fortune and I.

"Good afternoon Ns. Norde."

Fortune's voice echoed in the two-bedroom condominium as I followed him and Jonathan into a narrow passageway. He had briskly kissed the caregiver and was already removing his extra-large jacket. As if on cue, Jonathan remove and shifted aside to permit me to enter.

"Ms. Norde **ce nennenn** Vivian", Fortune stated, gesticulating in the caregiver's direction. Ms. Norde had cared for the caregiver's grandparents who were from St.Kitts and Barbados. It was her last stint of employment in Canada.

I peered tentatively ahead, looking for Ms. Norde. My eyes alighted on a dimly lit sitting room with well-worn couches draped by somber looking shawls. Straight ahead was an antique clock and radio, a gift from her grandparents, the caregiver declared proudly. Athwart, a table supported dozens of papers and documents which I had a terrible urge to peruse. Perched precariously on the table were pictures of the caregiver's family in various moments of family ecstasy. A wedding anniversary, first communion-all these were reminders of a past which had appeared brighter than the present.

"**Barbad,**" Fortune uttered knowledgeably, gesturing in the direction of the caregiver.

"How are you Ms. Norde?" he asked. He had proceeded through the kitchen to a small pantry-like room. It featured a table, a mobile tray overburdened by numerous grocery bags in varying stages of repose. Straight ahead was a glass window overlooking the street where we had previously driven and where we had painstakingly searched for a parking space. To the right, numerous flower pots contained various tropical plants. They appeared well cared for, alert, very much like the diminutive figure who sat beside the window.

I slowly made my way towards Ms. Norde where she sat with a commanding view of the street fifty feet below. The light from the window made it somewhat difficult to discern her features but they became clearer as I moved forward and stood three feet in front of her. I greeted her eagerly, looking at her carefully without creating the impression that I was prying.

Her voice was strong, though muted. She stared at me through brown-framed glasses. Her gaze was steady, probing. I gazed at her in return. Her hair had been neatly combed and was held in place by a thin black net. Her face lacked the wizened contoured look of persons her age. But her body appeared frail. On her feet were a pair of comfortable bedroom slippers draped over a pair of white stockings. She wore a loose-fitting pair of pants and matching vest with embroidered designs. A star-shaped gold pair of earrings augmented her face.

It was her hands which betrayed her age however. Her left held a walking stick although she did not require it as she sat next to the window. Her fingers were thin and the skin appeared stretched taut. She must have been in some distress since the caregiver advised that she had fallen a few weeks ago. If she was still suffering the effects of the fall she didn't show it. The only sign of weakness during our visit was her inability to hold a glass of gingerale. Her appearance became secondary and then inconsequential once we had started talking to her.

By then, I was seated beside her with my micro-cassette on the table next to her. Jonathan had set out his bigger contraption in a more strategic position even closer and had faithfully departed to the main sitting area. Fortune sat on a box directly in front of her where he would conduct the interview. A few comments, curtsies, a brief inquiry about Fortune's family and we were on a journey into the past of Octavia Norde.

She started slowly, matter-of-factly. Her voice had a mesmerizing quality causing me to lose the thread of her journey. Periodically, a name of a person, place or an event jarred my consciousness and forced me to keep pace with her life history.

She never gave her age but Ms. Norde was born in Pointe Michel in 1897. Her mother had died when she was only eight months old. Her father was a journeyman called Fergiste Norde who lived in Loubiere. As was customary in Dominica at the time, her father played no part in her upbringing.

Ms. Norde was raised by a Ma. Emmanuel, following the death of her mother. Ms. Emmanuel had a daughter, Tazzi Emmanuel, and two sons, one a painter, the other a mason. Octavia had a sister, Cecilia, who died before she was born, and two brothers, James and John. The latter died before she left Dominica in 1931 while James followed her to Canada after 1931.

Ms Norde recalled spending the first seventeen years of her life in Pointe Michel. It was a simple life of poverty alleviated only by the Roman Catholic Church where first Father Lillieve and then Father Moloy, both from Belgium, presided over the largely Roman Catholic population. The eating needs of the village population were more than adequately met by the bounty from the sea which tapped the village to the west and the **gardens** which spotted the highlands to the east.

Life in Pointe Michel in those seventeen years was rather uneventful, Ms. Norde remembered. It consisted of school, household chores, and walking to Roseau when the need arose. Religious festivals alleviated the daily routine of village life. A death would bring out virtually the whole village to the funeral. Mass was followed by nights of prayer. This **laveyea** would climax in ritualistic drinking and eating and the peace and tranquility would return to the village once more.

At seventeen, Ms. Norde's life in the small village would change forever. A few years earlier, a Portuguese businessman, one Mr. Ferreira, had moved to Dominica with his Dominican wife, Alexia Riviere. He had quickly established himself in Roseau by opening a string of businesses including an ice factory, a shop on River Street and Market Street and the Hotel La Paz.

The hotel consisted of rooms on the upper storey of the building and a bar and grocery store on the lower level.

In the narrow world of Roseau in the early twentieth century, a white person with money was someone of consequence. Persons of all colours gravitated towards the moneyed person and the relationships forged were not infrequently of the amorous kind. Public anger for this kind of behaviour was almost non-existent and in any event, could be assuaged by well-timed and well-placed acts of generosity.

Before long, Ferreira became "friendly" with Lucy Garchette, an attractive young woman of Pointe Michel. Garchette approached Ms. Norde with an alluring request.

"Monsieur Ferreira looking for a cashier but didn't want a girl from Roseau. Roseau girls too **konpawezon**. Is a nice young country girl he want. Octavia, is a good job **oui**!"

"What you staying in Pointe Michel to do, nuh! It doh have nofing here for you. Chile take de job eh!" her friend advised.

To move to Roseau was every country girl's dream and Ms. Norde was no exception. She would be paid wages, work in a hotel and avoid a life of hardship in the village. The prospect of completing her primary school education was never a serious consideration and Ms. Norde accepted the offer without any hesitation.

Ms. Norde worked at the hotel "Paz" for twelve years. She occupied a room upstairs and served as cashier for its customers. There she became acquainted with the cream of Dominica's society including Dr. Thaly, Dr. Nicholls, Ralph Nicholls and a few others. She was paid the princely sum of eight shillings a month. She bought a little house at Poree in Pointe Michel. She was also afforded the chance to travel to St. Kitts and Barbados where she had an eye operation in the early 1920s.

Ms. Norde lived a privileged life at the Hotel Paz. But she became painfully aware of another reality outside. Only whites were employed at the Barclays Bank and Royal Bank of Canada. She remembered the Caribs who used to bathe beneath the Police Station, then situated near the Anglican Church. The local population would jeer at them to the point where some had to be protected by the colonial authorities. Even at the Paz, the patrons were exclusively members of the town's elite.

It is her personal encounter with this world of privilege which would end Ms. Norde's employment at the Paz. The only refrigerator on the island was an ice factory owned by Ferreira in Roseau. The colonial bureaucrats including the Administrator, would bring various items to be refrigerated. Their maids would then retrieve these items but not before paying the requisite cost of refrigeration to Ms. Norde.

On a fateful Sunday in 1926-1927, the Administrator's **maid** came to retrieve the refrigerated items from the Paz. Ms. Norde dutifully gave her the bag and proceeded to write a receipt. Fatefully, Ferreira walked into the area and saw a number of customers with Ms. Norde seemingly unconcerned, writing on a piece of paper. He marched towards Ms. Norde and advised her that she was **fired**. Aghast, Ms. Norde proceeded to her room and immediately started packing her meager belongings. Exhortations from Ms. Ferreira did not shake her decision to leave since before long, the word that **Ferreira ladjé Ms. Norde** would be around town.

For a few weeks following her departure, it seemed that Ms. Norde's fairy tale story would end and she would have to go back to Pointe Michel, or to her small house at Poree.

Fortune smiled on Ms. Norde however. She got another job at A.C.S. Shillingford situated at Old Street and Market Street in Roseau. For the next four years, she would work with a number of persons including the manager Hugh Shillingford, bookkeeper Robert Royer, Noela Shillingford and head cashier, Ms. Maggie. While there, one of her friends, Darling, migrated to Canada as a **servant** through arrangements made by Dr. Nicholls.

After her fourth year at A.C.S., Darling invited Ms. Norde to come to Canada. A Canadian friend of Dr. Nicholls needed a **servant** from the islands to care for her six children. John Wright, an African American, had married Mary, a Norwegian and needed someone to assist with the care of the children. In Dominica, Ms. Norde was told that the job would not be a prestigious one but that she would **learn a lot** in Canada. Besides, Dr.Nicholls recommended the move so it must be good.

Ms. Norde paused at this point, breaking the conversation. The caregiver offered her some gingerale in a little red cup. Her grip on the cup was very feeble and I assisted her in picking it up with her right hand. She guided it to her mouth and had a few sips. In contrast, Fortune gulped down his serving as if impatient to continue the conversation.

I glanced at my cassette and opted to change the tape at this point. Jonathan did not have to do this since his was of the longer variety.

Ms. Norde continued her story. She couldn't remember the day or the month but in 1931 she boarded a steamer from Roseau, **Lady Nelson**, she believed it was called, bound for Canada. Her companion was Beryl Winston who would live in Canada for a number of years then move to the United States to live with her family.

The length of the journey, she could not remember. She believed the ship first arrived in New Brunswick, she then took a train to Toronto. There she was greeted by her friend "Darling" with whom she resided initially.

Although it was Ms. Norde's intention to work with the Wright family, she did not do so immediately. The family had six children who were all **spoiled like rats**. She would eventually work with the family as a **servant** for a long number of years after Mr. Wright's death in 1942. She remembered the family with fondness. They must have liked her also since one of the sons, an OPP officer called John Wright, visited her religiously every Christmas.

Life with the Wrights was difficult although the family treated her well. Her duties included taking care of the children. There were no fixed hours, she responded to their needs. She could not recall how much she was paid but remembers it to be a "few dollars."

Except for working in a munitions factory for two years during World War II, Ms. Norde worked as a **servant** for different families until her retirement in the 1960s. She took night courses in Chemistry to break the cycle of her employment, but found the portals closed. After the war, she worked at a furrier in Toronto called "Reliable Furs" but that employment did not last for "a very long time."

Ms. Norde recalled the racism she experienced in Canada without rancour or bitterness. When walking along the streets of Toronto, she would inevitably hear the comment, "There's a black cloud in the sky." In applying for a job, she would have to insert that she was "coloured". On occasion, she would have to respond to a question posed by a prospective employer. " How black are you?"

During World War II, she tried to find a more meaningful job. Her efforts were met with the comment that this is a "white man's war." That comment changed when Germans overran the Maginot Line, the seemingly impregnable line of fortifications which were supposed to protect France from German aggression. The fall of "The Line" woke up the western world to the threat of Nazism and the realization that all would be required in the war effort.

Ms. Norde remembered some of the early prejudice. She fondly recalled the experiences of a Jamaican friend, Menzies, who could pass for a white except for her "damned Jamaican" accent. Menzies tried to circumvent this by not indicating that she was "coloured" in her ads, much to the amusement of her friends. As one of them quipped, Menzies could pass for white but "as soon as she opened her **yap**", her coloured heritage was revealed.

Ms. Norde's sixty-five years in Canada were then, given her failing memory, compressed into a few important memories of her past. When I saw her, she was living with her caregiver whose mother she had befriended many years ago. She had been like a mother to the caregiver and living together was a perfect arrangement for both.

Ms. Norde never had a child and never married. Migration had effectively ended her life of traveling since she never left Toronto after arrival. She had seen lots of changes, many new faces of her own kind. She remembered meeting Dame Mary Eugenia Charles while she studied Law in Toronto during the 1940s. She had invited Charles to dinner back then.

In 1969, she sponsored a nephew and his family from England. The limited family reunion which ensued did not bring her any closer to the island.

Her memory is her most important possession. She held onto it since she had few worldly possessions. I asked whether she had any portraits, notes or momentos of the past. The caregiver promised to look but was not hopeful. The life she led had not afforded many luxuries.

While she had a clear memory of the life she left in Dominica, she had no desire to return. No one, she feared, would remember her. At her age, she could not deal with the uncertainty, the disruption. As alienating as life has been for her in Toronto, it was all she knew, all she could endure.

And so we left Ms. Norde that afternoon, gazing out the window of her condominium. We took some photographs, kissed her and took our leave. Although very grateful to talk to her, there was sadness over her plight. She was well cared for but that was not the point. I wondered whether she had ever questioned her decision to migrate; whether she had thought about the "lot of experience" which Dr. Nicholls had said she would gain in Canada. I looked at her before I left. For a moment, I thought that she would not have migrated then, had she known what she knew now. Migration. Was it for her an abortion or salvation?

Octavia Norde died peacefully in her sleep on November 29, 1997.

BIBLIOGRAPHY

PAMPHLETS

The Dominican Freedom Party. *Think it Over (1977).*
TWAVAY, Movement for a New Dominica (MND).
Dominica Labour Party, The Newtown Statement (August 28, 1977).

NEWS PAPERS

Le Monde.
London Times.
The National (Barbados).
The Toronto Star.
The Toronto Sun.
Trinidad and Tobago Express.
The Trinidad Guardian.
The Washington Post.
The Star (Dominica).
The Herald (Dominica).

ACTS OF PARLIAMENT OF DOMINICA

Abolition of Corporal Punishment (Amendment) Act, 1974.
Anti-Terrorist Act, 1981.
Bond and Securities Act, 1975.
The Dominican Constitution Order, 1978.
Extradition Act, 1980.
Foreign Incursions and Mercenaries Act, 1980.
Industrial Relations (Amendment) Act, 1979.
Praedial Larceny Act, 1975.
The Prohibited and Unlawful Societies and Association Act, 1974.

Treason Act, 1984.

MAGAZINES

Caribbean Week.
The Financial Times.

UNPUBLISHED THESIS.

Thomas, C.J. "From Crown Colony to Associated Statehood", Unpublished
PH. D Thesis. University of Massachusetts (1973).

BOOKS AND ARTICLES'

Achebe, Chinua, *Things Fall Apart*, 1958.
Adkins, M.M., *Operation Urgent Fury* (1989).
Andre, Francis, *Palm And Pine*, 1990.
André, Irving, "The Social World Of Phyllis Shand Allfrey's *The Orchid House"*, Carribean Quarterly, V.29, No.2, (1983), Pages 11-22.
André, Irving, *A Passage To Anywhere*, 1997.
André, Irving, *Distant Voices*, 2000.
André, Irving and Gabriel Christian, *In Search Of Eden*, Washington D. C, 1992.
André, Irving, *The Island Within*, 1999
André, Irivng, *The Jumbie Wedding*, 2001.
Angier, Carole, Jean Rhys, 1990.
Allfrey, Phylllis Shand, *In Circles*, England, 1940.
Allfrey, Phyllis Shand, *Palm And Oak*, 1950.
Allfrey, Phyllis Shand, *The Orchid House*, 1953.
Allfrey, Phyllis Shand, *Dashing Away*, (unpublished).
Allfrey, Phyllis Shand, *In The Cabinet*, (unpublished).
Atwood, Thomas, *A History Of Dominica*, London, 1971.

Baker, Patrick L., *Centring The Periphery*: Chaos, Order And The Ethnohistory Of Dominica, McGill, 1994.
Baptiste, Judith, *Caribbean Viewpoint*, 1992.
Bell, W. *The Democratic Revolution in the West-Indies* (1967).
Birge, William, *In Old Rosseau*, New York, 1990.
Blackman C. "The Economic Management of Small Island Developing countries". *Caribbean Affairs* October –December 1991, Vol.4, No. 1.
Brathwaite, Edward, *The Arrivants*, London, 1973.
Brathwaite, Edward *Contradictory Omens*, Savacou Publications, Kingston, 1974, pages 34-38
Browne, Ianthe W., Poems N.D..
Bruney, Eva, *A Little Bit Of Me*, Toronto, 1995.
Brytents, K.N. *National Liberation Revolutions Today*, (1977)
Burrows, R.A., *Revolution and Rescue in Grenada* 1988).
Burrows, Reynolds *A. Revolution and Rescue in Grenada*, (1989)

Campbell, Elaine, "Report From Dominica", *World Literature Written In English*, V. 12, #1, 1978.
Carpenter, H. P., *Aquarius*, N.D..
Carpenter H. .P., *In The Fifties, Bye And Bye*, London, 1982.
Carpenter H. P., *A Blossom of Sonnets*, 1995.
Casimir, J. .R. Ralph, *Freedom Poems*, N.D..
Casimir, J. R. Ralph, *Poesy*-Volumes 1-4, ed. 1948
Casimir, J. R. Ralph, *African Arise*, 1967.
Casimir, J. R. Ralph, *Pater Noster And Other Poems*, 1967
Casimir, J. R. Ralph, *Dominica And Other Poems*, 1969.
Casimir, J .R. Ralph, *The Negro Speaks*, 1969.
Casimir, J. R. Ralph, *Farewell*, 1971.
Casimir J. R. Ralph, *Black Man Listen*, 1978.
Casimir, J. R. Ralph, *Scriptum*, 1991.
Casimir, J. R. Ralph, *Hurricane*, 1995.
Caudeiron, Daniel, *Poems*, 1973.
Christian, G.J. *Rain on A Tin Roof*
Christian, G.J. *In Search of Eden*, 1992.
Christian, G.J. "Development Through South-South Trade and Cooperation" 1989.Unpublished Paper, Georgetown University Law Center.

Christian, Henckell, *Gatecrashing Into The Unknown*, 1994.
Colaire, Augustus. *Voices From The Mansion Of My Soul*, 1986.
Coleridge, H.N., *Six Months In The West-Indies* , London, 1825.
Conrad, Joseph, *Heart Of Darkness*, 1910.
Cracknell, Basil, *Dominica*, Harrisburg, 1968.
Cracknell, B.E., *Dominica* (1973).

Dabreo, D.S. *The Grenada Revolution,* (1979)
Davidson, Arnold, *Jean Rhys*, New York, 1985.
Daway, Dawen, *We Are Fighting*, 1983.
Demas W.G. "Towards a Development Consensus in Trinidad and Tobago".*Caribbean Affairs* January –March 1991, Vol. 4, No. 1.
Dies Dominica, Government of Dominica, 1967.
Dodsworth, Francis, *The Book of The West-Indies,* London, 1904.
Dominica Short Stories, Dominica Arts Council, 1974.
Douglas, Ian, *Inspiring Poems*, 1986.
Douglas, R. *Chairs or Charge* (1975).
D'Pope, Eddie, *Beyond Dark Clouds*, 1974.
Ducreay, Algernon, *Stepping Out*, 1994.
Durand, Helena, "The Boy's Story", *The New Chronicle*, May 3, 1991.
Durand, Helena, "The Paid Off Risk", *The New Chronicle*, May 10, 1991.
Durand, Helena, "The Crestfallen Gypsy", *The New Chronicle*, May 24 and 29, 1991.

Early, Eleanor, *Ports Of The Sun*, Boston, 1937.
Ellison, R. *Invisible Man* (1950).

Fanon, F. *The Wretched of the Earth* (1953).
Fanon, Traniz *The Wretched of the Earth* (1963)
Farrell, T. "Arthur Lewis and the Case for Caribbean Industrialization", *Social and Economic Studies* v.29, #4, December 1980, page 52.
Fermor, Patrick, *The Traveller's Tree*, 1950.
Forsythe, Dennis, *Let The Niggers Burn*! The Sir George Williams University Affair and its Caribbean Aftermath, (1971)

Frontline, *Ramparts I*, 1981.
Frontline, Ramparts II, *As We Ponder*, 1988.
Froude, J. J., *The English In The West-Indies*, London, 1888.

Galeano, E. *We Say No: Chronicles* 1963-1991 (192).
Gomes, A. *Through a Maze of Colour* (1974).
Government of Dominica, Aspects of Dominican History, 1972.
Gurney, J. J., *A Winter In the West-Indies*, London, 1841.

Harrington, M. The Next Left: *The History of the Future* (1986).
Haywood, H. *Autobiography of an Afro-American Communist* (1978)
Hawys, Stephen, *Mountjoy*, London, 1968.
Heines Jorge. *A Revolution Aborted:* The Lessons of Lessons of Grenada (1991).
Hellinger, S. "Failings of The CBI: Reflections from the Caribbean". A Development Group for Alternative Policies (D-Gap) Report on a visit to the Commonwealth Caribbean, January 5-19, 1986.
Henderson, Felix, *Pale Kweyol – Donmnik*
Henderson, Felix, *Basil*, N.D..
Henderson, Gordon, *Zoukland*, 2002.
Honeychurch, Dr. Lennox, *Green Triangles*, 1979.
Honeychurch, Dr. Lennox, *Our Island Culture*, 1982.
Honeychurch, Dr. Lennox, *The Dominica Story*, 1995.
Honeychurch L. Dr., *The Dominica Story* (1984),
Honeychurch, L., Dr. Isles of Adventure 1991.

Jackson, Ian, *Of Thoughts Confusing*, 1982.
Jackson, Ian, *Broken Images*, 1995.
Jackson, Ian , *Soukouyant*, 2002.
Jacob, Jenaud, *Ghetto Prisons*, 1984.
Jacob, Jenaud, *Columbus Came Third*, 1983.
James, C. L. R., *The Case For West-Indian Self Government*, 1932.
James, C. L. R., *Minty Alley*, 1934.
James, C. L. R. *Spheres of Existance* (1980).
James, Louis, *Jean Rhys*, 1978.

John, Giftus, *The Dawn*, 1978.
John, Giftus, *Words In The Quiet Moments*, 1981
John, Giftus, *The Island Man Sings his Song* 2001.
Jolly, Dorothy, *Heartaches And Roses*, 1995.
Jolly, Father Clement, *Rainbow Man,* 1994.
Jolly, Father Clement, *A Time To Remember*, N.D..
Jolly, Father Clement, *Song Of The Dove*, 1997.
Jolly, Father Clement, *Children of The Sunset*, 2002.
Jolly, Father Clement *"Building Bridges"* A Magazine
Joseph, Emanuel, "Him", *Dies Dominica*, 1972.
Joseph, Leonard, *From Thorny Bushes To Green Pastures,* 1977.
Joyce, James, *A Portrait Of An Artist As A Young Man*, 1916.

Kennedy, Julien, *As We Pondered*, N.D..
Keith, Nelson et al. *The Social Origins Democratic Socialism* (1992)
Kincaid, Jamaica, *Annie John*, 1983.
Kincaid, Jamaica, *The Autobiography Of My Mother*, New York, 1996.
Knight, F., and C. Palmer, *The Modern Caribbean* (1990).
Knight, F., and The Caribbean : *The Genesis of a Fragmented Nationalism* (1984).
Kwame, Roosevelt, *Whispers Of Passion*, 1994.
Kwayam, O., *The Rubaiyat* (1909).

Laing, R. D., *The Politics Of Experience*, 1968.
Lamming, George, *In The Castle Of My Skin*, Longman, 1953.
Lamming, George, *Water With Berries*, Longman, 1971.
La Ronde, Christabel, *From Dreams To Reality*, 1983.
La Ronde, Christabel *Llseypwé Fanm*, 1995.
La Touche, Gerald J. Jr., *To Catch A Life*, 1996.
La Touche, Gerald J. Jr., *The Burden Of Flight*, (Unpublished).
Lazare, Alick, *Native Laughter*, 1985.
Lazare, Alick, *Nature Island Verses*, 2001.
Lazare, Alick, *Carib*, 1996.
Leblanc, E.O., *Poems*, 1967.
Leevy, Alfred, *The Mountain Sings*, 1973.
Lewis, S. J., *Memories*, N.D..

Lewis, Sir W. Arthur, "*Industrialization in the West-Indies*", (1951).
Lockhart Anthony, "The Old Man And The Horse", *Wahseen,* March 2, 1974.
Lockhart, Anthony, *Two Heads*, 1977.
Lockhart, Anthony, " A Place Of Her Own*", Wahseen,* V. 2, No. 2, 1980.
Lockhart, Anthony, *Man In The Hills*, 1985.
Lockhart, Anthony, "Exile" in *New Writing From The Caribbean*, Erika Waters ed., 1994.
Lockhart, Anthony, *Midlife*, (unpublished).
Long, F. "Industrialization and the Role of Industrial Development Corporations in a Caribbean Economy: A Study of Barbados, 1960-1980 *Inter-American Economic Affairs*", v. 37 91983), page 33.

Mais, Roger, *The Hills Were Joyful Together*, 1954.
Malone, Alvin, *A Silver Lining*, N.D..
Malone, Alvin, *The Angel Of Death*, 1994.
Malone, Alvin, *Whispers In Solitude*, 1995.
Maloney, A.H., *After England – We* (1949).
Manley, M. *Up the Down Escalator* (1987)
Martin, Tony *Literary Garveyism* Garvey Blacks Arts and the Harlem Renaissance (1983).
Martin, Tony, *Race First*, The Ideological and Organizational Struggles of the Universal Negro Improvement Association (1976)
Mckaque, O. ed., *Racism in Canada* (1991).
McKay, Claude, *Banana Bottom*, 1933.
Melville, Herman, *Moby-Dick*, 1850.
Mitchell, Carlton, *Islands To Windward*, New York, 1948.
Mordecai, J., *The British Caribbean. From the Decline of Colonialism to the End of Federation* (1977)
Morris, Mervyn, "Oh, Give The Girl A Chance", Jean Rhys and *Voyage In The Dark*, 1988, (unpublished paper).
Moses, Desmond, (Ras Mo), *Crossroads*, 1982.
Moses, Desmond, *Melting Pot*, 1990.
Moses, Desmond, *The Mask*, 1995.

Musgrave, Evelyn, *On Clouds Of Love*, (unpublished).

Naipaul, V. S., *In A Free State*, 1971.
Naipaul, V.S, *Mimic Men* (1967).
Naipaul, V. S., *Guerrillas*, 1975.
Naipaul, V.S., *The Overcrowded Baracoon* (1972).
Nassief, Gilda, *Glimpses*, 1976.

Oakley, Army, *Behold The West Indies*, New York, 1951.
O'Connor, Teresa F., *Jean Rhys – The West –Indian Novels*, New York, 1986.

Palmer, C.A., *The Modern Caribbean* (1984).
Paravisini-Gebert, Lizabeth, Phyllis Shand Allfrey – *A Caribbean Life*, New Jersey, 1996.
Paton, Agnew, *Down The Islands*, 1890.
Pawol, Kweyol, Movement For Cultural Awarness, 1989.
Phillips, Caryl, *A State Of Independence*, London, 1986.
Piper, Peter, *Piper's Dilemma*, 1992.
Piper, Peter, *Neutralize*, 1993.
Piper, Peter, *Really and Rarely*, (unpublished).
Polydore, Dr. Kay, *Reflect And Chuckle*, 1990.
Polydore, Dr. Kay, *The Facetious And The Sublime*, 1991.
Polydore, Dr. Kay, *Pause To Ponder*, 1992.
Polydore, Dr. Kay, *For Mirth And Meditation*, 1993.
Proctor Jr. J., "Britian's Pro-Federation Policy in the Caribbean. An Enquiry into Motivation". *The Canadian Journal of Economics and Political Science* (1956).

Rabess, Gregory, "Waraka Christmas", *Wahseen*, V. 2, No. 2, 1980.
Rabess, Gregory, *Eruption*, 1983.
Rabess, Gregor, *Woch-La*, 1992.
Ramchand, Kenneth, An Introduction *To The Study Of West-Indian Literature*, 1968.
Rampersad, F. "Growth and Structural Change in the Economy of Trinidad and Tobago,1951-1961"
Rhys, Jean, *Quartet,* 1928.

Rhys, Jean, *After Leaving Mr. Mackenzie*, 1930.
Rhys, Jean, *Good Morning Midnight* (1939)
Rhys, Jean, *Voyage In The Dark*, 1934.
Rhys, Jean, *Wide Sargasso Sea*, 1966.
Rhys, Jean, *Tigers Are Better looking*, 1968.
Rhys, Jean, *Sleep It Off Lady*, 1976.
Rhys, Jean, *Smile Please*, 1979.
Richards, A.H., A. *Gem of Dominica,* N.D.
Riviere, Bert, "A Moment With Sandra", *Fields Of Gold*, ed.C.A.
Riviere, Raglan, *Rumpunch And Prejudice*, 1998.
Riviere, W. " A Special Report on Dominica", Trinidad and Tobago Review, March 1979.
Rogozinski, Jon *A Brief History of the Caribbean.* From the Arawak and the Carib to the Present (1992)
Royer-Meade, Jocelyn, *Cries Of My Soul*, 1994.
Ryan, S. *Race and Nationalism in Trinidad and Tobago* (1972).
Ryan, Selwyn, PNM: *Perspectives in the World of the Seventies*, (1970)

Salmon, C.S, *The Caribbean Confederation. A Plan for the Union of The Fifteen British West-Indian Colonies.* (N.D.).
Savory, Elaine, *Jean Rhys*, Cambridge, United Kingdom, 1998.
Selvon, Samuel, *A Brighter Sun*, 1952.
Selvon, Samuel, *Lonely Londoners*, London, 1956.
Shukman, Henry, *Travels With My Trombone*, Flamingo, London, 1992.
Singham, Archie, *The Hero And The Crowd In A Colonial Polity*, 1968.
Smith, Bradley, *Escape To The West-Indies*, New York, 1956.
Sorhaindo, Paula, *Pulse Rock*, 1994.
St. Cyr, "On Lewis, Theory of Growth and Development", *Social and Economic Studies,* 1980, v.29, No. 4.
St. Johnson, T.R., *From a Colonial Governor's Notebook* (1970 Reprinted)
St. Omer, Garth, *Nor Any Country*, 1969.
St. Omer, Garth, J. *Black Bam And The Masqueraders*, 1972.
Staley, T. E., *Jean Rhys*, Austin, Texas, 1979.
Stevens, The National Library Of Poetry, 1996.

Sylvester, Mark, *When I Awake*, 1977.
Sylvester, Mark, *The Road I Walk*, 1986.

Tavernier, Fitz, *Voices,* 1986.
Theophile, Alice, *Dreams And Visions Of A Schoolgirl*, N.D..
Thomas, Carole, " Mr. Rochester's First Marriage", *Wide Sargasso Sea*, by Jean Rhys, *World Literature Written In English,* 1968, V.17, No, 1, pages 342-357.
Thomas, A. Lockhart, A. *Two Heads* (1977)
Trilling, L., *The Liberal Imagination* (1950).
Trouillot, M.R. *Peasants and Capital.Dominica in the World Economy* (1988).
Toulon, Anthony, *The Gardens Of Attainea,* New York, 1995.

US DEPT of the ARMY, Regional Handbook: *Island of the Commonwealth Caribbean* (1989)

Walcott, Derek, *Omeros*, 1990.
Wallace, E., *The Economics of Nationhood* (1959)
-British Historians and the West Indies (1966).
Wally, Look Lai, "The Road To Thornfield Hall", *New Beacon Reviews*, 1968, pages 38-52.
Watty, Frank, "Marchand Poisson", *The Dawnlit*, 1964.
Waugh, Alec, *The Fatal Gift*, N. D..
Waugh, Alec, *The Sugar Islands*, New York, 1958..
Waugh, Alec, *Love and The Carribean*, 1986.
Wilcox, Ella Wheeler, *Sailing Sunny Seas*, New York, 1909.
Williams, Albert, One Dominica-*Odes For I Beloved*, 1982.
Williams, Augustus, *Today I Rise*, 1991.
Winston, Theodore, *Sautiqua Mwafrica*, 1983.
White, Michael, *Voices Of The Seed*, Toronto, 1994.
Woodward, B., Veil: *The Secret Wars of the C.I.A. (1987).*
Wright, Michael, *Morne Trois Pitons National Park in Dominica.* A Case Study in Park Establishment, (1985)
Wylie, Johnathan, "The Sense Of Time, The Social Construction Of Reality, And The Foundations Of Nationhood in Dominica And The Faroe Islands", *Comparative Studies In Society And History*, V. 24, No. 3, July 1982. 438.

Wyndham, F., ed., *Jean Rhys Letters*, London, 1984.

Zinn, Howard. *A Peoples History of the United States* (1990).